WITHDRAWN

Twelve Englishmen of Mystery

Twelve Englishmen of Mystery

Edited by
Earl F. Bargainnier

Bowling Green University Popular Press
Bowling Green, Ohio 43403

Copyright © 1984 by Bowling Green University Popular Press

Library of Congress Catalogue Card No.: 83-72499

ISBN: 0-87972-249-5 Clothbound
0-87972-250-9 Paperback

Contents

A Personal Preface Earl F. Bargainnier	1
Contributors	5
Wilkie Collins Jeanne F. Bedell	8
A.E.W. Mason Barrie Hayne	34
Gilbert Keith Chesterton Thomas E. Porter	64
H.C. Bailey Nancy Ellen Talburt	88
Anthony Berkeley Cox William Bradley Strickland	120
Nicholas Blake Earl F. Bargainnier	142
Michael Gilbert George N. Dove	170
Julian Symons Larry E. Grimes	196
Dick Francis Marty Knepper	222
Edmund Crispin Mary Jean DeMarr	250
H.R.F. Keating Meera T. Clark	276
Simon Brett Earl F. Bargainnier	302

A Personal Preface

Earl F. Bargainnier

This book had its genesis, though no one present—certainly not myself—had the least inkling of it, on an April afternoon in 1979. Three friends and I were having a drink at the annual conference of the Popular Culture Association, which that year was in Pittsburgh. I had been thinking for some time of a collection of critical essays on women mystery writers, and since my three friends happened to be women scholars of mystery fiction—Jane S. Bakerman, Nancy C. Joyner and Kathleen Gregory Klein—I tentatively stated my ideas. I was pleasantly surprised by their enthusiasm and grateful for their suggestions of authors to be included and of writers for the essays, but I was astounded when later that same afternoon I presented the proposal to Pat Browne of the Popular Press and she said, "Great, do it." The result was my editing *Ten Women of Mystery*. Its success has led directly to *Ten More Women of Mystery*, edited by Jane S. Bakerman, and now this volume, and plans are underway for two more volumes: *First-Rate Second-Raters*, on neglected American mystery writers, and *The Continental Ops*, on mystery writers from non-English speaking countries. Few drinking sessions can have been so productive of so much criticism by so many.

The past twelve years have produced a considerable amount of criticism of mystery, detective or crime fiction. Reference works have been especially important, for they have begun to provide the basic information with which criticism must begin. Jacques Barzun and Wendell Hertig Taylor's *A Catalogue of Crime* (1971), Chris Steinbrunner and Otto Penzler's *Encyclopedia of Mystery and Detection* (1976), and John M. Reilly's massive *Twentieth Century Crime and Mystery Writers* (1980) are three works that have saved anyone studying the detective genre much, much time. John Cawelti's *Adventure, Mystery, and Romance* (1976) has offered at least one theoretical framework for the study of popular fiction, and several significant histories and surveys have also appeared: Colin Watson's *Snobbery with Violence: Crime Stories and Their Audience* (1971), Julian Symons' *Mortal Consequences: A History From the Detective Story to the Crime Novel* (1972), Ian Ousby's *Bloodhounds of Heaven: The Detective in English Fiction from Godwin to Doyle* (1976), Leroy Panek's *Watteau's Shepherds: The Detective Novel in Britain 1914-1940* (1979), Patricia Craig and

Mary Cadogan's *The Lady Investigates: Women Detectives and Spies in Fiction* (1981) and George N. Dove's *The Police Procedural* (1982). Book-length studies of a few of the most prominent mystery writers have been written, notably on Raymond Chandler, Agatha Christie, Dashiell Hammett, Ellery Queen, Dorothy L. Sayers and Rex Stout, with the number on Christie and Sayers leading all others. Nevertheless, there are hundreds of other mystery writers of the past one hundred and fifty years, whose work is still read or is of historical importance in the development of the genre, who have yet to be examined seriously.

To fill that lack for at least some of these writers—often for the first time—is the purpose of this series of volumes. As I stated at the beginning of *Ten Women of Mystery*, the essays provide both an introduction to the body of the writer's work and analysis and evaluation of characteristic and distinctive elements within that work. Of course, the number of writers included is miniscule in relation to the number of possible choices. I regret particularly not being able to include in this volume Freeman Wills Crofts, Arthur Upfield, Andrew Garve, Cyril Hare, Henry Wade, Colin Watson, Peter Dickinson and Peter Lovesey, to name just eight. Others will have their own "flagrant omissions." However, the range of the twelve writers chosen, who are presented chronologically, covers over one hundred and twenty-five years of mystery fiction from Wilkie Collins to Simon Brett and indicates the evolution of British detective fiction from its beginnings to the present.

This short preface is hardly the place to take up that long-standing question: which is better, British or American detective fiction? As every freshman rhetoric book states, it is futile to argue matters of taste. The same is true for the writers selected for inclusion. With two exceptions (A.E.W. Mason and H.C. Bailey), the authors to be studied were chosen by me before I asked colleagues whom I knew to be knowledgeable in British detective fiction to take on the writing of the essays. Therefore, if the volume is skewed in any way as to the twelve Englishmen chosen, the bias—that is, the taste—is mine.

Without apologies, my preference is for the "traditional" British mystery, whether one calls it Golden Age, puzzle or whodunit. A principal reason for the preference is that works in that category, nebulous as it may be, consist, in John Cawelti's words, of a "basically comic literary universe." Even those who dislike the type and dismiss it as "cosy" are unconsciously recognizing its essentially comic nature. The vast majority of British *detective* fiction is comic in the broadest sense of the word. (The world of the thriller is generally quite the opposite; it is thrilling because it is terrifying or nightmarish. The superb comic thriller is rare; more often the introduction of the comic into the world of the thriller results in, and from, weakness of plot and inane characterization.) The relationship between detective fiction and comedy of manners has been studied by George Grella in "Murder and Manners: The Formal Detective Novel" (1970), and Hanna Charney in *The Detective Novel of Manners* (1981), but yet to be examined thoroughly is detective fiction's relation to—and use of—other forms of the comic, such as farce, wit, satire, romantic comedy and tragi-comedy. In any case, readers of this volume will find comments in a number of the essays on comic crime.

Likewise, there is much on the formulas and conventions of the genre. One will read of locked rooms, perfect alibis, red herrings, great (and not so great) detectives, innocence in distress, public murders, bizarre murders, chase and escape, closed circles of suspects, master criminals, suicide thought to be murder—and vice versa—inverted mysteries, murderless mysteries, policemen as murderers, vanishing bodies (and toyshops) and misdirection and clues of all sorts, from transvestism to the manuscripts of *Love's Labours Won*. The list could go on for pages, for repeated formulas and conventions have multiplied over the years until they number in the many hundreds. A taxonomy of them would be a helpful tool, if anyone is prepared to tackle such an immense and sure-to-be-attacked project. One convention these writers never—well, hardly ever—break is that demanding the principle of fair play; however much they may mystify, they still provide the necessary information for the reader to solve the case, though most readers probably do not.

The solvers in the works are most often amateurs. Only four policemen serve as series detectives, repeated in more than one work—though the single appearance of the inimitable Sergeant Cuff in *The Moonstone* requires mention: Inspector Hanaud, Sergeant Petrella, Inspector Bland and Inspector Ghote. On the other hand, there are seven amateur detectives in series: Father Brown, Reggie Fortune, Joshua Clunk, Roger Sheringham, Nigel Strangeways, Gervase Fen and Charles Paris. Also, Berkeley, Blake, Gilbert, Symons, Francis and Keating have many amateurs as protagonists in single novels. The freedom the writer has with an amateur and the chance to bring in special interests, such as racing, acting or religion, are probable reasons for the preponderance of amateurs, but, of whichever type, they all must deal with violence. They must find the culprit, deliver the innocent and restore community harmony—for that is the *raison d'etre* of their fictional existence. (The lack of detailed descriptions of murders, other forms of violence, or the victims afterwards by all the writers, excepting Dick Francis, is another significant convention of British mystery fiction.)

Even though formulas and conventions are present of necessity, for otherwise the works would not be in the genre, the crucial factor is the writer's ability to turn them into a form of theme and variations, to employ structure, point of view, setting, motifs, style, characters, *whatever* to make his fiction distinctively his own. Memorable writers, no matter their genre, bring to their works their personal qualities and interests, and the best writers of detective fiction are no exception. The essays document these individual elements, as well as the works' generic features. The range is from the religious implications of Chesterton's Father Brown stories so well explored by Thomas Porter through the combinations of erudition and comedy of Crispin analyzed by Mary Jean DeMarr and the risktaking of Francis examined by Marty Knepper to Meera Clark's delineation of Keating's philosophical concerns and his presentation of the people and languages of India. In other words, there are all sorts of works, and the essays provide all sorts of insights.

I must express my thanks to my fellow contributors for their knowledge, thoroughness and cheerful acceptance of my perhaps too "schoolmarmish" set of guidelines. They can be justly proud of their essays, and I am proud to have mine in such scholarly criminous company. Finally, we all share a deep debt of gratitude to that lady from Alabama who now resides amidst the winter blizzards of northern Ohio and who has done so much to encourage the serious study of detective fiction: Pat Browne.

Contributors

Earl F. Bargainnier is Fuller E. Callaway Professor of English Language and Literature at Wesleyan College. A former president of the Popular Culture Association in the South, he now serves as editor of that association's journal, *Studies in Popular Culture.* He has served twice as vice-president of the Popular Culture Association. He has published nearly fifty articles, as well as *The Gentle Art of Murder* (1980). He is editor of *Ten Women of Mystery* (1981).

Jeanne F. Bedell is on the faculty of Virginia Commonwealth University. She has published articles on Conrad, Alcott and composition as well as on detective and espionage fiction. Her special interests are nineteenth-century sensation fiction and mysteries before and during the early twentieth century. This study was begun at an NEH summer seminar at Stanford University.

Meera T. Clark is an Assistant Professor of English at North Adams State College. A native of India, she specializes in Shakespeare, but she has also published articles on Harold Pinter, Margaret Atwood, and detective fiction. Her poems have appeared in "assorted obscure journals," and she is now at work on her first novel.

Mary Jean DeMarr is Professor of English at Indiana State University. She has published articles in *The Indiana English Journal, The Mystery Fancier* and *Clues.* Recently she served as contributor to and member of the committee of consultants for *American Women Writers, I-IV,* and she is a member of the advisory board of *Clues.* Additionally, she is American editor for the Modern Humanities Research Association's Annual Bibliography of English Language and Literature.

George N. Dove is Dean Emeritus of Arts and Sciences at East Tennessee State University. The author of *The Police Procedural* (1982), he has published on mystery fiction in *Popular Culture Methods, The Armchair Detective, The Popular Culture Scholar, The Mystery Fancier* and *Studies in Popular Culture.* He was a contributor and member of the advisory board to *Twentieth Century Crime and Mystery Writers* and is on the advisory board of *Clues.* He wrote the chapter on Dorothy Uhnak for *Ten More Women of*

Mystery (1983). He is also the author of a forthcoming book on Ed McBain and co-editor of the volume *Cops and Constable,* both books to be published by the Popular Press.

Larry E. Grimes is Director of Liberal Studies and Head of the Department of English at Bethany College. His recent publications include articles on Hemingway, John D. MacDonald and Julian Symons, among others, in *Studies in Short Fiction, Clues, The Popular Culture Scholar, Twentieth Century Crime and Mystery Writers* and *Dictionary of Literary Biography.* In addition, he has written articles exploring the relation of crime fiction to religion and the adaptation of crime fiction to film.

Barrie Hayne is Associate Professor of English and Associate Chairman of the Department of English at the University of Toronto. He has published a number of articles on Cooper, Poe, Mrs. Stowe and other writers of nineteenth-century America. He contributed several articles to *Twentieth Century Crime and Mystery Writers* and is currently chairperson for detective-mystery fiction in the Popular Culture Association.

Marty S. Knepper is Adjunct Assistant Professor of English at Augustana College. She teaches detective fiction and has presented a number of papers on the subject. Her article "Agatha Christie—Feminist?" is forthcoming in *The Armchair Detective.* Currently she is revising a book-length manuscript on the theory, style and politics of feminist literary criticism.

Thomas E. Porter is Dean of the College of Liberal Arts at the University of Texas at Arlington. As circumstances permit, he teaches in the departments of English, philosophy, fine arts and the honors programs. His years as a Jesuit priest insure a continuing interest in both theology and mystery which come together uniquely in Chesterton's Father Brown series.

William Bradley Strickland is Director of the Program in English at Truett-McConnell College. He has published articles on American literature in various journals, and his fiction has appeared in such diverse places as *Harper's, Isaac Asimov's Science Fiction Magazine* and *Ellery Queen's Mystery Magazine.* Although he reads all detective fiction with pleasure, his favorite writers remain always Ross Macdonald and Ellery Queen.

Nancy Ellen Talburt is Professor of English and Associate Director of Libraries at the University of Arkansas. She has presented papers on detective fiction and other subjects at meetings of the Popular Culture Association and has contributed articles to *Twentieth Century Crime and Mystery Writers, Dictionary of Literary Biography, 10 Women of Mystery,* and *Objects of Special Devotion: Fetishes and Fetishism in Popular Culture.* She serves on the advisory board of the *Journal of Popular Culture* and as an editorial advisor for *Clues: A Journal of Detection*; she is co-editor with Lyna Lee Montgomery of *A Mystery Reader: Stories of Detection, Adventure, and Horror* (Scribners, 1975).

Wilkie Collins, 1850, reprinted with the permission of the
National Portrait Gallery, London

Wilkie Collins

Jeanne F. Bedell

1824	William Wilkie Collins born in London, first son of William Collins and Harriet Geddes Collins
1833	Attends Maida Hill Academy.
1836	Collins family departs for Italy in September.
1838	Return from Italy; Collins attends school in Highbury
1841	Apprenticed to Antrobus and Son, Tea Merchants
1843	First verifiable publication, "The Last Stagecoach," appears in Douglas Jerrold's *The Illuminated Magazine*
1844	Trip to Paris with Charles Ward
1846	Released from apprenticeship, enters Lincoln Inn as law student
1847	Death of William Collins
1848	Publication of first book, *Memoirs of the Life of William Collins,* Esq., R.A.
1850	First novel, *Antonia; or, The Fall of Rome,* published to generally favorable critical comment
1851	Meets Charles Dickens and participates in amateur production of Bulwer-Lytton's *Not So Bad As We Seem* presented 16 May 1851 at Devonshire House in the presence of Queen Victoria and Prince Albert; *Mr. Wray's Cash-Box,* first work to reflect influence of Dickens, published in December
1852	Joins staff of *Household Words*
1853	Tours Switzerland and Italy with Dickens and painter Augustus Egg
1856	Becomes an editor of *Household Words*
1857	*The Dead Secret* is serialized in *Household Words,* Collins' first serial publication *The Frozen Deep,* a melodrama, is produced under the management and with the help of Dickens at Tavistock House in January and before the royal family in July.
1859	Begins liaison with Carolyn Graves
1863	Resigns as editor of *All The Year Round,* successor to *Household Words*
1868	Death of Collins' mother; Carolyn Graves marries Joseph Clow, and Collins begins liaison with Martha Rudd, future mother of his three children
1869	First child, Marian, is born
1871	Second child, Harriet Constance, is born.
1873	Death of Collins' brother Charles; tours U.S. to give a series of readings
1874	Return from U.S.; third child, William Charles is born
1889	Dies 23 September; buried in Kensal Green cemetery under a tombstone whose inscription reads, at his direction, "Author of The Woman in White and Other Works of Fiction." Collins' will acknowledges his children and leaves his property divided between Carolyn and Martha.

Nobody who admits that the business of fiction is to exhibit human life, can deny that scenes of misery and crime must of necessity, while human nature remains what it is, form part of that exhibition.

"Letter of Dedication," *Basil*

Today books are marketed like toothpaste, romance fiction is advertised on television as an antidote to domestic boredom, and sharp distinctions are commonly made between "serious" novels and thrillers. But in the mid-nineteenth century when Wilkie Collins wrote, as T.S. Eliot has reminded us, "the best books *were* thrilling."[1] Eliot's statement emphasizes a fundamental and enduring characteristic of popular literature and offers salutary advice to critics who substitute classification for evaluation. Collins' reputation as a master of suspense has long been secure; his stature as a serious novelist, the "artist" he considered himself, has, for equally as long, been eroded by that very mastery, which has led generations of critics to praise the intricacy of his plots and to ignore the substance of his themes. Any discussion of Collins must acknowledge that he was noted in his own time, as he is remembered in ours, for the consummate skill with which he created atmospheres of mystery and suspense. Yet suspense and seriousness are not incompatible. And, as Collins' career demonstrates, it is possible to write suspenseful fiction that treats human life with perception, truth, and integrity.

As early as 1865 the young Henry James praised Collins for "having introduced into fiction those most mysterious of mysteries, the mysteries which are at our own doors."[2] A key figure in the development of sensation fiction, which domesticated the Gothic romance and established an atmosphere of mystery and terror in ordinary middle-class settings, Collins fused the romantic and the realistic in a manner crucial to the history of subsequent suspense writing and established plot techniques of such importance that Dorothy L. Sayers maintains that without his contributions "The English novel of intrigue would either never have developed at all or would have developed much later and upon much narrower and more Gothic lines."[3] Few critics would wish to dispute Sayers' claim, but to dismiss Collins, as two recent commentators have done, as a "first-rate thriller writer who could deal capably with melodramatic effects"[4] or to see him solely as a grandfatherly progenitor of detective fiction ignores the breadth and diversity of a career that spanned more than forty years and a series of books that, as David Blair has happily put it, "are in the great tradition of the Victorian novel in their insistent generosity."⁵

Yet the elements of this generosity—Collins' attention to important social issues; his careful and accurate descriptions of middle-class mores and values; his spirited and loving portrayals of independent women, so strangely ignored by feminist critics; and his innovative narrative techniques—have been neglected by the majority of commentators from his own day to the present. Typical is the *Saturday Review's* discussion of his first great success, *The Woman in White*: "Mr. Wilkie Collins is an admirable story teller, though he is not a great novelist. His plots are formed with artistic ingenuity ... and each chapter is a most skillful sequel to the chapter before. He does not attempt to paint character or passion."⁶ Although no other Victorian critic dismissed him as "not in the least imaginative," the substance of the anonymous *Saturday Review* essay, that Collins was a "good constructor," a puzzle-maker, and an "architect" of plots, represents a consensus of contemporary criticism, one summed up in Anthony Trollope's often quoted remark: "The construction is most minute and most wonderful. But I can never lose the taste of the construction."⁷

Collins himself, as the argumentative and frequently self-defensive prefaces to his novels reveal, was upset by his critical reception and, like many a popular author before and afterwards, professed to esteem the opinions of "readers in general," the public, instead of those of "readers in particular," the professional critics. This division of his audience, employed explicitly in the prefaces to *Armadale* and *Heart and Science*, was no doubt an emotional response to fault-finding critics, but it also reflected Collins' long-standing interest in the nature of audiences and the art of fiction. His analysis of penny-novel journals and their readers, "The Unknown Public," in *Household Words*, 21 August 1858, anticipates the methods and conclusions of George Orwell's noted essay, "Boys' Weeklies." "A Petition to Novel-Writers," which appeared in *Household Words*, 6 December 1856, satirized romantic excess and stock characterization in contemporary fiction and chided readers who objected to descriptions of deathbed scenes as "painful," inclusion of criminal activities as "morbid" and oblique references to childbirth as "improper." A defender of realism from the beginning of his career, Collins insisted on the artistic freedom to select his own subjects. In the Preface to *Armadale* he defended the book against those who would impose "narrow limits" on "the development of the novel"; he objected to the indirect censorship of circulating libraries like Mudie's and Smith's, which he called "twin tyrants of literature,"[8] and refused to accept "young people as the ultimate court of appeal in English literature"[9] or to succumb to "this wretched English clap-trap" that forbade an author to "touch on the sexual relations which literally swarm around him."[10] Such remarks tended to antagonize critics, many of whom found his fiction morally offensive.

Warned against the "vices of the French school" and "catering for a prurient taste"[11] with the publication of his first novel, *Antonina*, in 1850, Collins sustained critical attack for supposed immorality throughout his career. The *Atheneum* accused him of adopting the "aesthetics of the Old Bailey"[12] in *Basil* and of choosing "vermin" for his subject in *Armadale*, a novel which H.F. Chorley, long an opponent of Collins' "indecency," felt contained material better suited to "the police-cells" than "pages over which honest people should employ their leisure ...."[13] Collins' iconoclastic attitude toward Victorian morality, especially as expressed through his female characters, angered many reviewers. Chorley believed that Magdalen Vanstone in *No Name* did not suffer sufficiently for her moral transgressions, and Margaret Oliphant chastised Collins for his portrayal of Anne Sylvester in *Man and Wife*. Mrs. Oliphant found the "suggestion" that Anne might retain "moral dignity" after she had lost her chastity and "degraded herself to the lowest humiliation possible to a woman" to be "as horrible as it is impossible."[14] Collins' sympathetic treatment of fallen women is perhaps his most obvious deviation from the Victorian moral code, but his consistent attacks on social snobbery, class bias and religious hypocrisy led Charles Dickens to note that he was often "unnecessarily offensive to the middle class."[15]

Collins did not ignore critics who questioned the morality of his books. He had a firm sense of artistic integrity and told his friend Albert Caccia that "I respect my art far too sincerely to permit limits to be wantonly assigned to it" (*Jezebel's Daughter*, 6), and in an 1862 addendum to the original "Letter of Dedication" to *Basil* he said that since he had designed his story "with strictest regard to true delicacy," he knew that he had "nothing to fear from pure-minded readers." His most overt response, however, appeared in the preface to *Armadale*: "Estimated by the clap-trap morality of the present day, this may be a very daring book. Judged by the Christian morality which is of all times, it is only a book that is daring enough to speak the truth." Numbers of reviewers mentioned this remark in their generally unfavorable comments on the novel, but its popular success reassured Collins, as had that of *Basil* when he felt justified because "my story forced its way through all adverse criticism to a place in the public favor which it has never lost since" (vii).

As this statement indicates, Collins' commitment to "truth" was balanced by a high regard for the opinion of his popular audience. As late as 1880 in the dedication to *Jezebel's Daughter* he attributed the failure of *Fallen Leaves*, his worst novel and a book so bad that Swinburne called it "ludicrously loathsome,"[16] to forms of publication that limited its circulation and added, "When the book is finally reprinted in its cheapest form—then, and then only, it will appeal to the great audience of the English public." In later years when ill-health and declining popularity had made him excessively sensitive, there is a note of pathos in his comments. The preface to *Heart and Science* tells readers:

> The two qualities in fiction which hold the highest rank in your estimation are: Character and Humor. Incident and dramatic situation only occupy second place in your favor. A novel that tells no story, or that blunders perpetually in trying to tell a story—a novel so entirely devoid of all sense of the dramatic side of human life, that not even a theatrical thief can find anything in it to steal—will nevertheless be a work that wins (and keeps) your admiration, if it has humor which dwells on your memory, and characters which enlarge the circle of your friends (6).

"I have myself," Collins assured his audience, "always tried to combine the different merits of a good novel, in one and the same work," but implicit in the passage quoted above is his belief that his own particular talent for depicting the "dramatic side of human life" was not appreciated as he wished. His admission that the emphasis on character and humor in *Heart and Science* did not "happen accidentally" is pathetic evidence of his desire to please, doubly sad because his subject, an attack on vivisection, was not suitable for humor. The preface, however, remains noteworthy for its indication of Collins' estimation of his readers' taste and the indirect insight it offers into the effects of the Victorian debate over novels of incident vs. novels of character.

This distinction brings condescending smiles to the faces of post-Jamesian critics, but it was real to Collins, who had too often smarted under accusations of over-reliance on dramatic incident to the detriment of characterization. His own view of the relationship between character and incident, set forth in the preface to the second edition of *The Woman in White*, seems considerably more modern than that of many of his contemporaries:

> I have always held the old-fashioned view that the primary object of a work of fiction should be to tell a story; and I have never believed that the novelist who properly performed this first condition of his art was in danger, on that account, of neglecting the delineation of character—for this plain reason, that the effect produced by any narrative of events is essentially dependent, not on the events themselves, but on the human interest which is directly connected with them. It may be possible in novel-writing to present characters successfully without telling a story; but it is not possible to tell a story without presenting characters: their existence and recognizable realities, being the one sole condition on which the story can be effectively told (39).

This emphasis upon the interrelationship of character and incident is an important aspect of Collins' theory of fiction. Of equal importance is his belief that drama and fiction are closely intertwined. In the preface to the 1852 edition of *Basil* he wrote that "the Novel and the Play are twin-sisters in the family of Fiction ... the one is a drama narrated, as the other is a drama acted ... and all the strong and deep emotions that the Play-writer is privileged to excite, the Novel-writer is privileged to excite also ..." (v).

Collins' appreciation of the role of drama in narrative is crucial and accounts, in many ways, for both his greatest strengths and his major weaknesses. His first novel, *Antonina*, a turgid historical romance set in ancient Rome, received moderate praise because of its author's "dramatic instinct,"[17] and later Edmund Yates compared Collins' characters with "the *dramatis personae* of an Adelphi drama."[18] Since the Adelphi was the major London theatre specializing in melodrama, Yates' comment was highly uncomplimentary. Juxtaposition of these critical remarks does, however, highlight a significant aspect of Collins' reputation, one addressed by Eliot when he wrote that melodrama, as well as the "craving" for it, is "perennial" and attributed Collin's success to his mastery of "plot and situation, of those elements of drama which are the most essential to melodrama."[19] That Collins used the techniques of melodrama, often very effectively, is unquestionable, but those who label him a melodramatist are as mistaken as those who refer to him as the author of detective stories. Collins wrote only one novel, *The Moonstone*, which features a professional detective, only three, *The Law and the Lady, My Lady's Money* and *"I Say No,"* which emphasize the process of detection, and four short stories, "A Stolen Letter," "The Biter Bit," "Anne Rodway," and "Mr. Policeman and the Cook," in which detection is significant.

Themes of secrecy and deceit and an atmosphere of mystery pervaded his work, as they did those of his more famous contemporary, Charles Dickens. But just as he usually integrated suspense with serious discussion of Victorian life, so did he usually temper melodramatic effects with irony or filter them through narrative voices which offer the intelligent reader a rational and sophisticated view of both action and characters. First-person and multiple narratives, letters and documents, and the personal foibles and eccentricities of narrators provide readers with sufficient perspective to understand that lurid incidents, melodramatic of themselves, are changed by the author's attitude toward his material.

There is little doubt that Collins often sacrificed characterization to the exigencies of plot or credibility to the creation of suspense; the Bluebeard-like conclusion of *Man and Wife*, where the heroine waits in peril of her life for a last-minute rescue, has affronted common sense since the book's publication in 1870. At his worst, in the climax of *Jezebel's Daughter*, set in a Frankfurt morgue, when a supposed corpse with bells attached to its extremities awakens in time to frighten a poisoner into suicide, Collins deserved the accusations levelled against him. At his best, seemingly melodramatic scenes or techniques are charged with psychological or social significance. The "shivering sands" of *The Moonstone* represent a stunning use of foreshadowing to create suspense; but just as they are necessary to Collins' plot, so are they crucial to his theme. The instability of the sands forms a metaphorical parallel to life at the Verinder estate after the disappearance of the Indian diamond has disrupted its placid serenity; the "unknown depths" below the sands provide a symbolic counterpart not only to the central event of the novel, Franklin Blake's "theft" of the moonstone while under the influence of laudanum, but also to the hidden desires which motivate other characters and cloud their perceptions of reality. Such subtlety is not characteristic of melodrama; nor is Collins' ability to infuse overtly melodramatic scenes with symbolic import.

In *The Woman in White* Laura Fairlie denies her love for Walter Hartright and marries Sir Percival Glyde in obedience to the wishes of her dead father. The reward granted this dutiful daughter is to stand beside her own grave, her physical and mental health shattered, her fortune lost, and her identity destroyed. Visually, this is a tableau upon which any melodramatist would be happy to ring down the third-act curtain. Symbolically, it is one of the most powerful scenes in sensation fiction, a sub-genre that challenged Victorian attitudes about women and revealed their discontent with the limited sphere to which they were confined.[20] Collins dramatized the destructive effects of self-abnegation and thereby indicated his disapproval of a virtue commended in women and enshrined in numerous fictional heroines, a disapproval doubly effective since the only defense of woman's traditional role is given by the arch-villain, Count Fosco.

Pliable, obedient and innocent, Laurie Fairlie is both an ideal lady and a typical Victorian heroine; her virtue is not, however, an adequate defense against the conspiracy designed by her husband and his accomplice, Fosco, to steal her fortune and incarcerate her in an insane asylum. *The Woman in White* is not a fictional predecessor to John Stuart Mill's *The Subjection of Women* (1869), but it demonstrates just as clearly the legal plight of married women. That such telling and important social criticism was achieved in a novel that was an immediate popular success and has long been considered a classic of suspense fiction surely counters the view that Collins was a mere architect of plots whose books were read only to satisfy readers' curiosity about the outcome of the action.

In September, 1860, a *Spectator* reviewer dismissed this belief as "palpably absurd,"[21] but the idea that intricate, suspenseful plotting and serious artistry are inimical was commonplace in criticism of Collins, as it is in that of modern mystery fiction. Most Victorian critics, unfortunately, ignored Collins' social commentary when it was implicit and carefully embedded in successful characterization and condemned it, often justifiably, when it was overt and didactic. Modern critics have praised Collins' portrayals of women as a refreshing change from those typical of his period, but few have observed how skillfully these portraits challenge Victorian values. Marian Halcombe, Laura Fairlie's half-sister, is not, by our standards, a liberated woman; yet the "masculine" force of her character, her independence in thought and action, and her willingness to defy authority to rescue Laura from imprisonment reveal, by contrast with the helpless Laura, Collins' dissatisfaction with the sheltered, submissive woman idealized in mid-Victorian England.

Even more strikingly iconoclastic is Magdalen Vanstone in *No Name*. The child of an illicit but happy union (in itself a shocking deviation from Victorian morality), Magdalen is deprived of her inheritance because of illegitimacy. Flaunting the conventional belief that a lady accepts misfortune with resignation, she joins forces with a swindler, gives a series of dramatic performances to earn money, and later marries her cousin in order to regain her name and her fortune. Because she is both a persecuted victim and a revenge-pursuing temptress, the stock melodramatic situation of an orphan deprived of her rights is transformed into a study of a complex woman willing to use unconventional or even immoral means to achieve her goal. Inventive, active, assertive and aware of her sexual power, she says, "I can twist any man alive round my little finger ... as long as I keep my looks!" (256). She is clear-sighted enough to admit to her own maid that it is behavior, not birth, that distinguishes them and bluntly defines a lady as "a woman who wears a silk gown, and has a sense of her own importance" (510). H.F. Chorley condemned Magdalen as a "perverse heroine,"[22] but here, as in the later and less successful *Jezebel's Daughter*, Collins implied what Victorian women well knew: deceit is often the only weapon of the powerless.

In fact, as the action of *No Name* emphasizes, social convention, "respectability," forces Magdalen into the scheme to trap her repulsive cousin in marriage. Her success as a professional actress is, says her ex-governess, "a suspicious way of life to all respectable people" (262) and causes her sister to lose her job. Aware of the irony in her position, Magdalen promises to "make the general sense of Propriety" her "accomplice" (266) in the future and replace public with private impersonation. John Stuart Mill's astute comment that "An active and energetic mind, if denied liberty, will seek for power; refused the command of itself, it will assert its personality to control others"[23] provides insight into Magdalen's motivation and into that of Madame Fontaine in *Jezebel's Daughter*, where Collins presents a compelling if flawed portrait of a frustrated woman whose natural abilities have no outlet. Married to a physician who devotes himself to chemical research in a provincial German town, Madame Fontaine finds her marriage unsatisfying, her social ambitions thwarted, and her financial position impossible. She writes a friend, "Gossip and scandal, with an eternal accompaniment of knitting, are not to my taste, and ... I do not consider them, in connection with tea drinking, the one great interest of a woman's life" (111). When she begins her career as a poisoner, she feels the excitement of the power so long denied her. Just as Collins here sharpens his social commentary by contrasting Madame Fontaine with Mrs. Wagner, whose talents are fulfilled in business association with her husband, a man who believes that many employments usually reserved for men could be performed by "capable" women, so does he gain sympathy for Magdalen through contrast with her miserly cousin whose only real aim in life is the accumulation of possessions. Both his uncharitable parsimony and her rebellion against an unfair legal system are placed in wider social context when Collins describes Vauxhall Walk in London. Here, where "miserable women, whose faces never smile, haunt the butchers' shops ... with relics of the men's wages saved from the public-houses clutched in their hands, with eyes that devour meat they dare not buy" and where the London vagabond acts as an "unheeded warning of social troubles that are yet to come," Collins reveals the underside of Victorian prosperity and "warns the Monarch, Money, that his glory is weighed in the balance, and his power found wanting" (218).

Such overt moralizing is rare in Collins' major novels, where social comment is usually laced with humor or carefully integrated with character and incident. He did, however, become increasingly didactic at the end of his career when he turned to topical studies of such subjects as divorce, heredity vs. environment, and the fallen woman. His heavily moralistic treatment of issues occasioned Swinburne's famous couplet:

> What brought good Wilkie's genius nigh perdition?
> Some demon whispered—Wilkie! have a mission,[24]

and drew criticism from the same reviewers who had previously accused him of lack of seriousness.

Collins' "mission" did not, however, preclude attention to suspense. Even *Heart and Science*, which is as close to a polemical tract as anything he wrote, includes elements of mystery; in *The Legacy of Cain* he considers, to reject, the possible influence of heredity upon a murderess' daughter, and *"I Say No"* centers on a crime committed in a lonely inn, though the *Saturday Review's* comment that "the mystery is not a mystery, and should never have greatly exercised the minds of any of the characters" is just. Writing in 1884, the same reviewer repeats the commonplace idea that Collins' novels "attract chiefly by their ingenious construction and ... are almost invariably excellent displays of invention and artifice." He adds, "In all of them mystery is the thing."[25] While this view is limited and implies that fiction which contains suspense and mystery is read only for the unravelling of its plot, it does emphasize Collins' skill in narrative construction, undoubtedly his greatest talent.

Collins himself believed that "the primary object of a work of fiction should be to tell a story," but his emphasis upon the importance of characterization and his insistence upon the role of the "Actual," realism, in so doing present a different view from that of his critics. As early as 1852 in the "Letter of Dedication" to *Basil*, he says that "I have founded the main event out of which this story springs, on a fact within my own knowledge" so that the novel "would touch on something real and true in its progress" (iii). Throughout his career he remained true to his belief that telling a story meant exhibition of "human life" and "truth to Nature." The novels do, of course, contain exaggeration; the characters are often eccentric (a method of creating humor Collins learned from his friend Dickens) and sometimes ill-conceived or ill-developed; the plots on occasion are artificial or even incredible. *Poor Miss Finch,* in which the blind heroine harbors a horror of dark colors and regains her sight only to learn that a course of medical treatments has turned her fiancé dark blue, has perhaps the most implausible plot in English fiction. But that the novels are flawed or the plots "almost as ingenious as the knot of Gordius"[26] does not mean that they are without merit; nor is the inclusion of romantic elements necessarily incompatible with realism. Collins admitted that "I have not thought it either politic or necessary, while adhering to realities, to adhere to every-day realities only" (*Basil*, v). Like Dickens, he saw "the romantic side of familiar things"[27] and understood that elements of romance—the strange, the exotic and the criminal—have greater impact on readers when they are presented in ordinary, even mundane, settings. The results of this technique were described by one of the most perceptive of Collins' early critics in a review of *Basil*:

> There is a startling antagonism between the intensity of the passion, the violent spasmodic action of the piece, and its smooth, common-place environment. The scenery, the *dramatis personae*, the costumery, are all of the most familiar every-day type, belonging to an advanced stage of civilization, but there is something rude and barbarous, almost Titanic, about the incidents; they belong to a different state of society. But this very discrepancy enhances the terror of the drama....[28]

This critic's feeling that the action of *Basil* suggests a "different state of society" anticipates U.C. Knoepflmacher's essay, "The Counterworld of Victorian Fiction and *The Woman in White*," where he maintains that Collins offered the counterworld as an "attractive alternative to the ordered, civilized world of conventional beliefs" and argues that the novel "depicts a collision between a lawful order in which identities are fixed and an anarchic lawlessness in which these social identities can be erased and destroyed."[29] This collision destroys Laura Fairlie's identity, but it also alters those of Marian Halcombe and Walter Hartright, who discover the truth of Count Fosco's statement that "English Society ... is as often the accomplice as it is the enemy of crime" (238). Hartright learns that "the Law ... is in certain inevitable cases, the pre-engaged servant of the long purse" (33) and finds that his struggle to restore Laura's identity has altered "me to myself almost past recognition" (87). Candid, outspoken Marian dissembles before Fosco and admits to herself, "I, who once mercilessly despised deceit in other women, was as false as the worst of them" (328). Hartright refuses to don disguise during his "secret inquiries" because of its association with "spies and informers"; yet he himself turns informer when he reveals Fosco's presence in London to the secret Italian brotherhood the Count had betrayed and thus ensures his death.

Lying and concealment became second nature to Marian; wearing dark clothes, she creeps from her room in the dead of night to eavesdrop on Fosco and Sir Percival—thereby earning the admiration of Fosco, who calls her "this unparalleled woman." His admiration for Marian and her fascination with him are perhaps symptomatic of the blurring of values and identities which occurs in the novel. As unconventional behavior becomes essential and deception necessary, the boundaries between civilized society and the criminal counterworld grow indistinct and the definition of morality questionable.

The contrast between what Knoepflmacher calls ordered and anarchic worlds is surely one of Collins' persistent themes, one he used frequently to show how fragile and illusory were the acclaimed stability and tranquility of Victorian domestic life and how untrustworthy our perceptions of reality. The juxtaposition of the two and the intrusion of the anarchic, false or criminal into the orderly create suspense and fear and reveal how easily the unwary can be deceived. Charming villains like Fosco find surface politeness and flattery an adequate substitute for honesty; concealed or assumed identities are commonplace, even necessary, and little is what it seems. Opulent Blackwater Park in *The Woman in White* is debt-ridden and the urbane Sir Percival Glyde hounded by debt collectors. Charming in courtship, he is despotic in marriage. The beautiful Lydia Gwilt in *Armadale* marries one man while planning to murder another and pose as *his* widow. Robert Mannion in *Basil* pretends friendship for a man he hates, seduces his wife and then attempts to kill him.

The opening description of Combe Raven in *No Name* exemplifies Ruskin's famous dictum that the home is "the Place of Peace; the shelter, not only from all injury, but from all terror, doubt and division."[30] Legally, however, the happy Vanstone family is no family at all, and only because the presumed Mrs. Vanstone has been able to "resolve firmly, scheme patiently, and act promptly" and to take "the needful precautions which her husband's less ready capacity had not the art to devise" (113) can they live as man and wife while he is still married to another woman. Deception here, Collins implies, is not only necessary but beneficial. The idyll ends abruptly, however, when Mr. Vanstone dies; his illegitimate daughters are disinherited and forced to leave the shelter of Combe Raven to earn their livings. The placid opening scenes of the novel disarm readers and lull them into a false sense of security, one they share with its characters. But security, as Gabriel Betteredge learns in *The Moonstone* when the mysterious Indian diamond "invades...our quiet English home" is only temporary. With irony unintentional on his part but clearly so on Collins', Betteredge asks, "Whosoever heard of it—in the nineteenth century, mind, in the age of progress, and in a country which rejoices in the blessings of the British constitution?" (67).

Deceptive identities, as well as the intrusion of unsettling, disturbing elements into an orderly world are, of course, stock ingredients of detective fiction, especially that of the English interwar period. But Collins, who wrote long before the detective story had hardened into formula, used these techniques not only to create extended puzzles but also to comment satirically on the conventional mores and values of his time and to indict Victorian society for what he felt were injustices. Mrs. Catherick in *The Woman in White* is a crucial figure in the novel and her background essential to discovering the secrets at the heart of its plot, but she also represents a type Collins often satirized, the person who confuses respectability with morality. An adulteress, co-conspirator with Sir Percival Glyde in concealing his illegitimacy and hence his illegal assumption of the title and fortune of his father, and a woman so attached to material security that she allows Sir Percival to place her weak-minded daughter in an asylum in order to retain the annual "pension" he allots her, she sees no reason to expose his wrongdoing because it "did no harm to me" (342) and boasts of her social achievement: "The clergyman bows to me" (542). Mrs. Catherick's elation with her facade of respectability is treated with contempt, but the efforts of Mercy Merrick in *The New Magdalen* to escape her past and move in ordinary middle-class circles are presented sympathetically. An ex-prostitute and product of the refuges for fallen women designed to rehabilitate those of her profession, Mercy assumes the identity of a "virtuous" woman in her search for acceptance. Her "false character" suits her much better than its owner, a woman whose *only* virtue is chastity. Genuinely repentant, Mercy marries a minister who appreciates her intelligence, courage and compassion. The two realize, however, that such Christian forgiveness is rare in England and emigrate to Canada where her past will remain unknown. Collins here derides the idea that woman's virtue is synonymous with chastity, a view also developed in *Man and Wife* where Sir Patrick Lundie marries the "lost" Anne Sylvester, whose courage, dignity and concern for others place her youthful affair in proper perspective. Her infatuation with national sports hero Geoffrey Delamayne enabled Collins to launch what Bruce Haley in *The Healthy Body and Victorian Culture* calls "the severest attack yet on the muscular ruffian"[31] and to satirize the English adulation of sports heroes. *Man and Wife*, which also attacks the ambiguities in Irish and Scottish marriage laws, is overburdened with didacticism and reveals the failure to integrate suspense and social criticism characteristic of many of Collins' later novels. Still, it does reflect clearly his desire to embed serious themes in his fiction while simultaneously providing suspenseful situations for his audience.

Man and Wife, like the earlier *Woman in White*, emphasizes the helplessness of women under the laws of patriarchal society. In its prologue John Vanborough, tired of his wife, Anne's mother, and desirous of entering Parliament, wants a "woman highly connected and highly bred—a woman who can receive the best society in England, and open her husband's way to a position in the world" (I, 11). To achieve this selfish goal, he takes advantage of a loophole in the Irish marriage laws and disowns his wife. Similarly, her daughter's Scottish marriage to Geoffrey Delamayne, contracted solely to save the pregnant Anne's reputation, is dismissed, though unsuccessfullly, by Delamayne when he wishes to marry a wealthy widow. In a subplot which meshes both thematically and structurally with the main action, Collins presents a vivid and moving portrait of Hester Dethridge, a battered, helpless wife whose efforts to improve her lot in life are thwarted by a drunken husband who squanders her inheritance and takes her wages. The law cannot, of course, help her since before the passage of the Married Women's Property Act in 1870, a husband had legal right to his wife's property. After years of abuse, Hester murders her husband, and although the method, which involves a complicated locked-room mystery, seems more in keeping with Collins' talents as a plotter than Hester's as an ill-treated and uneducated woman, the act of violence does underscore the lack of alternatives open to her or other women in similar situations. The conclusion of the novel is unabashedly melodramatic: Delamayne studies the *Newgate Calendar* as he holds Anne prisoner and plans to murder her; she waits anxiously for a last-minute rescue; and Hester erupts into a homicidal mania in time to dispatch Delamayne before he can kill Anne. Collins' concern for the victimized and the helpless does not excuse his piling up of sensational incident to create suspense, but no reader can finish the novel without respect for the compassion he showed.

This compassion extends to all classes. Unlike Dickens, Collins did not describe the plight of poor children or unfortunate clerks, but his sympathy for the "lower orders" is evident both in his characterizations of servants and his determined exposure of the absurdity of social pretensions and the destructiveness of class barriers. Sir Patrick Lundie refers to the "inhumane separation of classes" (I, 415), and Leonard Frankland in *The Dead Secret* learns that his wife's love is more important than her birth. Frankland has been referred to as the first blind detective, anticipating by seventy years Ernest Bramah's Max Carrados,[32] but his minor achievements in deduction are incidental to his thematic importance in the novel. Frankland is a "little given to overrate the advantage of birth and the importance of rank" (60) and tells his wife Rosamund that because of her birth she "ought to be the last person in the world to confuse these distinctions in rank upon which the whole well-being of society depends" (71). Despite these views, Frankland is a humane and gentle man, and when he discovers that Rosamund is actually the illegitimate child of a lady's maid and a coal miner, he acknowledges "the worth of my wife, let her parentage be what it may" (287).

Emotional and moral sensitivity, Collins clearly indicates, are not the sole prerogative of the upper classes. The tormented Sarah Leeson, Rosamund's mother, is filled with guilt because she agreed to relinquish her own baby when that of her mistress died and to keep the substitution secret. Like Roseanna Spearman in *The Moonstone*, whose hopeless love for Franklin Blake is dignified by its intensity, she is capable of great emotion.

Even those stories classifiable as detective fiction reveal Collins' ability to create characters who are both members of a specific social class and recognizable individuals. Intelligence, persistence and devotion enable the heroine of "The Diary of Anne Rodway," published in *Household Words*, 19 and 26 July 1856, to follow the slightest of clues and discover the murderer of her dead friend. Her story sketches in telling detail the life of a poor seamstress faced with an uncharitable landlord and confronted with callous police. She does not openly disagree with the clergyman who "said in his sermon . . . that all things were ordered for the best, and we are put into the stations in life that are properest for us" because "he was a clever gentleman who fills the church to crowding" (*Queen of Hearts*, 501); the capability and assurance which she brings to her task do, in themselves, however, implicitly question the "propriety" of conventional attitudes toward class distinctions. And the skill with which Anne tracks down the murderer is equal, if not superior, to that which the middle-class Valeria Woodville of *The Law and the Lady* brings to clearing the reputation of her husband. Valeria too lacks Anne Rodway's self-confidence: her devotion to a husband so weak-willed and cowardly that his own mother despises him is occasionally ridiculous, and she makes numerous self-deprecatory remarks which relentlessly remind the reader that she is "only a woman." *The Law and the Lady* is usually remembered as one of the first detective novels with a female protagonist, but its characterization of Valeria as a woman so imbued with conventional beliefs about the inferiority of women that she cannot recognize her own abilities or worth is far more memorable than her efforts at detection.

In *Basil* Collins mocks both the materialistic values and social pretensions of the *nouveau riche* Sherwins and the fanatical family pride of the hero's aristocratic father. *Basil*, the most important Collins novel of the 1850s, illustrates not only his critical attitude toward social stratification; it also reveals that at the beginning of his career, in his second novel, he used with a sure hand the techniques of suspense which he was to improve and refine in the major novels, *The Woman in White* and *The Moonstone*. The story opens with what was to become a classic suspense situation: the hero recounts his past as he waits on the lonely Cornish coast under the threat of "impending hostility, which may descend and overwhelm me, I know not how soon, or in what manner" (2). This approach creates a double suspense narrative: the reader knows the major effect of the novel's action before he knows its cause; therefore, the surface plot may build suspense on, as it were, a day-to-day basis, while the hero's peril at the time of writing increases interest in its outcome and builds an undercurrent of tension which remains continuous throughout. That is, the reader needs answers to two questions: what will happen next? and why is Basil threatened? This retelling of events acknowledged to be concluded before the writing begins is the approach used in both major novels, though the central difficulty of such a method, the acceptable concealing of information, is handled differently in *Basil*. Both *The Woman in White* and *The Moonstone* use multiple narrators who are expressly forbidden to relate events outside their personal experience and whose views, even of those, are limited by lack of information about their importance or individual preoccupations which cloud perception. *Basil* does not treat this problem directly, though the narrator's opening remarks that he is writing a "record" and a "history" prepare the reader for a chronological account which leads through the past to the present. This suspense is reinforced by promises to reveal why he has been forced to abandon his father's name and his rightful position in society.

Central to the plot of the novel is the pride of Basil's father who sees his ancestors as "the deities of his social worship" (8). When the young and inexperienced Basil falls in love with Margaret Sherwin, a linen-draper's daughter whom he meets by chance on a bus, he is wracked by guilt because he knows he dare not introduce her to his father or his beloved sister, Clara. His attraction is primarily sexual, but so infatuated is he that he proposes a secret marriage and consents to the stipulation of Margaret's father that the marriage not be consummated for a year. He feels "ominous doubts" on his wedding day, and during the year-long waiting period he comes to see "certain peculiarities in Margaret's character and conduct ... which gave me a little uneasiness and even a little displeasure" (111). Margaret, as the reader knows at once, is vain, shallow and materialistic; she feels no affection for Basil and cares only for his wealth and social position. The uncomfortable and unnatural situation of Basil, who calls on his wife in the evenings and is chaperoned during his visits, is further complicated by the appearance of Mr. Sherwin's clerk, Robert Mannion, a reticent and sinister figure whose relationship with Margaret creates a sense of foreboding. Basil's humiliation becomes complete when he follows Margaret and Mannion to a seedy hotel and learns that they are lovers. Infuriated, he attacks Mannion and permanently disfigures him.

To create suspense out of an awaited sexual encounter was rare in Victorian fiction, but the *Westminster Review* critic who said that *Basil* "dwells on the details of sexual appetite with persistence which can serve no moral purpose"[33] recognized one of the novel's most important sources of tension, one that is also the source of its undoubted moral ambiguity. The ordinary and rather dull Margaret Sherwin may seem an unlikely sexual temptress and her "oppressively" new suburban villa an unlikely setting for seduction, but here, as in Collins' other novels, what he tellingly calls "the secret theatre of home" (76) becomes as suitable a place for intrigue as the ruined castles of Gothic romance. Margaret's role as the "dark lady" is foreshadowed in a dream which occurs shortly after Basil meets her. Nearly crushed by the conflict between his "burning love-thoughts" of Margaret and the "social prejudice" of his family, he falls into a "feverish" sleep.

In his dream, which embodies traditional light and dark imagery and also anticipates Freudian usage, Basil stands on a wide plain bounded on one side by thick woods of "unfathomable depth" and on the other by high hills rising until they were "lost in bright, beautifully white clouds, gleaming in refulgent sunlight" (45). From the dark wood emerges a black-haired woman wearing a "dun-colored" robe and enveloped in mist and vapor. As she walks toward him, another woman, dressed in white, her face "illumined with a light," descends from the hills. Collins' description of the dark woman is essentially Romantic: "Her eyes were lustrous and fascinating, as the eyes of a serpent ... Her lips were parted with a languid smile; and she drew back the long hair, which lay over her cheeks, her bosom, while I was gazing on her" (45). And the dream precisely symbolizes Basil's internal conflict: the fair woman whose cooling, soothing presence resembles that of his sister beckons to him, but he cannot resist the "hot breath" of the other whose touch "ran through me like fire." Wrapped in the embrace of "the woman from the woods," he feels her long hair "spread over his eyes like a veil" as the fair one returns to the hills "wringing her hands and letting her head droop, as if in bitter grief" (46). The conclusion of the dream is conspicuously erotic:

> I was drawn along in the arms of the dark woman, with my blood burning and my breath failing me, until we entered the secret recesses that lay amid the unfathomable depths of trees. There she encircled me in the folds of her dusky robe, and laid her cheek

close to mine, and murmured a mysterious music in my ear, amid
the midnight silence and darkness all around us. And I had no
thought of returning to the plain again; for I had forgotten the
woman from the fair hills, and given myself up, heart, and soul,
and body, to the woman from the dark woods (46-47).

Although the use of dreams as foreshadowing devices was
common in Collins' later works, most noticeably in *Armadale*,
where a dream provides, somewhat mechanically, the structural
basis of the novel, he never matched the psychological validity of
Basil's dream, nor constructed one so profoundly sexual in nature.
Basil's infatuation for Margaret, as the dream prophesies, is
doomed. But in a reversal of conventional expectations, it is doomed
because his intentions are honorable. His worldly brother, who
admits to having "spent time very pleasantly among the ladies of
the counter" and has had several mistresses, considers Basil's
marrying Margaret "unparalleled insanity ... worthier of a patient
in Bedlam than of my brother" (259). Mannion supports this idea
when he tells Basil that his keeping the promise to "wait" a year for
Margaret made the seduction possible. The final touch to this most
unVictorian argument is placed by Basil's father, who condemns
the "foul stain of your marriage" and says that "such a record of
dishonour and degradation ... has never yet defiled" the family
history (203). Banished as "an enemy to me and my house,"
destroyed by his virtue, Basil goes into exile where he awaits the
vengeance vowed by Mannion.

The novel's conclusion, when Basil is chased by Mannion over
the Cornish cliffs, is melodramatic, but the novel is successful in its
mingling of secrecy and sex. Mannion's characterization, despite
Byronic undertones, anticipates such smooth-tongued and
plausible villains as Count Fosco and Godfrey Ablewhite, and
Collins skillfully conceals the secret in the past which accounts for
his original antipathy toward Basil. Kathleen Tillotson has aptly
defined sensation fiction as "the novel-with-a-secret,"[34] and
although several of Collins' books, especially *The Woman in White*,
emphasize the importance of a specific secret, he did not approach
the writing of fiction with such limitations. It is not, as he and other
outstanding practitioners of suspense knew, the secret that is
important but the fact and manner of its concealment: "Even the
crime itself is not more hideous and more incredible than the
mystery in which its evil motives, and the manner of its evil
ripening, were still impenetrably veiled" (*Basil*, 178).

Practically all the elements of Collins' fiction are discernible in

Basil. Within this unconventional account of the love affair between an aristocrat and a middle-class woman, he developed a suspenseful narrative that yet offered serious, even shocking commentary on contemporary mores and morality. Although subsequent novels achieved greater distinction in characterization and complexity in plotting, Collins' approach to fiction was clearly established in 1852. The friendship and influence of Charles Dickens, however, encouraged Collins to add humor to his narratives and to lighten his satire with comic touches or to embed it in eccentric characters. The absurd devotion to religious trivia of Drusilla Clack in *The Moonstone* made it possible for him to offer biting commentary on petty religiosity and organized charity without offending his audience. The officious, one might even say unChristian, nature of Miss Clark's favorite charities is deftly communicated: the "British-Ladies'-Servants-Sunday-Supervision Society," represents Grundyism at its worst; the "Mothers'-Small-Clothes-Conversion Society," whose goal it is to "rescue unredeemed fathers' trousers from the pawnbroker, and to prevent their resumption, on the part of the unreclaimable parent, by abridging them immediately to suit the proportions of the innocent son" (237), exemplifies a moralistic and useless approach to charity. Laura Fairlie's uncle, a neurotic hypochrondriac, is an irritatingly funny representative of his species and also important to a plot whose tension he serves to simultaneously break and enhance. Humor is also the distinguishing characteristic of the short detective story "The Biter Bit," first published as "Who is the Thief?" in *The Atlantic Monthly*, April, 1858. Told entirely in letters, the story focuses on a policeman, ironically named Matthew Sharpin, whose high opinion of himself is belied by a marked lack of ability which leads him to misinterpret evidence clear to the reader.

Collins' skill in fusing suspense and humor is best seen, of course, in *The Moonstone,* which Dennis Porter believes to combine "the forms and material of romantic comedy, comedy of manners, and mystery novel with those of the detective novel" and calls the first "comic detective novel of manners."[35] Considered the best novel in the genre by both T.S. Eliot and Dorothy L. Sayers, *The Moonstone* is perfectly plotted and rich in diversionary material.

From its opening scene in India where the diamond is stolen from a Hindu temple through a strikingly original denouement to the discovery of the villain murdered a squalid East End rooming house, every clue has been fairly given, but each is so enmeshed in the personal peculiarities of the narrators that the reader is apt to misinterpret its significance. Collins subverts the old maxim that seeing is believing and shows that truth is more complex and reality less easily discernible than one thought.

Although the novel's police detective, Sgt. Cuff, provided a model for what Eliot called "the healthy generation of amiable, efficient, professional but fallible inspectors of fiction among whom we live today,"[36] the process of detection is actually spread among several characters,[37] the most important of whom are Franklin Blake, whose attempt to prove his innocence established one of the significant conventions in the novel of intrigue, and Ezra Jennings, the doctor's assistant, who is an opium addict. Jennings discovers the series of clues that reveal the identity of the criminal through a process closely approximating Freudian word association and emphasizes the importance of the unconscious in human action. To this psychological perceptiveness, Collins added witty social satire and sophisticated narration, a combination that sets *The Moonstone* apart from detective stories of its time and ours.

Fusing the romantic and the realistic, the mundane and the exotic in the "secret theatre of home," Collins created an approach to suspense fiction to which modern writers are still indebted. He also set a standard at which they still aim, one *Harper's New Monthly* described as "the faculty of constructing a story in such a way that while it is in progress no one can guess at its winding-up, yet when all is done the reader will wonder why he had not anticipated the end of the plot."[38] To make one's conclusion both surprising and inevitable is the mark of outstanding mystery fiction. To create plots "as closely-knit and logical as the plot of classical drama"[39] and to place within those plots memorable characters is a significant achievement. But Collins did more than this: at his best, he wrote original, exciting, suspenseful novels which offered richly detailed pictures of Victorian life and subversive, challenging criticism of Victorian society. He was, as Algernon Swinburne said in 1889, "a genuine artist."[40]

Notes

The editions of Collins' works used for the study are listed below, preceded by the original date of publication. In order to avoid repetition, I have provided publication information about the *Works of Wilkie Collins* only once and have thereafter referred only to *Works* and the appropriate volume number. All quotations will be cited in the text, followed, where necessary, by the abbreviation given after selected entries.

1848   *Memoirs of the Life of William Collins, Esq., R.A., with Journals and Correspondence* (London: Longmans, 1848).
1850   *Antonina; or, The Fall of Rome: A Romance of the Fifty Century* (London: Bentley, 1851).
1851   *Rambles Beyond Railways; or, Notes in Cornwall Taken A-Foot* (London: Bentley, 1851).
1852   *Mr. Wray's Cash-Box; or, The Mask and the Mystery: A Christmas Sketch* (London:

Bentley, 1852).
1853 *Basil: A Story of Modern Life* (New York: Dover Press, 1980).
1854 *Hide and Seek*, Vol. XI of *The Works of Wilkie Collins* (New York: Peter Fenelon Collier, n.d.).
1856 *After Dark*, Vol. XIX of *Works*. Contains six stories connected by "Leaves from Leah's Diary":

"A Terribly Strange Bed"
"A Stolen Letter"
"Sister Rose"
"The Lady of Glenwith Grange"
"Gabriel's Marriage"
"The Yellow Mask"

1857 *The Dead Secret* (New York: Dover, 1979).
1857 *The Frozen Deep*, in *Under the Management of Mr. Charles Dickens: His Production of "The Frozen Deep,"* ed. Robert Louis Brannan (Ithaca, NY: Cornell Univ. Press, 1966).
1859 *The Queen of Hearts*, Vol. XIV of *Works*, Connecting narrative for ten stories:

"The Siege of the Black Cottage"
"The Family Secret"
"The Dream-Woman"
"Mad Monkton"
"The Dead Hand"
"The Biter Bit"
"The Parson's Scruple"
"A Plot in Private Life"
"Fauntleroy"
"Anne Rodney"

1860 *The Woman in White* (New York: Penguin, 1974).
1862 *No Name* (New York: Dover, 1978).
1863 *My Miscellanies*, Vol. XX of *Works*. Collection of non-fiction essays.
1866 *Armadale* (New York: Dover, 1977).
1868 *The Moonstone* (New York: Penguin, 1966).
1870 *Man and Wife*, Vol. III, IV of *Works*.
1872 *Poor Miss Finch*, Vol. XV of *Works*.
1873 *The New Magdalen*, Vol. VII of *Works*.
1875 *The Law and the Lady*, Vol. V of *Works* (Law).
1876 *The Two Destinies: A Romance*, Vol. XVIII of *Works* (Destinies).
1878 *The Haunted Hotel: A Mystery of Modern Venice; to which is added My Lady's Money*, Vol. XXII of *Works* (Hotel, Money).
1879 *A Rogue's Life: from His Birth to His Marriage*, Vol. XXX of *Works*.
1879 *The Fallen Leaves—First Series*, Vol. XXI of *Works*.
1880 *Jezebel's Daughter*, Vol. XXVII of *Works*.
1881 *The Black Robe*, Vol. XXIII of *Works*.
1883 *Heart and Science: A Story of the Present Time*, Vol. XXV of *Works*.
1884 *I Say No*, Vol. XXIX of *Works*.
1886 *The Evil Genius: A Dramatic Story*, Vol. XXIV of *Works*.
1886 *The Guilty River* (New York: American Publishing Corp. n.d.)
1887 *Little Novels* (New York: Dover Press, 1977). Collection of stories:

"Mrs. Zant and the Cook"
"Miss Morris and the Stranger"
"Mr. Cosway and the Landlady"
"Mr. Medhurst and the Princess"
"Mr. Lismore and the Widow"
"Miss Jeromette and the Clergyman"
"Miss Mina and the Groom"

"Mr. Lepel and the Housekeeper"
"Mr. Captain and the Housekeeper"
"Mr. Captain and the Nymph"
"Mr. Marmaduke and the Minister"
"Mr. Percy and the Prophet"
"Miss Bertha and the Yankee"
"Mr. Policeman and the Cook"

1889   *The Legacy of Cain* Vol. XXVI of *Works*.
1890   *Blind Love* (completed by Walter Besant), Vol. XXVIII of *Works*.

[1]"Wilkie Collins and Dickens," in *Selected Essays* (New York: Harcourt, Brace & World, 1964), p. 409.
[2]"Miss Braddon," in *Notes and Reviews* (Freeport, N.Y.: Books for Libraries Press, 1968), p. 110.
[3]*Wilkie Collins: A Critical and Biographical Study,* ed. E.H. Gregory (Toledo: The Friends of the Univ. of Toledo Library, 1977), p. 38.
[4]Patricia Craig and Mary Cadogan, *The Lady Investigates: Women Detectives and Spies in Fiction* (New York: St. Martin's Press, 1981), p. 38.
[5]"Wilkie Collins and the Crisis of Suspense," in *Reading the Victorian Novel: Detail into Form*, ed. Ian Gregor (New York: Barnes & Noble, 1980), p. 38.
[6]Unsigned review, *Saturday Review*, 25 August 1860, in *Wilkie Collins: The Critical Heritage*, ed. Norman Page (London: Routledge & Kegan Paul, 1974), p. 83.
[7]*Autobiography*, in Page, p. 223.
[8]Quoted by Guinivere Griest, *Mudie's Circulating Library and the Victorian Novel* (Bloomington: Indiana Univ. Press, 1973), p. 116.
[9]Quoted by Kenneth Robinson, *Wilkie Collins*, A Biography (London: The Bodley Head, 1951), p. 232.
[10]Marginal note in Collins' copy of Forster's *Life of Dickens*, quoted by Duncan Crow, *The Victorian Woman* (London: George Allen & Unwin, 1971), p. 210.
[11]H.F. Chorley, unsigned review of *Antonina*, *Athenuem*, 16 March 1850, in Page, p. 41.
[12]D.G. Maddyn, unsigned review of *Basil*, *Athenaeun* 4 Dec. 1852, in Page 47.
[13]H.F. Chorley, unsigned review of *Armadale*, *Athenaeum*, 2 June 1866, in Page. 147.
[14]"New Books," *Blackwoods*, 1086 (Nov. 1870), 629.
[15]Quoted in Robinson, p. 119.
[16]A.C. Swinburne, "Wilkie Collins,' *Fortnightly Review*, 1 Nov. 1889, in Page, p. 261.
[17]H.F. Chorley, unsigned review of *Antonina*, *Athenaeun* 16 March 1850, in Page. p. 40.
[18]"The Novels of Wilkie Collins," in *Temple Bar*, August, 1890, in Page, p. 273.
[19]Eliot, p. 409.
[20]For discussion of the portrayal of women in sensation fiction see Elaine Showalter, *A Literature of Their Own: British Women Novelists from Bronte to Lessing* (Princeton: Princeton Univ. Press, 1977), pp. 153-181.
[21]Unsigned review, *Spectator*, 8 Sept. 1860, in Page, p. 92.
[22]Unsigned review, *Atheneum*, 3 Jan. 1863, in Page, p. 131.
[23]*The Subjection of Women* (Cambridge: MIT Press, 1970), p. 97.
[24]In Page, p. 262.
[25]Unsigned review, *Saturday Review*, 22 Nov. 1884, in Page, p. 218.
[26]Unsigned review, *Saturday Review*, 13 March, 1875, in Page, p. 203.
[27]"Author's Preface," *Bleak House* (1853; rpt. Boston: Houghton Mifflin, 1956), p. xxxii.
[28]Unsigned review, *Bentley's Magazine*, Nov. 1852, in Page, pp. 46-47.
[29]In *The Worlds of Victorian Fiction*, ed. Jerome H. Buckley (Cambridge: Harvard Univ. Press, 1975), pp. 353, 362.
[30]"Of Queens' Gardens," in *Sesame and Lilies* (New York: D.D. Morrill, n.d.), pp. 96-97.
[31](Cambridge: Harvard Univ. Press, 1978), p. 224.
[32]Gavin Lambert, *The Dangerous Edge* (New York: Grossman Publishers, 1976), p. 5.
[33]Unsigned review, *Westminster Review*, Oct. 1853, in Page, p. 52.
[34]"The Lighter Reading of the Eighteen-Sixties," Introduction, *The Woman in White* (Boston: Houghton Mifflin, 1969), p. xv.
[35]*The Pursuit of Crime: Art and Ideology in Detective Fiction* (New Haven: Yale Univ. Press,

1981), pp. 62, 61.

[36]Eliot, p. 413.

[37]Modern readers might be interested to note that *The Times*, 1 Oct. 1868, called Cuff "the inevitable detective, a character so regularly retained on the establishment of sensational novelists that it would be inconvenient for a due appreciation of new works to find appended to advertisements of them, along with extracts from critical journals, such remarks as 'Very true to life' and the like, dated from Scotland Yard." *The Times* did, however, add that " 'the great' Sergeant Cuff would almost reconcile us to the type."

[38]Unsigned review, *Harper's New Monthly*, Oct.1868, in Page, p. 178.

[39]Sayers, p. 84.

[40]"Wilkie Collins," *Fortnightly Review*, 1 Nov. 1889, in Page, p. 255. This was Swinburne's obituary essay.

A.E.W. Mason

A.E.W. Mason
(Arthur Edward Woodley Mason)

Barrie Hayne

1865	Born, May 7, in Camberwell; son of William Woodley Mason, chartered accountant, and wife, Elizabeth
1874	Attended Dulwich College, where he specialized in acting and debating
1884	Went up to Trinity College, Oxford
1888	June, graduated Third Class in Litterae Humaniores. August, made professional acting debut with Edward Compton's Company at Crewe
1894	His first published work, *Blanche de Maletroit,* a play based upon Robert Louis Stevenson's "The Sire de Maletroit's Door"
1902	*The Four Feathers*
1906	Elected Liberal M.P. for Coventry; at the end of the parliament (1910) did not stand again
1910	*At the Villa Rose,* his first Hanaud novel
1911	*The Witness for the Defence*, play, published as novel 1913
1914	December, joined Army
1915	Entered secret service (Major, 1917)
1924	*The House of the Arrow*
1927	*No Other Tiger*
1928	*The Prisoner in the Opal*
1933	*The Sapphire*
1935	*They Wouldn't Be Chessmen*
1936	*Fire Over England*
1946	*The House in Lordship Lane,* the last Hanaud novel
1948	Died, November 22

"All the great detective novels," A.E.W. Mason wrote in 1925,

> are known by and live on account of their detectives. Dupin, Sherlock Holmes, Monsieur Lecoq, above all Monsieur Lecoq in the novel that bears his name. Has not Father Brown joined that select company? The detective must be an outstanding person, actual, picturesque, amusing, a creature of power and singularity. Without such a being, the detective novel, however ingenious, will pass back to the lending library. With him it may find a permanent place on the bookshelf.

The setting of the detective novel must be realistic ("one touch of fairyland ruins it altogether"); there must be considerable reliance upon the "puzzle"; "the author must play fair." But "the greatest of all conditions" is the primacy of the Great Detective.[1]

Six years later, in his preface to an omnibus volume of his first three Hanaud novels, Mason emphasized the same point in a different way: "Detective fiction ... has been judged not so much by the ingenuity of its plots, but by the higher standard of its characterization."[2] The puzzle must give way to convincing characterization and psychology; and it is as a novelist of character that Mason's peers and critics have acknowledged him from the beginning. In 1929, Dorothy L. Sayers saw his novels as having "the convincing psychological structure of the novel of character"; in 1936 she underlined his psychological realism: "A few writers, such as ... A.E.W. Mason, still remembered that they were novelists and strove hard to keep the detective story in touch with life ...." And Howard Haycraft, with one more Hanaud case to come, expressed the view that Mason had been the first detective novelist after Wilkie Collins to make significant use of the psychological element.[3] Comparing Mason to Chesterton as a psychological novelist versus a philosophical one, Haycraft touches the essence of Mason's concern, for while Father Brown's cases turn upon moral questions, and are morally resolved by the little priest, Hanaud's cases track into the dark recesses of the criminal mind, an area Hanaud is well qualified to study. Brown talks at length of philosophical and theological questions, Hanaud of speculative and psychological ones. Echoing Holmes to Watson on the train journey to the Copper Beeches, perhaps, Hanaud speaks of the "pestilence" of the anonymous letter, especially in the rural setting:

> The little towns, my friend, where life is not very gay and people
> have the time to be interested in the affairs of their neighbours,
> have their own crimes .... The postman's knock, a thing so
> welcome to the sane life of every day, becomes a thing to shiver
> at, and in the end dreadful things happen. (HA, 324-425).

The tone here is plainly free of moral judgment; as always Hanaud is interested in the mind, not the morals of his criminal quarry; the note of psychological generalization is characteristic. Though his method of closing in on the criminal is frequently cat-and-mouse, he usually shows some sympathy, but transcended by a detached clinical interest in the way the criminal's mind works: "all great criminals who are women are great actresses. But never in my life have I seen one who acted so superbly ... while that story was being unfolded. Imagine it! .... Picture to yourself ---'s feelings during that hour in the pleasant garden, if you can! The questions which must have been racing through her mind!" (HA, 647).

These elements we have a right to look for, therefore, in Mason's detective fiction, judging his practice by his precept, and these we do find: realism, characterization, an emphasis on the psychology of the criminal, and above all, the central importance of the detective. What Willard Huntington Wright would grave in stone two years after Mason's 1925 pronouncement ("He is, at one and the same time, the outstanding personality of the story .... The life of the books takes place in him,"[4]) and what Raymond Chandler would further enscroll four years before Mason's death ("He is the hero; he is everything .... He must be the best man in his world and a good enough man for any world.")[5], Mason, in his insistence on the hero as center, articulates here.

Certainly Mason's own detective novels, however realistic, would be much less satisfying without his detective, the rotund, histrionic Inspector Hanaud of the Paris Surete, though much of their life comes as well from Hanaud's auxiliary, the finicky Julius Ricardo. This "incongruous" pair is an important and often overlooked link in the chain joining Holmes and Watson to Wolfe and Goodwin, and Hanaud himself has an important place in the development of the detective hero. He is the first important professional detective after Bucket, Cuff and Lecoq. When we remember that he made his first appearance in 1910, we know that few detectives, professional or amateur, as fully realized, had preceded him; only Dupin, Holmes, Gryce and Thorndyke come readily to mind. He may have been modelled upon Robert Barr's French policeman, Eugene Valmont (1907), though the more obvious (and fully acknowledged) model is Gaboriau's Lecoq, but he anticipated by one year Chesterton's momentarily prominent Valentin, and by a full decade Hercule Poirot.

Hanaud appears in five novels,[6] well spaced between 1910 and 1946: *At the Villa Rose* (1910), *The House of the Arrow* (1924), *The Prisoner in the Opal* (1928), *They Wouldn't be Chessmen* (1935) and *The House in Lordship Lane* (1946). Though he ages very little, there are references in the later cases to the earlier ones, usually to the affair at Aix-les-Bains which is the subject of *At the Villa Rose*. In the omnibus preface of 1931, Mason summed up his by now famous detective, specifying the four qualities he saw him as necessarily having:

> He should be first of all a professional, secondly as physically unlike Mr. Sherlock Holmes as he could possibly be; thirdly, a genial and friendly soul; and fourthly, ready to trust his flair or intuition and to take the risk of acting upon it, as the French detective does. (10)

The second and third of these specifications make Hanaud a big bear of a man (at a far remove from the lean and poker-faced). One character calls him a Newfoundland dog, and he has a disarming geniality which often enables him to entrap his adversary into damaging admissions—a kind of ur-Columbo. The first words of description applied to him show him as "stout and broad-shouldered, with a full and almost heavy face. In his morning suit at his breakfast table he looked like a prosperous comedian" (AVR, 37). So, to emphasize the lack of change in him, the last novel describes him as "a big, heavy man with thick black hair and a blue jowl. He looked rather like a French comedian. He appeared to be as clumsy as a rhino, but he moved as lightly as an antelope, and he had quiet eyes which saw everything and a voice which was of no account and suddenly had all the authority in the world" (HLL, 202).

Hanaud's sense of theatre is a quality returned to again and again. In the second novel, an experiment he engages in "savoured of the theatrical" (HA, 479). And in the third he confronts poor Ricardo in the guise of a brigand, terrifying him ("a sort of schoolboy impishness"): " 'I am Hanaudski. The King of the Tchekas' " (PO, 679). Yet his theatricality has no affiliations with Holmes' use of disguise. Holmes is an actor, who elicits information through his disguises; he even plays with schoolboy impishness on *his* Watson (most notably in his dramatic return to life in "The Empty House," which produces Watson's only swoon). But Holmes rarely—"Silver Blaze" comes to mind as an exception—engages in the *coup de theatre*. Hanaud frequently does, though less as an actor than as stage-manager, as Ricardo more than once notes: "It was the scene of three men, Ricardo realised; the inevitable great scene of the plays of Sardou; and this one stage-managed—produced was the modern word, wasn't it?—by Hanaud, chief dramatist of the Surete Francaise" (HLL, 266).

Moreover, Hanaud's theatricality is part of his disarming quality. He uses his folly as a stalking-horse, and under cover of it he shoots his cuffs, as it were. In the second novel: "A minute ago Hanaud had been the grave agent of Justice; without a hint he had leaped to buffoonery, and with a huge enjoyment. He had become half urchin, half clown. Jim could almost hear the bells of his cap still tinkling" (HA, 321). In the same novel, the hero, the center of conscious, notes that " 'Whatever he does and however keenly he does it, he sees a row of footlights in front of him' " (HA, 506), later remarking that "there was a strain of the mountebank about Hanaud" (HA, 517). In the last of the five novels in which he appears, this characteristic, which is a constant annoyance to Ricardo, draws from him the complaint, "you have melodrama in the tips of your fingers" (TWBC, 152). About Hanaud—and here of course the analogy with the similarly cat-and-mouse Columbo breaks down—there is something of the dandy as well as the actor and the jester. His physical type may readily be visualized through those who have played him on stage and screen: the formidable and grandiloquent Otis Skinner on the American stage, and, in his most recent appearance on film, Oscar Homolka, more elegant than usual (though Homolka's iconic untidiness again gives us a whiff of Columbo).[7]

Hanaud smokes neither Regies nor Meerschaum pipe, but black "Maryland" cigarettes, cleaving to them alone. (One of the most amusing scenes in which Hanaud appears—and one of the few occasions on which he is discomforted, though he manages to have his way—is the chapter in the last novel entitled "Hanaud Smokes a Cigar, or Does He?" Hanaud abhors cigars, but is presented with the polite necessity of smoking one for a stubborn host, from whom he is seeking information. Ricardo positively revels in *Schadenfreud*.) Hanaud apes English ways, but does not—at least according to the wine-fancier Ricardo—know a good port from a bad one. ("Porto was Porto, and the blacker it was and the stickier it was, the more Hanaud enjoyed it" [HLL, 134], though his theatricality will not allow him to admit his lack of taste to his host. " 'I am not like you'," he once says to Ricardo, " 'a continentalist. No, I have the English tastes. I will have a whisky and lemonade"[TWBC, 323]. Ricardo fastidiously shudders.)

But for one quality, which is rather imposed upon Hanaud through his dialogue, the detective is little of a foreigner, and clearly the projection of a very English writer. Indeed, the "continentalist" Ricardo, who still retains certain stereotypical "English" traits such as stuffiness, is more "foreign" than Hanaud, and his name, Julius Ricardo, underlines the point. But the quality that makes Hanaud French—for one meets few Frenchmen who would admit to patterning their behavior upon English models—is his mangling of English idiom. Though his use of English is beyond reproach in almost every other respect, he has a talent for giving a new twist to an old cliche which carries its own creativity; a talent, incidentally, which is almost completely missing in the first two novels, but which Mason works especially hard in the last two. Thus Paris is one character's "spirituous home" (PO, 748). Looking after a female character, Hanaud calls himself "her goat" (i.e., nanny—PO, 911); the unexpected appearance of a character "upsets the carriage of the pears" (PO, 979). A cathedral Hanaud visits in England has—to the startlement of his listeners—"what is rare, perhaps, the flying buttocks" (HLL, 126). To describe the indigence of a female character he indulges in what appears to be the language of sensationalism—" 'Mrs. Hubbard, she was naked. You understand?' " (HLL, 50). He occasionally lards his language with distinct Briticisms—"Gorblimey" (PO, 961) and "Arf a mo" (HLL, 94). But perhaps his most amusing flight of linguistic fancy is one involving both his languages. When the villainess, in demotic French, upbraids her accusers, she calls one of them "un professeur [i.e., fellow] sanguinaire." Hanaud translates the curse back into English to tell the villain what he thinks of him: " 'You are—prepare yourself!—you are a full-blooded professor' " (TWBC, 339-340). When the villain in turn calls him "barmy," Hanaud is bewildered. What has he to do with the tropics?

No more than with Poirot, however, does this unenglish language debase Hanaud. One may even suspect that he deliberately employs it to guy his friend Ricardo, as well as to be part of his genial entrapment. The one memorable time when Ricardo does not correct his friend is when he is seduced by the content of the unidiomatic phrase. " 'The cunning Mr. Ricardo is after it straight as the crock crows'," says the detective, and Ricardo is too busy "preening himself upon this admission of his perspicacity" to complain (PO, 730). Here, and often elsewhere, Mason's extension of

Hanaud's metaphor (Ricardo as the preening cock) draws attention to the creative and probably deliberate nature of Hanaud's "lapses," which are often witticisms, and not merely unwitting confusions like Mrs. Malaprop's.

If this creative use of unidiomatic English is part of Hanaud's theatricality as well as of his geniality, so too is his "detestable habit" (to the conventional Ricardo—PO, 884), of speaking of himself in the third person, and of signing with his surname only, "like a peer of England" (HLL, 8). "Am I not Hanaud? Ah my friend, the responsibility of being Hanaud! Aren't you fortunate to be without it? Pity me! For the Hanaud's must see something everywhere—even when there is nothing to see" (HA, 451). While these passages show clearly enough a great egotism which reminds us that Hanaud, physically unlike Holmes, is not so psychically unlike him, there is behind Hanaud's self-esteem and theatricality a saving touch of irony which is not directed exclusively at the interlocutor.

The fourth specification that Mason made for Hanaud (like the others, *ex post facto*) is his "flair," "intuition," prescience. Throughout the novels, Hanaud drops hints to Ricardo—and of course to the reader—as the investigation proceeds. Of such is fair play composed. He allows Ricardo to summarize the facts with the customary Watsonian obtuseness, and adds embellishments of his own, as he does to Jim Frobisher's set of questions in *The House of the Arrow*. After Ricardo, in *The Prisoner in the Opal,* has drawn up nineteen questions and answers, Hanaud leans over his shoulder to comment, " 'You almost write down there one most important question' " (759-763). Ricardo is the unassisted—Mason calls these notes of his "ineffectual"—reason. Hanaud, like the Bi-Part Soul of Dupin and all his descendants, is reason assisted by intuition. The most suggestive description of this faculty in him comes in the last novel of the five, when the character tells him that what is important is facts, not imagination. He replies: "Yes, facts, my dear Maltby, and a little imagination to interpret them. Imagination on a leash—he is the blind man's dog" (HHL, 100). The imagination must be held in check, but without it the reason is blind. Even Hanaud's famous statement about his dependence upon Chance, often read as an example of his modesty, is an acknowledgement of the power of the imagination, as the second of the two sentences makes clear: " 'We are the servants of Chance, the very best of us. Our skill is to seize quickly the hem of her skirt, when it flashes for the fraction of a second before our eyes' " (HA, 328).

Such then is Hanaud, in rough sketch, a professional policeman, and the first important example of one since Lecoq. In taking our leave of him for the moment, we may note that he received one of his highest commendations from Willard Huntington Wright. Taking the view of him which I have adopted here (that he represents "the psychological methods of crime detection, combined with an adherence to the evidences of reality"), Wright calls him "the Gallic counterpart of Sherlock Holmes," a view which, following Mason himself, I have not adopted here. Looking forward as well as back, however, Wright links him with a more modern detective—Philo Vance! Perhaps the kind of ingenuity devoted to seeing Holmes' paternity in Wolfe might be applied to tracing Vance back to the bachelor Hanaud. Between the Maryland blacks which Hanaud smokes and Vance's Regies we may have the makings of a relationship.

Though Mason's interests are indeed in psychology and characterization, and we do come to know Hanaud well by the end of the series, we are rarely inside his skin; his eccentricities make of him a character of humors, however, multi-dimensional. He is seen from outside. In the most admired of the Hanaud novels, *The House of the Arrow*, the young lawyer and leading man, Jim Frobisher, is our center of consciousness. But generally we are privy to the thoughts of the only other character, besides Hanaud, who sustains our interest throughout the series, Julius Ricardo, whom Mason himself, again retrospectively, described as "the dilettante from Mincing Lane, with his passion for entertaining interesting people, his trim propriety and his generous good nature ... partly as a foil and a butt for his friend Hanaud, and partly as a fairy godfather for the young suspect" (Preface, 10).

Ricardo is indeed foil and butt, taken into Hanaud's confidence "to know the inner terrible truth of a good many strange cases which remained uncomfortable mysteries to the general public," but also ridiculed by Hanaud's pranks, and invited to expound his own views, "which were then rent to pieces, and ridiculed and jumped upon." He is the prisoner in the opal, "dimly aware of another world outside," yet fully aware of the brittle opal substance beneath his feet. He is initiate to the terrors, but saved from their full impact by his imperceptiveness. In short, a further evolution of Dr. Watson, but with Mason's greater insistence upon "fair play." As E.M. Wrong long ago noted, "Mr. Mason's *Hanaud* ... is like *Holmes* in one way—while his actions are not described by his admirer, only such actions are recorded as his admirer has seen."[8] Watson is a selective reflector; Ricardo is the refraction of what Mason wishes to tell us of Hanaud's actions. The effect of the difference, with Ricardo the more passive reporter, is to reveal more of the investigative method.

Like Hanaud, Ricardo changes little through the five novels. The only notable change occurs in a brief appearance he makes in a novel not in the series, *No Other Tiger* (1927), where his function is merely to identify the villainous central character, and to bore some ingenues at a dinner party. Here he is "a thin, narrow-shouldered elderly man with *pince-nez* bridging his nose" (84), and moreover an "amateur of the horrible" who haunts the scenes of crime "to reconstruct with a delicious shiver of fear the horrors which had there taken place" (126). This is mere caricature of the Ricardo of the Hanaud series, as are his tedious flirtations with his young dinner companions. He is, it is true, as the hero of *The House of the Arrow* says, " 'a rather finicking person' " (314). He is a creature of habit; he must travel to the South of France at the same late summer time each year; he recognizes a gentleman by his ability "to distinguish at a first sip the virility of a Chateau Latour from the feminine fragrance of a Chateau Lafite" (PO, 659). He drives—or has driven for him—a Rolls Royce (he has two by the last novel; though perhaps he has always had, since this is the only time we see him at home in London); Hanaud uses the car with a good deal of official freedom. There is some sign of aging in the next-to-last novel, though he seems unchanged again in the last; he tells the heroine, who is aqua-planing, that "my youth was spent in the age of bathing-machines on wheels" (TWBC, 137). But as Mason's retrospective sketch makes clear, he is not a contemptible character; Hanaud is as reliant on him as Holmes is on Watson. In one of his more creative non-idioms, Hanaud calls him "the power behind the sofa" (PO, 739). He is "the germ-carrier. I [Hanaud] get the disease and you give it to me without knowing what you are doing" (PO, 777). He travels "first on a second-class ticket" (HLL, 178). But he is not, as Julian Symons says, "uxorious," nor is he, as Daniel P. King says, a bachelor.[9] When Mason first introduces him, in the opening paragraphs of *At the Villa Rose*, he states quite plainly: "in condition he was a widower—a state greatly to his liking, for he avoided at once the irksomeness of marriage and the reproaches justly levelled at the bachelor" (AVR, 23). He does not have Mary Morstan and her successors as encumbrances he must drop when the game is afoot, but he does have an independence, financial and emotional, which enables him to keep Hanaud at psychological arm's length; Billy Wilder would have great difficulty in linking the two as he plausibly linked the archetypal pair in *The Private Life of Sherlock Holmes*. He is a very rich man, a connoisseur ("a Maecenas without a Horace"—AVR, 24), and leads an idle cafe-society life. But behind him there is a business fortune amassed, we assume, by himself: "Though he lounged from January to December, he lounged with the air of a financier taking a holiday" (AVR, 23).

Most crucial of all, he is trusted not only by Hanaud, but by Mason as well. Center of consciousness in all but *The House of the Arrow*, and even there his appearance precedes the detective's, so that he is still a reflector, he is above all the advance man, who first sees the strange behavior of the heroine at the gambling tables in *At the Villa Rose*; who is approached by the lawyers over the threatening of the heroine in *The House of the Arrow*; who is the recipient of the heroine's confidences about her fey fears in *The Prisoner in the Opal*; who is holidaying in July—it is too early for Aix—and meets the heroine as she is caught in the villainous moves of *They Wouldn't be Chessmen*; and who, in *The House in Lordship Lane*, is present when the young revolutionary is fished from the sea, an event which in its ramifications brings Hanaud to the solution of a related murder.

Such then is Julius Ricardo, and between them he and Hanaud provide the main character interest of the five novels in which they appear together. Though Ricardo does not directly relate his friend's adventures, we are most of the time in his mind (though sometimes ironically distanced from it so as to see him as Hanaud sees him). He is not the foil-convenience that Dupin's friend is. He is as obtuse as Watson or Hastings, and guyed by his principal as much as they, but he serves the additional purpose Mason mentions: he is a fairy godfather, an avuncular figure who in the first novel takes the heroine under his—or more precisely his sister's—wing when she is bereft at the end. Thereafter he shares with Hanaud the fairy godfather's role—bringing together the two lovers in *The House of the Arrow*, checking Hanaud's archness in observing the lovers in *The Prisoner in the Opal*, comforting the heroine when her hero is killed in *They Wouldn't be Chessmen*, but in the end being surprised by Hanaud's recognition of the lovers in *The House in Lordship Lane,* a novel which reverses several of the earlier formulas.

But these duties remain peripheral, as the love interest in Mason's fiction—a carry-over from his romantic and historical novels—remains peripheral. Again setting aside the Wilder shores of love, the real partnership in the Hanaud series is the mutual friendship of the detective and his auxiliary, bound by a variety of ties—Hanaud's self-esteem, Ricardo's vanity, each feeding the other through Ricardo's obtuseness and Hanaud's ostensible willingness to encourage his friend. Hanaud's most theatrical entrance is the one he makes in *They Wouldn't be Chessmen*, and it sums up the qualities of the two men, and what joins them. In the open-air restaurant Ricardo is enjoying his croustilles, when a dirty feather floats on to his spotless table cloth, to be followed by Hanaud's voice—"Birds with a feather flock together" (139). But as Hanaud later explains to his friend, there is more than mere waggishness impelling him to his physical-linguistic joke: "I who live amongst crimes and squalor must laugh when I find friends to laugh with" (148). With Ricardo "in silent communication with his companion," Hanaud continues:

> "Once or twice ... accident, destiny—God—has brought us together. And each time there has been something"—he hesitated for a word and found it—"fantastic in its horror, and dark because of some queer strain of cruelty.... I pick up a dirty feather from the gutter and do my waggishness. And at once you tell me much that I want to know."
>
> Mr. Ricardo was more than a little moved.

Ricardo, to sum him up, is a safety-valve, a sounding-board, but also a collaborator. Absolutely the descendant of Watson, he has more appealing human qualities which make him live more vividly as an eccentric. Hanaud is quite as egocentric as Holmes, and as theatrical in a different way, but his eccentricities—he is, after all, a professional, who must to some extent conform to social norms—are shared with his auxiliary. There is a greater merger of qualities in these two than in the archetypal pair. When in the last novel Ricardo acerbically objects to the use of his house in the investigation, Hanaud says, "Ah, ah, you make fun of your poor Hanaud. Well, well! .... After all, we are twins." To which Ricardo replies, "I should prefer to say 'quits' " (HLL, 220). Twins they are, but the running friendly antagonism between the two makes them duellists as well, in much the way the second most famous pair, Wolfe and Goodwin, later will be. We leave the pair at the end of the last novel not duelling, however, but showing for each other the concern which underlies all these relationships:

> "You are quite yourself, eh?" cried the anxious Ricardo.
> Hanaud nodded. He had remembered. He laughed. He answered:
> "I am all Sir Garnet." (HLL, 320)

So Hanaud goes out on a linguistic pun.

By most accounts, and by shrewd conjecture, Mason himself was a combination of Hanaud and Ricardo. He resembles Hanaud in his theatricality and flamboyance, though not in his rotundity; he resembles Ricardo the bon-vivant, and he *was* a bachelor. Mason was also a figure of great fun and bonhomie, whose "laugh was famous in both hemispheres."[10] He had an immensely retentive memory, and could marshal facts and retain details in much the same way as his detective. He was a dandiacal figure, and it was as an actor, in fact, that he began his career: in school and at Oxford he neglected his studies for amateur acting, and on going down from the University he walked the professional stage in secondary but not minor roles—Orsino in *Twelfth Night*, Falkland in *The Rivals*, and smaller parts in two notable premieres by young playwrights, Yeats' first play, *The Land of Heart's Desire*, and Shaw's second, *Arms and the Man*. Whereas his almost exact contemporary, E. Phillips Oppenheim, projected his thrillers and novels of world intrigue from his palatial quarters, on land and on sea, on the Riviera, Mason, like John Buchan, himself led an adventurous, even a cloak-and-dagger life. Explorer, yachtsman (his craft was called *The Sleuth*), mountaineer (he annually in his middle years essayed the Alps), he was also a member of parliament, and in the first world war a secret agent in Spain and Mexico. Finally, as the sociable man he was, he mixed easily with most of the literary famous of his day, being especially friendly with Andrew Lang (with whom he collaborated on one novel), J.M. Barrie (of whom he wrote a memoir), Anthony Hope Hawkins (the author of *The Prisoner of Zenda*, of whom he also wrote), Arnold Bennett, and Gilbert Murray, another writer-statesman. Mason was an initiate of the same circles to which Ricardo gained access by his wealth and position, but he entered them through Hanaud's brilliance and flair.

While it is not germane here to discuss at length Mason's fiction outside the detective field, it is unquestionable that much of his continuing fame does belong outside that field. His most famous works are *The Four Feathers* (1902), his first great bestseller, and, at least in England, *Fire Over England* (1936). Both were made into highly successful films during the heyday of British film in the 1930s. These two novels, moreover, represent two important sides of his character as a writer: *The Four Feathers* the study of imperial Britain at its apogee, so often explored by Oppenheim, Sapper, Buchan; *Fire Over England* the costume drama which also breathes the power of the English at a time of greatness (here 1588, and the Spanish Armada).

Most of his novels before *The Four Feathers* are in fact costume dramas: *The Courtship of Maurice Buckler* deals with the Monmouth Rebellion and its aftermath; *Clementina*, following the Dumas pattern closely, deals with the Old Pretender, his bride-to-be, and the hero, servitor of one and lover of the other, after the failed rebellion of 1715. These two novels, indeed, parallel the more conventional patriotic romanticism of *Fire Over England* with the romanticism of the Lost Cause: romantic swashbuckling often casts Mason in the role of a nostalgic aristocrat, and the hero of *The Four Feathers*, Harry Feversham, is very much a Mason hero, the idealist who proves himself in practical terms. This novel needs no explanation to little British boys who read it forty years ago, but perhaps for an American audience it ought to be briefly identified as dealing with a young man of principle who quits his regiment on the eve of the Egyptian War, is given four feathers denoting his cowardice by his—now former—fiancee and his three closest friends. He proceeds to expiate his "cowardice" by acts of great heroism outside the army, directed at his accusers; and, most notably, disguised as a native, he leads his principal detractor, Durrance, blinded by exposure to the sun, through the North African desert. In the novel, too, Mason's biographer sees in Durrance's attempts to bring his wits together in his blindness a foreshadowing of Mason's detective fiction;[11] there is justice in this view, but the episode seems rather to testify to Mason's pervasive interest in the way the mind works. Similarly, many of the works listed in the *Crime and Mystery Writers* encyclopedia as "Crime Publications"[12] are very tenuously so, except in the sense that *The Scarlet Pimpernel*, or *These Old Shades* (both written by occasional practitioners of detective fiction) are crime publications.

The keynote of all Mason's fiction—as it was the keynote of the life he lived—is adventure, theatrically heightened above reality, while still attached to it (essentially Henry James' commodious car of the imagination, somewhat more commodious than for James, with its cable grounded in terra firma). And that is the keynote of mystery and detective fiction as much as it is of adventurous costume drama. An early novel, *The Watchers*, will serve as an example. Listed in the encyclopedia as "crime" fiction, it is set in late eighteenth-century England and centers on a monstrous villain, Cullen Mayle, who is a mesmerist, a smuggler, a pirate, and who is eventually murdered by his own associate. There are, obviously, elements of mystery in the plot, but the main emphasis lies upon adventurous and rapidly moving incident, to which even the criminality is secondary. Such "secrets" as there are unfold as the exciting incidents proceed, and there is no percipient character with whom the reader may identify. The hero is something of a bumbler, without the other existence of Sir Percy or the Duke of Avon.

All of which suggests that while there is a kind of "adventure" connection between Mason's other fiction and the Hanaud novels, it is no more than the kind of connection that exists, say, between *The White Company* and *The Hound of the Baskervilles*. It testifies, as with many of Mason's contemporaries—Doyle, Orczy, Heyer—to the parallel popularity, in the early twentieth century, of detective fiction and the kind of romance—even the Graustarkian—that Henry James dismissed in his preface to *The American*.

There are, however, a handful of genuine crime novels, dealing directly and in a characteristically psychological way with the criminal mind, not part of the Hanaud-Ricardo series, and of these, three novels and one collection of short stories should be mentioned here. The first of these, *The Witness for the Defence*, was written first as a play in 1911, just after the success of the first Hanaud novel. Published as a novel in 1913, it continues the theme so successfully treated in *The Four Feathers*: the act of cowardice—though Harry Feversham's act is not precisely that—which must be expiated. But here there is a crime. The central character, Thresk, having led the heroine to believe that he is paying court to her, out of worldly ambition fails to propose. She goes to India, marries unhappily a husband who brutalizes her, and whom, after meeting again with Thresk, she kills. She is tried and acquitted on Thresk's perjured evidence. She plans to marry again, but Thresk insists that she expiate *her* crime (though the whole course of events represents *his* expiation) by telling the full story to her fiance. She tells Thresk instead: she had planned to kill herself, and the killing of her husband was an accident. Thresk then self-effacedly blesses her union with her new husband. *The Witness for the Defence* is, as a novel, not one of Mason's important works: its dramatic origins are obvious in its chapter/curtain lines, its prepared confrontations between characters, its trial scene, its stridency of tone. As a play, one can easily visualize its success; as a novel its keynote is excess. There is little mystery—it is, of course, a crime, not a detective novel, unless Thresk be seen as an investigator who fails to solve the mystery—and its real affiliation, suggested by its principal setting, is again with the Oppenheim school of the outpost of empire (through the empire is not here endangered) of *The Great*

Impersonation, or *The Four Feathers* itself.

No Other Tiger (1927) is much closer to the genre of detection, and shows its closeness by the—albeit distorted—appearance of Ricardo, and at least the references to Hanaud, who does not appear. As with so many of Mason's novels, however, it never quite lives up to its opening (in this case the first three chapters), which finds a famous hunter in Burma, persuaded to watch at night for a tiger who is laying waste a local village. He is about to shoot the beast he stalks when he sees it is not a beast, but a man, with a face "horribly evil, evil to the point of majesty" (26). "No other tiger passed that way that night." The rest of the novel is anti-climax, as the hero finds favor in the eyes of the heroine, who is, in her thoughtless flapper way, caught up in the plot, which has already involved murder, and which has at its center this diabolic and tigerish villain, whom the hero does at last shoot. Unlike *The Witness for the Defence, No Other Tiger* is still occasionally read and has not been so long out of print; it is arguably Mason's best thriller outside the Hanaud series (Dorothy L. Sayers named it, and no other, beside *The House of the Arrow*). In a graphic way it illustrates what Hanaud often perceives, that there are "people who take their orders from their lusts and hates" (TWBC, 292), indeed most people are so impelled. Julian Symons regards the Hanaud novels as an outlet for "dark imaginings"[13] which had no place in the swashbuckling costume dramas. No other novel in Mason's canon illustrates such an impulse better than *No Other Tiger*.

Finally, in this category is *The Sapphire* (1933), the last truly "crime" novel Mason wrote before the last two novels of the Hanaud series; it would be followed only by them and more costume novels. Again the opening is spectacular, and not thoroughly connected with what follows. A gem is stolen from a Burmese temple, and two votaries follow its progress as it moves through English country life. *The Moonstone* is inevitably called to mind, and there is an atmosphere of fate and mystery, but the emphasis is different, lying rather on the enigmatic character of Michael Crowther, a moral degenerate who is redeemed at the end and who is instrumental in securing the return of the sapphire. While a contemporary reviewer thought that Crowther had a "Conradian pathos,"[14] this now seems excessive, suggested only by his isolation and the locale; and the chief interest of *The Sapphire* seems rather that it again shows Mason in his adventurous Oppenheim mood. The brooding atmosphere of evil, though it is pervasive rather than located in one tigerish villain, links the novel with the "dark imaginings" of *No*

Other Tiger.

It is the short story collection *Dilemmas* (1934) which most clearly embodies those dark imaginings, and shows Mason's talent, not elsewhere exploited, for a genre far removed, traditionally and appropriately, from the detective genre. These are stories of the occult, and as Mason noted, "one touch of fairyland" ruins the detective novel altogether. But there are elements of detection here. In "The Strange Case of Joan Winterbourne," a surgeon by slow degrees—while deploring the methods of psychoanalysis, "the heresy of heresies" (9)—tracks through the past of a young woman given to fainting spells, and finds his solution in her traumatic witnessing of a farmhouse murder. The method is absolutely that of the crime investigator. In "The Chronometer," an observer pieces together the story of a young woman shipwrecked and sold into a harem from the presence of the ship's chronometer in a jeweller's shop. But because most of these stories deal with crimes in commission rather than crimes detected by investigator and reader in concert, this collection illustrates better than any of Mason's other work his unbridled psychological interest in man's darker side. "A Flaw in the Organization" describes the Jekyll and Hyde life of an eminent solicitor who has embezzled from the inheritance of a young client; his daughter and the client fall in love and plan marriage. Fleeing to a new identity, with his daughter, he is destroyed by his own imaginings. "There was, you see, after all, a flaw in Julian Clere's organization. He had not organized against fear" (153). Throughout this story, we are in Julian Clere's mind, a mind already divided between respectable normality and covert criminality; when that mind collapses, the effect is both chilling and satisfying. But the chill is uppermost; except for occasional glimpses of the *rational* mind—as in "The Strange Case of Joan Winterbourne" (the title recalling Stevenson)—seeking to impose an order on the *irrational* mind, these stories belong to a different genre. The dark imaginings without Hanaud's therapeutic presence.

It is finally, however, on the five Hanaud novels that Mason's fame as a detective or mystery writer must rest, so as the climax to this study we return to them.

In the 1931 preface, Mason describes at some length the impulses that led to the creation of *At the Villa Rose* (12-14): the fictional case from a story told him which telescoped with the details of a trial he attended; his recollection of a conjurer and his daughter which gave him his heroine, who is a spiritualist; the memoirs of certain police officials which suggested Hanaud. What remained was the telling of the story, and it is the method used, in this first novel, which has caused the most controversy these past seven decades. For in his aim "to combine the crime story which produces a shiver with the detective story which aims at a surprise"—and he seems here very much engaged in *ex post facto* self-justification—Mason abandoned the latter, at least in the orthodox way of having the surprise come at the end, in favor of the former. *At the Villa Rose* is of course a detective story, but it is a detective story—hence the frequent critical application of the word "psychological"—in which the emphasis upon the criminals' minds and their workings prevails over the wish to postpone the solution for the reader. Thus in a novel of twenty-one chapters we are told who the criminals are at the end of the thirteenth chapter, and much of the last eight chapters is taken up with the reconstruction of the crime by the heroine, before "Hanaud Explains" (the title of Chapter XXI).

There is something quite formulaic about these five novels, only the last one being to some extent *sui generis*. To none of the first four cases is Hanaud actually assigned. In *At the Villa Rose*, on holidays, he is invited by Harry Wethermill, the young inventor who is the lover of the suspect-heroine, to investigate the facts and clear her name. In *The House of the Arrow* he is investigating a rash of poison-pen letters in the region where the murder is committed (though this becomes a cover operation as the murder becomes the main object of his attention). In *The Prisoner in the Opal* he is brought to the case by Ricardo's interest, and in *They Wouldn't be Chessmen* he is looking into a case of naval incendiarism near where the plot to steal a pearl necklace is hatched. Only in *The House in Lordship Lane* is he assigned directly to the principal crime, and that crime so quickly proliferates into something much larger that the consistency of the formula is not really jeopardized. In the first novel, true to what the formula would become, Ricardo sits in the hotel garden, outside the gaming rooms, and sees the distracted behavior of a girl who has evidently lost at the tables. He shortly meets up with Wethermill, a much younger acquaintance. Then occurs the murder, at the villa, of the elderly rich woman who has recently taken up as her companion Celia, the distracted girl of two nights earlier. The old woman has been murdered for her jewelry; her maid, who has been displaced from favor by Celia's arrival, has been chloroformed; and Celia herself has disappeared. Wethermill approaches Hanaud, whom he has met at one of Ricardo's London dinner-parties, to undertake the case. While I will not here reveal the secret that Mason prematurely reveals, and while to the avid reader of detective fiction there is no such person as the least likely suspect (especially here, where there are only two possibilities), it will be enough to say that there is some surprise in the explanations which follow the revelation of the criminals. Hanaud's solution turns on some nice points by now familiar to detective story readers: footprints have been made with a certain person's shoes to cast suspicion in the wrong direction; the crime is discovered by an astute policeman on his rounds seven hours before the murderer intended its discovery. What seems to have struck a lot of readers of *At the Villa Rose* as a true *coup de theatre*—from which Hanaud is necessarily but unfortunately absent—is the scene of the murder itself, at a seance. As the old woman feels the ghostly hand move from her forehead to her cheek to her throat, where it remains until the task is accomplished, there is genuine terror, not least because the only person in the room with goodwill towards the victim has been tied up and immobilised at the old woman's command. But the main defect of *At the Villa Rose* lies in its odd construction, which leaves the last third of the novel predominantly explanation, with little surprise. "I wanted," Mason says, "that the surprise which is the natural end of a detective story should come in the middle and that the victims and the criminals should between them ... tell a story which, while explaining, should transcend in interest all the doubts and even the alarms which a good mystery is able to provoke" (Preface, 11).

In the face of the standard criticism, one must ask, is there anything wrong with this aim? The essential difference between sensational fiction and detective fiction has always lain in the revelation of the secret, or surprise. In sensation fiction, it is often sprung upon the reader for the mere thrill of it; in detective fiction, we are as much in the way of discovering it, if the author does play fair, as the detective himself. While Mason's method in *At the Villa Rose* is clearly unorthodox, it will be condemned more strenuously by those readers who look, not for the revelation of the mystery by rational means, but for the thrill and the *frisson*. And that is not the province of detective fiction, which has rather dealt, since Poe, in the ratiocinative method. But *At the Villa Rose* does not quite play fair with the reader: the more orthodox detective novel would have supplied information withheld until the last third of the novel, so that the reader would have been presented with less of a surprise. Indeed, one may question how important surprise, as distinct from secret, is in detective fiction; the present discussion really arises out of an attempt to accommodate Mason's own insistence on its importance. But if the reader is in full if not always conscious possession of the facts, then the final surprise is more akin to a coincidence of view between reader and detective, and a consequent sense of self-satisfied intelligence, having little in common with the *frisson* of sensation fiction.

The next novel, *The House of the Arrow*, written fourteen years later, is more orthodox (in any case, three lustra of the Golden Age had hardened the orthodoxy), though in all of the Hanaud novels the criminal is identified well before the final chapter. Though critics have complained that in this second novel the criminal's identity is too obvious too early, this is again the complaint of readers widely and subsequently read in a genre then in its infancy: for readers accustomed to seeing the criminal in the least likely person, Mason does cast so much suspicion around that the least obvious becomes the obvious. This is, however, the most complex novel of the five, not least in its narrative method, where it interposes the young lawyer Frobisher between Ricardo and the audience as an alternative reflector of the events. The novel opens in a law office, with rapidly telescoped action revealing the death of a wealthy woman in Dijon and her brother-in-law's accusation that her niece-companion is responsible for her murder. The novel takes its name from the weapon, infected with poison, which is used in the murder. That weapon, incidentally, for which a long search is conducted, turns up in a tray of pens, hidden according to a method as old as Poe. As Hanaud says, "The old rules are the best. Hide a thing in some out-of-the-way corner, and it will surely be found. Put it to lie carelessly under everyone's nose and no one will see it at all" (HA, 502).

The plot similarities between *The House of the Arrow* and *At the Villa Rose* are striking. In each novel there is a pair of heroines, each in love with the hero; in each, suspicion, almost incontrovertible, is cast upon one of them, before the guilt is affixed to the other, who seems at the outset indisputably innocent. In each novel a rich old woman is murdered, but *The House of the Arrow* turns upon a tricky psychological point. "The murder could not be that of a mother," Mason wrote in his preface. "Such a thing might be matter for a tragedy, not for a detective story" (13). In spirit if not in fact, however, the murder of Mrs. Harlowe is a matricide, and in its details the more terrifying—Mason's "dark imaginings" once more—because of this. As in *At the Villa Rose* we are present by way of the suspect-heroine's narrative as the old woman is killed, but what was Grand Guignol in the earlier novel—melodramatic death at a seance—becomes here the terrifying death of a dependent at the hands of one from whom she has every right to expect only comfort and protection; a death, moreover, done with cool calculation—"and Madame's voice died to a mumble and then silence"—and then the other voice in a low, clear whisper, "That will do now" (424).

The House of the Arrow is an advance on *At the Villa Rose* in other respects as well. In the earlier novel the plot was simple; here two plots converge, the murder and the spate of anonymous letters which descends upon Dijon and which it is Hanaud's ostensible purpose to investigate. It is especially suggestive that Mason's development of the second plot seems to have applied the goad to his writing ("*The House of the Arrow* began then really to build itself in plan"). These two parallel plots interweave throughout the novel, and climax at the same time, when the one person is revealed as the culprit in both cases. But there is a metaphorical connection between the two crimes as well, as when Hanaud expounds the crime of anonymous letter-writing:

> Suddenly *out of a clear sky* they will *come* like a *pestilence* .... For a while these abominations flow into the letter-boxes and not a word is said .... If it is only sheer wickedness which *drives* that unknown pen, those who are *lashed* by it none the less hold their tongues (324-325; italics added).

The violent, disease-ridden metaphors suggest the common factor in both crimes: poison, fluid and death-dealing, and hurtling through the air like an arrow. Moreover, the incident which triggers the plot, Boris Waberski's letter of accusation to the lawyers, parallels, once the novel is read, the seeming innocence of the actual criminal's letter of appeal (these are the "letters of mark" of the opening chapter's title). In its *lack* of anonymity, Waberski's letter ought to have been taken at face value. This was "the basis" of the plot as Mason saw it in 1931—"Suppose that after all the accusation was true, but the blackmailing uncle, relying upon the little discreditable secret, didn't know that it was true!" (13). Or as Hanaud puts it at the denouement, somewhat disingenuously: "Waberski? He is for nothing in all this. He brought a charge in which he didn't believe, and the charge happened to be true. That is all" (630). That Waberski is a crank, however, and also the possible murderer, for long diverts the reader's attention from the real criminal. Open, suspected guilt and covert, poisonous, actual guilt run through the novel both as technique to deceive the reader, in the traditional way of the detective story, and as metaphor linking these two vicious crimes, murder and the anonymous letter—in Hanaud's words, "the most pernicious" of all crimes.

To those who look for the surprise of detective fiction at the end of the work, *The House of the Arrow* is again the more orthodox novel, though the criminal is unmasked in Chapter XXI of twenty-six chapters. "My aim," Mason says, "was to keep the secret, if I could, until the end of the novel was reached." *But,* and this is the transcendant consideration in Mason's method always, with mystery yielding to character: "The solution was ... so to depend upon the interplay of characters ... that it would provide a second story of greater interest than the story of the mystery to be solved" (12).

The device on which much of the surprise turns, corresponding to the weaker devices in *At the Villa Rose* of the meter in the car and the villain's possession of a road map, is much more ingenious here. It depends upon a crucial mistake in time being made when a clock is seen in a mirror; half past ten is registered as half past one. Even as the device strikes the reader as being based on solid, if not immediately apparent, reality, Mason's preface reminds us that this key to the mystery was based on mundane observation: sitting up late writing, he makes the same mistake himself as he goes to bed— "a few days later I realized that one of my chief difficulties in framing the story smoothed itself out" (14).

In the next novel, *The Prisoner in the Opal*, we are again on familiar formulaic territory: the damsel in distress approaches Ricardo, *mutatis mutandis,* for the third time, and so Hanaud enters the case. It is arguable that, given his titular importance—he is the prisoner—and given Mason's statement that he wrote the novel after "a few of my friends clamoured for the reappearance of Mr. Ricardo, and I had a tenderness for him myself" (15), Ricardo is, in this third novel, the more important character. Hanaud solves the mystery of course, but Ricardo is much more involved in it than before, actually seeing the light go out as the victim's life is extinguished (though he does not know it at the time).

The Prisoner in the Opal embodies the darkest imaginings of the five novels, being concerned with a group of Satanists. But the formula continues: again there are two heroines, though one is quickly murdered; again the murder is directly described in the retrospective narrative of the principal heroine—on an altar of devil worship this time, naked, with her body in the form of a parodic cross. At the end of the twenty-second of twenty-nine chapters, the solution is in hand, but the darker nature of this novel dictates that Hanaud "allow" one of the criminals to take poison rather than face the exercise of the law:

> "You executed him," said Mr. Ricardo with a shiver of terror.
> "Better I than the man with the guillotine," Hanaud answered solemnly (948).

The two heroines of this novel, befitting its more romantic quality, are those polar opposites of romantic stereotype, the light-haired and the dark: Joyce Whipple, a wholesome English girl with brown hair and lips "healthy red" (662), and Evelyn Devenish, "dark of hair," with "black liquid eyes," suggesting to Ricardo "storms and wild passions." "It passed through his mind that if he ever had to take a meal with her alone, it should be tea and not supper" (692). On his usual August vacation in the south of France, Joyce asks Ricardo to look after a friend whose letters suggest she is in the grip of some mysterious power; and so Ricardo becomes involved with the murder of Evelyn Devenish, found in a box, still naked, her hand severed. Before the body is actually discovered, there is some doubt whether Evelyn or Joyce has been murdered, for Joyce, like Celia in *At the Villa Rose*, has disappeared. Though Hanaud, at *his* romantic best, dressed as a brigand *pour le sport*, shortly arrives and eventually solves the case, Ricardo's centrality is suggested first of all by the role he adopts at the beginning, similar to the adviser-mentor of the earlier two novels, but less auxiliary. He is more—though this is treated slightly satirically by the author—the knight serving the lady in distress. "For all his finical ways and methodical habits he was at heart a romantic" (671). "But romance must nevertheless be reasonable .... (672). Hanaud's rationality solves the crime, but Ricardo's skeptical yet involved observation of the diabolical terrors are what set the tone of *The Prisoner in the Opal*.

One of the most striking scenes in the novel occurs in the chapter "The Cave of the Mummies," the grotto beneath St. Michel, when, in safe retrospect, Ricardo describes to Hanaud his subterranean first sight of Evelyn Devenish (I have assumed, in this discussion, that the suggestive nature of the heroines' names needs no comment). While the frame of this scene, as Ricardo and Hanaud motor in the Rolls through the summery French countryside, insulates it, it is one of Mason's most terrifying moments, with a suggestion of the supernatural, and the omnipresence of the macabre, reinforced by the cry Ricardo hears from Evelyn's lips—"a low cry of desire, savage and primitive, the desire to hurt as no one had yet been hurt, to punish as no one had yet been punished, a whisper of regret that not such punishment was possible" (737). It is the sense of Satanism and thwarted human passion, for Evelyn is killed partly because she has lost the love of the principal villain, which takes *The Prisoner in the Opal* at times outside the customary logic and rationalism of detective fiction. The end of the novel, with Hanaud logically explicating the crime and doing his usual part in bringing together the hero and the heroine, does not quite reverse the irrationality of the rest of the novel.

Seven years after *The Prisoner in the Opal* came *They Wouldn't be Chessmen* (1935). The title, which Sutherland Scott listed amongst the cleverest in the genre,[15] is nonetheless delphic, and needs some explanation. The plot revolves around the attempt of Major Scott Carruthers—surely a trustworthy name in clubland!—to steal from an Indian princeling his ancestral pearls. This young Rajah has given them to a showgirl, and they have become "sick," tarnished by a reaction to her skin (this is evidently a possible phenomenon). Carruthers undertakes to have them worn, and so "cured," by another woman, the famous opera singer Lydia Flight. Lydia is not in on the plot, but she and her lover are to be framed for the crime after the substitution of paste for real pearls is made. In a grand piece of Mason theatre which follows murder at the seance, murder in the sick-room, murder in the Black Mass, the theft takes place during a high-wire act at a very fancy dress ball (the timing, the effectiveness, of this scene—and the theft—at the moment of greatest audience distraction, recalls the assassination plot, at the moment of the striking of the cymbal, in Alfred Hitchcock's *The Man Who Knew Too Much*, the first version of which had appeared the year before this novel). But the title points to the reason for the ultimate failure of the conspiracy. It is less Hanaud's intervention which defeats the villains, than the failure of the various pawns in Carruthers' plan, who simply wouldn't be his chessmen, taking their orders instead, as Hanaud points out, "from their lusts and hates" (291-292).

Hanaud, it follows, and Ricardo, are less prominent in this novel than in the earlier three. It is Ricardo, as usual, who is the friend of Lydia Flight, who approaches him about the game in which she seems to be caught up. It is Hanaud, as usual, who comes in his wake and makes the connections between Carruthers and the rest of his gang. Hanaud, moreover, who in *The Prisoner in the Opal* began to reveal serious difficulties with English idiom which largely did not trouble him in the first two novels, has even more difficulties in this novel and the one to follow.

While *The Prisoner in the Opal* is the darkest and most macabre of the Hanaud novels, *They Wouldn't Be Chessmen* is the most pessimistic, and ends on the saddest note. The lovers are not given the blessing of Hanaud and Ricardo at the end, for the man is murdered as well as framed. "Let us leave it to time," Ricardo optimistically says of Lydia's sorrow as he gives "a Napoleonic sweep of his arm" to the gondolier who is propelling them through the Grand Canal, but even in that gesture there is sadness, and an acknowledgment of the emphasis on frustrated love, for this is the one novel which ends with Hanaud and Ricardo separated as well, their function as matchmakers gone. Of the five novels which make up the stories, this is the one which least shows the detective as analyser and investigator. He also is no chessman, but, except for his final act of *eclaircissement,* he is as subordinated to the march of events and individuals as Carruthers himself is.

There is now an eleven-year wait for the next Hanaud novel, only less than the wait between first and second. *The House in Lordship Lane* was published when Mason was eighty-one, two years before his death. This novel uncovers as many dark corners as the others; there is little sign of mellowing. The novel is, moreover, as I have remarked, odd man out of the five in many ways. It begins, as usual, with Ricardo on holiday, but not in Aix; he is en route home in a town with an "uncommon name," in Brittany. It is set, once Ricardo has returned home, and aside from a brief excursion of certain characters to Cairo, in London, whereas the main action of the earlier four never leaves France. Ricardo is approached by no lady in distress, nor is there any such character in the novel. There is, as usual, a female villain, but here she is more distinctly a supernumerary, a bystander rather than a participant when the crime is committed. As usual, the criminal is revealed five chapters short of the end (the twenty-ninth chapter of thirty-four), and then follows what Mason had condemned in Gaboriau, but used in Evelyn's letters in *The Prisoner in the Opal,* a written recapitulation of the crime by the criminal. But here, as perhaps only in *The Prisoner in the Opal* before, the revelation of the criminal comes as a genuine surprise. And finally, as we have seen before, *The House in Lordship Lane* departs from the pattern in showing Hanaud on specific assignment to the principal case.

In the telling of *The House in Lordship Lane*, few of Mason's old skills are gone. As only in *The House of the Arrow*, there is a double plot, though it is not bound together so effectively in the last novel. There is no metaphorical connection between the young revolutionary rescued from the sea at the beginning and then sent to a new life in Egypt, and the main murder. There is some suggestion of the poisonous evil in man's darker nature in the subplot, which deals with drug trafficking. But the real emphasis of the plot lies on the murder of the member of parliament who was once linked in an illegal transaction with the young revolutionary, and escaped with the profits of it. *The House in Lordship Lane* gives more glimpses of the world of power than the other four novels in the series, and it is for this reason more effectively grounded in familiar England, with the excursion to Egypt as a reminder of the international nature of the drug conspiracy. It is also this feature that makes it, of all the series, the most like an Oppenheim novel.

One of the most interesting characters in *The House in Lordship Lane* is the old shipping magnate who is kidnaped into solitary confinement and whose iron nerve is broken as a result. But in the very interest he generates there is unbalance in the plot, for he ought to have been principally a plot device. However, an incident during his imprisonment gives Hanaud his principal chance of deductive reasoning in the novel: the old man has a watch which strikes the hours, and he is able, even in the complete darkness, to determine that an airplane passes over his prison at certain fixed times. But Hanaud's deductions are based less upon intuition here, or even logic, and more on a simple reading of a timetable, a calculation of where the airplane would be at the particular time, and a consequent identification of the place of imprisonment.

The House in Lordship Lane is perhaps the one inaptly named novel in the series, though the title does refer to the scene of the principal murder. This is where the emphasis of the novel does lie, but because of the creative energy which the aged Mason lavished on the aged cantankerous millionaire, it is less than a comprehensive title. What one sees, overall, in the titles Mason gave to the five novels of the Hanaud series is their sense of place, and restriction. In the first two, Hanaud's field of activity is largely confined to the villa or house, and we are firmly in the realm of the closed circle of suspects which reached its *reductio* in Christie's *And Then There Were None* (1939). In the third novel, *The Prisoner in the Opal*, what is emphasized is the immobility and impotence of Ricardo; the confinement is his, as he watches the events of the novel with only less than his customary obtuseness, but also with little power to alter their macabre and irrational momentum. In *They Wouldn't be Chessmen*, we see again Mason's underscoring of the importance of character over circumstance, and, in contrast to *The Prisoner in the Opal*, a lesser impotence for the individual, but a greater sadness, for where one can checkmate the moves of the game-master one can regret the more one's own mistakes.

These then are the five novels which feature Inspector Hanaud of the Paris Surete. Only rather loosely, and by those who are seduced by Mason's excessive admiration for Gaboriau—"The best detective novel ever written is the first volume of Gaboriau's *Monsieur Lecoq* taken with the last chapter of the second volume"—can these five novels be taken as *romans policiers*, still less as police procedurals in the manner of McBain or Sjowall and Wahloo. For Hanaud is never seen in his office, and the tedious paperwork of a precinct room is entirely missing. Indeed, in the country house setting especially of the first three novels, and in the contrast which is drawn, to some extent, in all five novels between Hanaud and more plodding professionals, there is the strong suggestion that Hanaud is, after all, yet another Dupin or Holmes, unofficial, with the honorary title of Inspector. Mason drafts no floor plans, and Hanaud, unlike Lecoq, Bucket, Cuff or Ebenezer Gryce, has easy entree to the aristocratic circles he investigates. Though such considerations may be used to show Mason advancing and adapting the *roman policier*, it is probably more apt to see him working outside it altogether, while using a police official as his detective.

The true exponent of the *roman policier* in this period, of course, was Freeman Wills Crofts, the "best plodding detail man," as Chandler called him: Julian Symons assigned him to "the Humdrum School."[16] His novels, checkered with floor plans and railway timetables, remind us of the limitations of the factual method in detective fiction. His Inspector French proceeds with the factual caution of all fictional policemen down to that time, using his understanding without much aid from the intuition. As the contempt for the plodding policeman which Mason carries over into the Hanaud novels should remind us, Hanaud has little in common with French, and much more with his amateur forebears. Haycraft's linking of Mason and Chesterton has more than a chronological aptness, and finds its justification in Mason's listing of the great detectives which I quoted at the beginning of this study: "Has not Father Brown joined that select company?" Both Brown and

Hanaud, in the different ways that can be taken for granted, reach their solutions by intuition as much as by deduction. The blind man's dog ultimately does the leading.

Mason's admiration for *Monsieur Lecoq* is, in fact, scarcely at all for its detectival method, but all for its construction. Mason reads Gaboriau's two novels, *Monsieur Lecoq* and *The Honor of the Name*, quite reasonably, as one novel, and uses such a reading to justify his own revelation of the surprise before the psychological explanations and clues which in more orthodox detective fiction precede it. He does this most spectacularly in *At the Villa Rose*, but, as we have seen, in all the novels in the series surprise is secondary to character. The last two novels are markedly weaker than the first three, and the most obvious reason for their weakness is that *They Wouldn't be Chessmen* lacks, except for the two principals, the interesting characters of the earlier three, though Mason continues his study of the criminal mind in Carruthers and his associates; and that *The House in Lordship Lane* contains a character so interestingly presented that he attracts more attention than is tolerable away from the main plot.

The reasons, therefore, for the reluctance of the more casual historians of the detective genre to give Mason a more prominent place, or their willingness to ignore him altogether, are by now inherent in my discussion. He cannot ultimately be called an exponent of the *roman policier*, and his detective has suffered by comparison with more popular and archetypal figures. Moreover, his fame is more closely attached to a school of adventure and occasional intrigue in which Oppenheim, in his own time and probably since, surpassed him. But Hanaud is more than a copy of Sherlock Holmes—Mason's determination to differentiate him shows this—and Hanaud and Ricardo do advance the Holmes-Watson archetype in important ways. Moreover, to underline the single most important fact about these novels—which Mason himself went out of his way to do—their psychological study not only of their criminals but also of their detective shows Mason bringing something back into the genre that had been missing since *The Moonstone*.

And there is a final analogy with Chesterton: Mason, as his expertise and success in other kinds of novel demonstrate, is a serious writer. As Sutherland Scott somewhat rhapsodically noted, his style "seems to flow like a limpid stream over its bed of smooth, rounded pebbles."[17] Mason's elegance of style, as well as his considerable constructive powers, take him above such contemporaries as Freeman Wills Crofts, R. Austin Freeman, Robert Barr, Arthur B. Reeve, J.S. Fletcher, and place him very properly with the principal writers, those who have had their proper due, of the Golden Age. If readability is a criterion, Hanaud and Ricardo should not lack devotees.

Notes

[1] "Detective Novels," *The Nation and the Atheneum*, (Feb. 7, 1925), 645-646.

[2] *The A.E.W. Mason Omnibus: Inspector Hanaud's Investigations* (London: Hodder & Stoughton, 1931), "Preface," pp. 5-15.

[3] Dorothy L. Sayers, *The Omnibus of Crime* (New York: Harcourt, Brace, 1929), "Introduction," p. 33; *Tales of Detection* (London: Dent, 1936), "Introduction," p. xii. Howard Haycraft, *Murder for Pleasure* (New York, 1941), pp. 72-74.

[4] S.S. Van Dine, *The World's Great Detective Stories* (New York, 1927), "Introduction," pp. 9-10.

[5] "The Simple Art of Murder," *The Simple Art of Murder* (1950; new ed., New York: Norton, 1968), p. 533.

[6] Here follows a list of the detective and mystery novels and short stories of A.E.W. Mason, with editions used. All are the first editions, with the exception of the first three Hanaud novels, where for ease of reference I have cited *The A.E.W. Mason Omnibus* (London: Hodder & Stoughton, 1931). Mason's use of the "mystery" genre is often a matter of fine judgment (see Note 12); I have construed the term very strictly here.

At the Villa Rose (London: Hodder & Stoughton, 1910) (AVR) *Omnibus*.
The Witness for the Defence (London: Hodder & Stoughton, 1913).
The House of the Arrow (London: Hodder & Stoughton, 1924), (HA) *Omnibus*.
No Other Tiger (London: Hodder & Stoughton, 1927).
No Prisoner in the Opal (London: Hodder & Stoughton, 1928) (PO) *Omnibus*.
The Sapphire (London: Hodder & Stoughton, 1933).
They Wouldn't be Chessmen (London: Hodder & Stoughton, 1935), (TWBC)
The House in Lordship Lane (London: Hodder & Stoughton, 1946) (HLL).

Short stories:
The Four Corners of the World (London: Hodder & Stoughton, 1917).
    "The Clock"
    "Green Paint"
    "North of the Tropic of Capricorn"
    "One of Them"
    "Raymond Byatt"
    "The Crystal Trench"
    "Peiffer"
    "The House of Terror"
    "The Brown Book"
    "The Refuge"
    "Pfeiffer"
    "The Ebony Box"
    "The Affair at the Semiramis Hotel"
    "Under Bignor Hill"

Dilemmas (London: Hodder & Stoughton, 1934)
    "The Strange Case of Joan Winterbourne"
    "The Wounded God"
    "The Chronometer"
    "Sixteen Bells"
    "The Reverend Bernard Simmons, B.D."

"A Flaw in the Organization"
"The Law of Flight"
"The Key"
"Tasmanian Jim's Specialities"
"The Italian"
"Magic"
"The Duchess and Lady Torrent"
"War Notes:
　"Mati Hari"
　"The Cruise of the Virgen del Sorocco"

[7] Both *At the Villa Rose* and *The House of the Arrow* have been filmed three times. In 1939-40, the role of Hanaud was played twice by Kenneth Kent, of whom Mason himself strongly approved. Both novels also had early stage versions, in 1920 and 1928 respectively.

[8] *Crime and Detection* (Oxford: The World's Classics, 1926), "Introduction," p. xv.

[9] *Bloody Murder* (London: Faber & Faber, 1972), p. 95; King, article on Mason in *Twentieth-Century Crime and Mystery Writers*, ed., John M. Reilly (New York: St. Martin's Press, 1980), pp. 1016-1017.

[10] Roger Lancelyn Green, *A.E.W. Mason* (London: Max Parrish, 1952), p. 71. I am indebted to this book, the only biography of Mason, for the details contained in this paragraph. It is E.V. Lucas who is quoted here.

[11] Green, p. 166.

[12] Reilly, p. 1014.

[13] Symons, p. 95.

[14] "Cecil Roberts in the *Sphere*," as quoted in the end papers of most of the volumes that followed *The Sapphire*.

[15] *Blood in Their Ink* (London: Stanley Paul, 1953), p. 158.

[16] "The Simple Art of Murder," p. 525; *Bloody Murder*, p. 114.

[17] *Blood in Their Ink*, p. 32.

FINAL NOTE: Hanaud and Ricardo appear in two short stories: "The Affair at the Semiramis Hotel" and "The Ginger King." The first of these, which appeared in *The Four Corners of the World* (1917), is more easily accessible in *Ellery Queen's Mystery Magazine* (Jan. 1950). It adds nothing to the portraits of the two characters; its only interest being its earliness, published between *At the Villa Rose* and *The House of the Arrow*. Barzun and Taylor call it "this rather tedious novella," which seems just. "The Ginger King" appeared first in *EQMM* in August 1950. This later story also has little to recommend it, as Hanaud investigates a fire insurance case; though the method of arson used is ingenious, it is not likely to appeal to cat lovers.

G.K. Chesterton

Gilbert Keith Chesterton

Thomas E. Porter

1874	Born May 29, son of Edward Chesterton and Marie Grosjean, in Campden Hill, Kensington, London
1881	Attended Colet Court [Bewsher's] school, London
1887	Attended St. Paul's School, London
1892	Attended Slade School of Art and University College, London
1895	Proof-reader for publishers (Redway; Fisher Unwin); free lance journalism
1900	First book published: *The Wild Knight and Other Poems*
1901	Married Frances Blogg after a five-year courtship; writing regular weekly columns for *Daily News*
1904	Meeting with Monsignor John O'Connor, alias "Father Brown"; published *The Napoleon of Notting Hill* (novel)
1905	Began contributing *Our Notebook* weekly column to *Illustrated London News*.
1907	*The Man Who Was Thursday* (novel)
1908	*Orthodoxy* (essay)
1909	Move from London to Beaconsfield, Sussex; published *The Ball and the Cross* (novel)
1911	*The Innocence of Father Brown*
	The Eye Witness founded by G.K.C., his brother Cecil and Hilaire Belloc; later became *The New Witness* (1912-23), then *G.K.'s Weekly* (1925-1936), finally *Weekly Review* (1936-)
1914	*The Wisdom of Father Brown*
1918	Death of Cecil Chesterton in France
1921	Lecture tour of U.S.
1922	Reception into Roman Catholic Church by Father John O'Connor; published *What I Saw in America*
1923	*St. Francis of Assisi* (biography)
1925	Editor of *G.K.'s Weekly*; *The Everlasting Man* (essay)
1926	*The Incredulity of Father Brown*; founding of the Distributist League, a liberal populist society. Frances Chesterton received into Roman Catholic Church.
1927	*The Secret of Father Brown*
1929	Founding of the Detection Club by Anthony Berkeley; Chesterton a charter member; *Omnibus Volume-Father Brown Stories*
1930	Second visit to U.S.
1933	*St. Thomas Aquinas* (biography)
1935	*The Scandal of Father Brown*
1936	Died at Beaconsfield, 14 June; publication of *Autobiography* (For a complete list of G.K.C.'s publications, see Maisie Ward, *Gilbert Keith Chesterton*, New York: Sheed and Ward, 1943)

In the opening sequence of a recent Paul Newman film, *Fort Apache: the Bronx,* two rookie cops are eating a coffee-and-doughnut breakfast in a parked patrol car.[1] A black woman in a pink dress teeters across the deserted street and banters with the officers. As she straightens up to go, she draws a .38 from her purse and fires point-blank in their faces. With the shots the street comes to life; out of the alleys and the storefront doorways come scavengers who pull the bodies from the car, strip them of guns and shields and leave them bloody on the asphalt. The woman melts away among the grey buildings.

The fate of the murderess constitutes a sub-plot through the remainder of the film. Plying her trade, she takes a fat "john" to her flat and slits his throat with a razor. In her subsequent search for a fix, she falls out with her suppliers. They kill her, wrap her body in a carpet and dump the roll on a garbage heap. As the final shot in the initial sequence showed the dead policemen sprawled on the pavement, so the disposing shot of this sub-plot pans back to show the carpet roll on the dump.

This scenario of sudden death and senseless violence is a cinematic antithesis to the "mystery" or "detective story" genre. The opening sequence, however shocking and motiveless, offers the ingredients for a typical mystery plot—a violent crime in which law officers are the victims. In the classic mode of mystery-genre development, brother officers of the slain rookies would rally round to track down the killer. The community would—however reluctantly—yield information about the crime. If the murderess were herself discovered to be a victim, the "real" criminals—the dope dealer or the vice lord—would be uncovered and punished. In *Fort Apache* nothing of the sort happens and the viewer is left with a brassy taste in his mouth. This world is quintessentially chaotic; the omniscient camera eye, in following the murderess to her fate, makes it clear that no other eye could possibly connect the body in the carpet with the murdered policemen or the throat-cut customer or even with the dope dealer who murdered her. The police, by this cinematic device, are pronounced powerless against the forces of destruction and dissolution; indeed, those forces attack the department itself with impunity. For the citizenry and the law officers in *Fort Apache: the Bronx,* there is only one law: *suave qui peut.*

It is instructive to counterpoise against this contemporary scenario the substantive arguments of Gilbert Keith Chesterton's "A Defence of Detective Stories," written at the turn of this century. With his celebrated long-view of cultural matters, he argues that a principal value of the detective story lies in its sense of "the poetry of modern life." The city bears the imprint of human purposes and consciousness; the detective story imbues what might otherwise seem prosaic and routine in urban living with a sense of mystery and adventure. In this context he establishes an equally long perspective by viewing police activity as romantic and policemen as the white knights of contemporary society. The "natural" state of mankind is barbarism, he affirms, and civilization is the most sensational of departures from nature and the most romantic of mankind's rebellions. The detective hero thus attains epic proportions:

> When the detective in a police romance stands alone, and somewhat fatuously fearless amid the knives and fists of a thieves' kitchen, it does certainly serve to make us remember that it is the agent of social justice who is the original and poetic figure, while the burglars and footpads are merely placid old cosmic conservatives, happy in the immemorial respectability of apes and wolves.[2]

The imbedded paradoxes in this view of the genre are hardly surprising, considering the source; like all paradoxes, they provide food for thought. The detective, stereotypically regarded as the conservative representative of the status quo, appears here as romantic liberal; his dogged sleuthing is discovered to be a bulwark against the animality latent in human nature. Indeed, this presentation implies that the *roman policier*, far from being a mere escape to be enjoyed or simply a puzzle to be solved, epitomizes the triumph of the human spirit over the powers of chaos and old night. Without this view of the detective hero as knight-errant and this exercise of the romantic imagination, this interpretation implies, we would have Fort Apache, and apes and wolves would rule the Bronx.

When, some ten years after the appearance of this essay, the first volume of Father Brown stories appeared, Chesterton's own detective-hero bore small resemblance to this romantic figure. A dumpy, dough-faced cleric, J. (or perhaps Paul) Brown, Roman Catholic diocesan priest, lacks the dash and polish of sleuths like Lord Peter Wimsey or Hercule Poirot and the eccentricity and deductive brilliance of Sherlock Holmes or Nero Wolfe. He does not sniff either orchids or cocaine. Since it is not altogether improbable that a clergyman be both brilliant and eccentric (Chesterton had personal clerical acquaintances who were both), Father Brown's "ordinariness" draws attention to itself. In fact, only his clerical garb singles him out in a group:

> How long the fourth figure had stood there none of the earnest disputants could tell, but he had every appearance of waiting respectfully and even timidly for the opportunity to say something urgent. But to their nervous sensibility he seemed to have sprung up suddenly and silently like a mushroom. And indeed he looked rather like a big, black mushroom, for he was quite short and his small, stumpy figure was eclipsed by his big, black clerical hat; the resemblance might have been more complete if mushrooms were in the habit of carrying umbrellas, even of a shabby and shapeless sort.[3]

The broad-brimmed hat and the shapeless umbrella regularly precede Father Brown onto the scene; the one proclaims him a Roman clergyman—as the collar alone would not—and the other declares him a proper Englishman—since the umbrella is omnipresent, rain or shine. Chesterton frequently underscores Father Brown's Englishness; one example will serve:

> "See here, Father Brown," he said. "I consider you about the wisest and whitest man I ever met."
> Father Brown was very English. He had all the normal national helplessness about what to do with a serious and sincere compliment suddenly handed to him to his face, in the American manner. (355)

So it is that Chesterton's detective combines odd contraries: an undistinguished appearance in distinctive clerical garb, a thoroughgoing Englishness in the service of the Romish creed. Top this off with Father Brown's remarkable powers of detection, and one must suspect that these contrasts make a point.

Chesterton himself has commented on the reconciliation of opposites that mark his detective hero. In his autobiography, which he describes as a "mystery story," he speaks about his inspiration for the persona. The chief feature of Father Brown was to be his featurelessness and his point to appear pointless, a "Suffolk dumpling from East Anglia."[4] Chesterton then indicates that the description of Father Brown functioned as a deliberate disguise for a priest-friend, Father John O'Connor.[5] Father Brown's anonymity, his protypical English character and his religious affiliation in fact constitute a kind of disguise for a unique culture-hero. In a crowd Father Brown would have no more individuality than an egg; as a

Roman cleric in a determinedly Protestant culture, he might be viewed as a suspect outsider. There is an abiding mystery behind the mysteries of the individual tales which the reader is left to penetrate as best he may: what does this combination of the commonplace and the unusual in the Father Brown persona represent; does the priest in any way approximate the romantic sleuth of the essay? Who, then, *is* Father Brown?

The clues that Chesterton provides to his hero's identity and function are scattered over five volumes and (counting "The Vampire of the Village") fifty-one stories. The titles of the collections all focus on qualities and attributes of the priest-detective: *The Innocence of Father Brown* (1911), *The Wisdom of Father Brown* (1914), *The Incredulity of Father Brown* (1926), *The Secret of Father Brown* (1927) and *The Scandal of Father Brown* (1935). Presumably the stories in each collection illustrate the quality or property of the title. They also promise, by implication, that dictionary definitions of these virtues (innocence, wisdom, incredulity) may not apply, that Father Brown's virtues will have special characteristics. The secret he harbors and the scandal he gives will likewise be unique. *The Memoires of Sherlock Holmes* illustrate, in a series of case studies, a method of detection by a master; by contrast Chesterton's titles focus attention on personal qualities of his hero.

The reader, however, looks in vain among the tales for an explicit or systematic treatment of Father Brown's titular virtues. The stories conform superficially to the formulaic pattern of the genre: the commission of a crime, the investigation by the detective, the discovery of the guilty party and the consequent renewal of society. This skeletal outline may be elaborated in a number of ways: W.H. Auden, in his celebrated essay "The Guilty Vicarage," sees the detective story (the garden-variety English type, at least) as conforming to the Socratic daydream: "Sin is ignorance."[6] Jerry Palmer, who lumps the detective story with other types of "thrillers," describes the structural elements in terms of a conspiracy which is seen as an unnatural or pathological disruption of an otherwise ordered world discovered and destroyed by a competitive hero whose competitiveness isolates him from the rest of society.[7] The bare bones of the formula can be fleshed out with a variety of perspectives, e.g., psychological, mythic or Marxist. Any kind of interpretative elaboration of the formula, however, precludes the discontinuity depicted in *Fort Apache*.

Chesterton's adaptation of the formula contains a number of

variations, the emphasis on the personal qualities of the hero being principal among them. In the typical mystery story, although the detective is an outsider, a "genius" who sets things right, he also has some obvious affinities with the milieu. The corpse in the vicarage cries out for a detective whose qualities suit the village atmosphere; Miss Marple, for instance, fills the bill nicely. Hercule Poirot has an ineluctable cosmopolitan flavor that matches the ambience of the Orient Express. Philip Archer displays a hard-bitten, pragmatic cynicism consonant with the mean streets down which he walks. Sherlock Holmes would cut a ridiculous figure in downtown Los Angeles. In short, the detective, though set apart by wit, method or point of vantage, generally makes a match with the type of world he is to set right.

Father Brown, however, as we shall see, has no specific milieu to call his own. He ranges widely in time and space, and through a spectrum of socio-economic classes. Along with various settings in the English countryside, London and the suburbs, he will appear at a castle in Scotland, in a South American village, in a mansion outside Chicago, aboard an Atlantic luxury liner and on a road in the Apennines. He moves comfortably into the past, settling cases involving an eighteenth-century Puritan general and a feudal Lichtensteinian king, and deciding the provenance of ancient curses at Exmoor and on the Cornish coast. Whatever the circumstances, Father Brown is never at a loss; whatever the company, he relates, in appropriate fashion, to the membership. He gains the confidence of the professor, the milionaire, the secretary, the upstairs maid and the thief without pressing for it. He is "the kind of person people talk to." Even his clerical attire, because it precludes fashion, is a uniform for all occasions. It will pass for a tuxedo if circumstances warrant. Thus the milieux in which Father Brown operates embrace a wide variety of cultural situations; his ability to function in such disparate environments is a comment on the universality of both his clerical status and his personal qualities.

The "criminals" that Father Brown encounters are as varied as the geographical and the cultural circumstances of the tales; they do not fit neatly into socio-economic categories. They include the professional policeman, manservant, millionaire, aristocrat, vicar, artist, doctor, lawyer, merchant-chief. As Father Brown ranges to the continent, to North and South America, the villains cover a wider range of occupations, social classes and nationalities. Since the purely formulaic dimension of the mystery does not demand much of the criminal, simply that he initiate the process of detection by committing the crime, specific characteristics of the criminals and their motive(s) serve to determine the type of universe the detective is to order. Like the milieux, these culprits belong to a wide spectrum of race and class.

This is not to say that the criminals in the tales do not run to type; it is simply that the type is not racial or socio-economic. With the exception of the professional thieves, all the real culprits are, to some degree, ideologues; that is, they subscribe to an idea or a system of ideas that controls their interpretation of experience and dictates their reactions to it. The professional thief is the exception simply because his ideology is a practical one that yields to circumstance; the world owes him a living and he takes the direct approach toward exacting it. When, however, the thief finds himself hardening in his habit, he too takes on an ideology: to protect himself first. Father Brown points this out to Flambeau in "The Flying Stars."

> Your downward steps have begun. You used to boast of doing nothing mean, but you are doing something mean tonight. You are leaving suspicion on an honest boy with a good deal against him already; you are separating him from the woman he loves and who loves him. But you will do meaner things than that before you die. (53)

Flambeau responds to this exhortation by returning the gems he has stolen; he repents and reforms. The criminal action *per se* then can afford an occasion for repentance, but the criminal action that expresses an ideological mind-set never does. The professional detective who is also an ideologue is not above corruption; in "The Secret Garden" an anti-religious fanaticism leads the "most famous investigator in the world," Valentin of the Parisian Sécurité, to decapitate an American millionaire who is considering conversion to Roman Catholicism. When Father Brown divines both his method and his motive, the master detective does not consider reformation; he can only, in his pride, take poison (30). So, in the first tales of the first volume of the Father Brown series, the priest begins his career in detection by converting the master thief and convicting the famous policeman. The distinction implied in these solutions obtains throughout the canon: the evil-doer who is not set in his ways may repent and reform, but the ideologue involved in evil will generally persevere in his evil doing. Throughout the classes of society, in the bosom of every occupation, in all nationalities this tendency to evil is operative and is expressed not only in the simple appetites of greed or lust or power, though these motives often lie on the surface. Its expression is often the *idee fixee,* an ideology based on a narrow view of experience and reality that provokes a destructive course of action and results in the "crime to be solved."

Other tales in this first volume present villains of a similar stripe. In "The Wrong Shape" Dr. Harris, atheist and scientist, murders Quinton, poet and Orientalist. The doctor lives by Nature and by that creed he is free to kill the poet, "that tormenting little lunatic" (88). The Puritan general whose memory is graced by numerous monuments in "The Sign of the Broken Sword" stages a battle to conceal a murder he has done: what better place to hide a body than on a battlefield? According to the priest, the general found his justification in his own interpretation of an "Oriental book," the Old Testament (135). Kalon, the priest in "The Eye of Apollo," schemes to murder his mistress and benefactress for her money. He sends the blind heiress down an open elevator shaft. The prophet's "new religion" is a cover for his "meanness" (Father Brown's word for the psychological effect of habitual criminal activity). Though his missionary zeal is a sham, at root this confidence man lives as a pagan stoic, and it is his stoicism that gives him away. Father Brown observes that, of all the on-lookers, he alone does not flinch as his lover hits the pavement (126). Like Valentin, these malefactors are supported, in varying degrees, by their ideologies.

Even where no crime has been committed, but only the appearance of crime obtains, explanations depend on an understanding of the mind-set or ideology of the personae. In "The Honour of Israel Gow" the piles on the table of the Ogilvie castle: precious stones, heaps of snuff, minute pieces of metal, twenty-five candles, challenge the priest-detective's powers; Father Brown offers a number of imaginative possibilities connecting these items. In fact, the servant Israel Gow, a true Scot and descendant of the Ogilvies, has collected all the gold on the premises, including the gold in the teeth of his deceased master. An absolute sense of justice, an ideology of sorts, leads the old manservant and rightful heir to gather this bizarre collection: as even his name indicates, he is entitled to *all* the gold and he systematically retrieves it. "The Three Tools of Death" provides a plethora of murder weapons and a number of potential murderers, but Father Brown discovers in the personality of the deceased a suicidal mania that was not to be denied. The cause of his desperation was his religion, the religion of Cheerfulness that "would not let him weep a little, like his fathers before him" (148). Too much obligatory merriness drove him to drink and, finally mad, to self-destruction. In these stories the appearances of evil, as well as the actuality, depend on dedication to some consuming absolute.

These instances—all from the initial collection *The Innocence of Father Brown*—establish the type of culprit with which the priest continues to deal throughout the five volumes. Given Father Brown's profession, it should not come as much of a shock to recognize that the majority of these evil-doers are atheists; it is noteworthy that they are as often "men of science." When the criminal is neither, like Flambeau or the Anglican vicar who murders with the "hammer of God," then contrition and reformation may follow (115). The confirmed ideologues however do not take this path; the implication is that it is not open to them. Three of those noted above commit suicide rather than suffer public humiliation. The matrix from which the criminal action emanates is then not simply an individual urge to steal these diamonds or to revenge this insult or to possess that woman, nor even an idiosyncratic malevolence, but rather the consequent of a philosophical stance. There are no motiveless Iagos, no Moriartys or Doctor Nos in the tales.

Counterpoised against the destruction that closed systems foment is, in the first instance, the "innocence" of Father Brown. This quality at first blush suggests the the stereotype of the otherworldly cleric, a combination of naiveté and ignorance of the ways of the world. His unprepossessing appearance, rusty clerical attire and bumbling ways reinforce the image of the naif. In the first encounter with Flambeau, when the thief is shocked at Father Brown's knowledge of "foul practices," the priest responds: "Has it ever struck you that a man who does next to nothing but hear men's real sins is not likely to be wholly unaware of human evil?" (15)

Ignorance of evil is not a component of Father Brown's brand of innocence. In "The Blue Cross," from the outset he suspects the tall cleric traveling with him, and, later, when Flambeau has turned detective, he warns him about the danger lurking beneath the fairyland appearance of the Saradine castle. With all his experience Flambeau cannot imagine foully enough to detect the truth in the matter of the Puritan general; Father Brown can. In the case of the "hammer of God" the neighbors view their vicar as above suspicion. Father Brown finds his penchant for high places and his attempt to fix blame on the village idiot suspicious. The tendency to evil, to assume absolute control, to play God, does not exclude the clergyman. "Awareness of evil" is a constituent element of Father Brown's "innocence." Without it his nimble wit and capacity to reason would presumably trust unused.

Wisdom, the titular virtue of the second collection, is hardly absent from the perceptions of the little priest in the first volume. Its outlines, however, take more definite shape in the investigations of the second series. In the plurality of tales in this volume, conventional perspectives, accepting things as they appear, provides the knot that the priest-detective must unravel. The case of "The Man in the Passage" turns on Father Brown's ability to distinguish appearance from actuality. All the witnesses tell a different story about an elusive figure in the passage—presumably the murderer. The distinguished actor, under arraignment for the crime, describes the figure of a woman; the soldier describes a beast. Father Brown has the impression of a "devil with horns," but hastens to add that he recognized the apparition—it was himself. The actor and the soldier each caught a glimpse of his own reflection and saw a woman and a beast, respectively. When the judge asks Father Brown to explain his ability to recognize his own image, he replies: "Really, my lord, I don't know ... unless it's because I don't look at it so often" (198). (In this tale, the murderer—no ideologue—dies penitent of his crime.) Self-knowledge is clouded by the narcissistic projection of one's own image on the cosmos; *e contra*, it is cultivated by a reflective regard for others.

This brand of wisdom accepts the limitations of both theory and method. It holds suspect conventional opinion and cultural stereotyping. In "The Absence of Mr. Glass," Dr. Hood, an advocate of racial determinism, discredits his own theory. He accuses the Celts of "wild imaginings" and then constructs a scenario of blackmail and mayhem to explain the disappearance of "Mr. Glass" who turns out to be a juggled set of wine glasses and a ventriloquist's voice. The doctor's method is a parody of Holmesian deduction, as he assembles a detailed description of the missing "Mr. Glass" from a battered hat and fragments of glass. Father Brown solves the mystery by looking into the suspect's eyes and discovering that he is laughing. The scientific approach—both theory and method—makes a mountainous crime of a comic molehill.

"The Paradise of Thieves" and "The Mistake of the Machine" transport the problem of appearance and stereotype abroad—to Italy and America respectively. In the mountain passes of the Apennines brigands abound—at least in the popular imagination. The twist in this tale reveals as the true brigand the banker who has made a career of embezzling. When the false brigand (an actor in the banker's employ) announces that he will depart for such places as Manchester, Liverpool and Chicago, the poet remarks: "In short, to the real Paradise of Thieves" (175). Father Brown is not taken in either by the mustachioed "bandit chieftain" or by the distinguished millionaire. The pen in the hand of an embezzler can be as powerful an instrument for piracy as the cutlass. "The Mistake of the Machine," set in the Chicago area, illustrates, in Father Brown's view, the limits of technology in diagnosing psychic phenomena: "how sentimental must American men of science be. Who but a Yankee would think of proving anything from heart-throbs?" (199). The American detective, "a cadaverous, careful-spoken Yankee philosopher," makes the mistake of assuming that English nobility is necessarily noble and that a convict could not possibly belong to the peerage. The convict's pulse-rate leaps at the mention of the lord's name, not because the lord was his victim, but because the name is his own. "Lie detector," as the priest points out, is a misnomer; it is the operator of the machine who detects (or fails to detect) the lie. Father Brown insists on the human element as a principal factor in the equation of detection.

The priest's brand of wisdom also questions the validity of simple dichotomies, neat oppositions. "The Duel of Dr. Hirsch" offers a scientist-villain who creates a mirror-image opponent. The moralist and pacifist, a "saint of science," reports a confrontation with a chauvinist colonel who accuses him of selling secrets to the Germans and challenges him to a duel. Both the doctor and the colonel appear totally convinced of their positions. Father Brown is troubled by the exclusivity of the alternative possibilities: the note containing the secret information "was written by a French officer to ruin a French official; or it was written by the French official to help German officers; or it was written by the French official to mislead German officers" (182). Father Brown discovers a fourth possibility: that the note was written by Dr. Hirsch, the scientist-saint, to convince the public of his own magnanimity and courage. The colonel turns out to be Dr. Hirsch in disguise. The little priest notes that opposites do not quarrel, that there can be no real argument between black and white because there is no common ground between them. Absolute good and absolute evil are fictions of the platonic imagination and a playground for monistic ideologues.

Two tales in the *Wisdom* collection anticipate the theme of the third volume, *The Incredulity of Father Brown*. They deal with a peculiar version of cultural determinism: the hereditary curse. The Pendragons, in "The Perishing of the Pendragons," reputedly fall under an old Spanish curse; two of the family have perished at sea. The Admiral, the last but one of his house, disclaims any validity for the curse—he is a "man of science" and an atheist. The appearance of a flaming tower leading ships to their destruction is simply superstition, according to the Admiral. Father Brown discovers that the devil is indeed at work, but in the Admiral's machinations. The Admiral by torching the tower simulates a lighthouse beacon and draws the sailors on the rocks. The efficacy of the ancient curse is reduced to the present plotting of the villain. In "The Purple Wig" an imposter draws on the "legend of Exmoor"—the lord of the manor has a diabolically deformed ear. The wig presumably hides the deformity and lends credence to the legend. Father Brown reveals a guttersnipe solicitor under the wig and points out that journalists and the public itself enjoys fostering these legends about aristocratic families. Preternatural phenomena make sensational headlines and produce pleasurable *frissons* among the public, but the deviltry is often much more mean and mundane.

This wisdom, it is clear, can be more easily described in terms of what it avoids than what it embraces. It is wary of monistic views at face value; its principles exclude any simplistic reductions. Father Brown relies on reason, though he can hardly be called a rationalist. He looks for the rational and the humane features in events on the grounds that human beings operate consistently according to their natures and that the beliefs of people influence their actions. Thus he is able to see the millionaire as thief, the moralist as glory-hound, the lie detector as machine, the scientist as poet and the peer as convict. Because scientism and atheism are, in his view, inhumane, that is, because these ideologies disregard capacity for free choice and the need for community, their advocates are likely to abuse reason. The tendency to evil, to act or judge inhumanely, is thus given free rein.

The title of the third volume highlights a quality not usually included in the canon of conventional virtues. Incredulity ordinarily refers to a temporary state of disbelief; in a clergyman—even one so idiosyncratic as Father Brown—it is calculated to raise questions, if not eyebrows. An early commentator on Chesterton remarks on a shift in emphasis in the later stories:

> People who had refused to believe in Orthodoxy, because it was supernatural, were now disinclined to believe in it because it was

not supernatural enough .... Christianity was too wild for the old-fashioned scientist, it was far too tame for the new-fashioned Christian scientist. It was too spiritual for the materialist, but it was not spiritual enough for the Spiritualist.[8]

Six of the nine tales in this collection deal with curses of some variety, three concern the possibility of other preternatural occurrences—oracles or miracles. In every case Father Brown is incredulous; he is unwilling to accept *prima facie* an explanation based on the operation of occult or supernatural causes. So there is the apparent anomaly of the minister of the supernatural who is reluctant to believe in its operation. The tales themselves, of course, specify various grounds for this reluctance.

The opening narrative in the collection is curious enough in its own right—it serves two functions. "The Resurrection of Father Brown" reintroduces the detective after a twelve-year absence; he is resurrected for the reading public, and it is an "incredulous" Father Brown who rises. A motley and diverse community witness the "miracle." In a South American village, where the priest is doing missionary work, an American reporter who displays an Ingersollian contempt for religion, an American engineer who shows a simple Puritan regard for it, the atheist alcalde of the town and a conservative politician, more ecclesiastical than the Pope, come together over the apparently deceased body of the missionary. When the alcalde demands that God raise the priest and he awakes, the credulous are eager to proclaim the "miracle." Father Brown quickly telegraphs his bishop: "No miracle here," and adds: "Miracles are not as cheap as all that" (298). The sham would have provoked boom and bust among the religionists and have provided ammunition for the atheist alcalde and the cynical reporter. The engineer, who serves as observer, confidant and commentator, asks whether the conservative religionist was also part of the plot; Father Brown indicates that he would not be surprised. The little priest is back on the scene after a dozen years' absence, resurrected but not transmogrified, the same sane and sensible spokesman for reason.

Three of the tales in the *Incredulity* volume, like the "Resurrection," have settings in America (one on a liner in passage from America to England). The American personae represent a curious collection of types, with the most prominent variety the millionaire/philanthropist. "The Arrow of Heaven" is a "sealed room" mystery in which the millionaire is found with an arrow in his neck. Among the suspects are an old frontiersman who goes on knowledgeably about the bowmanship of "Red Indians" and an aviator from the underworld who is blackmailing the millionaire. "The Miracle of Moon Crescent," set in an "elder city on the eastern coast of America," presents a variant on "The Arrow of Heaven" situation and has a philanthropist disappear from a locked room guarded by four witnesses. Among the suspects in this tale is a Westerner, an advocate of wide-open-spaces religion and practical action. Among the sleuths on the case is a scientist who suggests that the witnesses should, on psychological grounds, doubt their testimony that the victim did not leave the room by the passageway they were guarding. The details of both cases educe a good deal of credulity from suspects, witnesses and would-be detectives. A mysterious and valuable *objet d'art*, the Coptic Cup, acts as curse-carrier in "The Arrow of Heaven," and a ranting Irishman with a blunderbuss serves the same function in "The Miracle of Moon Crescent." When other explanations fail, the atheists and scientists come to the brink of belief in the preternatural. In "The Miracle of Moon Crescent" the Westerner and his companion witnesses call on Father Brown to sign a testimonial, acknowledging spiritual causality: "We've stated how the curse was spoken out in the street; how the man was sealed up here in a room like a box; how the curse dissolved him straight into thin air, and in some unthinkable way materialized him as a suicide hoisted on a gallows." Father Brown replies that he would rather not sign such a statement and that one in his position does not joke about miracles (351). The Americans seem, by comparison, more quaint and credulous than any of their English counterparts; it is noteworthy that the millionaire victims in each case turn out to have richly deserved their fates. The mystical aura that gathers around wealth contributes to the Americans' simplistic view of these affairs—to which the priest refuses to subscribe.

Father Brown's incredulity, in two other tales, is focused on another class whose members enjoy a similar aura—the artists. "The Ghost of Gideon Wise" and "The Doom of the Darnaways" both present a murderer who is an artist. The family curse in the second is interpreted by the man of science; it is a matter of heredity. Father Brown points out that this hypothesis simply exchanges one set of superstitions for another; for his part, he believes in free will, reason and daylight. The artist-criminal works in the dark, both by faking a portrait from a photograph and by executing the murder in a "darkroom." Here the ego of the artist is his undoing; he is forging masterpieces and using his position as assessor for the Darnaways' collection to establish their authenticity. He testifies, with secret satisfaction, that a portrait is "by Holbein—or somebody of the same genius" (404). The artist in "The Ghost of Gideon Wise" is a socialist and a poet—in short, the sort of person the public would credit with integrity, high ideals and little pragmatic sense. The conflict in the tale is ostensibly between capitalists and communists, three millionaires intent on maintaining their monopolies *vs* the socialists who would destroy them. In the end the "ghost" turns out to provide an alibi for the two murderers, the artist and his socialist companion who are co-conspirators with one of the millionaires. When the reporter-confidante comments to Father Brown that the fictive adventure of the poet with the ghost was painted in brilliant detail, the priest notes that the artist can be "a sneak and a skunk" without ceasing to be an artist. His incredulity here extends to the mystic powers and elevated character often attributed by the public to the artistic personality.

None of these tales includes a genuine instance of the supernatural, as Father Brown would describe it. He argues that it is necessary to have an orthodox and circumscribed belief in the supernatural in order to avoid being taken in by bogus versions. In "The Miracle of Moon Crescent" he declares that "it's natural to believe in the supernatural. It never feels natural to accept only natural things" (352). To fill the vacuum of disbelief, the atheist tends to attribute supernatural qualities or functions to other sources: science, occultism, nature. Father Brown's incredulity in these matters is balanced by a complementary set of beliefs: God, free will, reason, history and daylight.

The Secret of Father Brown, published in 1927, is the only collection of stories with explicit narrative continuity, a frame story. Flambeau, ex-criminal turned private investigator, is now retired on a Spanish estate. Father Brown and an American, Mr. Chace, are visiting. The American proposes the thesis that Father Brown's method of detection must be "spiritual," i.e., gnostic and occult. Nothing would be more calculated to rouse the little priest's ire than such an implication. And indeed, his language in addressing the case runs to a number of oratorical devices: repetition for emphasis, rhetorical questions, slang and ellipses:

> A real live man with two legs said to me: "I only believe in the Holy Ghost in a spiritual sense." Naturally, I said to him, "In what other sense could you believe it?" and *then* he thought I meant he needn't believe in anything except evolution, or ethical fellowship, or some bilge.... (426)

His secret is indeed spiritual, but only in the sense that the spirit does the detecting from inside, assimilating to the mind and emotional state of the criminal in everything but the action. This identification with the criminal Father Brown calls, much to the American's amazement, "a religious exercise." Science deals with the criminal from outside, as if he were an ape or an aborigine or an insect; Father Brown's method demands the humility (a word he does not use) to recognize those murderous tendencies and motivations supplied by the detective's own psyche. The following tales in the volume are proposed as illustrations of this unique approach to criminology.

The underlying features of the little priest's method, as exemplified in the tales, include, with this critical employment of one's own criminal potential, careful reservations of judgment. The criminals in a number of these tales all look respectable: a prosecuting attorney ("The Mirror of the Magistrate"), a businessman ("The Man With Two Beards"), a leading actress ("The Actor and the Alibi"), a trusted servant ("The Song of the Flying Fish"), while the suspects tend to be outlandish: a wild Irishman, a professional burgler, a jailbird. In two tales, occultism, with an Oriental flavor, is invoked to explain the mysteries. In "The Song of the Flying Fish" an Arab with a stringed instrument causes fish made of gold to fly; in "The Red Moon of Meru" a guru allegedly exercises his psychic power over time and space to steal a ruby. In both instances Father Brown turns up a plausible explanation for the theft that debunks the operation of occult powers.

Three other tales deal with a particular kind of diabolism: "The Worst Crime in the World" is parracide, with the murderer impersonating the father-victim in order to insure his inheritance. The malice of the deed doubles as the son delights in his impersonation, a grisly joke shared with the devil. "The Vanishing of Vaudrey" turns on vengeance and irony; Sybil, a marriageable young woman, turns down a suitor who is a jailbird, only to accept, all unknowingly, the proposal of a murderer. In "The Chief Mourner of the Marne" the mourner has presumably fallen under "monkish influence" and cut himself off from the world because he was responsible for killing his brother in a duel. Father Brown discovers to the company bent on saving the recluse that the duel was no fair fight, that, indeed, the brother supposedly slain actually faked his fall and then shot the other at close range. The company is horrified at this treachery and totally unwilling to forgive such a miscreant. Only Christian charity, notes Father Brown, can forgive *real* crimes.

The priest's "secret" looks for the key to detection in a knowledge of good and evil—malice, revenge, treachery—that is not restricted by class, race or kinship. When he insists in his conversation with Chace that "I was the murderer," he is making his point. To exempt oneself or one's circle from the consequences of the Fall is to invite deception and disaster. The frame story comes to closure with "The Secret of Flambeau," in which "M. Duroc," alias Flambeau, vouches for Father Brown's contention that the most effective deterrent to crime is the individual's awareness of his own criminal potential. Once the master thief understood the grounds and the consequences of his activity, he was able to reform. Either to explain crime away or to see the criminal as irredeemable is a disservice to the individual and to society.

The final volume of stories, *The Scandal of Father Brown* (1935) consists of a reprise of themes now familiar from the earlier works with the exception of the title story. This tale deals with the issue of public opinion and reputation. Father Brown, visiting Mexico, encounters a domestic triangle that includes a poet, an actress and a businessman. The actress has presumably struck up a liaison with the poet; her businessman-husband is apparently odd man out. The priest assists the actress and her husband to reunite. This activity, in itself hardly scandalous, is misinterpreted by a bilious American reporter who hates romance, divorce and "dagoes." His misinterpretation results from the fact that Mr. Potter from Pittsburgh looks like a poet, while the poet looks like Mr. Potter from Pittsburgh; his press release reflects this confusion. Thus the press reports that Father Brown promoted an illicit affair and no subsequent retraction ever quite kills the first story. So a grave scandal is attached to the priest's name, about which he is little concerned, accepting, as he does, "the world as his companion, but never as his judge" (554).

Of the villains who appear in this collection, businessmen and scientists predominate. In "The Quick One," an old Scot Tory is murdered; Father Brown spends some choice rhetoric in eulogizing this type of old-fashioned curmudgeon as a man of principle who resisted the Whig mercantile movement. A traveling salesman does the old gentleman in simply to protect his swindle. "The Point of a Pin" offers a nouveau riche who murders his contractor uncle for property. The old aristocrat who impedes progress and the laborers who oppose exploitation would not stoop to murder or collusion; both have a conscience as the embezzling middle-class nephew does not.

The Mandeville College setting in "The Crime of the Communist" allows Father Brown to comment from the high table on capitalism, communism and science. He points out that Capitalism is a heresy that is taken for granted whereas Communism is a heresy under constant surveillance. The Bursar, a businessman, murders two philanthropists in order to cover his embezzling. His involuntary accomplice is the scientist who is experimenting with poisons "for the next war" in his laboratory. The communist faculty member is exonerated because, in spite of his desire to unbutton Western civilization and all its works, he would never light an after-dinner cigar before finishing his port. In "The Blast of the Book" a spiritualist/scientist argues both sides of the case for epiphenomena; he is taken in by his clerk who presents him with a book that causes people to disappear. While the professor has his eye on the epiphenomena, Father Brown solves the mystery by talking to the clerk.

The little priest, in this final collection, displays more of his personality than is usual in the earlier tales; he can rhapsodize, engage in whimsy, indulge in irony. After solving the case of Mr. Blue, he concludes with this apostrophe to his child-companion:

> One more penny left in the world . . . and then we must go home to tea. Do you know, Doris, I rather like those revolving games that just go round and round like the Mulberry-Bush . . . . I like to think of Mr. Red and Mr. Blue always jumping with undiminished spirits; all free and equal; and never hurting each other. "Fond lover, never, never wilt thou kiss—or kill." Happy, happy Mr. Red. (607)

He points out to the Professor in "The Blast of the Book" that, while seeking out the fakes, he ought occasionally to pay attention to honest men. In defense of the crime of the communist he employs wry and ironic understatement:

> He only wanted to abolish God . . . . He only wanted to destroy the Ten Commandments and root up all the religion and civilization that made him, and wash out all the common sense of ownership and honesty; and let his culture and his country be flattened out by savages from the end of the earth. That's all he wanted . . . . And you come here and calmly suggest that a Mandeville Man of the old generation . . . would have begun to smoke, or even strike a match while he was still drinking the College Port, of the vintage of '08—no, no; men are not so utterly without laws and limits as all that. (620)

Instances like this round out the Father Brown persona by etching in emotions; for example, he concludes his reflections on the College by remarking that it is, like England, a "funny place." At this stage he is occasionally playful, perplexed and even irritable. The "featurelessness" that characterized his presence and appearance in the earlier volumes is, in *The Scandal of Father Brown*, supplanted by a unique personality. The dumpy, little blank-faced figure fills out till his emotions are showing. So the character is complete.

Through the five volumes Chesterton unfolds the qualities and characteristics of his detective-hero in a fashion unique among mystery writers. From the stereotype of the cleric in the first volume, the bumbling innocent abroad, through the responsive and reflective commentator of the final series, a distinctive and specific personality emerges whose ability to solve mysteries remains constant. The vacant-faced dumpling of the early stories is as acute a sleuth as the alert and worldly-wise companion of the last volume. So the character of Father Brown develops through the tales; his identity is revealed in the aggregate.

The mystery of his identity is related to an aspect of the stories that transcends the whodunit formula. It is evident, even to the casual reader, that each tale illustrates a truth or set of truths or highlights a principle of common sense or an insight that has application beyond the solution of a particular mystery. As the tales include such illustrations, they move, in function, toward a venerable literary genre: the parable.

Using the obvious Biblical analogue, the parable proper is a story drawn from common experience that leaves the mind in sufficient doubt about its precise application to provoke thought. Gospel narratives like the Good Samaritan or the Prodigal Son come immediately to mind. The purpose of the parable is to teach by vivid illustration.[9] Critics have not overlooked this dimension of Chesterton's work; Hugh Kenner, amplifying a remark of Hilaire Belloc's, states that the parable is "Chesterton's chosen form."[10] In the Father Brown stories the "common experience" on which the author draws is the familiar whodunit formula; he weaves his teaching into the data, illustrating as he goes. The lessons of the tales, that the Old Testament is an Oriental book needing careful interpretation, that scientific explanations, zealously adopted, can become superstitions, that the irrational makes for bad theology, that capitalism can be as heretical a doctrine as communism are properly thought-provoking. These lessons, and others similar to them, unfold along with the solution to the crime.

Given this parabolic effect in the tales, Father Brown emerges, not only as sleuth, but as teacher. By and large, his *dicta* carry the burden of the parable's impact; he is the one who points out, for example, that the Puritan general misreads the Old Testament and that heredity may be as magical an explanation of evil as a curse is. Chesterton makes it clear that, though Father Brown's virtues are his own, he teaches also by reason of his office. That is, in action and attitude Father Brown represents a Christian point of view. He speaks of "sin" and of "charity" and, while his truths often reflect plain common sense, they are shaped by religious perspectives. The suicidal old man, for instance, who could not feel grief is labeled a "devotee of the Religion of Cheerfulness." All this suggests that a principal "truth" of Chesterton's detective stories is the revelation of the detective as a model of Christianity in action.

Thus in the parabolic aspect of the tales Father Brown is the Christian confronting the world.[11] Much of what would ordinarily fit that kind of model is missing in that nothing of his interior life or his sacramental ministry (with the exception of occasional references to confession) appears. The collar and the Roman hat announce his affiliation and specify a source for both his attitudes and his teaching. Just as the Christian as such does not belong to any special class or race, so the priest's activities cut across all such barriers. He goes about, doing good, dispensing justice and teaching the truth to all comers in all climates.

Chesterton's Christianity, as exemplified in Father Brown, is not everybody's. While most Christians might agree with his rejection of scientism, atheism and occultism, not all would agree with the substance of his critiques. Father Brown is too much the humanist and his teaching somewhat too rationalistic for broad acceptance among certain types of believers. He relies very heavily on common sense and reason. Those denominations that hold to basic tenets of Reformation theology tend to view the intellect as essentially corrupted by the Fall and logic as an instrument of prideful self-justification. They would doubt that repentance is possible without a dramatic and explicit experience of grace. Conversions like Flambeau's are too intellectual to be genuine and Father Brown's advocacy of them too "natural." For those sectaries who see a sharp dichotomy between the sacred and the profane, the little priest's traffic with the world (in the Pauline sense) would be suspect. He belongs in the pulpit, the sacristy and the rectory, dispensing spiritual counsel, not abroad in the marketplace, on the rostrum or in the pub. In significant ways, Father Brown is not only in the world, but also of it.

In contemporary theological terms, then, Chesterton's Christian is an incarnationalist, a believer who sees nature and mankind as redeemed in all its aspects and the potential for evil in human beings as repressible. This is why Father Brown's Christianity seems sensible and attractive and why his opponents, the ideologues, appear to be short-sighted, narrow and mean-spirited. This humanness is catalogued by the sum of the priest-detective's virtues: innocence, trust in reason, investigative incredulity, belief in individual freedom to choose and change. If Father Brown is a model Christian, then these qualities are presumably indispensable to the type. If more spiritual qualities are required, then they must build on these. At the very least, the priest represents a humanizing and Christianizing force in a society threatened by inhumane systems and attitudes.

The rhetoric of the tales, Chesterton's narrative voice, promotes this incarnational view; the fictive world of Father Brown fits him as he fits it. The landscape is humanized, indeed, romanticized, with rich and varied impressions that sometimes verge on the baroque:

> Outside, the last edges of the sunset still clung to the corners of the green square but inside a lamp had already been kindled; and in the mingling of the two lights the coloured globe glowed like some monstrous jewel and the fantastic outlines of the fiery fishes seemed to give it indeed something of the mystery of a talisman; like strange shapes seen by a seer in the crystal of doom. (461)

High color and chiaroscuro typify the descriptive passages; vivid images highlight the characterizations of the personae: "Everything about [Dr. Hood] and his room indicated something at once rigid and restless, like that great Northern Sea by which (on pure principles of hygiene) he had built his home" (153). Chesterton describes the perspective of his narrator in his autobiography: "[The primary problem for me was] how men could be made to realize the wonder and splendor of being alive in environments which their own daily criticism treated as dead-alive, and which their imagination had left for dead."[12] This lively imagination produces, in the tales, strongly defined impressions and sensations rather than a distanced reproduction of phenomena. The country manors, the village streets, pubs and sitting rooms are not Raymond Chandler's "mean streets" or Agatha Christie's homogeneous parlors. A feature of Chesterton's parables is this highly colored picture of a world invested with feeling and pregnant with life.

To come full circle as mysteries must, we return to the opening scenario. Even a Father Brown could do nothing in the discontinuous, live-dead world of *Fort Apache: the Bronx*. In it the imagination does not humanize and unify, but rather disjoins and fragments. In the Bronx of the film, anonymous and uncaring forces have long since rubbed out any traces of a civilizing imprint. As the violence there is irrational, its consequences are inexplicable; the blue knights who should maintain order for the common good can only hope to defend themselves. In an absurd world like this one, Father Brown would be a supernumerary, like a chaplain on the battlefield. It does little good among this chaos to believe in God, daylight and free will.

Finally, then, Father Brown's reasonable Christianity depends on a creative imagination that humanizes the landscape. The conventional formula itself proclaims ultimate intelligibility; by virtue of the whodunit structure the crime is explained and the criminal discovered. The basic mission of the detective is "to make narrative sense out of the data."[13] The assumption underlying the mission is patent, to wit, that sense *can* be made of the data. Father Brown's mission is to make common sense of the data and Christian sense of its implications. In a world of the "live" imagination he can comment on the roots of evil, principally the propensity to construct a closed system in which the architect is god. Chesterton's narrative style creates a cosmos with a human impress and so one with the potential for christianization. Whatever one thinks of this kind of cosmos, it does not fade noticeably with the passage of time. Like the parables of the New Testament, Chesterton's tales and his hero retain their savor.

Notes

[1] *Fort Apache: the Bronx*, starring Paul Newman and Edward Asner, directed by Daniel Petrie, produced by David Suskind, Martin Richards, Tom Fiorello, a Time-Life Film of David Susskind Productions, 1981.

[2] "A Defence of Detective Stories," in *The Art of the Mystery Story*, ed. Howard Haycraft (New York: Simon and Schuster, 1946), p. 6.

[3] G.K. Chesterton, *The Father Brown Omnibus*, (New York: Dodd, Mead & Co., 1951), p. 399. All subsequent references to the Father Brown stories will be to this volume, cited in the text.

[4] *The Autobiography of G.K. Chesterton* (New York: Sheed and Ward), p. 334.

[5] *Autobiography*, p. 339.

[6] *The Dyer's Hand* (New York: Random House, 1948), p. 158.

[7] *Thrillers* (New York: St. Martin's Press, 1979), p. 100.

[8] Emile Cammaerts, *The Laughing Prophet* (London: Methuen, 1937), p. 210.

⁹C.H. Dodd, *The Parables of the Kingdom* (London: The Religious Book Club, 1942), pp. 16-7.
¹⁰*Paradox in Chesterton* (New York: Sheed and Ward, 1947), p. 111.
¹¹Father Brown as Christian is not sectarian, that is, he need not represent Roman Catholicism as such. Chesterton converted to Roman Catholicism in 1922; the rationale for his conversion was unique in that he discovered that the church agreed with him rather than that he agreed with the church. See Margaret Canovan, *G.K. Chesterton: Radical Populist* (New York: Harcourt, Brace, Jovanovich, 1977), pp. 117-20.
¹²*Autobiography*, pp. 133-34.
¹³Robert Champigny, *What Will Have Happened?* (Bloomington: Indiana Univ. Press, 1977), p. 46.

H.C. Bailey

H.C. (Henry Christopher) Bailey

Nancy Ellen Talburt

1878	Born, 1 February, in London, only son of Henry Bailey
1901	B.A., Corpus Christi College, Oxford, 1st Class Honours in Greats.
	My Lady of Orange, first novel, published
	Begins career as dramatic correspondent, war correspondent, and leader writer for *The Daily Telegraph,* London
1908	Marries Lydia Haden Janet Guest, daughter of Dr. A. Hayden Guest, a Manchester physician
1920	*Call Mr. Fortune*, first collection of detective short stories, introduces the character of Reginald "Reggie" Fortune, medical consultant to Scotland Yard
1930	*Garstons,* first detective novel, introduces the character of "shyster" lawyer, Joshua Clunk
1933	*The Man in the Cape,* only non-series detective novel
1934	*Shadow on the Wall,* the first Reggie Fortune novel
1940	*Mr. Fortune Here,* the twelfth and last collection of Reggie Fortune stories
1946	Retires from *The Daily Telegraph* and moves to Llanfairfechan, Carnarvonshire, Wales
1948	*Saving a Rope (Save a Rope* in New York) the last Reggie Fortune novel
1950	*Shrouded Death,* the last Joshua Clunk novel and the last work by Bailey
1961	Dies, 24 March, in London, leaving an estate of about 15,000 pounds
1968	"A Matter of Speculation," only known non-series story, featuring a woman detective, the Honourable Victoria Pumphrey, published in *Ellery Queen's Anthology 1968 Mid-Year*

> "*Providence expects a lot for its money.*"
> Reggie Fortune

The age of the Great Detective—the agent of Providence—is past. The classic and colorful mystery fiction which was his customary vehicle survives only in muted versions of the originals. More nearly mortal champions creep to Pyrrhic victory where once their predecessors took longer strides to Edenic restoration. In its movement from tale to short story, and from romance to novel, detective fiction has acquired more of that realism praised by Raymond Chandler but lost much of its romance and much that was heroic (and melodramatic) in its earlier forms. Tastes shaped on contemporary detective fiction and related works find early mysteries dated—lacking not only in immediacy and suspense but in protagonists who are recognizably human or credible. Accordingly, much pre-World War II detective fiction is out of print today.

There are those works—standards and classics—which appear immune to such fluctuations in taste by virtue of some stamp of originality, some unique accomplishment which raises them to the level of enduring myth, or by virtue of some complexity which enables them to present different congenial elements to a new audience. Sherlock Holmes has become a legend—the archetypal figure against whom all others are measured—and continues to inspire imitators and reincarnations. Agatha Christie is a preferred adversary to a new generation in works whose fair and cunningly-wrought plots diminish the distance created by their period settings. Dorothy L. Sayers' novels exhibit a wit and feminist philosophy attractive to present-day readers who might not otherwise enjoy the exploits of a titled detective. But the list is short. It is a legitimate concern of readers of the diversifying genre of detective fiction to ask whether there are other works once widely praised and read which might appeal to a new generation of readers on the basis of qualities sufficiently remarkable to compensate for a distinct period flavor. An obvious corpus for reexamination along such lines is the detective fiction of Henry Christopher Bailey.[1]

H.C. Bailey was born and raised in London. He was already the published author of a novel, *My Lady of Orange* (1901), written as an undergraduate, when he came down from Oxford in that year to take a position in London on the *Daily Telegraph*. This early venture into print had not been his only non-academic effort—he served as coxswain for his college boat crew—nor did it prevent his being graduated with a First in Greats from Corpus Christi College. He served at different times as dramatic correspondent, war correspondent, and leader writer, remaining on the staff of the *Telegraph* until his retirement in 1946. Fellow detective fiction author E.C. Bentley (*Trent's Last Case*, 1913) was also a staff member of the *Telegraph* for 25 of those years.

Of Bailey's personal life, little is known. He married Lydia Haden Janet Guest, daughter of a Manchester physician, in 1908, and they had two daughters, Mary and Betty. Bailey, like Reggie Fortune, loved his garden. In 1946 he retired to Llanfairfechan in Wales, taking up residence in Bernina, a cottage formerly used by his wife's family as a holiday home. Neighbors recall the perfectly-dressed gentleman, a shy man who kept to himself. He is reported to have collected postal cards and to have enjoyed riding in his large automobile. In contrast to Reggie Fortune, however, he let his wife do the driving. Henry Christopher Bailey died in 1961.

While pursuing a full-time career as a journalist, Bailey published fiction for 50 years, producing a total of 50 novels, 12 volumes of short stories, a play, a history and a work for juveniles. His fiction falls into three classes: historical romances, detective short stories and detective novels. From 1901 to 1920 he published only historical romances, and he continued to write them regularly until he began to publish detective novels in 1930. He began writing detective short stories in 1920 when Reginald Fortune was introduced in a collection of six stories, *Call Mr. Fortune*. Bailey's sixth collection of short stories was published in the same year, 1930, in which he published his first detective novel, *Garstons*. This novel introduced a second series figure, solicitor Joshua Clunk. The last collection of new short stories, *Mr. Fortune Here*, appeared in 1940, but novels about Clunk and Fortune continued to be published until the appearance in 1950 of *Shrouded Death*, Bailey's last work. Bailey wrote no short stories featuring Clunk and only one is not about Fortune. In "A Matter of Speculation," a woman detective is introduced. She never reappears. Only one novel, *The Man in the Cape*, contains neither Clunk nor Fortune.

Mr. Reginald Fortune was "perhaps the most popular sleuth in England between the World Wars," according to the *Encyclopedia of Mystery and Fiction*, and Julian Symons calls his creator the "most often praised of the authors of the detective short story in the years after World War I."[2] But Reggie Fortune has suffered the common fate. Cast in the mold of the Great Detective, and medical consultant to Scotland Yard, Mr. Fortune appeared in 85 short stories and 10 novels. Ellery Queen points out in *101 Years' Entertainment* (1941)[3] that Bailey had written more detective short stories about a single detective than any other author. Today, only three Fortune works are in print. Fortune is similarly absent from such current "Who's Who" compilations as *The Great Detectives, The Book of Sleuths* and *The Private Lives of Private Eyes*.[4] Since H.C. Bailey was identified by Howard Haycraft in 1941 as one of the semi-mythical "big five" of Golden Age detective fiction authors,[5] his present obscurity raises the question of whether he has suffered a just fate (having been over-valued by readers of his own day) or is the victim of an unfortunate neglect. The question can be approached by a reexamination of the Bailey canon with a view to establishing three things: the degree of success of his characterizations of his series detectives; the ingenuity and sureness of his employment of other stock elements and preferred conventions of detective fiction; and the particular and distinct features of his writing, especially those which appear to have lasting aesthetic value. The results of such a reexamination should indicate the degree to which the period qualities of Bailey's fiction detract from—or promote—the participation and enjoyment of contemporary readers in his fictional world.

I. Rebel Disciple

'Yes, my job's sin. What sin's this?'

Reggie Fortune

Chief among the required elements of Golden Age detective fiction is the towering figure of its centerpiece and mastermind, the Great Detective himself. Penetrating in intellect, absolute in judgment, eccentric if not bizarre in taste and habit, and standing apart from the common herd in all things, he is its raison d'être. Next to Sherlock Holmes among Great British detectives, (in force of personality) stands Mr. Reginald Fortune, although no closer than cleverness ever is to genius. Still, as works of genius are rare, the genuinely clever is a not unattractive second best. It is in an analysis of the character of Reggie Fortune—his typical methods and comments—that the nature of Bailey's contribution to detective fiction is most clearly revealed.

Milward Kennedy is among the early reviewers of Bailey's

fiction to appreciate Reggie: "Has any sleuth since Sherlock Holmes had so strong a personality as Reggie Fortune?"[6] However, it is Erik Routley who first specifies the nature of the relationship between Fortune and Holmes when he labels Reggie a "rebel disciple."[7]

An aesthetic concern motivates most detectives. The beauty of the solution or the completed pattern drives individuals from Holmes to the Continental Op by what amounts to compulsion to find it. The disinterested and emotionless intellectual drive is embodied in Holmes who is described to Watson as being cold-blooded: "I could imagine his giving a friend a little pinch of the latest vegetable alkaloid, not out of malevolence ... but simply out of a spirit of inquiry ...."[8] The Continental Op describes himself to one of his adversaries as being out of the range of the human feeling she sought to arouse: "I'm a manhunter and you're something that has been running in front of me. There's nothing human about it."[9] For the rebel disciple of Holmes, there is a different concern. The mainspring of his character is a moral, not an aesthetic, an intellectual, not an instinctive compulsion to discover truth or a particular solution. His relationship to weak and helpless victims of crime and malice is personal, human and passionate. His being a doctor underscores this concern which takes precedence over pure detecting. Reggie's is a fierce if not militant outrage at the injustice and cruelty allowed to exist in the world. He has a ruthlessness which results from his double function in many stories: he not only reconstructs past actions to solve crimes, but, when legally admissible evidence of the crime is lacking (or when the immoral act was not illegal), he arranges to protect the innocent from the further depredations of those who were too clever to be caught at their initial forays into crime.

As much as a detective, he is, like the hero of adventure or sensational mysteries, a preventer of crimes. Often there is imminent danger to someone kidnapped or otherwise threatened. Like Ross Macdonald's Lew Archer, Fortune is often involved with mistreated children, the helpless young woman, or the dependent adult. Also, like Archer, he has an appreciation of the potential for perversion in parental feeling and domestic relationships. Despite the ferocity of his response to the injuries inflicted upon defenseless victims, Fortune is by no means eager to take up the cause of the downtrodden by doing literal battle, and he strongly resents the physical attacks which often occur when he does: "Self-sacrificin' heroine not my job. No intention to get knocked on the head. Painful surprise. And much resented" (Land, 166-7). As an agent of Providence, Reggie combines the functions of ministering angel and merciless avenger, achieving a happier fate for the threatened but misfortune for his antagonists.

Reggie is neither amateur nor professional detective, strictly speaking. As a member of another profession, the medical, he combines expertise in it with the demands of detection. In having a different primary profession as in his commitment to moral concerns, he resembles G.K. Chesterton's Father Brown. He belongs to the same social class and has the same "Oxford" manner (so much appreciated by Mr. Smithers in "The Two Bottles of Relish") as Lord Peter Wimsey and Philip Trent. He will also be found by some to have the same disturbing affectations of speech and manner. Unlike Lord Peter, Reggie "goes on cutting bread and butter"[10] rather than suffering agonies of conscience over the fate of his adversaries. Like Holmes, Reggie makes frequent use of physical clues (especially plants), employs scientific methods (especially in his laboratory and dissecting room), and does important investigative work on his own. He is very much his own man and moves as confidently among the guests of the King or while posing as an amateur botanist as he does in dissecting a cadaver. Perhaps most important, he has an irreverent if not sarcastic vein of humor.

Fortune views "crime" not in legal terms: "Crime as handled by the police, murder and theft and what not, only symptoms of disease," but in moral terms: "Worst effects in crime not forbidden by law: destruction of happiness, breakin' people's souls" (Wonders, Lilies, 89). As a physician, he also views crime in medical terms. In a short biographical sketch of Reggie, often appended to later works and editions, Bailey describes him as having no more mercy for the cruel criminal than for the germs of disease and as believing that the measures taken against both must be such as to diminish the danger of further infection (Meet, Fortune, 4). Reggie repeatedly points out that he is not (in contrast to many of his contemporaries) "playing the game" but doing something more important:

> "Playing the game for the sake of the game. I know. You would feel that. Well, you've found your line in life now, Fortune."
> "You think so?" Reggie said slowly. "I wonder."
> "Great game, manhunting, isn't it?"
> "No," said Reggie. "Not a game. And I wasn't manhunting. I was working for the woman—savin' what could be saved of her life. So little, my lord, so little. However. That is my job." He hung up with a clash (Clue, Stocking, 1).

While a decent respect for the expectations of a complex

readership requires Bailey (and Fortune) to reveal the truth and present solutions, a certain dramatic effect is sometimes achieved by having the final facts revealed almost off-handedly. The climax of a Reggie Fortune work, time after time, is not a solution presented to a rapt circle of participants in a drawing room but a high-speed car chase or the general convergence of the forces of justice upon some obscure attic, chapel, cellar, cottage or other covert where an incidental victim of the antagonist of the work lies awaiting death: drugged, beaten, subdued, bound. Reggie's brilliant analysis of clues and circumstances has led him in the nick of time not only to the solution of who-, what-, how-, or why-dunit, but to an intended victim. His focus is upon the rescue, not the solution. In a case that presents an extreme example, "The Yellow Diamonds," it is a full two days after a young woman is rescued and the thieves and murderers captured that Reggie stirs himself to point out the probable location of the stolen diamonds which have been the ostensible object of his and the police's search since the beginning of the investigation. To Reggie, the restoration of stolen property is clearly secondary.

It is not only in his moral rather than aesthetic drive, or his focus on the rescue rather than the solution, that Reggie is a rebel disciple. In physical appearance and manner of living, Reggie is the polar opposite of Holmes as well as of the tall, dark and handsome stereotype of the masculine romantic hero. Described as cherubic in appearance, or said to resemble a small boy (Holmes' profile is hawklike), Mr. Fortune is also round where Holmes is lean, and inclined to lie recumbent when Holmes would be pacing restlessly. Reggie, in fact, has several traits in common with the most successful of the American rebel disciples of Holmes, Nero Wolfe. While his rotundity does not approach in bulk Wolfe's one-seventh of a ton, he has a similar love for flowers and gardening and an encyclopedic knowledge of them, a similar love of good food which is often described at some length, and a similar indolence and love of ease which makes him reluctant to work or to leave home. It is impossible to imagine him saying "The game is afoot." He is far more likely to be found groaning a resentful "Oh my aunt" when summoned to help the police. Unlike Wolfe, Reggie can move fast when the occasion requires (although he dislikes walking) relishes driving fast and comes to share the comforts of his home not only with his cat, Cyrus, but a wife. It is easy to imagine Wolfe's sympathy, however, when Reggie, exiled to a country inn during an investigation, wishes the police could hang the cook—or when he makes a characteristically caustic comment about police officialdom: "the police, like the undertaker, do nothing until the only thing to be done is clearing up the remains with pomp and circumstance" (Explains, Milliner, 45). Finally, there is a Peter Pan quality in Reggie, an agelessness, a childlike straightforwardness and simplicity which is at odds with his sophistication but perfectly consonant with his restless impatience with protocol and his anarchist's disregard for troublesome laws. In contrast, Holmes and Wolfe represent the complete adult; it is impossible to imagine either of them as a child—and equally rare to find a child as a character in their works.

In several stories, Reggie has a factotum and chauffeur, Sam, who combines some of the qualities of Bunter and some of Archie Goodwin. This relationship is never developed, however, and Reggie's "Watson" figure is finally established in the person of Sidney Lomas, who is the chief of the CID and who regularly enlists Mr. Fortune's aid in the endeavors of Scotland Yard. A more morganatic but similar relationship develops with the Inspectors Bell and Underwood, who most often direct the investigations Reggie aids. Lomas, a social equal, shares Reggie's taste for good food and is a frequent guest in Reggie's house. He not only provides logical access for Reggie to the facts of a case but is an example of the foil so often used the better to display a detective's brilliance. Lomas escapes this stereotype in a number of ways, for example being capable of landing a jab it would never occur to Watson to throw—as when he responds to an unusual visit by Reggie (who is attempting to get information for his own purposes) with the comment: "Are you making conversation or will there be a point?" (Meet, Goddess, 346). In a similar vein is his response to Reggie's lament about the nature of things: "It's a wicked world, Lomas." "Thank you, I've been here some time" (Speaking, Zodiacs, 16). This relationship, like that of Holmes and Watson, is an important device for sustaining interest in the central character and creating a climate for exchanges and activities amusing for their own sake, apart from any particular plot or tale.

It is a curiosity of the works by Bailey that Reggie's scathing and regular attacks on the impotence of institutions, a characteristic more typical of hardboiled fiction than the classic detective story, is combined with special friendships with the police. Indeed his misgivings about the whole enterprise of criminal investigation extend to his own endeavors on behalf of the police. His towering arrogance of action has no corresponding arrogance of accomplishment. He talks of a "failure" in which the police, to their complete satisfaction, have, with his help, caught a murderer:

> Frightful. Exemplar of futility. We shall never know the truth of old Colborn's death. We've let a poor wretch of a woman get murdered. And all we do is hang another. An awful warning. Hopeless trade, our trade. Change the uniform of the police. Should be sackcloth and ashes (Clue, Pool, 84).

And of another case he remarks, "Yes, Justice has been done,.. no thanks to me or you" (Meet, Finger, 408). Reggie's criticism of the police focuses upon their refusal to do anything until confronted with a corpse: "Never see anything till it's over. Then you'll be the perfect policeman" (*The Best of Mr. Fortune Stories*, New York: Pocket Books, 1942, p. 269) and their failure to reason from evidence.

Mr. Fortune's method of crime solving and victim-saving is to regard all and only the evidence (usually supplemented by his own efforts), to avoid theories and to keep an entirely open mind. He believes that crime grows out of conceit, out of a person's desire to have more than he's got and to take it. He describes himself as a common man or a natural man, by which he means that he avoids specialization, intuition or imagination, and concentrates on the facts. He says that nobody understands detective work and nobody can: "You never know what you're looking for, so you have to look for everything" (Meet, Play, 325). His method is commonly mistaken by friends among the police (as well as a generation of critics). Inspector Bell says: "Very odd how he knows men .... As if he had an extra sense to tell him of people's souls, like smells or colours" (Eight, Murderer, 33). Bell, however, like Lastrade and Prefect G. before him, mistakes his man. More surprising are the many critics who have followed Bell with an observation that Fortune is an intuitive detective. Bailey seems to feed the notion, as when he has Lomas remark: "You're an uncanny fellow, Fortune" (Eight, Murder, 65). The fact is, the stories are full of clues, both physical and psychological, and Reggie's usual technique is to observe, make an inference, test his theory, and find the answer. The rarity of this approach accounts for Bell's and Lomas' attribution of special gifts to Reggie—a further indictment by Bailey of the poverty of police methods. The quality Reggie most often disclaims is imagination, something he may appear to have in abundance. He would argue that considering all the possible explanations of phenomena is logical and has nothing fanciful about it. Not only is the nature of his genius misunderstood by his associates, it is not taken seriously by him:

> Mr. Fortune was once persuaded to speak at a world conference on the detection of crime. What he said has been

hushed up. But out of the horror of experts from Washington to Tokyo it leaks that he told them never to believe they knew what they were doing (Here, Paint, 213).

In method, Mr. Fortune is a true disciple of Holmes, despite some appearances to the contrary. More than most detectives Reginald Fortune, M.A., M.B., M.Ch., F.R.C.S.,lives up to his name—a force or power that determines events and issues. While the classic detective and his hardboiled successor characteristically administer their own "justice" on occasion, seldom before the advent of Mickey Spillane does one so thoroughly and consistently do so as Reggie Fortune. Holmes is mentor to Reggie in instances of absolving the legally guilty of moral blame and shielding them from punishment. But in devising the punishments, most often death, of those whom the law could not touch, Reggie goes much beyond any predecessor. His is an Old Testament, if not ancient Greek, justice of retribution. His ruthlessness is at odds with his appearance and manner, but it is one of his most consistent traits and makes him a terror to the guilty and an object of awe to his police associates, insofar as they know what he is doing.

Reggie's essence is found in his comments and a quotation expressing his philosophy often provides the pungent beginning to a tale:

> When he feels life hard, Mr. Fortune is apt to argue that one of the chief causes of crime is the desire of people to be good. Too often, he points out, this tempts them to a life of doing good which is bad for everybody (Wonders, Cigarette, 1).

Such comments are not merely provocative: they express an ironic truth illustrated by the story. They also reveal a quality of mind which is both modern and timeless.

After thirty years of writing fiction, H.C. Bailey wrote his first detective novel. All his detective works had been in the form of the longish short story and had featured the same series hero. Wisely recognizing that he had found, or made, a very good fit between his pathologist-detective and the short story, Bailey chose to initiate his detective novel writing effort with a new character. Wisdom seems to have lessened at that point. Joshua Clunk's mannerisms are not only anti-heroic, they are downright silly. It is true that the novels which featured Clunk sold on both sides of the Atlantic, though not so well as the Reggie Fortune works. It may also be true that Clunk's character was less unpalatable to readers of the 1930s than it will be to most readers today. Clunk is impressive in the effects he achieves, and he shares with Reggie a confidence in his own moral sense. This allows him a wide latitude in the dispensing of justice, although his decisions more often protect the legally guilty than punishing the actually guilty. It is in Clunk's personal characteristics that Bailey hits wide of the mark in his detective. These traits, if peculiar to the point of being revolting, are also at least as unforgettable as they are odd. Consistent with his name, Joshua Clunk's avocation is that of preacher. He has built a Gospel Hall with his own money and "there, three times on Sundays and once in the week, Mrs. Clunk played the harmonium and Mr. Clunk preached the Larger Hope, when business allowed" (Garstons, 2). His ivory-yellow face, grey beard, and grey eyes also suggest a venerable deacon. He habitually sings or hums hymns, snatches of which take the place of the incredibly dizzy range of quotations which fill Reggie Fortune's mouth. He drinks quantities of tea, has gourmand, rather than gourmet, tastes and fuels himself steadily with sweet candy between meals and mountains of sugar at them. There is some suggestion that he soon bored Bailey as much as his readers, for his wife (clearly the same one—unless this is a clue to a deeper mystery) is variously called Maria, Emma and Rachel.

Joshua Clunk is introduced as a shyster lawyer. Thus, like Reggie, he is neither policeman nor detective but has a profession of his own. Unlike Reggie, he ostensibly works at cross purposes with the police and therefore has to rely very often upon his own resources in gathering information. Clunk's involvement seldom centers upon a client. More often, his initial hiring serves only to bring to his attention what is an interesting and puzzling situation. His closest fictional relative is Anthony Gilbert's lawyer, Arthur Crook, who first appears in 1937.

In the first Clunk novel, *Garstons*, Clunk is challenged by the son of a former client to explain where all the client's money went (Clunk was trustee). Clunk is introduced by figures familiar to Bailey readers, Inspectors Bell and Underwood:

> "Don't you know him, Underwood? You will. He's Clunk and Clunk, Joshua Clunk."
> "What, the crook's solicitor?"
> "That's the fellow. I'd say he's given us more trouble than any man that's never gone to gaol" (Garstons, 2).

Bailey goes on to say that Clunk makes more of the hopeless cases of criminal small fry than any other lawyer, giving them a run for their money, if not acquittal: "It is commonly said that he knew more of what was going on underground than any man in London, and not uncommonly believed that he was up to the neck in most of it" (Garstons, 3).

Howard Haycroft points out in *Murder for Pleasure* that "a villainous detective is something of a contradiction in terms" (p. 127), but the early descriptions suggest that Bailey, tiring of chronicling the exploits of an agent of Providence, conjured up Clunk as an agent of the devil. In fact, he is described by the police as being able to show the devil the way to hell. However, it is as much a mistake to take Bell's view of Clunk as it is to trust his analysis of Reggie Fortune's method. Clunk is revealed in the course of the novels to be a different sort of character: he helps Bell and others (including Lomas) with information; he is referred to as a champion of widows and those menaced by society; and he receives kind words from Reggie in *The Great Game*, a novel in which he plays a minor role.

Both A.E. Murch, in *The Development of the Detective Novel*, and Haycraft pay tribute to the excellent and intricate plots of the Clunk novels.[11] As a matter of fact, the plots sometimes defy analysis, even after the conclusion is reached. At least one source of the intricacy of the plots is the presence in them of a group of investigators. While there is insufficient personal attractiveness in Clunk to compensate for the peculiar nature of the eccentricities with which he is endowed, some of his employees are more interesting and appear in most of the novels. The romance of Victor Hopley, Clunk's chief investigator, forms an important subplot in *The Red Castle*. The pretended romance of Fay Delicia, "Madge" John and Jock Scott, one-armed war veteran, is a cover in *The Wrong Man,* and Madge does more investigating, being wounded in the final free-for-all, in Clunk's last novel, *Shrouded Death*.

It is not easy to establish the mainspring of a character such as Clunk. He says his method is to "scatter manure as well as seed" (Sky, 186), and he shares with Vidocq a thorough knowledge of the criminal underworld and the methods of its inhabitants. In these two respects he is able to draw on sources of information different from those used by Reggie. Clunk digs up information then passes some of it on to the police, but he never calls off his own workers or reveals all of what he knows to anyone. He rescues innocent women and children and exhibits Reggie's passionate concern for the helpless, but he always manages to make a profit and back the winning heir. There are more characters from the underworld, including more who were framed and sent to prison rather than being rescued, than in the Fortune novels. Would-be clients and former clients seek him out for help or with information to offer. Clunk's world is the world of big and little criminal alike, not the world of Ascot, club and house party.

Joshua Clunk is not a Great Detective, although the novels in which he appears are, insofar as plot and detection are concerned, not inferior to those in which Reggie Fortune appears. While there are some courtroom scenes—for example in *The Great Game*—that suggest Perry Mason's tactics, as a character Clunk is never taken quite beyond chirping sanctimony. Bailey had a good idea in beginning a series of novels about a criminal's lawyer on the other side of the well-explored fence from the Fortune territory. Like Erle Stanley Gardner, he wanted to provide a view of how "justice" looks from the receiving end. Whether because of a failure of conception in the character of Clunk or because of the different demands of the detective novel as opposed to the short story, the good features of the Clunk series have little to do with the presence in them of the solicitor-detective.

In the one novel written by Bailey which features neither Clunk nor Fortune, one of the main detectives suggests Gideon Fell in appearance and is given a strong personality and profession, that of painter. But there is no suggestion, in *The Man in the Cape* or elsewhere, that Bailey ever considered having him make a return appearance.

In contrast, in a short story Bailey introduces the Honorable Victoria Pumphrey, from an old respectable family gone broke: "The Pumphreys came over with the Conqueror and did very well out of it" (Speculation, 141). The story records Miss Pumphrey's first case. Although it is the only story published about Victoria, there is a reference in the story itself to further adventures: "Thus, Miss Pumphrey is wont to say, was she launched on her present profitable career of crime. But she considers that she always had a bent for it" (Speculation, 18). The conclusion of the story reveals Victoria's plan to set up as: "The Hon. Victoria Pumphrey, Friend of the Family: relations discovered or destroyed; domestic quarrels settled; mysteries solved—family skeletons a specialty" (Speculation, 27). Whether Bailey actually intended at some point to begin a series of works about a woman private detective seems impossible to discover. Miss Pumphrey shares with Madge John an active detecting role and with Reggie a love of food and ease. She is quick witted and observant, and promises much as a series character. The introduction of Victoria Pumphrey, and the success of her debut, is of considerable interest despite the fact that she appears in only one work.

H.C. Bailey created one Great Detective, Reggie Fortune. But for that achievement—his creation of the cynical and sybaritic rebel disciple of Sherlock Holmes—he deserves recognition as one of the masters of Golden Age detective fiction.

II. Convention and Formula

"Hanging's too good for the man."

Inspector Bell

"You may be right. However. Try it."

Reggie Fortune

The classic detective story has been variously dismembered and anatomized and found to consist of assorted vital and supplementary parts. Depending upon one's hermeneutics, the parts constitute a formula, a comedy of manners, a tragedy or an elaborate puzzle. Whatever the critical perspective, at the center of the work is a problem and a detective. **Almost equally important is the immediate periphery, composed of villain, victim and suspects.** Assorted conventions, rules and secondary elements may be significant, the most often discussed of these being the convention of fair play, which provides the clues to allow the reader to match wits with the detective. In assessing the accomplishment of any author of detective fiction, it is necessary at some point to focus explicitly upon the handling of basic elements and conventions of the genre.

In his 107 works of detective fiction, H.C. Bailey achieves considerable variety in the management of basic elements while creating his own patterns and typical usages. Specifically he makes use of such individual variations as: 1) assigning unusual and bizarre motives to criminals, 2) dividing the role of victim among more than one character, 3) focusing upon physical clues examined at the scene of the crime and recording the detective's inferences from them, and 4) emphasizing the counterplot and rescue aspects of his detective's actions.

The time-honored but socially deplored practices of heir- and obstacle-removal dominate the catalogue of classic crimes, and they have their place in the plots and motives of Bailey's criminals, but simple greed and ambition are embellished in convincing and surprising ways in his fiction. More than most contemporaries, Bailey depicts the obsessed criminal, one bent on malicious destruction, violent revenge or some awful altruism. While there are also recognizable examples of such criminal types as the professional criminal, the architect of business frauds, the practical joker and the odd spy or hunter after treasure, Bailey's accounts of the deeds of the obsessed antagonist make the best reading.

Quite a number of the criminals in the Bailey works are motivated by irrational hatred. They are not, however, excused on the grounds of insanity. In a riveting story, "The Unknown Murderer," Bailey presents an exquisite murderer, Lady Chantry, who is a talented organizer and philanthropist. She is motivated by a desire to enjoy someone's intense emotional hurt, and she kills those who have someone to feel the loss intensely. Other examples of the irrational criminal include the woman in "The Broken Toad" who, having murdered father-in-law, husband, policeman (by accident) and daughter-in-law, commits suicide after having framed her daughter for her "murder." The object of her crimes is to leave her beloved son the entire estate. A more awful altruism can hardly be imagined. Similar parental devotion compels a mother to attempt to murder her grandchild so as to have the love of its father, her son, for herself in "The Oleander Flowers." Obsessed by a desire to save poor children from starvation and give them a chance for life, the proprietor of a boys' school in "The Long Dinner" infects those wealthy heirs among his charges with disease germs and sends them home to die. With the money paid him for these murders, he brings larger numbers of poor children to the beneficial climate of his school. In other stories, vengeful criminals go to elaborate lengths to right real or fancied wrongs. In "The Little House," a child is tortured by criminal drug distributors because of enmity for her parents; children of a murderer are brought up to hate Fortune for his part in their father's death and attempt to kill him in "The Furnished Cottage"; and young men who were cheated out of land or money return to kill the men who built fortunes at their expense in "The Pink Macaw" and "The Nice Girl." Benevolently motivated perhaps, the fathers of two vicious children kill them: in "The Key in the Door" a father kills his daughter after discovering that she murdered her brother and has attempted the life of a lover who spurned her; in "The Bicycle Lamp," a father kills his son after discovering him to be a criminal and a murderer. By the creation of such criminals as these, Bailey produces his own atmosphere of horror, not by overstatement but by simple statements of the emotions that apparently ordinary domestic relationships can produce. Among his ordinary, professional and occasionally attractive criminals, the almost mad are the most memorable.

In both novels and short stories, Bailey makes consistent use of what may be called divided victims. This is not an original device, but the regularity and manner of its employment in his works make it one of the distinguishing features of his plots. There is frequently a victim who is dead and one who is threatened in a Bailey plot. Thus the concern for the victim is split, and the attention to the victim as an object of attack is multiplied. The presence of a potential victim changes the character of a detective story, giving immediacy to the need to find the criminal, something which may otherwise become more an intellectual or abstractly moral pursuit. The menace may be immediate, when planned victims are abducted, as in "The Magic Stone," "The Wistful Goddess," "The Picnic," and many other works. It may be implied, as when Reggie determines that his own fiance is the intended victim of Lady Chantry. It may be contingent upon the criminal finding out the potential victim's whereabouts (as in *The Man in the Cape*). The victim may be endangered by those to whom he or she would naturally go for help, rather than by strangers or apparent enemies: a husband is almost buried alive by his "bride" (and her husband) in "The Long Barrow," and children are tortured by their stepfather and mother in "The Yellow Slugs."

A particularly intricate use of the divided victim occurs in stories such as "The Business Minister," which has as its antecedent Conan Doyle's "The Problem of Thor Bridge." In such instances the real object of malice is someone who can be "framed" for a crime (in this case actually suicide) which he or she did not commit. "The Quiet Lady" has a similar plot. While not every criminal is willing to become a victim in order to destroy an enemy, in these stories an apparent murder masks the intention of the apparent victim to destroy the apparent criminal. Thus the roles of victim and criminal are reversed, dividing the real from the false victim, the real from the false criminal. In other less extreme examples of this kind of divided victim, the plot succeeds in disgracing the intended victim by his conviction for a crime he did not commit. In *The Sullen Sky Mystery*, a young man is wrongly convicted of setting fire to hay ricks to remove him as a rival in love. In "The Brown Paper," and "The Little Finger," men who are also successful rivals of the criminals are framed for theft and arson. In these cases, the object of the crime is to injure the rival: the crime itself is incidental. By creating a set of stories and novels in which there is a great number of injured and potentially injured victims of malice, Bailey defines both his detectives as protectors of the innocent as well as bringers of justice and confers a more than academic interest in their endeavors.

A crucial part of a Reggie Fortune story is his visit to the scene of the crime. Like Sherlock Holmes, he is able literally to pick up important clues which have escaped the attention of the police. In addition, he brings to the post-mortem examination the same thoroughness, often instructing the divisional surgeon or other pathologists in their work. Because Fortune is a man who professes to know a little of everything but not to be an expert in anything, the clues found are seldom esoteric. Fortune traces one of his own assailants by a sprig of heather; he determines the approximate date of death of a badly decomposed body by noting the state of development of the flowers (some in bud) upon which the body lies; he knows how butterflies are captured, and where, and the habitat of the gipsy moth; he can differentiate Dutch tobacco from German, and he recognizes the sort of slime which comes from a neglected pool. He also knows the habitat of slugs. Like Holmes, Fortune is capable of inferring a great deal from slight evidence. It is the visit to the scene of the crime and the clues always to be found there which form the basis for a Fortune story, although such clues are often supplemented by laboratory analysis. H.C. Bailey is at his most classic and conventional in presenting physical evidence which in nearly every work forms the primary basis for investigation and solution of crimes. Fortune asks questions, but he does not believe the answers. He believes, as he often says, evidence.

If H.C. Bailey's detectives proceed by a careful examination of evidence and the drawing of inferences which permit no other possibility, they conclude their investigations in a more active than cerebral way. The resolution and solution in the typical Bailey work is the result of his detective's counterplot. Once having ascertained the facts of the case and formed an hypothesis, Fortune or Clunk typically leaks a story to a newspaper, sends a faked message, gives misinformation to suspects, or sets in motion other activities which precipitate responses by the criminals. Very often the counterplot includes having suspects followed or suspect places watched. Counterplots are designed to elicit the whereabouts of kidnapped victims, confirm the guilt of the malefactors, turn criminals against one another, or to produce the punishment suitable to the crime. Whatever the mechanism used, the counterplots flush the quarry, make clear the plot, and not infrequently dispatch the criminal.

Not every counterplot is devised by the detective. Two "Robin Hood" figures lend a hand to justice in "The Little Finger" and *Honour among Thieves*. The Smiler is a burglar who falls during the course of a crime and is saved from the police by a good samaritan.

He pays his debt by "framing" the old adversary of his benefactor's father so as to accomplish his punishment for an earlier crime. Reggie condones the unusual method of achieving justice. Similarly, Alf Buck is successful in defending himself against a "frame" by former criminal associates, and he "frames" a set of counterfeiters for their own crimes.

While achieving a distinctive treatment of these basic elements of the detective story—motive, divided victims, clues and counterplots—Bailey is less innovative in his handling of others. In structure, his short stories are simple or compound, but his novel plots are complex. In most of both there is more than one crime or attempted crime. In the short stories, however, one criminal or pair, often lovers, is the rule. Often also the story begins with an account of what turns out to be the second or middle crime in a sequence. It is the middle crime which causes Reggie to hypothesize the existence of earlier crimes so that he must work both backward, to discover and prove the identity of the criminal, and forward, to protect the next victim. There is less consistency in the novels, except that plots are very tangled and the novels are very busy. In four of the twenty-one novels there is a single plot line, although more than one crime and victim, and in three of these, heirs try to improve their circumstances by removing other heirs. The fourth, one of Bailey's best, concerns a hunt for church treasure.

The clues in *The Bishop's Crime* include a code in a fourteenth century Dante manuscipt, and the chief criminal is a scholar from Oxford, a beautiful young woman. The book is flawed by the lack of explanation for the murders and attacks which occur periodically, but it makes good use of red herrings, something at which Bailey does not excel, and has an effective double resolution, disposing of the criminals and later discovering the treasure. In other novels, there are more than one criminal and usually more than one criminal scheme. In *Dead Man's Shoes*, for example, there are three different criminals with three different motives for the three lines of criminal activity. Other novels are also cluttered by the simultaneous operation of large groups of criminals, spies, traitors and their associates. Such plots bulge the acceptable lines of the classic mystery.

There is considerable conscious variation within the collections of short stories, and each contains a variety of story types. In most collections there is at least one "light" story whose plot begins as a joke or issues in amusing rather than menacing results. The first such story published is "The Hottentot Venus," in which a Prince and amateur archeologist tries to arrange a marriage for his English daughter by kidnapping her. Reggie invites himself along on this and another "kidnapping" in which a tyrannical woman is made to pay for her mistreatment of her charges in what Jane Gottschalk calls a "Wodehousian romp."[12] In addition to the latter story, "The Hermit Crab," other examples are "The Snowball Burglary," planned to amuse Reggie, and "The Love Bird" in which a young woman successfully thwarts a financial scheme and Reggie reunites two love birds. It is usual for each collection to have one story in which professional crime and criminals replace the usual amateurs. Among the best of these are "The Yellow Diamonds," "The Yellow Cloth," and "The Long Barrow." Diamond theft, a thieves' disagreement and a kidnapped girl figure in the first, while silver thefts and a bad policeman are principals in the second. American criminals round out the trio of stories. Finally, in each collection there is at least one very serious story, one in which the crime threatened or committed is shocking or emotionally disturbing. Bailey's best stories belong in this category, of which some important examples are "The Long Dinner," "The Yellow Slugs" and "The Unknown Murderer." Because of a tendency in later collections to make the serious story one concerning a menaced child, Bailey has become linked with such an emphasis. In fact, fewer than twenty percent of his stories treat child or adolescent victims.

In criminal method, Bailey leans heavily upon various blunt instruments and introduces a noticeable number of drownings and near drownings. In fact, a character in a Bailey novel stands a better than even chance of ending up in the water. There are exceptions, such as the criminal who punctures the gas tank in a victim's car, allowing the gas to drip upon the exhaust pipe until sufficiently heated to explode the tank. There are also poisonings, including at least two cases of death from an unknown and untraceable poison and several with such imaginative and homely substances as salts of lemon (a cleaning product) and laburnum and oleander which can be gotten from one's own garden. While the methods are the designs of a fairly well varied lot of villains, insofar as sex, class, age and occupation are concerned, too often the criminal is a business tycoon and a humorless, boorish member of the nouveau riche.

Among other conventions and secondary elements of the classic detective work, Bailey finds little to use. He does regularly incorporate into the novels a set of lovers, and they occasionally figure in the short stories especially as a means of stirring up interest in the fate of the one kidnapped, usually the young woman. His handling of such figures is usually stilted and unconvincing, and his most successful employment of this convention may be in *The Great Game*, where, after introducing them and allowing them to become engaged at a village bonfire, he allows them to die. Bailey provides clues but does not play fair with the reader since confessional behavior often provides the final clue. He also makes little use of locked rooms or closed circles of suspects.

Bailey is at odds with practice among his peers in a number of ways. He uses untraceable poisons—a clear violation of the rules of detective fiction—and employs suicide, natural death and accident with some regularity to explain causes of death. He makes little use of timetables and maps, although he employs several ingenious codes, one involving book catalogues, another based on "Mignon's Song" from Goethe. A more serious departure from practice is his failure, especially in novels, to offer detailed and convincing explanations of exactly why or exactly how a crime was committed.

Despite a lack of highly dramatic plots and criminals, H.C. Bailey makes a craftsman's use of the elements and conventions of detective fiction, rising above the ordinary in a number of ways and offering a wide range of inventive and varied problems for solution. His treatment of victims, and the spirited and passionate intensity of his detectives on their behalf, is the main distinguishing feature of his handling of the genre's staple elements, but his use of physical clues and the medical analysis of evidence and bodies is also consistently good.

III. Crimson Patches, Parables and the Good Life

"Here's who's who. What's what?"
                                            Sidney Lomas

The Purple Patch approach to critical appraisal enjoyed a measure of popularity for which it has paid with a greater amount of ridicule. Questionable as the touchstone theory of high literary art may be, the related but different technique of locating characteristic passages in a detective writer's work—such passages as seem typical because they embody the techniques and subjects most associated by the public with the writer's special qualities—can be useful. Especially in works of formulaic or other highly conventional genres, the identification and analysis of such key passages may provide important clues as to the way in which the writer bends convention or stretches stereotype in order to wrench a new meaning from formula and convention. It is the double obligation of the writer of formula fiction to satisfy the formula (meeting expectation) while exceeding it in some allowable and individual way (creating suspense and surprise). The effect is to create a new pattern which falls partially within but slightly outside the set of conventions which define the genre. This new set of features constitutes the sub-formula of the writer. Detective fiction also requires a writer's most characteristic elements to be prominent in his works, and the ability to originate a sub-formula of unmistakably colorful features can spell great success for a writer in this field.

It should be useful to have a term by which to indicate any of those prominent passages which contain or constitute the sub-formula of a writer. For obvious reasons, Crimson Patch has much to recommend it, suggesting critical tradition as well as the site of some crucial—if not fatal—encounter. Such a passage will most often carry the stamp of a personal voice or style and will focus on a characteristic situation, exchange or observation. It may contain only one of the author's favorite devices or topics, but it should have the essence of the author in that particular element. The Crimson Patch is author-specific, not genre-specific. It captures at least a part of the vitality and individual vision which shape the author's sub-formula and serves as a concrete example of what distinguishes that author from others who write in the same genre. While certain authors' works cannot be successfully approached by such a technique, the scores of parodies and what might be called pale pastiches of certain authors and schools of detective fiction, in particular Sherlock Holmes stories and hardboiled fiction, suggest that there are a variety of uses to which Crimson Patch identification may be put, patterns for imitation being one. A Crimson Patch from Doyle and one from Chandler will illustrate:

> "Is there any point to which you would wish to draw my attention?"
> "To the curious incident of the dog in the night-time."
> "The dog did nothing in the night-time."
> "That was the curious incident," remarked Sherlock Holmes.[13]
>
> ...He was worth looking at. He wore a shaggy borsalino hat, a rough gray sports coat with white golf balls on it for buttons, a brown shirt, a yellow tie, pleated gray flannel slacks and alligator shoes with white explosions on the toes. From his outer breast pocket cascaded a show handkerchief of the same

brilliant yellow as his tie. There were a couple of colored feathers tucked into the band of his hat, but he didn't really need them. Even on Central Avenue, not the quietest dressed street in the world, he looked about as conspicuous as a tarantula on a slice of angel food.[14]

Few writers of detective fiction have left so personal a mark. But it is possible to find important motifs in key passages by many writers. Three quotations from the works of H.C. Bailey will serve as examples:

> "Come on, let's have it," Lomas exclaimed. "What do you make of the fellow?"
> "This interest is flattering. To me and him. Well. Not one of our cleanest fellows. Clothes not his strong suit. Except to the nose. But generously nourished. Too generously. Age fifty or so. Middle height, strongly built, fair skin, when washed, which he hadn't been for some time. No organic disease but the beginnings of resentment of drink in the liver. Man of crude, greedy tastes...."
> "Congratulations. Scotland Yard always gets its man. Alive or dead. Speakin' officially, you can say your hunting der-rove him to his doom. And I wouldn't deny it. Rather stern punishment for the crime. But these little excesses will happen" (Meet, Crime, 12, 15).
> "I find the people so dear and interesting," Mrs. Mervyn explained.
> Reggie's amazement was mingled with apprehension. "Dangerous state of mind. Leads to a lot of trouble."
> "You do love to talk wickedley, Reggie." Mrs. Marvyn smiled at him. "I know you too well to listen."
> "Yes. Makes you very soothing company. But I thought you were fairly safe here. Opportunities of doing good to people very limited." He turned and looked over the bare cliffs to the sea. "Nice uninhabited country" (Wonders, Case, 3).

One further example comes from a discussion involving the nature of goodness in which Lomas has said that goodness consists of good taste and Joan Fortune has suggested that it is being kind:

> "Yes. Both have glimpses of the truth," Reggie murmured. "Bein' kind isn't adequate. You've got to be kind within reason.

That's where sound taste is useful. Love's done about as much harm in the world as hate. Devotion—self-sacrifice—dangerous, delusive virtues. Made some of the worst horrors" (Meet, Toad, 198).

It is not true, as is sometimes supposed, that the creation of a convincing Great Detective figure is sufficient to insure the success of the author. Neither is it sufficient to add to that conception a familiarity and dexterity in manipulating a plot, a villain, a victim and assorted suspects. More likely to confirm the talent and assure the audience is the creation of an unmistakable voice, a narrative manner so much one's own that Crimson Patches would almost as surely betray authorship as a fingerprint. No writer of Golden Age detective fiction has so singular a voice as H.C. Bailey. While it is most often the character of Reggie Fortune who speaks in elliptical and obscure telegraphic phrases, Bailey's own statements, or those of his narrative voice, are similarly distinct and pointed. The mannered, clipped and article-or-verb-free prose may become tiring, even to the appreciative, in a novel, but it is effective in the short stories, compressing a great deal into a few suggestive or summarizing words. Bailey's command of language is sound, and he writes with the ease and confidence of learning and extensive practice, but because of its highly individual quality, his prose will be as maddening to one kind of reader as it is interesting to another. Not only cryptic and epigrammatic, the prose is clever, arch and highly allusive as well as affected. There are rather too many "old things" or "old boy's" for the American ear, and the so-called drawl (a "dropped" *g* in spelling which is a dialect marker rather than an affectation) will be equally grating to the snobbery-with-violence school of criticism. The writing is, however, unmistakably Bailey, many Crimson Patches marking each work as precisely as a signature. To achieve a stamp so nearly unique is remarkable in a genre best known for its content and convention.

Hardly separate from the texture of Bailey's prose are the satire and sarcasm which pepper it. No institution escapes, not even those to whom Reggie owes apparent allegiance: "Because the old ruffian was beastly wealthy, it's suspicious that he doesn't die in his bed with a specialist or two to kill him decently" (Trials, Profiteers, 218); "In spite of Eton and Oxford, Geoffrey disturbed his father by showing signs of originality" (Call, Assassin, 90); "It was a marriage made in haste and even less explicable than marriages generally are" (Sentence, 95); and "They have the one English virtue—though they do not live, they let live" (Man, 41). Even among parodies of classic detective mysteries, it would be hard to surpass the comment by a Bailey butler upon the violent murder of his prominent and wealthy master: "It is most distressing for the mistress, and, if I might say so, a shock to us all, being quite sudden and unexpected and the circumstances not what could be wished for nor thought of . . . ." (Vineyard, 136).

Next to humor and satire, the most consistent inclusion in Bailey's prose is the allusion. Allusions generally create a common ground in Bailey. Rather than providing a basis for exclusion of the uninitiated, as do the more consciously literary allusions of Nicholas Blake, Michael Innes and Amanda Cross, they are inclusive, ranging widely enough to include hymns, popular verse and that which is more cliche than allusion. It would take a treatise to explore the allusions in Bailey, for there are hundreds. Most come from the mouths of Reggie or Joshua Clunk, but Sidney Lomas and Inspector Bell also contribute upon occasion. The sources range from nursery rhymes, such as Old Mother Hubbard, to the Bible; from Shakespeare to Schiller; from Julia Ward Howe to Gilbert and Sullivan; and include Spenser, Milton, Tennyson, Keats, Wordsworth and Swinburne, among scores of others. Many allusions are freely and humorously adapted; most contribute to the tone of the stories; and, at best, they characterize the speaker and situation through the analogies they introduce.

Often allusions are part of the banter and the play between Reggie and Sidney Lomas. They contribute to the tone sought by Bailey of sophisticated men diverting themselves from frustrating or depressing crimes by means of a learned game. The frequent quotes from the Bible underscore a parable quality of the stories. "Way to hell, I presume?" (Clue, Pool, 44), spoken on a thronged road, is typical, as is the reference to "brother's blood, crying from the ground" (Eight, Ascot, 23), used by Reggie to justify his own vengeance against a killer. The use and misuse of quotations and references to the high and the low in literature supports the effect of irreverence which is one of the most consistent attitudes in Bailey. Some favored passages are quoted almost ad nauseum and others are less than totally apt in their contexts. Sometimes allusions substitute for dialogue or more serious exchanges, becoming padding or filler where none should be required. The range of Bailey's references is wide, and their use extends the richness and suggestiveness of the stories in which they occur. The total effect is to produce a fictional scene peopled by readers (or by those who have indulged in that pastime), and such a scene will have a definite appeal to many other readers.

While H.C. Bailey's rich and humorous prose is a significant accomplishment and the most distinctive feature of his writing apart from the character of his detective, there are other aspects of his work which deserve attention. One obvious feature is his mastery of the short story of a favorite length, about one and one-half to twice the length of a typical Sherlock Holmes story. Though an awkward length for anthologizing, such stories suit him, his style, and his detective exactly and allow development and comment without requiring artificial complexities or multiple murders. Few writers today make their mark as writers of the short story, although there are always some novelists who venture into the shorter form. It could hardly be incidental to the decline in Bailey's popularity that he was best at the short story, a form which is far less popular and less often available today than in his lifetime. Bailey's distinctive features surfeit when experienced at length; the pungent and mannered Reggie Fortune is not only terribly British, he is better savored in measured amounts.

In another more significant way, the works of H.C. Bailey are alien to the current trends in fiction. Northrop Frye's separation of fiction into four categories is useful in pinpointing this feature of Bailey's work: what he writes is closer to the tale than to the short story and closer to the romance than to the novel. There is a strong sense of the told and a narrator who speaks familiarly of characters and directly to the reader. The narrative point of view achieves a sense of memoir. Bailey, in comparison with near contemporaries such as Christie, Crofts, Freeman and Sayers, is less given to surface realism. There is a tendency toward allegory in plot and abstraction—as well as stereotype—in character. Good and Evil, not crime and punishment, is the subject. Starting with the name Fortune, one can enumerate other examples of descriptive names. Bailey writes of the villain called Nastiche; a suburb, Totsbury, in which a mother and baby were murdered and buried; and Nosy Parker, an ex-con who intervenes in plans to ensnare his daughter. Chatty Brown is an informer; Lady Sancreed is a reformer; Wanshire is the home of a pale young curate; and Sunshire is a resort area fancied to "have the climate of the Riviera but the morals and comfort of England" (Garstons, 43). There are also a Bill Sikes (a nickname), an Elizabeth Arden (a housekeeper), and a Randolph Hirst (a flashy Crook). The result is to generalize and distance the action but also to add to the farce and fun element of the fiction.

The specific locus occupied by Bailey's work in the rather broad territory of romance and allegory is suggested by Thomas Waugh who describes the stories as parables.[15] It is an acute observation. The moral urgency, the biblical quotes, and the approach to allegory in plot and character create such an effect. The generalized settings, the character names, even in some cases, the nature of the crimes, place the stories, like parables, in a timeless present. The philosophy which they convey is expressed in no specific religious terms, but reinforces humanity and stern justice. On the other hand, the larger-than-life-sized hero, Reginald Fortune, who is mistaken for Mr. Greatheart and confesses to being in the same line of business (Meet, Crime, 173), and the distressed damsels so often aided in the very nick of time suggest a dimension of the knightly romance. The combination of the heroic and the parable give to Bailey's works a quality of their own.

Bailey's accomplishment can be summed up in one final observation about the fictional world he creates. He depicts, with well-chosen detail, what can only be called the good life. We are told by Sidney Lomas that in Reggie's garden one can ring for the servants from the hammock or the lawn. In this domestic and pastoral setting, he fashions marionettes, entertains his friends, and dines well. Under his supervision, foods are prepared, and food is described more specifically than anything else in Bailey's fiction: cakes made from saffron and filled with clotted cream and fresh berries, a perfect omelet, crepes Joan, excellent claret. Even in the temporary home he makes of an inn, Reggie eats well:

> Over the soup and the cod, both watery, he despaired of England. The beef comforted him, over the partridges he rejoiced and with the aid of Burgundy, a Pommard, 'not great but good,' he became enthusiastic on the simple life. But he said no word of Badon until they had finished the herring roes (Meet, Crime, 57).

At another place on the social scale, Joshua Clunk and Mrs. Clunk, who prepares her own delicacies, eat and reside in similar ease, appropriate to their humbler station but no less lavish. While Reggie often seems aggressively indolent, and Joshua Clunk spends an awesome amount of time at tea, such scenes are a conscious counterpart to the criminal investigations which provide the main actions of the fiction.

Reggie is periodically summoned from the warm fireside to the drafty scene of yet another crime, but he is just as often rescued from a tedious social function by the call to investigate. The summons or the rescue frees Reggie from what would otherwise be a dull though comfortable existence as well as a less productive one. More than most detectives, those in H.C. Bailey's fiction work to make things better, to protect the innocent, to promote the general good. Reggie lives a good life, and the seemingly rascally Joshua Clunk does, too, because they do good things. The paradox inherent in Bailey's celebration of the good life is that, despite Reggie's protestations at being called from it to work, what makes the good life *good* is detecting.

The period flavor of H.C. Bailey's detective fiction may be so marked as to make his work unpalatable to a reader of the 1980s. There is no denying the presence of clumsy dialogue between minor characters, melodramatic situations, outdated social comment, stock figures and affectation. While these qualities in modest amounts might not be sufficient to discourage those acquainted with similar qualities in contemporary works, the parable quality of his stories could prove a barrier to the pleasure of many readers. Sin, after all, is no longer in, as an object of reprehension. On the other hand, for the more eclectic collector and reader of mystery fiction, the highly individual prose style, with its wit, satire and playful allusions; the soft-living, tough-thinking and tart-tongued detective; and the careful attention to clues, unusual puzzles and detecting will make Bailey's evocation of the good life attractive despite a certain quaintness. The qualities which made H.C. Bailey a favorite author in his own day are present, in his best works, in sufficient quantity to continue to deserve a measure of that original recognition.

Notes

[1]The editions of Bailey's works used for this study are listed below, preceded by the original date of publication. References to them will be included in the text by title of novel or collection and story, using, where necessary, the abbreviation given after each entry.

1920 *Call Mr. Fortune* (London: Methuen, 1920). (Call)
        "The Archduke's Tea" (Archduke)
        "The Sleeping Companion" (Companion)
        "The Nice Girl" (Girl)
        "The Efficient Assassin" (Assassin)
        "The Hottentot Venus" (Venus)
        "The Business Minister" (Minister)
1923 *Mr. Fortune's Practice* (London: Methuen, 1923). (Practice)
        "The Ascot Tragedy" (Ascot)
        "The President of San Jacinto" (President)
        "The Young Doctor" (Doctor)
        "The Magic Stone" (Stone)
        "The Snowball Burglary" (Burglary)

"The Leading Lady" (Lady)
"The Unknown Murderer" (Murderer)
1925 *Mr. Fortune's Trials* (London: Methuen, 1925). (Trials)
"The Young God" (God)
"The Only Son" (Son)
"The Furnished Cottage" (Cottage)
"The Hermit Crab" (Crab)
"The Long Barrow" (Barrow)
"The Profiteers" (Profiteers)
1929 *Mr. Fortune, Please* (London: Methuen, 1927). (Please)
"The Missing Husband" (Husband)
"The Cat Burglar" (Burglar)
"The Lion Party" (Party)
"The Violet Farm" (Farm)
"The Quiet Lady" (Lady)
"The Little House" (House)
1929 *Mr. Fortune Speaking* (London: Ward, Lock, 1929). (Speaking)
"Zodiacs"
"The Cat's Milk" (Milk)
"The Pink Macaw" (Macaw)
"The Hazel Ice" (Ice)
"The Painted Pebbles" (Pebbles)
"The Woman in Wood" (Wood)
"The German Song" (Song)
"The Lion Fish" (Fish)
1930 *Mr. Fortune Explains* (London: Ward, Lock, 1930).
"The Picnic"
"The Little Milliner" (Milliner)
"The Wedding Ring" (Ring)
"The Football Photograph" (Photograph)
"The Rock Garden" (Garden)
"The Silver Cross" (Cross)
"The Bicycle Lamp" (Lamp)
"The Face in the Picture" (Face)
1930 *Garstons* (London: Methuen, 1930); as *The Garston's Murder Case* in New York. (A Joshua Clunk mystery)
1932 *The Red Castle* (London: Ward, Lock, 1932); as *The Red Castle Mystery* in New York. (Castle) (Clunk)
1932 *Case for Mr. Fortune* (London: Ward, Lock, 1932) (Case)
"The Greek Play" (Play)
"The Mountain Meadow" (Meadow)
"The Pair of Spectacles" (Spectacles)
"A Bunch of Grapes" (Grapes)
"The Sported Oak" (Oak)
"The Oak Gall" (Gall)
"The Little Dog" (Dog)
"The Walrus Ivory" (Ivory)
1933 *The Man in the Cape* (London: Benn, 1933). (Cape)
1933 *Mr. Fortune Wonders* (New York: Doubleday, 1933). (Wonders)
"The Cigarette Case" (Case)
"The Yellow Diamonds" (Diamonds)
"The Lilies of St. Gabriel's" (Lilies)
"The Gipsy Moth" (Moth)
"The Fairy Cycle" (Cycle)
"The Oleander Flowers" (Flowers)
"The Love Bird" (Bird)
"The Old Bible" (Bible)
1934 *Shadow on the Wall* (London: Gollancz, 1934). (Wall) (A Reggie Fortune mystery)
1935 *The Sullen Sky Mystery* (London: Tom Stacey, 1971). (Sky) (Clunk)
1935 *Mr. Fortune Objects* (London: Gollancz, 1935). (Objects)

"The Broken Toad" (Toad)
"The Angel's Eye" (Eye)
"The Little Finger" (Finger)
"The Three Bears" (Bears)
"The Long Dinner" (Dinner)
"The Yellow Slugs" (Slugs)
1936 *A Clue for Mr. Fortune* (London: Gollancz, 1935) (Clue)
"The Torn Stocking" (Torn)
"The Swimming Pool" (Pool)
"The Hole in the Parchment" (Hole)
"The Holy Well" (Well)
"The Wistful Goddess" (Goddess)
"The Dead Leaves" (Leaves)
1937 *Black Land, White Land* (London: Gollancz, 1937). (Land) (Fortune)
1937 *Clunk's Claimant;* as *The Twittering Bird Mystery* (New York: Doubleday, 1937). (Twittering) (Clunk)
1938 *This is Mr. Fortune* (London: Gollancz, 1938). (This)
"The Yellow Cloth" (Cloth)
"The Children's Home" (Home)
"The Lizard's Tail" (Tail)
"The Cowslip Ball" (Ball)
"The Burnt Tout" (Tout)
"Key of the Door" (Key)
1939 *The Great Game* (London: Gollancz, 1939). (Game) (Fortune)
1939 *The Veron Mystery;* as *Mr. Clunk's Text* (New York: Doubleday, 1939). (Text)
1939 "The Thistle Down," in *The Queen's Book of the Red Cross* (London: Hodder & Stoughton, 1939). (Thistle)
1940 *The Bishop's Crime;* in *Meet Mr. Fortune* (New York: Book League of America, 1942). (Crime)
1940 *Mr. Fortune Here* (London: Gollancz, 1940). (Here)
"The Bottle Party" (Bottle)
"The Primrose Petals" (Petals)
"The Spider's Web" (Web)
"The Fight for the Crown" (Crown)
"The Point of the Knife" (Knife)
"The Gilded Girls" (Girls)
"The Brown Paper" (Paper)
"The Blue Paint" (Paint)
"The Bird in the Cellar" (Cellar)
1941 *The Little Captain;* as *Orphan Ann* (New York: Doubleday, 1941). (Orphan) (Clunk)
1942 *Dead Man's Shoes;* as *Nobody's Vineyard* (New York: Doubleday, 1942). (Vineyard) (Clunk)
1942 *No Murder;* as *The Apprehensive Dog* (New York: Doubleday, 1942). (Dog) (Fortune)
1942 *Meet Mr. Fortune* (New York: The Book League of America, 1942). (Meet)
(Materials in this collection were all published previously as listed above, except for the essay "Mr. Fortune.")
"Mr. Fortune"
The Bishops's Crime (Crime)
"The Broken Toad" (Toad)
"The Yellow Slugs" (Slugs)
"The Hole in the Parchment" (Hole)
"The Gipsy Moth" (Moth)
"The Greek Play" (Play)
"The Wistful Goddess" (Goddess)
"The Little Finger" (Finger)
"The Holy Well" (Well)
"The Yellow Cloth" (Cloth)
"The Point of the Knife" (Knife)
"The Yellow Diamonds" (Diamonds)
"The Brown Paper" (Paper)
1943 *Mr. Fortune Finds a Pig* (New York: Doubleday, 1943), (Pig)

1944 *Slippery Ann* (London: Gollancz, 1944); as *The Queen of Spades* in New York. (Ann) (Clunk)
1944 *The Cat's Whisker* (New York: Doubleday, 1944); as *Dead Man's Effects* in London. (Whisker) (Fortune)
1945 *The Wrong Man* (New York: Doubleday, 1945). (Man) (Clunk)
1946 *The Life Sentence* (New York: Doubleday, 1946). (Life) (Fortune)
1947 *Honour among Thieves* (New York: Doubleday, 1946). (Thieves) (Fortune)
1948 *Saving a Rope* (London: Macdonald, 1948); as *Save A Rope* in New York. (Rope) (Fortune)
1950 *Shrouded Death* (London: Macdonald, 1950). (Clunk)
1968 "A Matter of Speculation," in *Anthology 1968 Mid-Year,* edited by Ellery Queen (New York: Davis, 1968). (Speculation) (No earlier publication recorded)
1976 *Mr. Fortune: Eight of His Adventures,* edited by Jacques Barzun and Wendell Hertig Taylor (New York and London: Garland, 1976). (Eight)
(Materials in this collection were all published previously, as listed above.)
"The Ascot Tragedy" (Ascot)
"The Unknown Murderer" (Murderer)
"The Long Barrow" (Barrow)
"The Hermit Crab" (Crab)
"The Greek Play" (Play)
"The Angel's Eye" (Eye)
"The Long Dinner" (Dinner)
"The Dead Leaves" (Leaves)

[2]Chris Steinbrunner and Otto Penzler, (New York: McGraw-Hill, 1976), p. 17; *Mortal Consequences* (New York: Schocken Books, 1973), p. 171.
[3]Queen (New York: Modern Library, 1945), p. 324.
[4]*The Great Detectives*, ed. Otto Penzler (Boston: Little, Brown, 1978); Janet Pate, *The Book of Sleuths* (Chicago: Contemporary Books, 1977); *The Private Lives of Private Eyes, Spies, Crime Fighters and Other Good Guys* ed. Otto Penzler (New York: Grosset & Dunlap, 1977).
[5]*Murder for Pleasure* (New York: Appleton-Century, 1941), p. 125.
[6]*Daily Telegraph* (London), Sept. 13, 1936; in a review of *Clue for Mr. Fortune*.
[7]*The Puritan Pleasures of the Detective Story* (London: Gollancz, 1972), p, 82.
[8]Arthur Conan Doyle, "A Study in Scarlet," in *The Complete Adventures of Sherlock Holmes* (New York: Doubleday, n.d.), p. 17.
[9]Dashiell Hammett, "The Gutting of Couffignal," in *A Mystery Reader*, ed. Nancy Ellen Talburt and Lyna Lee Montgomery (New York: Scribners, 1975), p. 249.
[10]Reggie quotes Thackery's "Sorrows of Werther" in "The Yellow Diamonds," (Meet), p 487:

"Charlotte, having seen his body
Carried past her on a shutter,
Like a well-conducted person
Went on cutting bread and butter."

[11]Murch (London: Peter Owen, 1958), p. 221; Haycraft,p. 127.
[12]"H.C. Bailey," in *Twentieth Century Crime and Mystery Writers*, ed. John M. Reilly (New York: St. Martin's Press, 1980), p. 70.
[13]Doyle, p. 347.
[14]Raymond Chandler, *Farewell, My Lovely* (New York: Ballantine Books, 1971), p. 1.
[15]"The Parables of H.C. Bailey," *The Armchair Detective*, 6 (Sept. 1973), 75.
[16]Symons, p. 171.
[17]*Whodunit?* (New York: Van Nostrand Rheinhold, 1982), p. 117; Routley, pp. 81-88.
Additional note: sources for epigraphs are: *Shadow on the Wall*, p. 12; "A Bunch of Grapes" (in *Case for Mr. Fortune*), p. 122; *Black Land, White Land*, p. 271; and *The Apprehensive Dog*, p. 140.

Anthony Berkeley Cox

Anthony Berkeley Cox

William Bradley Strickland

1893	Anthony Berkeley Cox born in July, son of Dr. A.E. Cox of Watford
1900-14	Educated at Sherborne College and then University College, Oxford
1914-17	War service in France; invalided out of the army with health permanently impaired
c.1920	Begins writing career with humorous sketches for *Punch*
1925	*Jugged Journalism* (A.B. Cox)
	Brenda Entertains (A.B. Cox)
	The Family Witch (A.B. Cox)
	The Layton Court Mystery, first Roger Sheringham mystery (published anonymously)
1926	*The Professor on Paws* (A.B. Cox)
	The Wychford Poisoning Case (Anthony Berkeley)
1927	*Roger Sheringham and the Vane Mystery* (Anthony Berkeley)
	Mr. Priestley's Problem (A.B. Cox, reissued as by Anthony Berkeley)
1928	Founds Detection Club and becomes its first honorary secretary
	The Silk Stocking Murder, (Anthony Berkeley)
1929	*The Poisoned Chocolates Case* (Anthony Berkeley)
1930	*The Second Shot* (Anthony Berkeley)
1931	*Malice Aforethought* (Francis Iles)
	Top Storey Murders (Anthony Berkeley)
	Contributor, *The Floating Admiral,* a collaborative novel by the Detection Club members
1932	Marriage to Helen Macgregor
	Before the Fact (Francis Iles)
	Murder in the Basement (Anthony Berkeley)
1933	*Jumping Jenny* (Anthony Berkeley)
1934	*O England!* (A.B. Cox)
	Panic Party (Anthony Berkeley)
1937	*Trial and Error* (Anthony Berkeley)
1939	*Death in the House* (Anthony Berkeley)
	As for the Woman (Francis Iles)
	Retires from mystery writing, although he continues to review mysteries for the Sunday *Times* and later the *Guardian*
1971	Dies on 9 March following a protracted illness

Anthony Berkeley Cox, perhaps more than any other writer of his time and place, well deserves to be called a man of mystery. Cox was a living contradiction in terms: a popular writer who loathed publicity, a celebrity who kept his private life so intensely private that very little of his biography is known.[1] We have enough for a bare sketch, no more: Cox was born in July, 1893, the son of Dr. A.E. Cox of Watford. He received his education at Sherborne and at University College, Oxford. Cox saw active service during World War I in France, was invalided out of the army toward the end of the war, and found himself a civilian with health permanently impaired.

During the immediate postwar period, Cox apparently trained for the bar and at the same time began to write, his first literary efforts being a series of humorous pieces for *Punch*. He later published a great many books, several of them comic novels written under his own name, the remainder a series of entertaining detective and crime novels written between 1925 and 1939 and published under the pseudonyms "Anthony Berkeley" and "Francis Iles."

Cox moved in lofty circles, criminologically speaking, and in 1928 was instrumental in founding the Detection Club, together with such luminaries as G.K. Chesterton, John Dickson Carr, Dorothy L. Sayers and Agatha Christie. According to one source, Cox not only set up the operating rules for the Club but also was the moving spirit behind its famous membership oath, with its dedication to fair play and the avoidance of jiggery-pokery. In the next few years, Cox married (he and his wife were to have no children), became the director of A.B. Cox, Ltd., a company whose purpose and function have never been clear, and lived quietly with his wife in St. John's Wood.

Cox retired, for obscure reasons, from writing fiction in 1939. One notion is that he found the burden of income taxes too heavy— and it is true that as Cox he railed frequently against the tax structure that seemed to him to penalize literary talent; another suggestion is that he came into a legacy which made him financially able to lay aside his pen, for he had once promised to stop writing as soon as he found something else more lucrative. For whatever reason, Cox did retire from the scene, and, except for book reviews, he maintained a literary silence for more than thirty years, until his death in March, 1971. Aside from these meager facts, we know very little about the man.

Cox's interests, then, must lie more in his accomplishments as a writer than in his biography. Here the record is much more clear, but for practical purposes incomplete, since his works are largely out of print and very difficult to come by. Still, we can trace his literary career with comparative ease. An early work, *Jugged Journalism*, points the way: it is a collection of pieces originally done for *Punch*, most of them concerned with instructing the reader in the art of becoming a successful popular writer. Each chapter satirically dissects some formula for one of many types of not-so-immortal prose, from the romance to the adventure yarn. Chapter nineteen is interesting, since it analyzes the detective story and does a nice job of identifying the typical impedimenta under which the British fair-play Great Detective novel often staggered during the first quarter of this century. Naturally, Cox suggests that each stumbling block and tiresome element—timetables, an idiotic Scotland Yard man, an omniscient detective—is an ironbound requirement for success in writing a detective story, and he indicates graciously how a writer of absolutely no talent may shine in this particular field by juggling these ancient elements.

Having begun with a facile indication of how easy it would be to create a popular success from mediocre materials, Cox took the next logical step. He began to write fiction, first three novels, published under his own name, of light comedy. But Cox found his true vocation anonymously, when in 1925 he published *The Layton Court Mystery*, written reportedly to amuse Cox and his father. To Cox's admitted surprise, this first adventure of Roger Sheringham proved popular enough to bring him more money than had his other literary endeavors. Accordingly, Cox embarked on a career that was to last fourteen years. Abandoning the anonymity that shrouded his first effort, Cox composed a series of Sheringham novels as Anthony Berkeley; and in 1931 he adopted his second pseudonym, Francis Iles, for the first of what was to become a group of three novels, more serious and more self-consciously psychological than the Berkeley novels.

Taken as a whole, the twelve Anthony Berkeley novels and the three Francis Iles books reveal quite a bit about the state of the British mystery story in that golden era between the world wars. Many of the books are flawed in one way or another, but some are outstandingly good entertainments. Moreover, the split between the

Berkeley-Iles personae, though at times more apparent than real, illustrates the parallel development of two branches of the English crime story. On the one hand, Berkeley was capable of putting together an intricate puzzle quite in the manner of Christie; on the other, Iles was concerned with the sort of psychological realism that we have come to expect of Julian Symons and other moderns. However, having made an initial differentiation between Berkeley and Iles, Cox eventually all but demolished it, mainly by making his Berkeley productions more Iles-ish as the years went by.

The works of Cox may be seen as examples of the transition of a genre. A closer examination of a few selected titles will help to clarify certain favorite approaches and devices used by Cox—in particular his recurring use of the Mistaken Detective, in the style of E.C. Bentley's Trent—and to place him more firmly in the tradition of the English crime novel. We may view his novels as falling into two broad categories, the formal puzzle and the inverted detective story, with their method of development normally a compromise between social comedy and satire on the one hand and psychological realism on the other.

Chronologically, the Berkeley persona claims precedence. *The Layton Court Mystery* of 1925 introduces for the first time the figure of Roger Sheringham, an amateur detective notoriously based on an offensive person of Cox's acquaintance. Cox has frequently been quoted as saying, "In my original innocence I thought it would be amusing to have an offensive detective."[2] Accordingly, Sheringham appears as a loud meddler, painted broadly as a beer-drinking, abrasive, self-centered, rude man, at once absurdly vain and cynically deprecatory of public taste and intelligence; and, above all, bullheaded to a fault. Sheringham is by no stretch of the imagination one of the many incarnations of the Holmesian Great Detective, for although his investigations can and do bring dark deeds to light, they almost as often leave large tracts of ground in murky shadow. In short, Sheringham's accuracy as a detective is none too consistent, and quite often he can be absolutely wrong about any number of key deductions. In *Layton Court*, for instance, Sheringham begins promisingly by reasoning that an apparent suicide is in fact a locked-room murder, which he promptly solves, except for one important detail: he finds it deuced hard to identify the culprit.

The initial fallibility of Sheringham continues, and in some later works such as *The Second Shot* and *The Poisoned Chocolates*,

Sheringham is simply wrong in his interpretation of facts. This eventually becomes a large part of the entertainment value of the novels: seeing how poor Roger is misled this time. Howard Haycraft is right on the mark when he characterizes Sheringham as a sort of elaboration of Bentley's Trent, and the Berkeley novels as set in the mold of *Trent's Last Case*: lightweight but thoroughly entertaining examples of elan and good storytelling.[3] But the figure of the Mistaken Detective is by no means confined solely to the Berkeley tales about Sheringham, for there are plenty of others, both in the non-Sheringham stories and in the Francis Iles books.

Having established Sheringham as something of a lout and a boor in his first novel, Berkeley felt compelled over the years to smooth the detective's rough edges. Sheringham, to the amusement of his creator, was taken seriously as a new amateur detective by readers of the genre, and consequently Berkeley was moved to "tone his offensiveness down" to the point of pretending it had never existed to begin with. Fortunately, the refining process did not eliminate the detective's engaging fallibility or his often totally unjustified high opinion of himself. These traits, and the failures they sometimes occasion, mark Sheringham out from the crowd and carry a suggestion, not overdone, of self-mockery. After all, Sheringham, like Cox, writes for the popular press: the amateur sleuth, we learn, writes about crime for the *Courier* and later becomes a best-selling novelist who jauntily attributes all his success to the nearly complete lack of taste or intelligence among the reading public. Then, too, as Cox founded and became the honorary secretary of the Detection Club in 1928, so Sheringham at about the same time founded and began to guide the fortunes of the Crimes Circle, a group of dedicated amateurs who tried their hands at criminology. On occasion—even when cheerfully deriding the public taste that moves people to read the drivel he churns out— Sheringham might be a spokesman for Cox. That the reading public did not in fact rise up against this literary abuse is a tribute to Cox's essential lightness of touch and to his amiable if at times acerbic humor.

As a detective, Sheringham finds an approach that combines the inductive methods of such Great Detectives as Holmes, Wimsey, and Poirot with simple routine legwork suggestive of the procedural novels of later days, or, perhaps more aptly, of Archie Goodwin's inquiries on behalf of Nero Wolfe. Though Sheringham greatly prefers the armchair method, his acquaintance with methodical, demanding Inspector Moresby of Scotland Yard (extending to a sort of semi-official status for Sheringham at times) often makes the more active approach necessary. As an example of Sheringham in full, and for once successful, cry, *The Silk Stocking Murders* stands up well.

The story begins when Sheringham, at his desk at the *Courier*, receives a forlorn request from a country vicar. The clergyman's daughter, Janet Manners, has disappeared in London, and the vicar wishes Sheringham to discover her whereabouts. Sheringham, moved by curiosity to follow up on the request, soon discovers that Janet has hanged herself with her own silk stockings. This is disturbing enough, but when other women begin to follow Janet's example, Sheringham reflects to himself that "this is too much of a good thing." Typically for Sheringham, his realization that the suicides are in fact a series of murders done by a maniac strikes him in a hit-or-miss fashion. Sheringham, having attended an inquest on the death of Lady Ursula Graeme, the latest victim, notes the presence of Inspector Moresby. Later, over his favorite refreshment, beer, Sheringham attempts to goad Moresby into dispensing information with a random remark: "So *you* think Lady Ursula was murdered, too, do you, Moresby?"

The results are spectacular. Moresby, the most phlegmatic of men, starts violently. Then, and only then, does light dawn for Sheringham:

> ...perhaps for the first time in his life, the Chief Inspector had been caught napping and had given himself away, horse, foot, and artillery. The very fact that he had been on his guard had only contributed to his disaster, for he had been guarding his front and Roger had attracted him in the rear.
> In the meantime Roger's brain, jerking out of the coma into which the Inspector's start had momentarily plunged it, was making up for lost time ... instantly that which had been a mystery became plain. Roger could have kicked himself that it should have taken a starting Inspector to point out to him the obvious. Murder was the only explanation that fitted all those puzzling facts!
> "Whew!" he said, in some awe.[4]

In conjunction with Moresby, Sheringham pursues the case. The two of them methodically examine the victims' movements over the past few months and narrow possible suspects down to three. One of these, Gerald Newsome, unites with Sheringham and Anne Manners, the sister of the first victim, to flush out the real culprit.

They are joined by a financier, Pleydell, a brilliant man in his own line and the bereaved fiance of Lady Ursula.

The three go to considerable trouble to set up an elaborate re-enactment of an assault Anne has narrowly survived. Only when Anne nearly dies in the pretend assault does Sheringham spring the trap he has prepared: in the excitement of the moment, the true murderer confesses to the crime. Sheringham explains his motive this way: "You must remember that [he] suffered badly from megalomania. I'd noticed that on several occasions; 'If I say a thing is, then it is; if I say the impossible shall be done, then it shall.' But he was so quiet about it, while the usual megalomaniac is so bombastic, that one simply didn't recognize it for what it was" (241).

This glib note of psychoanalysis deepened over the years as Cox continued to write. In his later books he moved steadily away from the detective story as puzzle and toward the detective story as a study in abnormal psychology. When this approach worked, as it did in the Iles books to a greater extent than in the Berkeley ones, it lent an air of increased realism to the novels. Unfortunately, for modern readers the method often does *not* work, for psychological thought and theory have changed in the past fifty years, and many of Sheringham's observations regarding the psychology of murder echo with the same flat, antiquated ring as his intensely class-conscious remarks on social standing or race. Thus Pleydell, a Jew, is summed up by Roger as typifying "the Jewish outlook":

> They'd give up everything in the world to save the life of a dying friend, or even to ensure that he had a really luxurious funeral if he wanted one; but that doesn't prevent them from asking the undertaker for a cash discount .... We can't distinguish between real and false sentiment. And the Jews do (216).

Later, in *Trial and Error*, Cox has a character sum up someone else as an "American German Jew, with a dash of anything else unpleasant thrown in." Again, a character in the Iles novel *Before the Fact* grudgingly concedes that Lambroso's method was somewhat mistaken, but maintains that it holds some truth, for although there is in fact no criminal type, there is a degenerate type; and though all criminals are not degenerates, certainly all degenerates are criminals. Such views mark the works as products of a particular time, place and class even more strongly than plot, characterization and settings do. Berkeley's now-and-again insistence on such old-fashioned notions of psychology as physiognomy and racial "types" tends to weaken the value of his books as serious studies in psychology.

Still, in his exploration of possibilities, Berkeley was trying in his own way to accomplish what Raymond Chandler later recommended: he was moving murder out of the idealized surroundings of the vicarage and into the real world, with believable characters acting from real passions and committing real murders. Because he chose to work within the same constraints as the stereotyped "vicarage" book regarding setting and types of characters, and because he was a quirky and individualistic personality himself, Cox was unable to achieve complete success at his self-imposed task, try as he might.

He does command our respect at least for trying. That he was consciously attempting something different is made plain by his preface to *The Second Shot*. After asserting that the detective-story writer has only two options before him, namely to experiment with the telling of his plot or to develop character and atmosphere, Berkeley plumps for the latter option:

> In my opinion it is toward this latter that the best of the new detective-writing energies are being directed. I personally am convinced that the days of the old crime puzzle pure and simple, relying entirely upon plot and without any added attractions of character, style, or even humour, are, if not numbered, at least in the hands of its auditors; and that the detective story is already in the process of developing into the novel with a detective or a crime interest, holding its reader less by mathematical than by psychological ties.[5]

The Second Shot itself is an account of the mysterious death of Mr. Eric Scott-Davies, shot dead in the course of a game of murder at a typical English house-party. The elements were old, but Berkeley attempted to enliven them by altering his usual method of presentation and adopting an unconventional approach, albeit one already explored by Agatha Christie, in the way he conceals the identity of the murderer.

The novel is narrated by Mr. Cyril Pinkerton, a man so achingly "correct" that he positively irritates the reader by the mere fact of his existence. Pinkerton, having first explained that he has often considered writing a detective novel, then maintains that such a work would best be written from a viewpont different from that of the usual detached onlooker: "This [point of view] may make for a good puzzle, but it certainly does not make for human interest. And in the art of fiction, even in so low a form of it as the detective story, human interest should to my mind be a *sine qua non*" (21). Further, Pinkerton tells the reader that to gain true human interest, the story should be told from the point of view of the person most intimately connected and concerned with the outcome of the investigation: the criminal himself.

Having fussily criticized many of the very conventions of the detective story formalized by Cox and his contemporaries in the Detection Club, Pinkerton then launches into the story of an "actual" murder, that of Eric Scott-Davies. As narrator, Pinkerton magnifies and exaggerates many quite real opinions of Cox: he regards himself as above the "oafs" and "the herd"; he expresses amazement at the dismal taste which allows detective stories, of all things, to become popular as literature; and in general he evidences enough unreasonable prejudices and mulish opinions to mark himself as a waspy, finicky, old-maidish little man undeserving of the reader's sympathy.

Yet Pinkerton seems to be an attempt on Cox's part to draw a fundamentally decent, though comical, fellow. He is attracted to Elsa Verity, a young woman on whom Scott-Davis has his own designs. On the other hand, we are given to understand that another young lady, Eric's cousin Armorel Scott-Davis, might be attracted to Pinkerton but for his crankiness and fanatical prudishness. Armorel is a competently-drawn character herself, a bit reminiscent of a Fitzgerald heroine in her atmosphere of jaded adventurousness and her sense of humor.

These people and others are drawn into a discussion of murder, detective stories, and actual detection, and as a lark they decide to enact a theoretical murder with Eric as victim. Eric, by the way, is typical of many of Berkeley's victims: coarse, abusive and unsporting, he has few redeeming social qualities and is certainly no loss to the world. It comes as no surprise to learn that in the course of the game Eric is in fact murdered, shot with the same weapon that was to figure in the pretend crime. The second shot of the title is a plot complication: Pinkerton was to fire a single shot at Eric, actually doing no damage. Later, while Pinkerton is in the company of another guest, a second shot is heard, evidently the fatal one. The make-believe puzzle becomes one in reality, with suspects aplenty, for, as Pinkerton observes, several of the guests have

> openly expressed to me their wish for Eric's death and at least two more might be considered also to have an adequate motive

for killing him—three more indeed, I thought still more cynically, if I included myself. If one is to believe the detective stories a person with a motive for murder is invariably innocent of the crime, and the larger the motive the more certain his innocence. Yet I could not believe that detective stories are always quite so true to life as they should be (111-12).

The possibilities have not escaped the police, and when they begin to look at several guests, including Pinkerton, with signs of interest, he and his host send for Roger Sheringham to lend a hand. At this point in the narrative, Berkeley almost duplicates the challenge to the reader that is part of the classic Ellery Queen tales of the same period; even before Sheringham comes upon the scene, Pinkerton declares that an alert reader "should now, at this stage in the story, be fully aware whose finger pulled the fatal trigger" (154).

Sheringham's arrival throws matters into an even more confusing state, for his investigation indicates that an exoneration of Pinkerton as the murderer may lead to the wrongful arrest of someone else—Elsa Verity—for the crime. In his persnickety way Pinkerton insists on shouldering the blame for the crime, but finds, somewhat to his exasperation, that no one will take him seriously. Armorel, who has alienated Pinkerton by laughing at him (among other things she learns from Sheringham that Pinkerton's old school nickname of "Tapers" is short for "Tapeworm"), finally disillusions him about Miss Verity by showing that Elsa holds Pinkerton in the utmost contempt.

As the investigation continues, altruistic confessions become the order of the day. At the inquest both Armorel and Pinkerton confess to the crime, and, as Sheringham observes "*that* means that neither of you did it. And so, as I say, we know at last where we are— or rather, I do. Somebody else did it."

But Sheringham agrees that Eric was one of those men who require murdering, and no one is dreadfully cut up when the coroner's inquest clearly heads toward a verdict of accidental death. By that juncture, Armorel and Pinkerton have married, and Sheringham has decided on the identity of the real villain. He carefully constructs his case, showing by dogged logic that Elsa Verity must have committed the crime. All parties agree to shield her.

Pinkerton's narration, however, has not ended. In an epilogue, he explains that he began the book at the time of the murder in hopes that it would be found by the police and would clearly indicate his own innocence, when in fact he was guilty all along. He has successfully used Sheringham to perfect his own escape from justice. This adaptation of the Roger Ackroyd device works neatly, though it would be more enjoyable if the reader felt that Pinkerton deserved his escape from the hangman. However, Berkeley tries to mitigate the unpleasantness of his narrator's personality at the end, indicating that marriage to Armorel has made a new man of him, and that he is no longer the dry stick he first appeared to be.

In *The Second Shot*, as in many of Cox's novels, we see one of his favorite figures, the Mistaken Detective. Sheringham is clever, rational, painstaking; and yet he is wrong. Cox returned to this tactic time and again, developing it most thoroughly in three novels, *Malice Aforethought, The Poisoned Chocolates Case* and *Trial and Error*. Sheringham figures only in the second book; the first is by Francis Iles, and the third features Ambrose Chitterwick, not Sheringham. A fourth novel, *Before the Fact*, contains no Mistaken Detective, but does mark Iles's greatest achievement in the inverted form.

Malice Aforethought is a carefully contrived inverted detective novel, "the story of a commonplace crime," as its subtitle promises. Unlike the Berkeley novels, it contains no interest as a puzzle *per se*, and so the use of the Iles pseudonym is fully justified by the book's nature; on the other hand, it clearly shows the determination earlier expressed by "Berkeley" to develop the detective story as a study of character and atmosphere at the expense of plot. Further, many of the touches evident in Berkeley's novels are visible here, too.

These touches include Cox's weaknesses. Most obvious is *Malice Aforethought*'s lack of a center. Pinkerton in *The Second Shot* is not himself compelling as a character, but his first-person account commands the reader's involvement. Dr. Edmund Bickleigh, the protagonist of *Malice Aforethought*, lacks this claim on the reader's attention. Bickleigh is a weak man, bullied by his truly awful wife, Julia. A womanizer, a hypocrite, and a vacillating, dithering sort of fellow, Bickleigh seems to the reader to deserve killing fully as much as his victim does.

The story follows Bickleigh's growing determination to murder his wife as the doctor becomes foolishly infatuated with Madeleine Cranmere, another of Cox's Modern Young Women. Bickleigh, already an adulterer of long standing and wide experience, hits upon a plan that seems at first to be foolproof: he will use a drug to induce severe headaches in his wife, accustom her to the use of morphia for relief, and have her die in the end of a drug overdose. He does so successfully, only to learn on the very day of the deed that Madeleine has become engaged to another man.

The doctor's plot holds for many months, but finally begins to unravel when Mr. Chatford, the embittered husband of one of Bickleigh's ex-mistresses, instigates a criminal investigation into Julia's death. Bickleigh has gained confidence as a murderer and spitefully attempts to do in Madeleine and Chatford by giving them sandwiches contaminated with botulin. They survive, but Bickleigh is shortly taken into custody for the murder of Julia. In a long trial sequence the doctor alternately exults in his forthcoming release and wallows in despair as he is sure he will be convicted. In the end, he does win acquittal for his one murder, that of his wife; but, ironically, Madeleine's husband has died in the meantime, from a case of typhoid contracted naturally, and Bickleigh is prosecuted for this second murder, found guilty, and executed, correctly protesting his innocence the whole time.

Malice Aforethought is in many ways a pioneering work, concentrating on the state of mind of the murderer, not on the working out of a set of clues and the presentation of a clever puzzle. As such a work, it points the way to later developments in the detective and crime novel. At the time of its publication, the book was attacked by some as breaking the rules of the Detection Club with malicious abandon—the very rules that Cox helped to create!— but in many ways this story has dated less than the Berkeley novels in the more traditional vein. The gradual unfolding of Dr. Bickleigh's scheme, his evolution from a henpecked little man struggling under a pronounced sense of his own inferiority to a would-be murderer with delusions of grandeur, still have power to engage the reader's curiosity—but not, unfortunately, his emotions.

One obvious problem with *Malice Aforethought* is a kind of weakness in its dramatic development. As a rule, we see Dr. Bickleigh during his ordeal at the trial; we witness and know the reasons for his swings from hope to despair. But too often Cox is content merely to tell his audience that Bickleigh is in a given state of mind, and the flat statement that the doctor suffers from an inferiority complex has the same unfortunately glib ring as Sheringham's pompous pontificating on matters psychological.

On the positive side, *Malice Aforethought* affords Cox many opportunities for his cynical, bleak, not to say black, humor. The police, with their accidentally triumphant arrest and prosecution of a murderer for the wrong murder, come in for their share of satire, as does the British court system, a favorite target of Cox's. A kind of Wodehousian comedy, too, finds a place in the book, as witness Iles' droll recounting of an escapade of Denny Bourne, the man whom Bickleigh will later falsely be accused of killing:

> Five days after the beginning of the summer term ... Denny had been sent down for three weeks for depriving an unpopular don of his trousers and painting his hinder parts scarlet. If the don had not been so unpopular Denny would have been sent down for good, but the rest of the senior common-room, who also did not love their colleague, had felt that a certain justification, and more, was to be found in the existence of the fellow at all. Still, the man was a don, and one cannot have dons going about forcibly disguised as mandrills; so Denny had been sent down for three weeks.
> To Dr. Bickleigh's disgust Madeleine seemed delighted with this exploit: that the idea of a trouserless don with a scarlet posterior is about as far removed from the spiritual as one can well get, Dr. Bickleigh pointed out; but Madeleine, though agreeing, and looking for a moment as a nun might on being confronted with such a spectacle, continued to give the impression that she thought Denny really had done something rather clever.[6]

The horseplay with the don, though the point of departure here, is not the whole point of the anecdote. Instead, the passage defines the difference between the falsely romantic Bickleigh and the trifling, "spiritual" Madeleine ironically, succinctly and neatly. Cox is usually ready to skewer pretense and hypocrisy, as he does here.

In *Malice Aforethought*, we see of course the figure of the Mistaken Detective, in the person of Superintendent Allhayes, a representative of the plodding school of the official British police. To be sure, the device is huddled here, for Cox brings it in as a last-minute twist; but all the same Allhayes, no less than Sheringham at his most dense, is a hound far off the scent.

Of all the Berkeley books, the one most satisfactorily worked out as a puzzle and at the same time the one displaying most obviously the Mistaken Detective is *The Poisoned Chocolates Case*. Contrary to his intent in the later *The Second Shot* and *Malice Aforethought*, Cox sets out here to ring changes on the classic puzzle story. Oddly, given the circumstances of his literary life, Cox succeeds in giving the reader the impression of reality, with his fictional Crimes Circle standing in for the Detection Club. The problem itself—an elaborate murder plot that was exactly prefigured by Berkeley himself in a brilliant short story called "The Avenging Chance"—is reminiscent of a Christie puzzler, but the real interest comes from the efforts of the six members of the Crimes Circle to solve the problem of who killed Joan Bendix, the evidently accidental recipient of a box of toxic candies. The amateurs—Charles Wildman, a well-known barrister; Alicia Dammers, a novelist; Mrs. Fielder Flemming, a playwright; Percy Robinson, a successful writer of detective stories; Ambrose Chitterwick, a flighty little man with a keen mind for details; and Sheringham himself—have a field day, turning in no fewer than six distinct and equally reasonable solutions to the same crime. On the one hand, this remarkable book is a perfect example of the fair-play Detection-Club type of mystery; on the other, as Julian Symons observes, the book is practically a parody of the same type of story.[7]

The Poisoned Chocolates Case is a tour de force, as meticulous in its examination of plausible alternate explanations for the same set of physical facts as the early works of Ellery Queen are in their elaboration of interpretation for a set of baffling clues. At the same time, it is more relaxed than some of Berkeley's works, with many touches of Cox's sardonic humor.

Readers may recognize thinly disguised portraits of Dorothy L. Sayers, Agatha Christie and John Dickson Carr in some of the characters presented herein; but at the same time Cox pokes fun at himself, both in the figure of Sheringham, magnificently and completely wrong here in his own solution, and also in the person of twittery Mr. Chitterwick, whose explanation is perfectly correct but who is perfectly incapable of bringing the killer to justice. Berkeley also has some amusing things to say about the form in which he was laboring, the detective novel; regarding the works of Percy Robinson, he says,

> he wrote under the pseudonym of Morton Harrogate Bradley, which had so impressed the simple citizens of the United States of America that they had bought three editions of his first book on the strength of that alone. For some obscure psychological reason Americans are always impressed by the use of surnames for Christian, and particularly when one of them happens to be the name of an English watering-place.[8]

Since only one of the six proffered solutions to the poisoning is correct, *The Poisoned Chocolates Case* multiplies by five the Mistaken Detective device. Taken as a whole, the work indicates

Cox's growing dissatisfaction with the very type of detective story he had helped to institutionalize, and insofar as it satirizes the conventions of the genre it indicates the weakening foundations of the Golden Age puzzle story. The humor saves the tale from depending on a mere mechanical device, and the touches of caricature add a dimension for aficionados of the form. Viewed together with *The Second Shot* and *Malice Aforethought*, the book indicates plainly the direction of growth taken by the detective novel in these years: away from the puzzle school and the figure of the Great Detective and toward the more realistic study of crime and its effect on lifelike characters.

The following Iles book, *Before the Fact*, takes the process one step further. Here, strictly speaking, is hardly a detective story at all. Like *Malice Aforethought*, *Before the Fact* tells the story of a tawdry criminal, a superficially attractive but morally vacuous murderer, but unlike its predecessor, *Before the Fact* centers on the figure of the victim, not the killer, and that shift of perspective makes quite a difference.

Lina Aysgarth, the central character of *Before the Fact*, is in some ways difficult to believe in as a personality, but given the context of the novel, her character works in a way that Dr. Bickleigh's does not to engage the feelings of the reader. In the cold light of day, her failure to avoid her own impending murder seems silly; but it is prepared for in the development of the story every bit as carefully as Berkeley would prepare a surprise revelation in a puzzle plot.

The villain in the piece, Johnnie Aysgarth, Lina's reprobate husband, is the best representative of a favorite type of Cox's: the amoral man, born and brought up with no sense of right and wrong. Johnnie marries Lina for her money. He lives with her for nearly ten years, in that time becoming a confirmed adulterer, a gambler, an embezzler and a murderer, killing both Lina's father and Beaky Thwaite, an old school chum of Johnnie's, for personal gain. Lina slowly becomes aware of her husband's guilt and his reptilian lack of human feelings; and yet Lina cannot bring herself to leave Johnnie permanently, to turn him in, or even to avoid death when, at the end, she dully realizes that she is the next victim on his list.[9]

In a strange way *Before the Fact* is a love story. Lina, the plain one in the family, falls desperately for Johnny early on, and during the course of their marriage she assumes a loving but often hostile, often maternal, stance toward him. Lina, like Dr. Bickleigh's wife in *Malice Aforethought*, is older than her husband, and also like Julia

Bickleigh she becomes an officious, demanding wife. The difference is that here we see the step-by-step development of her character, and so we can understand her more readily. Then, too, we view Johnnie as she does, from the outside, and we have no call or need to sympathize with him. Here Iles' problem is rather different: he needs to let us understand more exactly just why Lina is so hopelessly in love with her undeserving Johnnie that she puts up with his infidelities, his financial peccadilloes, even his career as a murderer—that, indeed, she even becomes an accomplice "before the fact" to her own death at his hands, though she would very much like to live.

Even though Cox in some measure fails to justify Lina's fanatical devotion to Johnnie, he does provide a compelling story in *Before the Fact*. Admittedly, the book is somewhat uneven in style— Beaky Thwaite, in particular, seems to have wandered in uneasily from the pages of a Wodehouse novel and is a living example of what one writer calls "silly assery"[10]—but in its way it is an excellent example of the new crime story, concentrating on atmosphere and character, not plot. Given the yielding nature of Lina and not questioning it too closely, we find Howard Haycraft's observation still true: "Iles' studies invariably point to the killer and say, 'There but for the grace of God go I.' It is this convincing *normality* of murder that transforms the Iles stories into something apart, which gives them their horrid particular fascination ...."[11] Again, Berkeley touches are apparent in the Iles tale: a minor character, for example, is Isobel Sedbusk, a detective-story writer who seems a composite of Sayers and Christie. As usual for such a character in Cox, Isobel wonders aloud at the public that applauds any detective-story writer of even mediocre talent; and, like certain members of the Crimes Circle, garrulous Isobel has only one topic of conversation: violent death and innovative methods of inducing it in others.

As befits a pyschological study, *Before the Fact* exhibits a more mordant sense of humor than its predecessors, with cynical, satirical jabs at everything from the public-school tradition to upper-class conventions on adultery and divorce. The satire never gets in the way of the story, though, and taken as a whole *Before the Fact* is the most successful exercise undertaken by Iles in the inverted form.

Even so, the most successful performance by Cox in either of his criminous incarnations is *Trial and Error*. Largely because it adopts the conventions of the detective story only to turn them inside-out, and because it achieves this with gusto and high humor, *Trial and*

Error has diminished less with time than any of Cox's work. It is a mad tea-party of a book, with the inverted form combined with the puzzle, the courtroom drama with near farce, the novel of suspense with the comedy of P.G. Wodehouse.

Trial and Error is the story of inoffensive Lawrence Butterfield Todhunter (tag names are the order of the day here), suffering from a terminal disorder and condemned to natural death within a matter of months. Todhunter decides to occupy his last days performing some act of public good as a way of giving his life meaning. In a discussion with some of his friends, who are unaware of his precarious health, he discovers to his astonishment that they unanimously agree that the best act a dying man could possibly perform would be the murder of an obnoxious person. By doing the deed, the dying man could bring happiness to those unfortunate individuals whose lives are blighted by the intended victim.

Todhunter toys with the idea of eliminating Mussolini or Hitler (shades of *Rogue Male!*), but finally discards this notion in favor of a domestic sort of crime. Like Sheringham and Cox, Todhunter is a journalist—and also like Cox, one might add, he is a semi-invalid; his initial prospective target is a thoroughly offensive "American German Jew," Mr. Fisher, who has been hired by the publishing concern as a hatchet man. As one reads of Todhunter's preparations to eliminate his victim (he goes so far as to purchase a revolver), one is struck by the absurdity of this Walter Mitty of a man, with his bony knees, egg-like bald head, and cackling laugh, having the gumption to plan *anyone's* murder. Indeed, when it comes to the point, Todhunter foregoes the assassination, only to learn to his dismay that a younger man has done the deed. He regards himself as the cause of the younger man's embarkation on a life of crime, and, pricked by his conscience, Todhunter at last settles on an alternate victim, the actress Jean Norwood.

Jean is in Mr. Todhunter's phrase a "poisonous bitch" who feeds her vanity by keeping her plays going past their profitable runs solely to break record after record. This activity consumes quantities of money, and to get it Jean becomes the mistress of the handiest rich man. She currently is being kept by Mr. Farroway, a popular novelist, whose closest rival for her favors is his son-in-law, Vincent Palmer. This time Mr. Todhunter succeeds in acting out his plot, stealing into Miss Norwood's garden and firing his revolver at her. She dies, a bullet having passed completely through her body, and Todhunter, having wisely prepared for the crime by reading detective stories, retrieves the bullet and throws it into the Thames, thereby making detection all but impossible.

Unfortunately, Vincent Palmer is arrested, tried and convicted of the crime, and Todhunter, to prevent a miscarriage of justice, must confess. No one believes him. Todhunter is thus placed in the absurd position of having to detect a murder he himself committed and having to struggle manfully to establish beyond all doubt his own guilt. To this end he calls in Ambrose Chitterwick, and between the two of them they succeed in initiating a civil trial for murder, one in which the state tries desperately to exonerate Todhunter, while he insists on his right to be hanged for murder. The defendant has one additional problem: with his deteriorating health he must keep himself alive long enough to be hanged.

The ironic reversals are not tacked on. They are the very essence of the novel, and they give it a dimension and a strength not present in much of Cox's work. Since the story is not "serious" in the Iles tradition, Cox swings his satirical blade freely, inflicting the most damage on the British system of jurisprudence. Even Sheringham's old friend Inspector Moresby comes in for some tweaking, for he makes up his mind early and firmly that Todhunter is either a harmless lunatic or else a man willing to sacrifice his own life to spare the feelings of Farroway's wife and daughters and to save the life of Farroway's son-in-law.

Todhunter's character, granted his eccentricity in his determination to commit an altruistic murder, is a delight. Hardly middle-aged yet compelled to behave like a doddering old man by his illness, Todhunter comes alive only when faced with his own imminent death. His brusque impatience with the asinine law, his crusty insistence on his right as a British murderer to be hanged for his crime, lend the novel a surreal humor quite unlike anything else Cox attempted. Other characters—Todhunter's doctor, who takes a morbid and ghoulish delight in counting down his patient's last days and in congratulating him on his impending departure from this world, Mr. Chitterwick's no-nonsense aged aunt ("Lawks," she says on hearing Todhunter's plaintive confession, "*I* believe yer. You're too big a fool to be a liar."), even the crew of laboring journalists down at the *London Review*—mesh well with one another, adding color and humanity to the slightly unreal but decidedly entertaining atmosphere of the novel.

If *Before the Fact* is Cox's best achievement as Iles, and *The Poisoned Chocolates Case* is his best Sheringham yarn, *Trial and Error* is far and away his most successful working of the detective story as social comedy. Yet, in saying so, we cannot ignore the touches that mark the book as distinctively Cox's own: the same targets are held up to ridicule here, though to better effect than ever before, and in the end we even have a Mistaken Detective.

In an epilogue rich with irony, Chitterwick reveals to the reader that Todhunter was not guilty after all; someone else was in the garden that night and fired the fatal shot, almost simultaneously with Todhunter's firing. It is Chitterwick's conviction that Todhunter heroically sacrificed his own life to protect the true murderer, Farroway's unmarried daughter, now a successful actress. Thus Todhunter, found guilty through great efforts of his own, is actually innocent. But there is one further turn of this particular screw, for the limited third person narration shows that Chitterwick is wrong. Todhunter, excited and overwrought, was not even fully aware that a second shot had been fired. Having manufactured evidence to convict himself of murder, he died believing himself the true culprit, and Chitterwick is mistaken. Once again, Cox's rational detective, with the best will in the world, has followed the wrong trail.

Anthony Berkeley Cox, a man of mystery in a double sense, suffers today from an unjust obscurity. This is in part the result of his early abandonment of the genre: after 1939 he wrote no more detective stories, though he lived until 1971. Most of his books are long out of print, though a scattering have recently appeared in paperback editions. They certainly bear reading.

Writing both as Francis Iles and Anthony Berkeley, Cox provides us with a bridge from the formal puzzle stories of the British Golden Age to the post-war realistic studies in crime and criminal psychology. As a constructor of formal puzzles, Berkeley was adept, though never the equal of Agatha Christie. As a satirical and often sardonic observer of the London literary scene, Cox was an incisive and often delightful writer. As a pioneer of the psychological method, Cox is both deserving of praise and a bit of a problem.

The fact that Iles' use of psychology wears thin at times or appears superficial at others is not, perhaps, so much his own fault as the result of his living in his particular era. Psychological theory has changed greatly since the thirties, and Cox's labored explication of outdated ideas has caused portions of his books to age poorly. Then, too, Iles (to a greater extent than Berkeley) apparently felt no call to create engaging and sympathetic characters. As a result, his books often lack focus. *Malice Aforethought* is indeed a landmark work, one deserving of praise for what it attempts, and yet one cannot help feeling that its protagonist is at least as deserving of being murdered as his repellent wife. Since the book lacks a clear center, its humor and social commentary seem scattered. In this respect, *Before the Fact* is the most successful work, for the reader finds Lina Aysgarth a more sympathetic character.

Still, the novel that manages to break out of all molds by cheerfully turning conventions upside-down is more effective than either of the two Iles works. With its engaging but absurd hero, its mad murder trial in reverse, and its free-swinging high-spirited assault on the British legal system, *Trial and Error* stands as the most successful of all Cox's works. It is a pity that he ceased to write shortly after completing this work. The final Iles work, *As for the Woman*, is frankly dull, centering on adultery and not murder. Had Cox continued to mine the vein of *Trial and Error*, he might easily have established his own peculiar niche rivaling, in his own way, Christie and Sayers.

But these observations may be too harsh. Cox was about something new and different, and explorers often take risks that later travelers easily avoid. Anthony Berkeley/Francis Iles is an unjustly neglected figure today, one whose works richly repay one's time. That he has worn not quite as well as some of his contemporaries is surely not his own fault; and the historical interest of his novels, not to mention their undeniable delights as detective and crime stories, commends them to the attention of any fancier of mystery fiction.

Notes

[1] Biographical information herein comes from the following sources: Chris Steinbrunner and Otto Penzler, eds., *Encyclopedia of Mystery and Detection* (New York: McGraw-Hill, 1976); Julian Symons, *The Detective Story in Britain* (London: Longmans, Green, 1969); and Cox's obituary notice, *The Times* (London, March 11, 1971), p. 18.

[2] A.B. Cox quoted in Steinbrunner and Penzler, p. 362.

[3] Howard Haycraft, *Murder for Pleasure: The Life and Times of the Detective Story* (New York: Appleton-Century, 1941), pp. 148-149.

[4] Anthony Berkeley, *The Silk Stocking Murders* (Garden City: Doubleday, Doran, 1929), p. 42. After initial citation, Cox's works will be identitifed by abbreviated titles and the appropriate page numbers in the text of this paper. And here I would like to thank Mr. Grane Keene, book collector, gentleman and scholar, for rallying round and generously providing me with some of the scarcer works of Cox.

[6] Francis Iles, *Malice Aforethought* (New York: Perennial Library, reprint of the 1931 edition, 1980), pp. 133-134.

[7] Symons, p. 24.

[8] Anthony Berkeley, *The Poisoned Chocolates Case* (New York: Dell, reprint of the 1931 edition, 1980), p. 13.

[9] When Alfred Hitchcock came to direct an adaptation of the novel in 1941, the ending was changed, because, as Hitchcock said, Cary Grant played the role of the murderous husband, and "Cary Grant couldn't murder anyone." The film was, of course, *Suspicion*.

[10] See Colin Watson, *Snobbery with Violence* (London: Eyre and Spottiswoode, 1971), p. 186ff. for a discussion of this phenomenon in Cox and others.

[11] Haycraft, p. 148.

Nicholas Blake (C. Day Lewis)
Photo courtesy Howard Caster

Nicholas Blake
(C. Day Lewis)

Earl F. Bargainnier

1904	Cecil Day Lewis born on 27 April in Ballintubber, Ireland, son of Reverend F.C. Day Lewis and Kathleen Blake Squires.
1908	Death of mother; raised by her sister who moved with Day Lewis and his father to the latter's various London parishes: Ealing, Notting Hill, Lancaster Gate.
1912-17	Attended Wilkie's School.
1917-23	Attended Sherborne School.
1923-27	Attended Wadham College, Oxford University; received M.A.
1927-35	Schoolmaster at Summers Fields, Larchfield, and Cheltenham Schools.
1928	Married Constance Mary King, daughter of Reverend Henry Robinson King, one of his masters at Sherborne; two sons, divorced 1951.
1935	*A Question of Proof,* first novel by Nicholas Blake, published.
1935-38	Member, Communist Party Great Britain (C.P.G.B.); never actually resigned; in his own words, "I just quietly faded out."
1941-46	Editor, Ministry of Information.
1950	Commander, Order of the British Empire.
1951	Married Jill Balcon; a son and a daughter.
1951-56	Professor of Poetry, Oxford University.
1954-72	Director, Chatto & Windus, Ltd., publishers.
1960	*The Buried Day,* autobiography.
1964-65	Charles Eliot Norton Professor of Poetry, Harvard University.
1968	*The Private Wound,* last novel by Nicholas Blake, published.
1968-72	Poet Laureate of England.
1972	Death on 22 May.

The many awards, honors and degrees presented to Day Lewis are not given, as they may be found in a number of biographical references, nor are the more than sixty works of his career as poet, translator, critic and editor, the most complete list is Geoffrey Handley-Taylor and Timothy D'Arch Smith, *C. Day Lewis, the Poet Laureate: A Bibliography* (London & Chicago: St. James, 1968).

As Nicholas Blake, C. Day Lewis published twenty mystery novels among the more than eighty volumes of poetry, fiction, criticism and translation he wrote or edited. His position as a novelist of mystery fiction is as high in that genre as his position among twentieth-century English poets, even if the official recognition as Poet Laureate is ignored. These dual writing careers offer an approach to the Blake novels. If this essay were to have a sub title, it should perhaps most appropriately be "The Poet as Detective Novelist," but limiting a study of the Blake novels only to their relationship to their author's being a poet would be to fail in acknowledging their excellence as novels of mystery—whatever their author's success in other forms of literature. Therefore, the essay is divided into three sections: "The Poet as Detective Novelist," those relationships between the two careers which affect the novels; "The Detective Novelist as Detective Novelist," Blake's handling of the principal features of detective fiction; and "The Poet as Detective," an examination of Nigel Strangeways, the protagonist of sixteen of Blake's novels.[1]

The Poet as Detective Novelist

We have turned inward for our iron ration;
Tapping the vein and sole reserve of passion,
Drawing from poetry's capital what we can.
                *   *   *
...Our exile and extravagances,
Revolt, retreat, fine faiths, disordered fancies
Are but the poet's search for a right soil
Where words may settle, marry, and conceive an
Imagined truth....
    "Dedicatory Stanzas," *The Georgics of Virgil,* C. Day Lewis.

As a third of the "Auden-Spender-Day Lewis triumvirate" of British poetry in the 1930s, Cecil Day Lewis was considered—and considered himself—a revolutionary, but with hindsight it can now be seen that the revolutionary was at war with the poet, and the poet won the war. This internal battle is chronicled in his autobiography, *The Buried Day*. It contains little on his detective fiction as Nicholas Blake, but it does recount the cause of his writing *A Question of Proof*, the first novel: a leaking roof. "We were told it would cost £100 to repair the roof properly. I could see no way of acquiring this sum honestly, until it occurred to me that I had read a vast number of detective novels and might be able to write one myself. I did so."[2]

The first result was that he nearly lost his teaching position for using aspects of Cheltenham College for the setting, but the second and happier result was the novel's success, which allowed him to quit the teaching he did not enjoy; in other words, the detective novels made the poet independent. In spite of the absence of detective fiction as such from *The Buried Day*, it is extremely valuable for understanding the reflections of the author's personality and the extensive use of his own experiences in his detective fiction. It has correctly been said that "the detective stories plainly have their source in the clear brain of the poet who can analyze his own complex thoughts and feelings in meticulous detail and unfold a metaphysical argument with persuasive lucidity and logic."[3] And it might be added that the pastoral lyricism that distinguishes his best poetry is also present in his fiction. Certainly, the novels would not be what they are if their author were not also a poet.

Blake was actively involved with the British Communist Party during the period he was writing his first four novels, and the first three reflect his left-wing political views of that time. (The only other one that could possibly be considered is the anti-fascist thriller *The Smiler with the Knife,* 1939, but even if it should be, it is clearly balanced by the anti-communist thriller *The Sad Variety,* 1964). What is most evident is that political statements are never made by Nigel Strangeways and rarely by the authorial voice; rather they are made by sympathetic lesser characters. Michael Evans, a young schoolmaster in *A Question of Proof*, looks at the crowd of parents visiting for Sports Day, and his thoughts are angry: "The spectacle of all this painted, feathered, complacent, chattering flock made him feel sick inside. It was to maintain this pretentious scum that millions sweated or starved beneath the surface" (27). He has similar thoughts throughout the novel. In the second, Sir John Strangeways, Assistant Commissioner of Police, says that he must dine with the Home Secretary, who has "suddenly developed Communist-phobia; thinks they're going to put a bomb under his bed. Ought to know they don't allow acts of individual violence" (Shell, 17). *There's Trouble Brewing*, the third, has more such statements than the others. When a rich, penny-pinching brewer is found to be a murderer, a character says, "It's an interesting comment on our social system that a fellow like Burnett, whose whole life was a series of more or less legalised crimes, has to kill three people before we put him where he can't do any more mischief" (184), and a doctor gives a mini-lecture on the evils of the capitalistic system:

> His eyes seemed to be looking ... into some vision of the future as he inveighed against social conditions—the under-nutrition of children throughout the industrial areas where he had first worked, the cynical way in which some employers of labour attempted to evade health regulations—"and you needn't go to the industrial areas to find that sort of thing.... For the price of a few battleships, we could give you a healthy nation. We have the knowledge, the skill, the material resources; but those in power prefer to use them for destroying their competitors and safe-guarding their own profits" (28).

To include such statements in British detective novels of the 1930s was daring, considering the genre's conservative outlook, but they are evidence of Blake's inclusion of his deeply held—if temporary—beliefs, and, in any case, they no longer seem obtrusive, only somewhat dated.

A major concern in *The Buried Day* is the meaning of the self and what the author calls "the clash of irreconcilables" which make and unmake a human being: old versus new, poetic versus political, private versus public, etc."[4] "I have called it the divided mind; but I am not a schizophrenic, only a man who tends to be victimised and activated, more than most perhaps, by inner conflict" (242). The resulting search for what he calls "single-mindedness" is a constant of his poetry and, accepting the autobiography, of his life. What is the relation to the detective novels? First is the sensitivity of characterization, especially in the repetition of the intensity and confusion of allegiances that passion brings. Second is the emphasis on the fear of schizophrenia. In novel after novel some suspect wonders if he might have committed the crime without knowing it because of a split personality. In one there is a true schizophrenic, in another a murderess attempts to become the person she has killed, and in six the murderer is insane. The divided mind may not be as significant to the Blake novels as to Day Lewis' poetry, but it is certainly present.

From the number of incidents, characters and places in the novels which can be identified as real in *The Buried Day*, the probability is that there are many more not mentioned, but, major or minor, those that can be identified show that as Day Lewis the poet used his experiences so did Blake the novelist. They can be as minor as his using the faculty-student hay-fights of Summer Fields school in *A Question of Proof*, his playing with his boat on the Round Pond of Kensington Garden as a child and using that as an opening for *A Whisper in the Gloom*, his introducing his classical scholarship into divergent characters of *The Widow's Cruise*, or his simply lifting his neighbor, Major-General Burton, who filled his hall with tiger heads and played Bach on a harpsichord wearing a fishing hat, and calling him General Shrivenham in *The Beast Must Die*. On the other hand, they can be as central in his placing *Minute for Murder* in the environment of his World War II work ("To have stood outside the war emotionally, even had it been possible, would have been to exile myself from my fellows and suffer, as exiles do, the worst impoverishment of all" [Day, 87]); placing *End of Chapter* in the publishing firm of Wenham and Geraldine, he being a director of Chatto and Windus, and making that firm the publisher of *The Buried Day*; his presenting his own Georgian home in Greenwich as the home of the victim in *The Worm of Death*; or his sending Strangeways to Cabot University in New England to study a Herrick manuscript after his year as Norton Professor of Poetry at Harvard.

Other instances could be cited, but nowhere is Blake's use of personal experience more telling than in his last and most intriguing novel, *The Private Wound*. It is intriguing for, if the murder is excluded, it is largely autobiographical. The story of a writer's affair in Ireland in 1939, it is obviously a fictional version of what is described as follows in *The Buried Day:* "During this year, too, I was sowing my first wild oats—at the age of thirty-five—a shameless, half-savage, inordinate affair which taught me a great deal about women, and about myself, that I had never known. It seems, as I look back, all of a piece with the desperate irresponsibility and the fatalism which had been in the air since Munich" (230), and ten pages later is the comment: "During the ten years after 1940...I was never long free from the sense of guilt."

Narrated by the central character, Dominic Eyre, an introspective, self-analyzing Anglo-Irishman, the plot recounts the intensity of his passion for Harriet Leeson—what he calls "the insolence of lust"—and recreates fictionally that similar experience of the author. Harriet's murder and the punishment for it exacted by her deceived husband, a "wrecked" hero of the Irish Republican wars, are interwoven with the love affair and with Irish religion, politics and culture to form an unconventional and disturbing work, both brutal and lyrical. The "Epilogue," supposedly written by Eyre's literary executor and explaining the finding of the manuscript after his death, is filled with suggestions that, though names have been changed, "something like this must really have happened":

So it may well be, I reason, that although the events of the book are fictional, they represent some conflict, some authentic experience, which Dominic underwent in his thirties. The central relationship, between him and the woman he calls Harriet Leeson, may have developed in another part of Ireland, in England, or somewhere abroad for that matter. He would want to "distance" himself from the experience, in place as well as time (223).

The Private Wound, Blake's valedictory to the detective novel, is his most personal and, for that reason, ultimately the most mysterious.

Also related to his being a poet are the many writers besides Eyre who appear in the novels. The most significant to the action are the poets Robert Seaton (*Head of a Traveler*) and Stephen Protheroe (*End of Chapter*), the novelists Felix Lane (*The Beast Must Die*) and Millicent Miles (*End of Chapter*), and the television dramatist Ned Stowe (*A Penknife in My Heart*), but there are a number of others who, though less important to the plot, give the works a "literary tone." One result is much conversation about writing, from the satiric to the thoroughly serious. The pseudo-intellectual Gertrude Amberley provides a kind of in-joke with her comment: "Auden and that lot have been dismissed long ago .... *Scrutiny* settled *their* hash long ago" (Web,59). More serious is *Head of a Traveler*, as much about the meaning of being a poet as it is about a murder. Crucial to the plot of *End of Chapter* is the drying up of a dynamic poet's talent, and it contains such literary criticism as Strangeways' agreeing with Keats that one quality of a great writer is "that negative capability which enables its possessor to take on the color of his environment, surrender himself to the personality of another" (105). Such comments may not add anything to murder and its investigation, but they do create a literate and literary tone, which is further developed in some of the novels by themes and motifs. These give their novels a depth of meaning beyond the mystery and serve as one of Blake's principal ways of structuring them. The theme of nemesis—in its most strict Greek mythological sense—in *A Penknife in My Heart* and the theme of mother-child relationships, plus the motif of repeated animal imagery in *The Worm of Death*, are two examples. Another is the macabrely comic motif of all sorts of heads and that of the mesmerizing lifelike house Plash Meadow—"ripe and bursting with the juice of human hopes, human graces and tragedies"—in *Head of a Traveler* (69).

The most striking example of Blake's use of a controlling theme is *A Tangled Web*, a novel which breaks most of the conventions of mystery fiction. It is a study of lust for power, betrayal and, above all, love, in which a murder happens to occur. The murderer, however, is not the villain; that role goes to his supposed best friend who betrays him to the police. That friend, Dr. John (Jacko) Jaques, is described by a police inspector as *"The only known specimen of a totally irresponsible man outside the loony bins"* (140). His determination to destroy the love between Hugo Chesterman and Daisy Bland is pathological:

> He did not hate Hugo, any more than a tarantula hates its natural prey .... No, the pleasure he now felt was unalloyed by hatred—the pure pleasure of power .... The sensation of controlling Hugo's destiny, and Daisy's, was almost physical .... Their love for each other, so ardent and exclusive, had always irked him; he felt an obscure need, not vindictive but dispassionately compulsive, to defile it—bring it down to his own level, as a hooligan may be driven to shatter a stained-glass window or a beautiful image, the mere existence of which he resents because it reproaches him with a kind of truth quite beyond his understanding (138).

He succeeds, and Hugo is executed for killing a policeman during an attempted robbery. Yet the reader wishes Hugo to escape, for he is seen through the eyes of Daisy, the other person caught in Jacko's web. In her innocence, devotion and utter selflessness, she is "a creature out of a fable ... a being from a legend, from a simpler, more luminous world where right and wrong had a different meaning and legal textbooks were unknown" (186, 187). The story is really hers—the original title was *Death and Daisy Bland*—and the theme of "the burden of responsibility which true love inposes" (211) is exemplified by her in this most lyrical of Blake's novels.

Other structural elements that are evidence of Blake's being more than "just" a detective novelist are the management of point of view, the intertwining of action and explanation, and the "symmetrical" beginnings and endings. Only two of the novels are first-person narratives: *The Deadly Joker* and *The Private Wound*. The two narrators, John Waterson and Dominic Eyre, are quite different. As noted, Eyre is a tortured soul, revealing the most traumatic experience of his life, whereas Waterson could be described as a somewhat older Nigel Strangeways, and the tone is correspondingly lighter. Though the other eighteen novels are presented in the third person, several are largely written as if from the consciousness of one of the major characters: Paul Perry in

Malice in Wonderland, Daisy Bland in *A Tangled Web*, Ned Stowe in *A Penknife in My Heart* and, to a lesser degree, Lucy Wragby in *The Sad Variety*. Since these four include a murderer, two "victims" and a "bystander," Blake's ability to manipulate point of view for characterization or suspense is obvious. In two other novels, he employs the diary of a character. The victim's diary provides an epilogue, affecting but unnecessary, to *The Worm of Death*. Much more impressive is "The Diary of Felix Lane," the first third of *The Beast Must Die*, a tour-de-force in misdirection, with its opening, blunt sentence: "I am going to kill a man." Blake also abruptly switches point of view, as in *The Morning After Death*, in which after focusing on Strangeways until the last chapter, he then switches to the murderer, with returns to Strangeways and jumps to the police to provide an exciting conclusion at a football game. Similar to this conclusion are those in which the final explanation is intertwined with action. Blake should have used this combination more often, for some of Strangeways' explanations are far too long. The confrontations between the two suspects in *Minute for Murder* and between Strangeways and a psychopathic murderer on a crumbling barge in *The Worm of Death* and the juxtaposing of Strangeways' explanation with a mob's chasing the murderer in *The Dreadful Hollow* are excellent illustrations of what can be done to prevent a tiresome lecture on whodunit and why. A third feature of Blake's structure is that whatever happens in the first few pages—rarely the murder—is much more important than it appears, and often the events or comments on these first pages return at the very end to create a symmetrical effect. The happening may seem totally unconnected to the plot as Strangeways and Clair Massinger's noticing "hysterical" swans in London on the first two pages of *The Widow's Cruise*, yet these swans provide a significant clue to a murder in Greece as explained in the last sentence of the novel. Without question, the best example of this symmetry of structure is *A Penknife in My Heart*, but to reveal its nature would be unfair to those yet to read it, for the symmetry is essential to both plot and theme.

As might be expected, the novels abound in literary quotations and allusions. Among the titles alone are included Shakespeare, Chaucer, Tourneur, Dryden, Scott, Carroll, Dickinson and Housman. (Blake is also particularly fond of connected or grammatically parallel chapter titles, using puns most wittily in *Minute for Murder* and *End of Chapter* and rime in *The Widow's Cruise*, whose chapters are "Embarkation," "Fraternization,"

"Annihilation," "Investigation" and "Elucidation.") A partial list of other poets alluded to or quoted from includes Vergil (in Latin), Wordsworth, Blake, Tennyson, Patmore, Baudelaire, Clough, Hardy, Eliot, Auden and Muir. The Bible, Ruskin's pathetic fallacy, Jane Austen, Henry James and a large number of American writers in *The Morning After Death* add to the list. Some of the quotations are important clues—Tourneur in *Thou Shell of Death,* Clough in *Minute for Murder* and Tennyson in *The Dreadful Hollow*; others are simply a natural part of the mind of the poet-author, and they help to make the novels distinctively his.

Also helping is the detailed description which gives such a sense of place. From many examples, the one that is most evidently close to the author occurs in *The Worm of Death*. The presentation of the Thames around Greenwich and the use of Blake's own home as the home of the victim provide a realized setting without detracting from the action. (The same feeling for the area is expressed in *The Buried Day*, 239.) Throughout the novels, a love of place, a love of England, is always present, understandable from a writer who celebrates it so often in his poetry. Related is his ability to differentiate the speech of his characters. Although in the early novels he can sound, fortunately rarely, as if unconsciously parodying Dorothy L. Sayers—"the utter caliginous inspissated fog in his own mind" (Shell, 87)—his ability to reproduce psychoanalytic and academic jargon, the American-learned English of a Greek cruise-manager, the dialect of Irish peasants or rural Dorset boys, and the solecisms of "the Martini-and-smoked-salmon brigade," such as "for my wife and I" (Worm, 95, 96), proves that Blake has the ear of someone who pays attention to language, to the poetry of the human voice.

No consideration of the novels' relationship to their author's being a poet would be complete without some notice of the figures of speech which are so prevalent. There are so many that the only conclusion is they, if nothing else, would justify the author as a poet. The repeated use of them for characterization is evident in *End of Chapter,* where Stephen Protheroe is "fishlike" or "minnowy" and Arthur Geraldine's mouth is always "sharklike."

But figures of speech are not just for characterization; they can describe action in an unexpected but exact way, as in the first love-making of *A Tangled Web*; "She felt impaled, powerless yet wildly acquiescent. He was a stranger, he was a hawk hovering to swoop down upon her. They came together as if whirled by a clap of wind out of a cloudless sky. She was naked, staring up at him transfixed, an animal in a snare shamming dead under the poacher's hands, then quivering and struggling" (18). Rather than try to describe Blake's figures of speech, I prefer to present ten, chosen with difficulty from dozens:

> Pride: "the white elephant of the emotions, very imposing and expensive, and the sooner one can get rid of it, the better" (Beast, 149).
> "he swarms with ideas, you know, like lice" (Chapter, 140).
> "Out at the sea's edge a flock of terns flashed and gyrated, like a mobile gone mad" (Wound, 51).
> "Her white fists lay beside her like tear-soaked, crumpled handkerchiefs" (Head, 148).
> "the man's never been nearer Scotland than the end of a whiskey bottle" (Cruise, 85).
> "Faulkner in Mississippi, absorbedly tracing the history of one small region, like a lover feeling along the contours of his mistress's face" (Morning, 118).
> "It was the kind of country town which goes into a coma between its weekly markets .... An exanimate group of village housewives stood at the bus stop, in the patient attitudes of the dead awaiting Charon's ferry" (Hollow, 105).
> "he seemed to carry his personality with gingerly caution, as if it were a priceless vase" (Morning, 63).
> "I felt the fine Irish rain, which always seems to have been poured through holes, infinitesimal in diameter, of the rose of a celestial watering can; threads of rain, all but invisible, which alight on one's face with the touch of spider-web filaments" (Wound, 85).
> Of a swan: "It looks like an Edwardian hat trying to walk" (Cruise, 2).

C. Day Lewis was a critic, editor, translator and *poet*. Nicholas Blake was a detective novelist. They were one man, and the detective novelist cannot be separated from the poet; or perhaps since he so often has been, one can only say he should not be.

The Detective Novelist as Detective Novelist

> *"... tell me, do you read detective fiction?"*
> *"Sometimes," said Nigel.*
>   *"I hope you are sound on it."*
> *"Sound?" asked Nigel.*
> *"As an art form."*
> *"It's not an art form. It's an entertainment."*
>   ..."Excellent, I have no use for those who seek to turn the crime novel into an exercise in morbid psychology...[Crime novelists today have] lost

the courage of their own agreeable fantasies, and want to be accepted as serious writers."...
  "Still, novels that are all plot—just clever patterns concealing a vacuum—one does get bored with them" (Morning, 17).

Though such byplay is amusing, it seems to reflect Blake's own views of detective fiction, for it differs little from the Introduction he wrote to the English edition of Howard Haycraft's *Murder for Pleasure: The Life and Times of the Detective Story* (1942), which states some of his principal ideas about the genre more seriously.[5] Blake describes detective fiction as the "the Folk-Myth of the Twentieth Century," with the detective as fairy godmother. Since he believes that guilt is present in all of us and that the force of religion has weakened for most, detective fiction offers a substitute for religious ritual in harmlessly releasing or absolving that sense of guilt. It is in this "fantasy-representation of guilt" that the value of detective fiction lies, but the fantasy is of equal importance: "evil must, both for myth-making and entertainment, be volatised by a certain measure of fantasy." He sees two possible ways of achieving the "fantasy-representation of guilt": the author may put unreal characters into realistic situations, as in the *roman policier,* or " 'real' characters in unreal, fantastic, or at least improbable situations." He cites as examples of the latter method the works of John Dickson Carr, Rex Stout, Ngaio Marsh and Michael Innes and, from the context, obviously his own.

Blake's novels may be categorized in various ways. Most obviously, there are sixteen Nigel Strangeways novels and four without him, but more is indicated about their nature if they are divided by type; on that basis the grouping is fourteen detective novels, the only one without Strangeways being *The Deadly Joker,* where he is replaced by the similar John Waterson; three thrillers: *The Smiler with the Knife, The Whisper in the Gloom* and *The Sad Variety,* all with Strangeways; and three crime novels, as defined by Julian Symons, in which the lives and psychology of the characters are central: *A Tangled Web, A Penknife in My Heart* and *The Private Wound,* none with Strangeways.

The fourteen detective novels are not widely different in technique from those of Blake's colleagues from the thirties to the sixties, except for the, to be considered, continual emphasis upon the past's effect upon the present. They contain such often repeated conventions as crimes other than murder to complicate the investigation (blackmail, possible treason, poison-pen letters), snowed-in country houses, time problems, body substitutions, public and bizarre murders (hydrocyanic acid inserted into a walnut shell, boiling in a vat of beer, prussic acid inhaled from a "trick" flower), red herrings (binoculars with spiked eyepieces, a *Playboy* centerfold, removal of a corpse by someone other than the murderer), long final explanations (on a few occasions, too long), a small number of suspects, and foreshadowings of what is to come (even versions of the Had-I-But-Known convention: "Had he gone to investigate that moment, it is just possible that the course of several people's lives might have been profoundly altered" [Beast, 179]). Occasionally novels contain coincidences or improbabilities, but there are more in the thrillers than the detective novels. On the other hand, Blake can play with conventions. *Malice in Wonderland* is a comic mystery in which the only death is that of a German spy toward the end of the novel. His use of themes and motifs for structural purposes has already been discussed, and to be considered later is what might be called the "if" technique, which consists of Strangeways spending several pages going over in his mind all possible solutions, what is described as "spinning theories out of thin air" (Morning, 55). After he has indulged in one of these speculative sessions, the reader is hopelessly confused. One structural theme repeated so often as to be distinctively Blake's is the effect of the past on the present. Seen at its best in *Thou Shell of Death, End of Chapter*, and *The Worm of Death*, it involves Strangeways in exploring the past and revealing some buried secret which is the motive for murder. Usually the secret is a part of a family's history, and the search for it opens wounds and causes tensions within that family. Whether an illegitimate child, a girl's suicide, the neglect of a mother, or the loss of a lover, the event of the past returns after years to precipitate murder. Revenge and/or insanity are nearly always directly related, and in some cases the murder is ritualistic or a form of "poetic justice" paralleling what happened in the past—another instance of Blake's fondness for "symmetry."

The three thrillers are, in my opinion, lesser works. *The Smiler with the Knife* is fun with all its action, and the same is true of *The Whisper in the Gloom*, although it contains more coincidence than any other Blake novel, so much that it is commented upon within the novel. *The Sad Variety* is the weakest; an inverted work dealing with the saving of a kidnapped girl, it is unwieldly from attempting to include too many disparate and incompatible elements. Far superior are the three crime novels. Enough has already been said of *A Tangled Web* and *The Private Wound*, except to note that the first is based, as far as plot is concerned, upon the killing of a policeman by John Williams, "the Hooded Man," in 1912; Blake moves the time to the 1950s, and the characterization of the three major characters is all his. *A Penknife in My Heart*, the third, coincidentally has essentially the same premise as Patricia Highsmith's *Strangers on a Train*, relating two men's agreement to commit murders for each other and the nemesis which overtakes them in the form of the guilt and gradual self-understanding of one of them. It is Blake's most ironic novel—with irony in all its forms—and, though difficult to discuss without "spoiling" it, deserves to be better known.

In spite of the differences between the detective novels, the thrillers, and the crime novels, certain characteristic Blake elements are found in all three; these include chases, melodramatic action and comedy and comic set-pieces. (One might expect romance to be on the list, but it is not. It is very much present, unhappily so, in the three crime novels and takes various forms in the detective novels—again unhappy, motivative, conventional, as red herring, or quite complex in *The Deadly Joker*—but it is absent from the thrillers.) The first novel, *A Question of Proof*, includes a wildly comic car chase, and the following *Thou Shell of Death* goes one better with an airplane chase, ending in a death. The last half of *The Smiler with the Knife* is nothing but chase, and other novels include briefer episodes in which the chase of a suspect or murderer is a plot device. Most often, these occur at the end of a novel to give it a slambang finish. Whether the search for an assassin in the Royal Albert Hall—one immediately thinks of Alfred Hitchcock's *The Man Who Knew Too Much* (Gloom), a murderer's attempt to escape at a New England college football game (Morning), the attack by tractor on a kidnap cottage (Variety), or others, these chases are one aspect of Blake's penchant for melodrama. He is not afraid to present action that would not normally be included in classical British detective fiction. There is even a ledge-hanging episode in *Minute for Murder*. The melodrama is sometimes comic, as in the battle of Portobello Road and the shoot-out at a stately home in *The Whisper in the Gloom*, but it can also be physically brutal, minor as in the hanging of a puppy (Joker) or major as in the final confrontation between the detective and murderer (Worm), as well as psychologically brutal as in the confrontation of the two suspects in *Minute for Murder*, which is called "a pretty naked exhibition of mutual antipathy" (234). The comedy can also be brutal; for example, the "fun" of a dog named Truffles being boiled in a beer vat or the "hilarious" questioning of a half-wit dwarf by a police inspector. However, most of the comedy is not brutal. Strangeways can have puckish ideas—"an insane desire to be able to produce a live mouse out of his breast pocket, with the immortal Boy Scout alacrity of Harpo Marx" (Shell, 154)—or the pretensions of psychoanalysis can be mocked through the precocious child of two practitioners (Cruise).

Also, the novels contain numerous comic set-pieces, some extraneous to the plot but all contributing to the distinctive tone that is Blake's. The "surrealist" interior of Mr. Sorn's room in *There's Trouble Brewing*, the "peace" meeting in *The Whisper in the Gloom*, the Greek cafe scene in *The Widow's Cruise,* the "Initiation of a Detective" in *A Question of Proof,* and "The Old Nurse's Tale" chapter of *Thou Shell of Death* are a few such set-pieces representative of the gentle, if rather wacky, comedy of the novels.

A specific way in which Blake differs from other British detective novelists of his generation or earlier is the large number of children and teenagers who appear in his work. How many children play even minor roles in the works of the other eleven writers in this volume or in the works of Sayers, Christie or Marsh? In nine novels, young people are conspicuously present, though some are more important than others. The schoolboys who provide the background of *A Question of Proof* and show Blake's understanding of boyish fantasies; the information-supplying rural Dorset boys of *There's Trouble Brewing*, and the delightful John and Priscilla Restorick, the precocious children of *The Corpse in the Snowman*, who trade slang and quips with each other, using such expressions as "spotted pard" and "infant cheeild," may not be absolutely necessary, but they would be missed. The same is true of such teenagers as Sally Thistlewaite, the comic love interest of *Malice in Wonderland* or the emotionally troubled twins Peter and Faith Trubody of *The Widow's Cruise.* On the other hand, children are murder victims in *The Sad Variety* and *The Widow's Cruise*, and in *The Beast Must Die,* a child hit-and-run victim is the motivation for all that happens. In the same novel, another child greatly complicates the plot for both murderer and detective. Finally, in two of the thrillers children are central to the action. In *The Whisper in the Gloom* Bert Hale, aged twelve, and his friends, Copper and Foxy, become involved in an assassination attempt on a visiting Soviet minister. Bert is a scientific "brain" and Foxy is streetwise; together they are the equal of the Hardy boys. Though they undergo considerable danger, they thoroughly enjoy the excitement of their adventures: witnessing a murder, being kidnapped, hiding in secret rooms and riding in helicopters. Adult peril becomes boyish fun in this rather improbable, but comic, novel. (Walt Disney modernized and

Americanized it as *The Kids Who Knew Too Much.)* Lucy Wragsby of *The Sad Variety* is another child of twelve; she is kidnapped by communists to obtain a formula from her scientist father. She is incredibly calm during her ordeal, and her intelligence enables her to get a message to the outside. At the same time, she is so appealing that her tough female captor, a woman whose "mental world was one of abstractions, slogans, diagrams, statistics" (13), succumbs to her charm and attempts to prevent her death. As unlikely as the ability of these children to survive their perils may seem, they are still children in their emotions, fears, superstitions and infectious innocent acceptance of their adventures. They are examples of that negative capability so admired by their creator.

Other characters include typical stereotypes such as the suspects listed by Georgia Strangeways in *The Corpse in the Snowman*: "A trollop, an Ango-Saxon squire, an American wife, a rolling stone, a fribble, and a quack" (18). Witty tramps, boorish interlopers into village life, faithful retainers, pompous teachers, dull doctors, flirts, spinsters, and all sorts of people acting guilty for personal reasons—the well-known types of Golden Age detective fiction are present. In essence, they are little different from hundreds of characters created by other writers. Yet Blake rarely resorts to exaggerated eccentricity; rather his subsidiary characters are carefully delineated to serve their functions as witnesses and suspects. And occasionally, they are original, amusing or horrible enough to remain memorable: Mr. Thistlewaite, an imposing Oxford tailor who reads detective fiction (Malice), Clarissa Cavendish, who lives in her private eighteenth-century world (Shell), Mrs.Hale, the roly-poly but acerbic wife of a bishop (Cruise), Daniel Durdle, a caterpillar-like Puritan who writes poison-pen letters (Hollow), Charles Reilly, a poet in residence at an American university, who seems an elderly Irish reincarnation of Dylan Thomas (Morning), or priggish but likeable Paul Perry, a "mass observer," who is a satiric portrait of a young leftist just before World War II (Malice). Together the stereotypes and the originals provide a colorful supporting cast for the duel between murderer and detective or the action of the thrillers.

Most of Blake's victims follow the unknown or unpleasant convention so that the reader feels little sorrow, the major exceptions being the multi-viewed Nita Prince (Minute), the beautiful and gentle Vera Paston (Joker), and most especially the pathetic little boy called Evan, who is left to die in a blizzard (Variety). Some victims are never seen or appear only for their murder, while others range from simply obnoxious, Millicent Miles

(Chapter), to the absolutely evil, Dr. Dennis Bogan (Corpse) and George Rattery (Beast). Like most of his colleagues, Blake does not make the victim the most interesting character in a novel, the only possible exception being Harriet Leeson in *The Private Wound*, who is a third of a triangle with her husband and Dominic Eyre; she is at least as interesting as they because of her sexual nature and the deep love both men have for her, but even she is less complex than her murderer.

In *The Buried Day*, Blake states, "As a writer of detective novels, I am interested in the criminal mind," and he lists three characteristics of that mind: "unreality, fatalism and unconscious need for punishment" (47). This interest is evident in the principal motives of his murderers: fear, revenge, sexual repression and insanity. The term most often used to describe the weakness of a murderer is "moral cowardice," the inability to face life as it is. What seems to fascinate Blake most is the point at which a person's fantasy of murder changes to the determination to commit the act, for most people somehow suppress any such fantasies. This flashpoint is discussed in *The Widow's Cruise* (177), *The Dreadful Hollow* (243) and *The Morning After Death* (170), but the most concise statement is in *Head of a Traveller*: "The chap who plans a murder never really means to commit it. Generally he never gets further than the planning: there must be thousands of murders committed in fantasy every year. But just now and then the point is reached where the fantasies take charge and push the bloke over the edge" (166).

Just as the flashpoint is different for different people, so are the personalities of murderers. Blake's vary from one who is "Maiden aunt, St. Francis, intrepid aviator; tender, reckless, fussy, Rabelaisian, ruthless" (Shell, 31) to a vain "buccaneer" with "no best to bring out," "to whom unexpected obstacles come as a personal affront" (Penknife, 75, 93) to the one in *The Beast Must Die* who has "a too sensitive conscience" and sees the tragic irony of the situation—but all are flawed with "moral cowardice." As a result of Blake's desire to study the psychology of his murderers, they are often rather obvious or are revealed earlier than usual. *The Deadly Joker, The Widow's Cruise* and *The Worm of Death* provide three examples. Another is in *End of Chapter*, and there Blake uses his most popular means of misdirecting the reader from the obvious, one could say only possible, suspect: Nigel Strangeways' liking or admiring the murderer. This device is used in five of the Strangeways novels: *Thou Shell of Death, The Beast Must Die, The Corpse in the Snowman, Minute for Murder* and *End of Chapter*.

(The "liking" of the murderer is also used in the three crime novels; in *The Private Wound*, Eyre repeatedly expresses his admiration for the person who is revealed as the murderer and afterwards says that he "remains a tragic figure for me" [213].) His friendship with the murderer in *The Beast Must Die* causes Strangeways to call the results, "my most unhappy case" (218), and the ending of *Head of a Traveler* is left open with Strangeways undecided as to revealing the murderer because of his admiration for a relation of that murderer. Such sympathy is, needless to say, unusual in detective fiction, for it could easily skew the thematic formula of freeing a society from the suspicion of guilt and eliminating the one responsible, but Blake is able to hold to that formula while still exhibiting the sympathy. One way he does this—and tied to plot—is the final disposition of the murderers. A list is informative:

Suicide	7 (Proof, Shell, Beast, Chapter, Penknife, Cruise, Morning)
Death by others	4 (Hollow, Worm, Variety, Wound)
Arrest	4 (Trouble, Minute, Gloom, Joker)
Execution	1 (Web)
Insanity	1 (Smiler)
Freedom (no murder occurs)	1 (Malice)
Escape (to spy for England)	1 (Corpse)
Undecided	1 (Head)

As can be seen, suicide or death by others accounts for over half the murderers' exits from the novels. Only one of those Strangeways likes is arrested, and the suicides in *A Question of Proof* and *The Beast Must Die* are the direct results of his pity or friendship for the murderers. Some of the suicides are spectacular and are one form of those slambang endings, but even more the suicides and a number of the other exits are revelatory of their author's own nature as a human being. In only two instances does the murderer apparently escape some "punishment," yet the novels are unique in the amount of sympathy the murderers receive from the detective or the narrative voice. Blake's interest in the "why" of the criminal mind and his innate sense of compassion, so evident in his poetry, are the obvious reasons.

Blake has been quoted as saying that when he decided to write his first detective novel he had already read "a vast number." His works prove that he had: that he knew the conventions and formulas and accepted most of them. He used them skillfully, combining them with his personal and poetic interests, to create twenty novels, among which are some of the classics of the genre.

The Poet as Detective

> "What do you think an amateur detective ought to look like?
> * * *
> "Well, I suppose my idea of a detective is based on Sherlock Holmes, Father Brown and Poirot."
> "A curious composite figure he must be! Long and short, fat and thin—"
> "Now don't interrupt. He has piercing eyes, that see exactly what you are thinking. He is always making sinister deductions from one's most innocent remarks. And of course he's wildly eccentric. Are you wildly eccentric?"
> "It's very difficult: some of my friends complain that I'm too eccentric, others that I'm not eccentric enough."
> "You look quite ordinary to me." (Trouble, 14-15)

Though Nigel Strangeways may seem quite ordinary, an effect he often plays up, he is really in the tradition of the brilliant amateur sleuth. Blake consciously based him on his close friend and fellow poet, W.H. Auden, as Auden has noted, "I must confess to a weakness for Mr. Day Lewis's Nigel Strangeways, because some of his habits were taken from mine."[6] It is also evident from *The Buried Day* that much of the author's own personality, particularly his compassion and introspection, and appearance are present in his detective.[7] Blake chose not to make Strangeways a poet as such, but he does "dabble," his word, in literature. He has written a couple of "charming" books, including a "delightful little book on the Caroline poets" (Trouble, 10). In *The Smiler with a Knife*, he is translating Hesiod and has a flat in literary Bloomsbury, and in *Head of a Traveler* is writing a "monograph on the subject of graphology in relation to the manuscripts of certain twentieth-century poets" (18). With his Audenesque genesis, his traits in common with his poet-creator, and his literary manner, it is not much of an exaggeration to use "the poet as detective" to characterize Nigel Strangeways.

He does not age appreciably. He is said to be in his early thirties in *Malice in Wonderland*, and that is the general impression throughout the novels. An untidy, stooped six-footer, who sprawls or strides like an ostrich, he looks a little flabby but is not. His face is furrowed, but "the childlike pout of his underlip" (Smiler, 5) combined with his shortsighted, pale-blue eyes, sometimes behind thick glasses, and his "lock of sandy-coloured hair dropping over his forehead" (Shell,11) give him a boyish expression. Though he can be brutal when angry, he most often gives the deceptive impression of naivete: "Nigel's pale-blue eyes held an expression of guilelessness; which had been misinterpreted by many and had been the downfall of some" (Morning, 53). His docile air hides an inordinate curiosity: "the passionate interest in human nature which precluded any taking offense at its more offensive manifestations" (Hollow, 5). His ability to mask his curiosity behind apparent docility is naturally one of his greatest assets as a detective. Occasionally, the underlying keenness of mind shows through the mask; for instance, when he is thinking hard, he stares ruminatively down his nose, but his eyes can at any moment "narrow and spark into the most concentrated attention" (Smiler, 5). But the overall effect is an "air of purposeful abstraction," suggesting "a lecturer of the less orthodox academic type" (Cruise, 105).

Like most British "great detectives," Strangeways is given qualities which prevent his being too forbiddingly superior, and again like those of the others, they are comic qualities of personality. In only one novel do they become obtrusive; in *There's Trouble Brewing* Strangeways very facetiously plays the great detective. There is altogether too much of "We must visit the scene of the crime. This is big stuff. Noted amateur bloodhound follows up the Clue of the Sabotaged Bell" (113). Fortunately, Blake curbed the extravagance, but that is not to say that Strangeways does not succumb to the everpresent temptation to show off. During a high-speed car chase, he can say it is better than the movies and break into an aria from *Israel in Egypt*. The comment is made in *The Beast Must Die* that he is "never above a nice piece of exhibitionism" (114), and that is especially true of his final explanations. On the other hand, he shuns publicity: his exhibitionism is for the small group, not the public. The greatest display of it is in verbal humor, which can range from his teasing his wife about her travel books with the suggested title, *Three Thousand Miles Through the Bush on a Tricycle*, to the twenty-two nonsense questions he devises in *The Beast Must Die*. Two examples are "How many stitches in time save ten?" and "How many lives has a cat o' nine tails?" His wife's comment after examining the list is "It must be a terrible thing to have received the benefits of a classical education," which leads to a sparring match about *llamas* and *lamas* (104-05). Since we learn that Strangeways did not take his studies seriously, perhaps that classical education is not responsible. In any case, he is excessively fond of puns and mixed metaphors. His best literary pun is "Marihuana of the Moated Grange" (Morning, 60). His fondness for such mixed metaphors as "his pre-war wild oats come home to roost" causes his uncle to groan, but Strangeways says that "they are signs of a vivid and proleptic imagination" (Shell, 16, 187). Proleptic or not, Strangeways does have a vivid imagination. One of his jokes with Inspector Blount in *Thou Shell of Death* concerning possible murderers can serve as an illustration of that imagination and Blake's ability to give his detective a quirky humor that makes him as amusing as formidable:

> What about the gardener, then? Name of Jeremiah Pegrum: and a name like that should lead one into the worst excesses. Spends most of his time meditating in the outhouses, but you've only to read T.F. Powys to discover that murder is the chief winter sport amongst English rustics. "The long winter evenings are coming. Buy a set of our guaranteed ever-sharp hatchets. It will keep young and old amused. Packed in fancy box, with directions, seven shillings and sixpence net. Packets of assorted hemlock, ratsbane, henbane and deadly nightshade, sixpence extra" (125).

Other comic aspects of his personality are his love of "blankets for three" on his bed and his enormous appetite, from tea-drinking in the first novel to eating American corn muffins in the last. Amazingly, since he hates to exercise, he never gains weight. As a final eccentricity, he likes American football—for the majorettes.

There are two women in Strangeways' life: Georgia Cavendish, who becomes his wife, and later Clare Massinger, who becomes his lover. They provide a way of roughly dividing the sixteen Strangeways novels into three chronological groups. Seven were written between 1935 and 1941, the last six of which might be called the "Georgia" novels. As Blake was working for the Ministry of Information during World War II, no other novel appeared until 1947. Of the nine written between then and 1966, the first three present Strangeways mourning Georgia's death, while in the last six his affair with Clare Massinger is a major element, and they can be termed the "Clare" novels.

Georgia Cavendish is "one of the three most famous woman explorers of her day" (Beast, 107). When she first appears in *Thou Shell of Death*, she is accompanied by a parrot and a bloodhound and is described as "attractively ugly, eccentric without being a frump, witty, a good cook, sensible and sensual, faithful, and a perfect seat—I am told—on anything from an armadillo to a camel" (70). Having been everywhere from the Sahara to the outer Hebrides, she is a competent, liberated woman. Like Harriet Vane before Wimsey, she has had an affair before meeting Strangeways, and like Lord Peter he is not bothered by that as much as saving her from a murder charge, which he does. In the next novel, they are married, Blake not following Sayers in tracing the romance. Strangeways discusses his cases with her, receiving helpful insights and suggestions, and uses her, in his own words, as an *agent provocateuse*; the same is true of his later relationship with Clare. In *The Smiler with the Knife* Georgia is the central character. She and Strangeways fake a separation so that she may infiltrate a fascist conspiracy and attract its leader: Strangeways is absent from most of the novel. *The Smiler with the Knife* is a thriller in which the leader of the conspiracy is revealed in the first half of the narrative. That half is quite effective in reflecting the social and political unrest in Great Britain just before World War II, but the second half is almost a parody of the thriller, with a cricket-playing martyr destroying himself and the conspirators' underground bomb factory, causing "the Nottingham earthquake," and Georgia's undergoing a hyperbolic chase-and-escape sequence. She obtains the plans of the conspiracy, is caught, sets a fire and blinds the villain, disguises herself as Father Christmas (Santa Claus), endures a chase in a huge truck, disguises herself again as a eurythemic dancer, and finally has to fight the blind villain in a totally dark room. Along the way, she has some delightfully comic helpers: Mr. Dickon, a Strangewayish department store manager who provides her escape from Manchester; and Miss Lobelia Agg-Thoresby and her Radiance Girls, the eurythemic group, which takes her in. Though Blake seems unable to decide exactly what he wants the novel to be, it is great fun, and notable as Georgia's only starring role.[8]

She is killed by a bomb while driving an ambulance during the London blitz. Her death is announced and the effect on Strangeways stated in *Minute for Murder*:

> Georgia's death had left him mentally crippled .... His lack of interest in the personal relationships of his colleagues—this, he realized now, was because he could not come home and talk to her about them. Georgia had helped him in so many of his cases, bringing her keen intuitive power to bear upon the facts and hints he collected. To become involved in a case again would be

to remind himself at every step of how much he had lost (55).

After the interregnum of three novels, Clare Massinger enters in *The Whisper in the Gloom*. She is a famous sculptor at twenty-six, who "doodles" by shaping spout-muzzled little horses. Although she has supposedly known Strangeways four years, she only learns that he is a detective in this novel, an unnecessarily improbable situation. She is cat-like in appearance: thin with a dead-pale face and coal-black hair. Strangeways finds her even more untidy than himself and thinks, "I could never cohabit with a woman who keeps an open pot of foi gras on a shelf next to an open tin of turpentine" (Chapter, 71). However, they do eventually cohabit, but without marriage. The choice is hers, as Strangeways explains in *The Worm of Death*:

> We live together. But Clare is tremendously old-fashioned. She believes that marriage is for the procreationof children and the raising of families. And her lifework is making her children out of stone and wood. She simply couldn't divide her attention between them and real ones. So we've never married. But it's all very respectable (4).

(In *The Morning After Death*, the last Strangeways novel, he is unfaithful to Clare with an American graduate student. My students in a seminar on detective fiction found this "shocking conduct" for a great detective. Perhaps his unfaithfulness is a way of emphasizing the *respectability* of the relationship with Clare.) Being a sculptor, Clare has great powers of observation, and, like Georgia, she is a sounding board for Strangeways' theories and is used by him as decoy and information-gatherer or, in her own angry words, "as a cross between a tethered goat and a call girl" (Gloom, 170). But her most significant actions are her saving Strangeways' life in three of the six novels: *The Whisper in the Gloom, End of Chapter,* and *The Worm of Death*—in the last of these, she hangs the murderer! In spite of the novels having been written between 1954 and 1966, this reversal of stereotypical male-female roles—he never rescues *her,* along with the refusal to marry, gives their relationship a very contemporary tone.

The two policemen with whom Strangeways works most often are Inspector, later Superintendent, Blount and Inspector Wright. Blount appears in six novels, and in the last of these, *The Whisper in the Gloom*, introduces Strangeways to Wright, who then returns in two more. Blount is a bald, dryly courteous Scotsman, who has "rather impersonal eyes" and who can bully witnesses if necessary, but whose principal method of gaining information is to present a Pickwickian exterior, which Strangeways knows camouflages "a mind as ruthlessly purposeful as a guided missile" (Hollow, 149). Repeatedly such phrases as "that bland-faced, granite-hearted Scot" (Beast, 113) or "Bloody old serpent in hen's clothing" (Hollow, 168) are used to describe his deceptive appearance and what it masks. In their deceptiveness Blount and Strangeways are brothers. Blount's favorite phrase is "bricks without straw," most often applied to Strangeways' ideas, for, though somewhat of an over-simplification, their essential working relationship is Blount for facts and Strangeways for theories. There is typical jovial byplay between them, but they work well together, their specialities complimenting each other. In fact, Strangeways always works well with the police, though he occasionally employs them for their information in ways they do not anticipate. Both Blount and Wright are usually ahead of him in considering physical evidence—*The Worm of Death* providing several instances—and he generally leaves that aspect of a case to them. Wright seems somehow more "professional" than Blount, and his sternness is emphasized by his saturnine hatchet-face and eyes "sharp as augers." But as with Blount, he and Strangeways work together. When Strangeways feels he must withhold information from Wright, he agonizes, "To lie to his old friend Wright was unthinkable" (Worm, 201). All in all, though Strangeways is the solver of the mutual cases, he and his official colleagues are friends and work without acrimony; there is no Holmes-Lestrade or Poirot-Japp belitting of Scotland Yard in these novels.

One of Wright's facetious comments about Strangeways is "The mad archeologist. Loves digging up the past" (Worm, 69). As noted in the previous section, Strangeways does spend much time delving into the past, but as a detective he does more. Other characters are continually fascinated by his reasons for being a detective. In *A Question of Proof* one of his friends says that he left Oxford after two years, as a result of answering his examination questions in limericks, and "settled down to investigate crime; said it was the only career left which offered scope to good manners and scientific curiosity. He's been very successful; made pots of money" (93). Strangeways always mentions that he is paid—and paid well—for his detection. He states in *There's Trouble Brewing* that "Twenty-five guineas retaining fee, and a refresher of five guineas a day is my minimum charge" (25). Of course, the answer of money does not satisfy his questioners, and so he has to explain:

"But *why* do you do it?" he asked.

> "Criminal investigation, you mean? ... It's chiefly that I'm curious about people—particularly the pathological states of mind ... Also, it's just as well that murderers shouldn't be allowed to indulge in their pastime.... I charge high fees" (Worm, 11).

In *Malice in Wonderland,* he gives one of the classic statements about detection—at least fictional detection: "I don't hire myself out to prove any one's innocence. I do it to discover the truth" (143). His longest statement of his reasons occurs in *There's Trouble Brewing* and is basically an explanation of the intellectual satisfaction he receives from solving a case, using the analogy of translating Latin to criminal detection:

> You have a long sentence, full of inversions; just a jumble of words it looks at first. That is what a crime looks like at first sight, too. The subject is a murdered man; the verb is the modus operandi, the way the crime was committed; the object is the motive. Those are the three essentials of every sentence and every crime. First you find the subject, then you look for the verb, and the two of them lead you to the object. But you have not discovered the criminal—the meaning of the whole sentence yet. There are a number of subordinate clauses, which may be clues or red-herrings, and you've got to separate them from each other in your own mind and reconstruct them to fit and to amplify the meaning of the whole. It's an exercise in analysis and synthesis.... (52-53)

Such a philosophy of detection places great demands on the person attempting to practice it. Nigel Strangeways possesses a number of qualities which enable him to do just that and which make him one of the great detectives. He is "a kind of human microscope" as a result of what he calls his "trained, scientific curiosity" and his "almost perfect verbal memory" (Proof, 100: Shell, 160). Other well-established characteristics are his lack of intimidation by the rich or powerful and his refusal to be bound by official rules: "Etiquette and convention meant nothing to him, when a problem had arisen which could only be solved by unorthodox methods" (Hollow, 218). Yet he can have great compassion—even for murderers. He is a firm believer in the use of shock tactics; his favorite expression is some variation of "I think it's time I put a cat among the pigeons" (Worm, 153; see also Variety, 47 & Morning, 83). He enjoys the consternation among suspects when he introduces some ambiguous remark or supposed discovery, for their reactions often reveal more than they intend. Such tactics are another instance of his exhibitionism, as are those long, drawn-out final explanations.

All of these characteristics aid his success, but the principal component of that success is his ability to reason. Like other detectives, he makes lists, especially of what he finds anomalous, and then his mind ranges over them to resolve the anomalies. He states in the first novel, "My clues are of the invisible, intangible sort" (164). Therefore, he leaves physical evidence to the police and theorizes, reasons, *thinks*. In nearly every novel there is a three to five page section in which he considers all the questions of the case and all possible solutions. Though Strangeways' head may become dizzy from his "tail-chasing arguments," the reader's becomes even more so, which is Blake's intent. The possibilities are so logical and yet so confusing by their number that the reader can only wait for Strangeways to identify the correct solution at the end.

In Strangeways Blake neatly balances the normal and the eccentric. He is a likeable character. His sense of fun—literary and otherwise—his tendency toward exhibitionism, and his romantic relationships combine to give him a human quality which belies his name. His ways are not strange, but thoroughly natural and believable. But above all, Nigel Strangeways is a ratiocinative detective in that long line beginning with C. August Dupin, and he justly deserves to be included among those called "the great detectives."

* * *

The twenty novels of Nicholas Blake from 1935 to 1968 are both typical and atypical of the period. The typicality lies in their generally following the formulas and conventions of the genre present when Blake began writing, as well as the three late crime novels indicating his recognition of new forms. His creation of a "great detective" is also typical. Much less so are the passion of lovers, the significant presence of children, the compassion for murderers, the presence of explicit themes, the use of the author's own experience, and the basic "normality" of Nigel Strangeways. Julian Symons has accurately described another quality of the novels: "their bubbling high spirits."[9] They give the impression that the author enjoyed writing them, and the enjoyment communicates itself to the reader. Finally, and to repeat, the fact that Nicholas Blake was also C. Day Lewis gives the novels—whatever else they may possess—a lyrical quality that comes from their author being a major poet. No matter what the ultimate judgment of them may be, they can only be considered as the work of the poet as detective novelist.

Notes

[1]The editions of Blake's novels used for this study are listed below, preceded by the original date of publication. All quotations will be cited in the text using, where necessary for clarity, the abbreviation given after an entry:

1935 *A Question of Proof* (New York: Harper, 1979) (Proof)
1936 *Thou Shell of Death* (New York: Harper, 1977). (Shell)
1937 *There's Trouble Brewing* (London: Collins, 1973). (Trouble)
1938 *The Beast Must Die* (New York: Harper, 1978) (Beast)
1939 *The Smiler With the Knife* (New York: Harper, 1978). (Smiler)
1940 *Malice in Wonderland* (London: Collins, 1940).(Malice)
1941 *The Corpse in the Snowman* (New York: Harper, 1977). (Corpse)
1947 *Minute for Murder* (New York: Harper, 1977). (Minute)
1949 *Head of a Traveler* (New York: Harper, 1976). (Head)
1953 *The Dreadful Hollow* (New York: Harper, 1979). (Hollow)
1954 *The Whisper in the Gloom* (New York: Harper, 1977). (Gloom)
1956 *A Tangled Web* (New York: Harper, 1956). (Web)
1959 *A Penknife in My Heart* (New York: Harper, 1980). (Penknife)
1959 *The Widow's Cruise* (New York: Harper, 1977). (Cruise)
1961 *The Worm of Death* (New York: Harper, 1976). (Worm)
1963 *The Deadly Joker* (London: Collins, 1963). (Joker)
1964 *The Sad Variety* (New York: Harper, 1979). (Variety)
1966 *The Morning After Death* (New York: Harper, 1980). (Morning)
1968 *The Private Wound* (New York: Harper, 1981). (Wound)

There are eight uncollected Blake short stories: "A Slice of Bad Luck," "The Assassin's Club," "It Fell to Earth," "A Study in White," "Mr. Prendergast and the Orange," "Conscience Money," "Sometimes the Blins," and "Long Shot." For their original publication, see the entry on Blake in *Twentieth Century Crime and Mystery Writers*, ed. John M. Reilly (New York: St. Martin's, 1980). The only two considered for this essay are "The Assassin's Club," *Masterpieces of Mystery: The Golden Age-II*, ed. Ellery Queen (New York: Davis, 1977), pp. 261-69, and "A Study in White," *Masterpieces of Mystery: the Forties*, ed. Ellery Queen (New York: Davis, 1978), pp. 252-69.

[2]*The Buried Day* (New York: Harper, 1960), p. 202. Further references will be cited in the text.

[3]Clifford Dyment, *C. Day Lewis*, Rev. ed. (London: Longmans, Green, 1969), p. 28.

[4]This "divided mind" and search for "single-mindedness" in Day Lewis's poetry is treated extensively and well in Samuel Hynes, *The Auden Generation* (New York: Viking, 1972). Hynes also gives a succinct summary of Lewis' Communist period: "Of all the 'thirties poets, Day Lewis was the one who tried longest and hardest to reconcile political commitment with a sense of the integrity of art; he was an active member of the Communist Party ... and yet he remained what he always was essentially, a lyric poet" (96).

[5]The Introduction is reprinted in part as "The Detective Story—Why?" in *The Art of the Mystery Story*, ed. Howard Haycraft (1946; rpt. New York: Biblo & Tannen, 1975), pp. 398-405. All citations are to this version. Though Blake takes the genre seriously, he does not allow it to overpower his sense of humor: "But we had better not be too solemn about the detective novel. Let us be content to say, as readers, that it is a form of escape more stimulating for some of us than bingo, and less harmful than heroin." Quoted in Winslow Dix, "The Second Incarnation of C. Day Lewis," *The Chronicle of Higher Education*, 19 March 1979, p. R14.

[6]Quoted in Jacques Barzun and Wendell Hertig Taylor, *A Catalogue of Crime* (New York: Harper, 1971), p. 576.

[7]After seeing Irving Penn's 1951 photograph of Blake for *Vogue*, it is impossible for me to imagine Strangeways looking any other way. The photograph is reproduced in Tage la Cour and Harald Mogensen, *The Murder Book: An Illustrated History of the Detective Story*(New York: Herder and Herder, 1971), p. 143.

[8]Though I admire much in Patricia Craig and Mary Cadogan, *The Lady Investigates: Women Detectives and Spies in Fiction* (London: Victor Gollancz, 1981), their view of *The Smiler with the Knife* seems unnecessarily harsh, particularly of Georgia Strangeways' role in it. It also seems naive in their wonderment that Blake could easily write an anti-fascist thriller using the same materials as those of anti-socialist thrillers. Their judgment that Blake's fiction has a "somewhat querulous and vindictive note" toward "feminine tendencies" is in my opinion unwarranted. See pp. 197-200.

[9]*Mortal Consequences* (New York: Harper, 1972), p. 126.

Michael Gilbert
Photo credit courtesy Jerry Bauer

Michael Gilbert

George N. Dove

1912	Michael Gilbert born on July, 17, in Billinghay, Lincolnshire
1937	Received law degree at London University
1939-45	Served in Hon. Artillery Company, 12th Regiment, Royal Horse Artillery, North Africa and Italy; mentioned in dispatches, 1943; captured by Germans and imprisoned near Parma, Italy, 1943; escaped and rejoined regiment, 1944; left service with rank of major.
1947	Joined law firm of Trower, Still and Keeling in London; married Roberta Mary Marsden; published first novel, *Close Quarters*
1957	Published *The Claimant,* non-fiction study of the Tichborne case
1959	Edited *Best Detective Stories of Cyril Hare*
1960	Served as Legal Adviser to the government of Bahrain
1982	Published most recent novel, *End-Game*

The critical consensus with regard to Michael Gilbert seems to have stabilized, to the extent that almost any review of his most recent book is likely to contain expressions like "understatement" and "restraint," "civilized writing" and "careful control." Critics apparently find his work relatively easy to categorize. Dilys Winn places him in the "Typical Cozy" class of a scale in which the broad groupings are the Cozy, the Paranoid, the Romantic, the Vicious and the Analytical. The basis of Winn's taxonomy may become a little clearer upon identification of some other writers in her "Typical Cozy" group, Elizabeth Lemarchand, Michael Innes and Edmund Crispin.[1] Less picturesquely, but apparently following the same kind of reasoning, Julian Symons assigns Gilbert to the category of Entertainers, a class in which, says Symons, Emma Lathen is the other outstanding practitioner. The Entertainer according to this definition is a writer who thinks primarily in terms of what will amuse his audience and who tries not to injure the susceptibilities of the reader. The Entertainer is an objective-minded writer who puts little or nothing of his own personality into his stories and who can treat lightly or amusingly subjects that could be disturbing or alarming. In a more specific discussion of Gilbert's work, Symons does modify his characterization a little by saying that Gilbert "has wavered between a wish to be fairly realistic ... and a feeling that one shouldn't be too serious in a crime story."[2]

Eight years later, Michael Gilbert answered with a question: "What," he asked, "is a writer to do if he is not allowed to entertain?"[3] Both the query and the implied answer are deceptively simple, and a useful appreciation of Gilbert's conception of the role of the mystery-suspense writer can be gained only in light of an understanding of what he has done in his own fiction.

Michael Gilbert is a writer of considerable versatility and scope who has not only declined to develop series of stories built around a single protagonist but has moved much at will from one type of narrative to another, with the result that he now has to his credit an impressive body of fiction in five popular areas. Most of his stories can be classed as professional detection, professional intelligence (more accurately, counter-intelligence), amateur detection, amateur intelligence, and a kind of tale Gilbert has developed as his own specialty, which might be called the social-theme-suspense novel. There are no "series characters" in the sense that roles are carried along from one story to another; rather, Gilbert will feature one of his detectives in one book, assign him a subordinate position in another, and then allow him only cameo appearances in several others. Thus Chief Inspector Hazlerigg, who has the starring role in the first novel, *Close Quarters* (1947),[4] makes brief appearances in other tales of detection, professional and amateur, and even in one of the social-theme stories, but he never again plays a lead. The same treatment is accorded the two lawyer-detectives, Henry Bohun and "Nap" Rumbold, who make several appearances of varying importance. The closest Gilbert has come to a conventional series, as a matter of fact, has been the one novel *Blood and Judgment* (1958) and the collection of short stories *Petrella at Q* (1977), featuring Detective Inspector Patrick Petrella, and the succession of short stories (some of them collected in *Game Without Rules* in 1977) about Mr. Calder and Mr. Behrens of counter-intelligence.

Close Quarters, the first of the novels of professional detection, belongs in the category of police fiction represented by the Jules Maigret stories of Georges Simenon and the Roderick Alleyn stories of Ngaio Marsh, the mystery resolved by a distinctively superior policeman. Chief Inspector Hazlerigg, who solves the problem with only perfunctory assistance from his subordinates, is a detective whose thought-processes can rise to levels of abstraction characteristic of the great classic sleuths of the Golden Age. *Close Quarters* is as strictly English-formal-problem as one could imagine, with the setting laid in the close of Melchester Cathedral and the *dramatis personae* composed of the dean, assorted canons, vergers and vicars and their families. The development of the mystery is also conventional, including an elaborate clue hidden in a crossword puzzle, a red herring that sends one of the policemen off on a fruitless chase, and, predictably, the situational device of the second murder committed while the most likely suspect is in prison. As "cozy" entertainment *Close Quarters* is a satisfactorily absorbing mystery, but it is characteristic of Gilbert's versatility that he never again undertook a novel of the vicar's rose garden vintage.

By the time he returned to the field of professional detection three years later, Gilbert had written two other mysteries and had developed sufficient confidence to break out of conventional molds, to the extent that *Smallbone Deceased* has such an air of bright originality that it is widely regarded as his most successful novel.

Smallbone has those qualities that are now considered Gilbert trademarks, including the plausible atmosphere of a solicitors' firm and the dry, whimsical wit associated with lawyers and their attitudes, and a characteristically serene initial atmosphere that is sensationally shattered by a murder. *Smallbone Deceased* is important to Gilbert's development in one other respect, as a transitional novel toward the police procedural story, a kind of narrative in which he was to excel with the later Petrella and Mercer novels. Once again, in *Smallbone*, Hazlerigg is the leading detective, only now without the mental gymnastics of *Close Quarters*, but with an inclination to work with the squad of policemen assigned to the case, as is typical of the police procedural. Significantly, much of the job of investigation is carried on by Henry Bohun, a lawyer who serves Hazlerigg as an informant, and there is some dispersion of narrative thrust into the complications of the law firm, but final resolution of the mystery is distinctly a police triumph.

Blood and Judgment (1958) was Gilbert's first police procedural novel, and it introduced his best-known policeman, Patrick Petrella. Petrella, whose father was a member of the political branch of the Spanish police and whose mother was of a respectable English professional family,[5] is himself an interesting combination of traits not attributable solely to heredity, with a sense of justice that insists upon re-opening an investigation in which he thinks the police have erred, and a gift for dodging the refinements of police protocol. *Blood and Judgment* is representative of the police procedural school of detection, with the police acting as a team instead of depending upon the achievements of one single superior detective, with strong reliance on such commonplace police methods as fingerprinting and the use of informants, and without parallel excursions into the detective efforts of amateurs or private enquiry agents. *Petrella at Q*, published in 1977, is a collection of short stories so closely related that the volume reads like an episodic novel which, with *Blood and Judgment*, belongs in the tradition of the procedural story.

It is typical of Gilbert's refusal to develop series of stories that he invented a new detective for his next tale of professional detection, *The Body of a Girl* (1972), another police procedural. Detective Chief Inspector William Mercer is a harsher and more outspoken policeman than Petrella, who shares Petrella's tenacity but lacks his idealism. This novel is rich in insights into the police sub-culture, particularly the rivalries and resentments that characterize the relationships of the uniformed and plain-clothes branches. The only other appearance of Mercer has been his assignment to the leading role in three short stories published in 1979, this time as an undercover policeman who infiltrates and demolishes a crime syndicate.[6]

We will consider *The Night of the Twelfth* (1976) to be a story of professional detection because the mystery is solved by the police, but not a police procedural novel, for at least two reasons: first, the involvements of the people at Trenchard House School tend to distract the reader's attention from the activities of the police, and second, the main detective has solved the case some time before the end of the story but withholds the solution, a device common to the classic tale of detection but not to the procedural.

Peter Manciple, the protagonist of *The Empty House* (1979), is not a policeman, but he is an insurance investigator and can thus qualify as a professional. Structurally and thematically, *The Empty House* is an exemplary thriller, heavy with the menace of scientific research into the almost-forbidden reaches of human knowledge, clashes between powerful international opposites, and a reasonably explicit sexual involvement.

In *The Killing of Katie Steelstock* (1980) Gilbert returns to the police procedural formula. Chief Inspector Charlie Knott is a Scotland Yard man sent out to a rural area to investigate the murder of a celebrated television star, but he is no superior Yard man of the class of Marsh's Inspector Alleyn or P.D. James' Inspector Dalgliesh. Instead, the solution of the Steelstock case is the result of a team effort, including the application of some clever methodology by the police laboratory.

Gilbert's tales of professional espionage are short stories featuring his two veteran intelligence agents who have retired from active service but are now attached to the highly secret Joint Services Standing Intelligence Committee, Daniel Joseph Calder and Samuel Behrens. Gilbert published eleven of these stories in *Game Without Rules* in 1967, but they continue to appear in magazine form fourteen years later. One reason for the lasting popularity of Mr. Calder and Mr. Behrens (who may justifiably be considered Gilbert's most successful creations) is the happy contrast in these two elderly men of the outwardly quiet gentility with which they seem to move and the forceful action of which they are capable. "Looks like a genial old cove," says a policeman viewing Mr. Behrens at a distance. "That's what he looks like," says another, who knows him.[7]

We should also mention the third member of the team, Mr. Calder's Persian deerhound Rasselas, whose quickness and ferocity save the day in more than one of the stories, and whose intelligence is at times distinctly superhuman, to the extent that he becomes a source of security; the presence of Rasselas in a story invariably gives Mr. Calder an enormous advantage. The Calder-Behrens stories should really be classed as professional counter-intelligence instead of intelligence, because they usually involve the thwarting of enemy agents.

Despite the broad variety of their personal traits, Gilbert's professionals—policemen and intelligence agents—share a system of standards which mark them as members of a professional brotherhood. They are, for example, bound together by a group loyalty that expresses itself in a feeling of elitism. We get a taste of the policeman's contempt for the layman's ignorance when Detective Pollock of Scotland Yard, attending a mystery movie in *Close Quarters*, is shocked by the improbability of the police procedures and sleeps through the latter part of it (57). All outsiders, as a matter of fact, are regarded with a degree of disdain, even when they are part of the larger professional system. Thus Mr. Fortescue, the ostensibly respected banker who is also the superior of Messrs. Calder and Behrens in counter-intelligence, can be ruthless with his subordinates, but he will not allow anybody else to interfere with them.[8]

An objective posture, with an attendant sense of detachment, is another of their principles, most pointedly stated by Mr. Behrens to a young agent who has been compelled to shoot a woman with whom he had made love: "In this job there is neither right not wrong. Only expediency."[9] In the same detached spirit, Patrick Petrella is no longer shocked by crime, any more than a doctor is shocked by disease.[10] Certainly one support of the objective attitude is the special knowledge and skill they bring to the job, which more than any other quality distinguishes the professional from the amateur. Sometimes the knowledge has been gained by their police experience, as in the case of Charlie Knott, who investigates the Steelstock murder, and who knows that it is possible to make a plaster cast of a print in moist earth if it is first coated with ordinary hair spray (56). Occasionally it is the result of hard self-discipline, as with Peter Manciple in *The Empty House*, who has taught himself how to organize his own memory (81). Almost invariably, the skill is employed with suitable restraint; the counter-intelligence agents know how to hit an opponent "scientifically," in order to induce just the proper degree of submission without resort to messy excess.

The professional's motto is vigilance: it is, says Kenneth Mainfold in *The Night of the Twelfth*, a policeman's unhappy duty to suspect everyone (140), an assumption in which the others would concur, especially Inspector Hazlerigg, who trained in a section of London where wise policemen face strangers at all times (*Close Quarters* 154).

The one quality that guides and informs them, though, is their calculating approach to law enforcement and intelligence work, almost invariably carried out with an eye to the odds and percentages. With the police, the calculation usually takes the form of an estimate of what a jury will accept: the court-wise Charlie Knott builds up a case by putting himself in the shoes of the defense, picking all possible holes in his own case, then setting to work to plug those holes (*The Killing of Katie Steelstock,* 136-37). Secret agents tend to think in terms of trade-offs between gain and loss, as Mr. Calder does when he offers a criminal a sensible bargain, knowing the chances are he will accept in defiance of the apparent logic of the situation.[11] The principle is so well understood that it can even be succinctly stated by the inept Major Piper in *Be Shot for Sixpence*: "You don't win a chess match by hanging on to all your pieces" (210).

Gilbert's use of amateur detectives begins with his second novel, *They Never Looked Inside* (1948). Inspector Hazlerigg and his associates make brief appearances in this story, but the reader's interest is centered upon Major Angus McCann, who is called in by Hazlerigg for some minor help in a case, is later used as an undercover operator, and finally becomes the main protagonist in the novel. The pattern is repeated in *The Doors Open*, published the next year. Once again the police are in the background, but the detection is in the hands of an amateur trio: Patrick Yeatman-Carter, an almost incredibly thick-headed type who becomes implicated in a murder by chance and feels obligated to clear himself; Noel "Nap" Rumbold, an almost incredibly energetic and astute young solicitor who becomes involved "for fun"; and Lord Cedarbrook, Nap's uncle, an almost incredibly resourceful former secret agent.

These two novels are important in the history of mystery fiction, because they belong to an era in which English writers who would later distinguish themselves as authors of police fiction seemed to resort to all kinds of stratagems to keep the narrative interest away from their policemen. This was the decade during which John Creasey began the series that eventually produced forty-three novels featuring Roger West of Scotland Yard, but in the early West stories Creasey brings in brilliant amateurs and private detectives and often places West in a position to operate—quite unnecessarily—as a loner. The same kind of avoidance is evident in a novel like Seldon Truss' *Always Ask a Policeman* (1952), in which most of the story-interest is carried along by non-policemen; there are policemen and policewomen at work on the crime, but they are under cover until the end of the story. Gilbert was not willing to take the action completely out of the hands of his professionals, but the only policeman who has much to do in *They Never Looked Inside* is Sergeant Catlin, who works under cover throughout the story; Hazlerigg in *The Doors Open* seems to spend much of his time in his office, wondering how to keep the amateur sleuths out of trouble.

Death Has Deep Roots (1951) is another story featuring the detective efforts of young "Nap" Rumbold, who is this time involved not merely "for fun" but because he must discover new evidence to clear a woman defended by his law firm. Following the practice mentioned earlier, Gilbert brings back into this novel Major McCann of *They Never Looked Inside*, who shares the work of detection with young Rumbold.

Death in Captivity (1952) is a cleverly sited novel, in the sense that the amateur detection is carried out in an Italian prisoner of war camp during World War II, in which the British prisoners must solve a murder-mystery in a setting from which the police and other agencies of the outside world have been excluded as neatly as in the traditional country house. The solution of the murder is merged with an espionage plot (the discovery of an informer among the prisoners) and a caper (the digging of an escape tunnel) to produce Gilbert's most suspenseful novel to that point.

Readers who are reluctant to recognize any quality other than high seriousness in mystery fiction may experience some perplexity with the next tale of amateur detection, *Sky High* (1955). What are we to make of a story in which a person is killed by high explosives, but in which each chapter is introduced by a quotation from the more eccentric characters in *Love's Labour's Lost*, and in which the titles of the chapters themselves are musical expressions, "Accelerando e Fortissimo" for the chapter in which the victim is blown apart, and "Marche Militaire" for the one in which old General Sir Hubert Palling sets forth on his own investigation? Or in which there is a minor character named Major General Rocking-Hawse? Once again, Gilbert turns the job of detection over to an amateur trio whose avowed motive is the premise that the police are not competent to solve the murder: "Liz" Artside, presumably worried lest her son be accused of the murder but too capricious and affected to be taken seriously as a protagonist; her son Tim, a World War II commando who realizes he may be under suspicion; and the serio-comic ramrod octogenerian General Palling, who relishes any action in defense of the security of the community. Anthony Boucher, whose reviews of Gilbert's books were almost invariably favorable, called *Sky High* "markedly lighter than Gilbert's best efforts."[12]

Gilbert did not turn back to the field of amateur detection until *The Etruscan Net* (1969). The structure of this book is the one Gilbert first used in *Smallbone Deceased*: a tranquil beginning in the British colony in Florence rudely shattered by the murder of an elderly Florentine artisan and the arrest of the Englishman Robert Broke, whose innocence his friends must prove.

Be Shot for Sixpence (1956) can be classed as amateur espionage because the protagonist, an English business man without training or experience in intelligence work, is drawn into a search for his missing friend (who *is* a professional agent), a search that takes him into Austria and results in his capture by operatives from the Eastern side of the Iron Curtain. "Phillip" (whose last name we never learn) is capable of holding his own in the face of most dangers, but he is essentially an innocent caught up in big movements he does not really understand until it is too late to do much about them.

A more thorough innocent is Laura Hart of *After the Fine Weather* (1963), sister of the British consul at Lienz in the Austrian Tyrol, who becomes ensnared in a local conspiracy as a result of having witnessed a political murder and of refusing to yield to pressure to change her story.

The 92nd Tiger (1973) is a choice example of Gilbert's celebrated "restraint," in the sense that he pointedly refuses to squeeze every possible sensation out of a gorgeous combination of circumstances. Hugo Greest, a fortyish actor who has played ninety-one episodes of "The Tiger," a television Superman-type series, finds himself out of a job when the series is discontinued. A loyal "Tiger" fan, however, is also the ruler of a small but wealthy Middle East kingdom, who hires Greest as his military adviser because he likes the image projected by the television role. Instead of following the obvious easy course and making Greest a parody of the actor who must finally face reality, Gilbert handles him as another serious-minded amateur who works hard at his job and is not averse to accepting a little windfall when one becomes available.

One special challenge to a writer who introduces amateurs into the business of detection or espionage is the problem of how to get them into the story in the first place. After all, if they are not professionals, it might plausibly appear that they have no business investigating murders or ferreting out secret information. Gilbert is generally successful in introducing his amateurs into their roles as protagonists with a variety of devices that are usually in harmony with the personalities of his characters and the situations in which they become involved.

Two of them are invited into the story because their situation has placed them in a position to be of assistance to the police: Major McCann in *They Never Looked Inside* because he knows a prisoner the police want to turn informant, and Henry Bohun in *Smallbone Deceased* because, as a member of the law firm under investigation, he can supply the police some information not otherwise available to them. A larger group consists of those who must involve themselves in order to protect their own interests, like Philip Yeatman-Carter in *The Doors Open*, who fears he may be a murder suspect, and Laura Hart in *After the Fine Weather*, who refuses to be intimidated into changing her story regarding the murder she has witnessed. Two are formally appointed to jobs of detection or intelligence. Goyles is ordered to investigate the murder in *Death in Captivity*, although he has no apparent qualifications for the job other than a love of detective fiction, and Hugo Greest finds himself hired for a sensitive government post in Umran because the ruler likes the way he has played "The Tiger." Friendship and family connections are the motivations for involving several of them, especially Lord Cedarbrook in *The Doors Open*, who steps into the story to help his nephew, or the trio composed of the loyal friends of Robert Broke in *The Etruscan Net*, who organize their own investigation when they are convinced that Broke has been falsely imprisoned. Finally, there are two who join in the chase primarily as recreation: "Nap" Rumbold, who substantially invites himself into the business of detection in *The Doors Open*, and old General Sir Hubert Palling, who is off and running after the murder in *Sky High*, with no other motive than that justice seems to be the natural proper occupation of a retired military man.

As Gilbert's professionals make their most consistent progress by calculating the odds and percentages, his amateurs tend to advance by determination and persistence. Thus Major McCann in *They Never Looked Inside*, after his offer to help the police has been politely declined by Inspector Hazlerigg, goes ahead with his own investigation because his "Scotch pride" will not accept the rebuff (45), and thus the friends of Robert Broke in *The Etruscan Net* forge ahead in the effort to release Broke from prison after he has resigned himself to an inevitable conviction of murder.

Naturally they lack the acquired skills of the trained professionals, but most of them possess resources that come in handy during the process of detection. "Nap" Rumbold is an extremely civilized young solicitor, but his experience with the Maquis during World War II has taught him how to disable an automobile while riding in the passenger seat, which he does in *The Doors Open*, much to the surprise of his captors (236). Henry Bohun of *Smallbone Deceased* enjoys the eccentricity of para-insomnia, which prevents his sleeping more than ninety minutes per night and enables him to spend fantastic stretches of time in research (60).

Of course they make mistakes and blunder into trouble. McCann, whose "Scotch pride" forces him ahead in *They Never Looked Inside*, gets himself captured twice by criminal gangs and at one point decides that private detection is "a more expensive hobby than he had imagined" (168). "Phillip" in *Be Shot for Sixpence* apologizes to one of the Hungarian underground for barging into the midst of some plans already carefully worked out by the real pros and almost ruined by him: "I'm beginning to learn," he says, "what a blundering nuisance I've been" (211).

The well-meaning but blundering amateur is a familiar figure in mystery fiction, but Michael Gilbert accents the spirit of professionalism by pointedly contrasting it with the disposition of amateurism. When Hazlerigg catches on to the fact that McCann is going ahead on his own in *They Never Looked Inside*, the thought makes him shudder, and he assigns a tail to McCann (47). Things get even worse in *The Doors Open*, when Hazlerigg is aware of not just one but three civilians trying to solve the case the police are working on, and he becomes convinced that he "can't move without stubbing his toes over a pack of amateur helpers" (154). Part of Hazlerigg's motive is to protect these dilletantes from danger, and such is the case with Evelyn Fiennes, a member of the British embassy staff in Vienna, who tells the youthful Laura Hart in *After the Fine Weather* that diplomacy is quiet work most of the time: "It's only when people like you come along that things start happening" (175). An ominous change in this pattern comes about in *The Empty House*, when Peter Manciple finds himself caught in a struggle between two foreign powers: the danger is no longer that of an innocent getting in the way of Right vs. Wrong, but of an outsider being hurt between the ignorant armies that clash by night in Matthew Arnold's "Dover Beach" (135, 156).

Gilbert writes one other kind of story, which in different hands would be called a social-problem novel but which he develops by use of the narrative techniques of suspense. The effect is achieved largely by means of selection and emphasis, with the result that, even though the stuff of the story is a predicament with social or political implications, the reader finds himself drawn by the kind of expectations normally found in the mystery. In a review of one of the novels in this class, Anthony Boucher characterized the story as "a lovely blend of two disciplines" and went on to explain, "You may read it as a straight novel utilizing certain techniques of suspense or as a suspense novel of unusual substance."[13]

We can illustrate the intent by reference to the way Gilbert handles his material in one of the stories in *Stay of Execution*, called "The Rich Man in His Castle," which has all the ingredients of a commentary on contemporary Britain: Sir Charles Pellat offers to exchange his manor house and the rest of his estate, including a tenanted farm, with his lessee Mr. Suggs, who lives in his lodge. Not long after the exchange is made, the Suggs family want to change back. Most of the rent paid by the tenant farmer (fixed, of course, by law) goes to improvements and the rest into taxes. Repairs, taxes and upkeep take up everything else, including fuel for the manor house, which simply can not be heated. Sir Charles has by far the better of the bargain, with low fixed rent on the lodge and no proprietary responsibilities. As he approaches the denouement of his tale, however, Gilbert turns away from the ironies of a system that has so inverted the traditional values, and he develops a surprise ending quite compatible with a tale of suspense but completely neutral on the question of social justice.

The first of these social-theme-suspense novels is *Fear to Tread* (1953), featuring Wilfred Wetherall, a London schoolmaster with a visionary dedication to rightness who single-handedly does battle with a crime syndicate that is using terror as a means of subverting the rationing system. The author recognizes, in the frontispiece, that the story is based on a problem with the real world ("The characters are fictitious. The problem is not."), but the structure is that of the standard thriller, with five separate plot-strands going as the climax approaches, the author switching back and forth among them, usually with resort to a cliffhanger.

Gilbert did not return to this kind of story until 1966, with *The Crack in the Teacup*. This time the theme is municipal corruption, but once again the attention of the reader is directed to the resolution of the struggles between the several warring factions and the removal of menace instead of the societal implications of the basic problem.

The technique is most fully developed in the next novel, *The Dust and the Heat* (1967). This book is sometimes misunderstood as a story of business ethics, whereas its real theme is war-during-peace, or the applications of the strategies of war to peacetime business operations. Oliver Nugent, who was a highly capable tank commander during the Second World War, applies his wartime skills to the development of a successful business, even gathering into his circle many of his old war comrades and deploying them as he had done in battle. The real purpose of the novel becomes apparent in the employment of a concealed plot-element, when Jennie, who has figured in the story as a competitor's confidential secretary, turns out to be the daughter of one of Nugent's men, and she has been planted in the competitor's office as a spy (227). The reader is then made aware that he has met this young woman on two occasions earlier in the story, without her name being mentioned. Such a trick on the reader's perceptions is quite acceptable in a novel where the intention is suspense, but it would be outrageous in a story in which the frame of reference is a study of business morality.

There is also a danger of misjudging the intent of Gilbert's other social-theme-suspense story, *Flash Point* (1974). What appears to be the main plot in this novel is the campaign of Jonas Killey, a solicitor, to discredit Will Dylan, a labor-boss and aspiring politician, who is in line for a cabinet post. Neither man wins; at the end of the story, Killey retires from the law and settles in a small village, and Dylan leaves politics and returns to the world of organized labor. Read as a tale of union corruption, the story falls flat,[14] because the real theme is the effort of the government to discredit Killey, and the broad implications center upon the threat of a government which on occasion commits injustices against its own citizens in order to preserve itself. Significantly, Gilbert used the theme of government-as-menace again five years later in an avowed thriller, *The Empty House*.

Any assessment of Michael Gilbert's ability as a writer must center upon his skill as a craftsman rather than his development of memorable ideas or characters. Earlier we spoke of his versatility, which has permitted him to range rather freely over a number of different kinds of narrative. One foundation of that freedom is his mastery of the techniques of construction, which makes him equally comfortable with the plot of the classic detective story, the thriller, and the straight suspense tale.

A few paragraphs earlier we mentioned *The Dust and the Heat* as a fully developed social-theme-suspense novel; it is what Boucher admired as the "blend of two disciplines," partly because of the richness of detail with which it deals with the world of competitive business and the tricks, stratagems, ambushes, even outright massacres that business men practice on each other, but partly also because of the way the author has constructed his narrative creation. One evidence of graceful structuring is the time-frame of the story, which encompasses some twenty years in the career of Oliver Nugent but is set within a few minutes of time, so that the entire narrative is a flashback. The first chapter and the last are both entitled "Postscript"; at the beginning, the narrator sits in front of Nugent's retirement home in Switzerland, watching a solitary cyclist toiling up the winding mountain road (9); at the end, after the whole story has been recalled, only a few minutes have passed, and the cyclist arrives with a message that would have placed an ironic finish on Nugent's career except that (as we are now told for the first time) Nugent has died during the night (243).

What the reader gets, during this long recollection sandwiched between minutes, is a recounting of the narrator's sense of wonder and surprise as the full measure of Oliver Nugent is revealed to him, and thus the achievement of suspense is facilitated by its being shared by narrator and reader.

The blending of structure and point of view in this novel is one of the most successful achievements of Gilbert's craftsmanship. The nameless narrator is one of Oliver Nugent's fellow tank commanders who keeps in touch with his early business career but is not himself involved until years later, after the real depth of Nugent's ruthlessness has become evident, when he joins the firm. He is a Jamesian observer-interpreter, sufficiently involved to be concerned (Nugent saved his life during the war), but detached enough to be objective (he is an honest accountant). To the benefit of the reader, he does not lose his balanced judgment after he joins the firm. The suspense is achieved, in large measure, by the way in which Gilbert moves this observer onto and off the stage: the method is for the narrator to begin a section of the account (his part usually represented as something he has heard from one of Nugent's immediate associates) and then to fade from the story, whereupon the narrative viewpoint becomes detached and shifts from one character to another. The effect is an easy, functional revelation achieved without resort to artificial devices: even the bombshell revelation of the identity of the spy Jennie gains some acceptance in the fact that the narrator is as surprised as we are.

Gilbert's handling of the thriller structure, with its dependence on sensation and the omnipresence of menace, and its episodic development, is fairly conventional. His second novel, *They Never Looked Inside*, is representative: this is the story in which Angus McCann undertakes the job of amateur detection and falls into peril twice, rescued on the first occasion by his own skill and on the second by Hazlerigg's men from the London Metropolitan force. The denouement of the book is patent thriller, in which the police move in on the gangster stronghold assisted by units of infantry with Bren guns (235).

There is one danger indigenous to the thriller structure, which is that the writer, not bound by the tight discipline of the ratiocinative tale of detection, may get carried away by the opportunity for stacking up one sensation upon another. Michael Gilbert succumbed to the temptation in *After the Fine Weather*, in which Laura Hart, having gone through crisis after crisis to escape across the Italian border, has almost reached her destination when she is captured by an unidentified man of the mountains, is carried to his cave and bound, and escapes rape only by stabbing her captor (182). The episode has no relationship to the rest of the story except to prolong the escape by a few pages.

In *Close Quarters* and in most of the subsequent tales of detection, Gilbert employs the classic seven-step plot first used by Poe in the Dupin stories, which has become the conventional formula for organization of formal-problem detective stories. The structure is fairly obvious in *Sky High* where, after some preliminary episodes to establish background and atmosphere, the Problem is introduced in the death of Lieutenant Macmorris, killed by an explosion in his home. Then comes the Initial Solution by the police (traditionally, in this type of story a mistaken one), to the effect that Macmorris was a burglar who kept in his home some explosives, which had been set off by accident. The third step is the Complication, in which the first solution proves to be mistaken: in this case the development of evidence that the accidental-explosion theory is untenable. Next is the Period of Confusion, wherein one of the three amateur detectives, acting on his own, follows up a clue with which he alone is familiar, another is almost killed in a thinly disguised accident, and the police continue with their own routine investigations. Step five is the Dawning Light, in which things begin to fall into place, the discovery of a vital piece of evidence and the apprehension of the murderer's accomplice, followed shortly by the Solution, the identification of the murderer, and the Explanation, this final revelation being an account of a highly ingenious means of setting off an explosion. Gilbert is fairly conservative in his use of the formal-problem plot structure. Although it is a tight formula it lends itself to almost unlimited variety in sequence (the Complication, the Period of Confusion, and the Dawning Light can be repeated several times, for example, and Solution and Explanation can be reversed), but Gilbert's detective tales customarily hold closely to the classic order.

There is one type of structure that has come to be a Gilbert specialty. This is the mystery that opens with a deceptively mild atmosphere, lures the reader into an attitude of serene security, and then jolts him rudely with the incursion into the story of violent death. A particularly happy instance may be found in the early chapters of *Smallbone Deceased*, where the locale is the quiet chambers of a firm of solicitors, and the action is chiefly lawyer-talk, centering around such conveniences as the Horniman Self-Checking Completion System, designed to keep infallible account of the whereabouts of documents. Incredibly, a scream resounds through these peaceful surroundings, announcing the discovery of the mortal remains of Marcus Smallbone in a most unexpected place. That scream, by the way, must be the best-heralded in mystery fiction: first, a conversation between two of the partners ends with one of them asking, "Is that someone screaming?" (37); five pages later a discussion of golfing is terminated with "What on earth was that?" "It sounded like a scream, didn't it?" (42). Early in the next chapter we are told the cause, and the shock of recognition is much sharper as a result of the contrast. The corpse of Marcus Smallbone is a considerably more shocking affair in the chambers of Horniman, Birley and Craine than if it had been found in an opium den or fished out of the Thames. The same device is employed (with modifications) in the opening chapters of *The Etruscan Net*, where the civilized security of the English colony in Florence is disrupted by murder, and in *The Night of the Twelfth*, where the locale is a boys' school. Of course the intrusion of violence into the peaceful community has always been basic to the myth of the detective story, but Gilbert has become a master of the art of heightening the effect by means of contrast, as we will see a little further along in regard to his handling of the device of juxtaposed images.

In general, there are two ways for a writer of mystery-suspense fiction to hold his reader. The first is to devise mysteries so complex, so obscure, so impossible of solution that the reader is gripped by the compulsion of seeing how the writer will work it all out. This is the case with several of Michael Gilbert's books, notably *Close Quarters, Sky High, Blood and Judgment, The Body of a Girl*, and especially *The Night of the Twelfth*, in all of which the problem has been so well chosen that the suspense is reasonably sustained by the skillful handling of the strategies of concealment and revelation.

It is not, however, as a spinner of perplexing puzzles that Michael Gilbert has achieved his reputation as a writer, but rather by his skill in the employment of certain techniques and devices. This is another area in which he has earned widespread recognition, to the degree that his handling of the craftsmanship of suspense deserves some detailed examination. The number of possible examples is large, but we will briefly inspect two novels widely separated in time of composition, *Be Shot for Sixpence* (1956) and *The Empty House* (1979).

Be Shot for Sixpence is one of the tales of amateur espionage, in which the narrator "Philip" is almost inadvertently drawn into a harrowing trip into central Europe in search of his eccentric schooldays-friend, whom he suspects of being in danger. At the very beginning of the story, long before Philip has any indication of the impending menace, the writer permits him to overhear a conversation on a train, in which a group of men are discussing labor strikes (4-5); the reader will hardly notice this casual episode, but Gilbert is already preparing us for the big development that will precipitate the crisis in the story, a general strike in Hungary. A few pages later our interest is whetted by an account of the background of the missing Studd-Thompson, especially what Philip calls his "medieval love of craft-for-craft's sake" (18), a richly evocative characterization that promises all manner of involvements. The appearance (26) of the mysterious Captain Forrestier ("some sort of civil servant") introduces a new element of suspense, reinforced shortly when the Captain tells Philip, "You mustn't interfere" (29), the first of a number of hints designed to suggest to the reader that the real truth of the situation has been concealed. Another such hint is delivered toward the middle of the story when Philip, now awaiting developments at Schloss Obersteinbruck in Austria, runs into a young woman he knows in a dark corridor and has hardly touched her arm when he feels a knife at his throat, a reaction obviously based on something stronger than need for self-defense

(87-89). The hints and suggestions are discontinued after a satisfactory level of suspense has been achieved, and Gilbert turns to the employment of another device, the totally unexpected development. The first such enters the story when Philip, working with a local ex-Nazi who seems willing to help him search for information about Studd-Thompson, suddenly chokes the man to death (124); the reader, if he has been paying attention, must be thunderstruck because, although the reason is shortly explained (134), there has been absolutely no earlier preparation. The second bombshell comes when Philip enters his room to find the beautiful and mysterious True ensconced in his bed (192), again without reader preparation. Finally, Philip, captured and held in a prison somewhere in Hungary, is able to escape because of his ability as a mountain-climber, in a detailed and almost painfully prolonged scene in which his ascent of the prison wall is achieved step by step upward as each improvised piton is drawn from one place and agonizingly inserted in the next (183-97). *Be Shot for Sixpence*, with its adroitly handled hints and suggestions, and even its bolts from the blue and literal cliffhangers, is a satisfactorily suspenseful novel, but it was to be superseded as Gilbert sharpened his skills.

The Empty House is a story of detection with strong overtones of international espionage: Peter Manciple, an insurance investigator assigned to the case of an eminent scientist presumably killed in an accident, soon finds himself dealing with forces obviously bigger than those of a merely felonious nature. Earlier we referred to this novel as the typical thriller, partly because it is intrinsically endowed with several of the paraphernalia of the thriller, which Gilbert uses as material for a highly effective framework of suspense.

The first of these is the presumed victim: Dr. Wolfe, carrying on DNA research possibly dangerous to civilization, so advanced that "there are not more than a handful of men in any country who are capable of comprehending it" (61). The second is the situation of the investigator Peter Manciple, who comes to recognize, half-way through the story, that he is caught in a struggle between Israelis and Palestinians. The third piece of thriller-apparatus is the ambiguous position of Government (represented by the military and the police): Is it menace or security? To complete the panoply, there is the sexual involvement between Peter Manciple and one of the Israelis, which does not intrude more heavily into the narrative than to round out the set of paraphernalia necessary to a full-blown thriller.

Having developed such promising raw material, Gilbert employs his very considerable skills as a story-teller to produce a novel in which suspense is sustained at a reasonably high level. The hints of danger and intrigue are less obviously delivered than those in *Be Shot for Sixpence* and are consequently more unsettling. Early in the story, for example, Peter conducts what appears to be a routine interview of Dr. Wolfe's sister, but as he is leaving he hears a car start up; it cruises slowly past him and passes on without incident (24), a small enough event except to suggest that something may be developing; but when at the close of a secret midnight interview with an Indian scientist who knew Dr. Wolfe, Philip hears another car start up and move on (65), the reader begins to feel the pressure of the suggestion. Besides these hints, Gilbert uses a wide array of the techniques of suspense, many of them familiar and time-tested in the traditional tale of detection. Hints regarding the solution of the mystery are interspersed throughout, as when it is suggested that Dr. Wolfe was leading two or three different lives (50), or when Anna mutters "something unintelligible" in her sleep (153), which later turns out to be Israeli. There are summaries, as when Philip reviews the situation for his own (and the reader's) benefit (133-34), complications, as in the disappearance of Dr. Bishwas, the Indian scientist (101), and an attempt upon the life of the investigator (195-96), all evenly spaced in such fashion that they periodically re-kindle the reader's involvement without awkward pile-ups of sensation. *The Empty House* is flawed by two sets of coincidences that are broad enough to be embarrassing (106, 216), but even they do not detract from the intensity of the excitement.

Because of his ability at handling the dynamics of suspense, Michael Gilbert does not often find it necessary to fall back upon such time-worn devices as the red herring, though there is a cliffhanger in *Death Has Deep Roots* which must be a record for duration, especially in view of the circumstances. On page 117, Nap Rumbold falls into the cold black waters of the Loire, from which he does not emerge until page 175—"very slowly."

Any discussion of Gilbert's craftsmanship must include some comment upon his ability to manage the English language, in which respect he is an obvious master. On occasion his sentences snap with the unexpectedness of a well-told joke, as when he observes in *The Doors Open*, "Living together, as Anne of Cleeves was once heard to remark, can be a trial to both parties" (52). His figures of speech are customarily not only richly suggestive but also neatly precise, as when Laura Hart in *After the Fine Weather* senses that the wine "had a resinous tang which touched the back of her throat as a man's hand will touch, for a faction of a second, the hand of a woman he desires" (101). It rarely rises to the level of pure magic, but when it does, it is singularly effective, as in one of the stories in *Game Without Rules*, in which Mr. Calder and Rasselas are sleeping in the open on a down. Rasselas growls softly:

> Mr. Calder raised his head. During the time he had been asleep the wind had risen a little, and was blowing up dark clouds and sending them scudding across the face of the moon; the shadows on the bare down were horsemen, warriors with horned helmets, riding horses with flying manes and tails. Rasselas was following them with his eyes, head cocked. It was as if, behind the piping of the wind, he could hear, pitched too high for human ears, the shrill note of a trumpet.
> "They're ghosts," said Mr. Calder calmly. "They won't hurt us." He lay down, and was soon asleep again. (29)

One quality that distinguishes the really superior writer of mysteries is his ability to develop important themes that go above and beyond the orthodox solution of the mystery and at the same time supplement and reinforce it. At several points in this discussion we have referred to Gilbert's ability to integrate a parallel theme into a suspense story: fantasy and reality in *The 92nd Tiger*; the legacy of war in *The Dust and the Heat*; and the clash of "ignorant armies" in *The Empty House*. There is one other example of a really fine handling which deserves comment, the theme of growing up in *The Night of the Twelfth*.

The scene of this novel is Trenchard House School for Boys, one of those peaceful environments that make menace seem so much more horrible, and the problem is a series of murders of young boys in the neighborhood. An air of perversion and ugliness hangs over the narrative, manifested in the tortures and sexual mutilations of the victims, and also in the relationships within the school, where there are strong hints of homosexuality and perversion. Gilbert objectifies this intimation in a Shakespeare play, which the One-A group is rehearsing for production at graduation time; the first reference to it is tucked in unobtrusively and without preparation, and the play itself is not named, though it is obviously *Twelfth Night* (22-23). A little later, when the air of evil is beginning to emerge in the story, we get two short rehearsal scenes, now with strong hints of sexuality, especially homosexuality and transvestism, set down beside references to premature death (39-40,

76-77). It is not until two-thirds of the way through that the name of the play is mentioned, and it is at the time of the final production that we get the first explicit statement of the fear that has been to this point only suggested, "—you know, homosexuality and that sort of thing" (185). Immediately Gilbert achieves a thematic shift through the introduction of a second play; the Two-A group, who will shortly succeed the class that has been touched by death and violence, is preparing *As You Like It*. Kenneth Manifold, the policeman serving undercover as teacher, is impressed by the friendly wholesomeness of this group, and as he listens to them read a scene involving changing sex roles, " . . . the disguised Rosalind—surely a disguise that deceived no one—" his feelings are untroubled (187). The statement of the theme is saved for the closing scene of the book, the presentation of *As You Like It*, in which a small boy sings the clown's song about growing up (229-30). Thus the two plays are made to reflect the idea of maturity and loss of innocence, but the outlook is in this context optimistic, as the nastiness that has menaced one generation gives way to the wholesomeness of the next.

Whatever his other abilities, Michael Gilbert is not a character-portraitist. Nor does he need to be; the kind of story he writes well demands the effects of careful plotting and the tone of melodrama, but no great depth or breadth in the development of people. Most of his people, as we have said earlier, are not on stage long enough to be drawn at much length: Hazlerigg and Petrella appear in a number of stories, but with only one or two starring roles, and his other recurrent characters, if they receive much attention in one book, are hardly mentioned in the later ones.

Many of Gilbert's most memorable people are caricatures. Some are as obvious as the obtuse Patrick Yeatman-Carter in *The Doors Open*, who considers everything enjoyable "a good show," and whose response to the possibility of a beating by gangsters is to suggest that he is quite capable of taking care of the situation: "—I mean, I've done a bit of amateur boxing—" (77). Another undisguised caricature is Wilfred Wetherall, the crusading schoolmaster of *Fear to Tread*. Gilbert is too skillful a writer to make Wetherall a buffoon, but he touches him with a distrait quality that manifests itself when, during conversation, he catches an example of a grammatical function in his own speech, stops and makes a note for use in his grammar class (4). The most fully developed character in a Gilbert novel is Oliver Nugent of *The Dust and the Heat*, who might have been the subject of a Gatsby-like portrait if the writer's purpose were directed toward the figure of a personality in society, but who becomes rather a vehicle for the development of suspense: actually, we never get a direct look at Nugent, but must see him through the eyes of the other people in the story, with the result that his image is never complete.

With the exception of Colonel Dru, who interrogates Philip after his capture in *Be Shot for Sixpence*, there are no accredited monsters in Gilbert's stories, and even Dru comes off as more travesty than menace (164-70). Gilbert has, however, brought forth one of the most terrifying fiends in suspense fiction, Elizabeth Shaw, the assistant matron at the school in *The Night of the Twelfth*, who can be sexually aroused only by witnessing the torture-murders of pre-adolescent boys. The most frightening quality of Elizabeth is her inoffensive outward demeanor, which is such that she might show up on the staff of the school in which the reader's own small son is enrolled. Another almost as chilling is Simon Benz-Fisher in *Flash Point*, head of a super-secret unit of government, whose responsibility is to protect the government from scandal, and who sets about, skillfully and systematically, to demolish the reputation of the reformer who is troubling a prospective cabinet member.

We can not leave the discussion of Gilbert's *personnae* without mention of his portrayals of the British lawyers who make such frequent and effective appearances in all kinds of his stories. The portraits have the mark of authenticity (Gilbert is an experienced and successful solicitor), but they are also touched with the same playful colors as we have noticed earlier. Their talent for solemn pomposity is especially strong in *Smallbone Deceased*, for example, when a law secretary sets out on a search for the missing Smallbone, armed with a letter that might have been addressed simply "Resident," but is directed to "Occupier, Head Lessor or Sublessor as the case might be of 20 Wellingboro' Road" (32). For the most part, though, they can recognize the absurdity in these situations in which the veneer of dignity cracks wide open over the basic incongruity of the occasion, as it does in the story "The Blackmailing of Mr. Justice Ball," wherein four of the litigants are kittens; their counsel announces with a straight face that, being without means of support, those kittens have received assistance from Legal Aid.[15] Most of them have a strong appreciation for drama, which in no way distorts their grounding in reality. At the opening of the climactic court case in *The Dust and the Heat* the attorney for the plaintiff elaborately deplores the necessity of bringing suit, wasting money and the valuable time of the court, then steals a quick glance at the presiding judge, who stares blankly back as if to say, "You didn't fool me. We're both getting paid for this" (215).

One narrative device which Michael Gilbert has developed to the extent that his handling of it is really unique, is a trick of inserting a contrasting image into a situation, with a resultant heightening of effect. The most explicit example is to be found in the Calder and Behrens stories, in the repeated references to the serene paintings on the walls of Mr.Fortescue's office, where so many meetings lead to forays into peril and injury. In the story "The Last Reunion," while Mr. Calder and Mr. Behrens are reading a highly secret document full of potential crisis, the author remarks that above the fireplace in the dignified office, Millais' "The Angel Child" and Landseer's "Tug of War" smile at each other.[16] These paintings are not just part of the scene. They are symbols of security and stability, even stolidity, in juxtaposition to the menace and insecurity of the world of espionage and intrigue. They, along with the similar examples in a number of other stories, are images of things that are almost always conventional, trite, even slightly ridiculous, and at the same time suggestive of a safe and dependable world undisturbed by current danger. A prime example appears in *The Etruscan Net*, where Commander Comber, the very acme of English stolidity, enjoys reciting passages from the *Lays of Ancient Rome* amid all the novel's atmosphere of Roman and Etruscan antiquity. The effect is that Macaulay's stout lines go marching through the apparitions of ancient intrigue as reminders that the bland world of English security lives on.

The device appears to fulfill two functions. First, it can serve to define the frame of the story, as it does in *Smallbone Deceased*. Earlier we pointed to the remarkably quiet opening of that story in the peaceful chambers of a law firm, whose center of organization is the Horniman Self-Checking Completion System; after the disruption of the intervening murder story, the reader is returned to the scene of peace, now objectified in another image, a letter being dictated by Henry Bohun to a laundry, inquiring about certain undervests missing from the wardrobe of the firm's client, Lady Buntingford (245). Used in this way, the images serve to specify the "state of grace" which the crime interrupts and to which the community is restored after the mystery is solved. The other function is to act as a reminder of the sane, stable world out there, in contrast to the anxiety of the present involvement. This is the role of the *Lays of Ancient Rome* in *The Etruscan Net* and also of *The*

Barretts of Wimpole Street, which the British inmates of the prisoner-of-war camp are rehearsing throughout *Death in Captivity*. The intention of the device seems to be confirmed by the fact that it appears regularly in the tales of espionage, amateur and professional, in the suspense-social-theme stories, and in stories in which the sense of menace is especially strong, like *Death in Captivity* and *The Etruscan Net*. Otherwise, it is almost completely absent from the ratiocinative tales of amateur or professional detection. Thus, the pattern of presence or absence would seem to be an illustration of the often-stated principle that the detective story in its "pure" form does not include terror or menace among its purposes, in contrast to the spy-story or the story with strong social and political implications.

With such an array of technical skills at his command, it is no wonder that Michael Gilbert does not object to classification among the Entertainers. Ultimately, he is not likely to be ranked with the portrayers of complex characters or the developers of great ideas. His excellence lies rather in his control of the art of suspense, in his ability to make the English language crackle, and in his command of those narrative techniques that produce the well-made story.

Notes

[1] "From Poe to the Present," in *Murder Ink*, ed. Dilys Winn (New York: Workman, 1977), p. 4.
[2] *Mortal Consequences* (New York: Harper & Row, 1972), pp. 199-200.
[3] *Twentieth Century Crime and Mystery Writers* ed. John M. Reilly (New York: St. Martin's Press, 1980), p. 666.
[4] The editions of Gilbert's novels and collections of short stories used for this study are listed below, preceded by the original date of publication.

1947	*Close Quarters* (New York: Walker, 1963).
1948	*They Never Looked Inside* (U.S. title, *He Didn't Mind Danger*, New York: Harper, 1948).
1949	*The Doors Open* (New York: Walker, 1962).
1950	*Smallbone Deceased* (New York: Harper, 1950).
1951	*Death Has Deep Roots* (New York: Harper, 1951).
1952	*Death in Captivity* (U.S. title, *The Danger Within*, New York: Harper, 1952).
1953	*Fear to Tread* (New York: Harper, 1953).
1955	*Sky High* (U.S. title, *The Country-House Burglar*, New York: Harper, 1955).
1956	*Be Shot for Sixpence* (New York: Harper, 1956).
1958	*Blood and Judgment* (New York: Harper, 1959).
1963	*After the Fine Weather* (London: Hodder & Stoughton, 1967).
1966	*The Crack in the Teacup* (New York: Harper, 1966).
1967	*The Dust and the Heat* (U.S. title, *Overdrive*, New York: Harper, 1967).
1967	*Game Without Rules* (New York: Harper, 1967).
1969	*The Etruscan Net (U.S. title, The Family Tomb,* New York: Harper, 1969).
1971	*Stay of Execution and Other Stories of Legal Practice* (London: Hodder & Stoughton, 1971).
1972	*The Body of a Girl* (New York: Harper, 1972).
1973	*The 92nd Tiger* (New York: Harper, 1973).

1974   *Flash Point* (New York: Harper, 1974).
1976   *The Night of the Twelfth* (New York: Harper, 1976).
1977   *Petrella at Q* (New York: Harper, 1977).
1978   *The Empty House* (New York: Harper, 1979).
1980   *The Killing of Katie Steelstock* (New York: Harper, 1980).

[5]Michael Gilbert, "Patrick Petrella," in *The Great Detectives,* ed. Otto Penzler (Boston: Little, Brown, 1978), pp. 167-8.

[6]"The Man at the Bottom," *Ellery Queen's Mystery Magazine*, April 1979, pp. 6-25; "The Man in the Middle," *EQMM*, May 1979, pp. 6-27; "The Man at the Top," *EQMM*, June 1979, pp. 6-24.

[7]"Dangerous Game," *EQMM,* 12 August 1981, p. 8.

[8]"The Last Reunion," *EQMM* 2 December 1981, p. 6.

[9]"The M Route," *EQMM*, 7 April 1980, p. 159.

[10]*Petrella at Q,* p. 182.

[11]"The Violence Peddlers," *EQMM*, 25 February 1981, p. 27.

[12]*New York Times*, 18 September 1955, p. 35.

[13]*New York Times Book Review*, 25 February 1968, p. 34.

[14]As it apparently did for Newgate Callendar, who wrote (*New York Times Book Review,* 19 January 1955, p. 36), "It is as though Gilbert did not know exactly how to resolve the plot, and there is the sudden, unconvincing reversal of character of several key figures."

[15]*EQMM*, April 1972, p. 155.

[16]"The Last Reunion," p. 8.

Julian Symons

Julian Symons

Larry E. Grimes

1912	Julian Symons born on 30 May in London, England
1929	Begins roughly a decade of work at Victoria Lighting and Dynamos, as a shorthand typist and secretary
1927-39	Founding editor, *Twentieth Century Verse,* London
1939	First volume of poetry, *Confusions of X*
1941	Married Kathleen Clark
1943	Publication of *The Second Man* (poetry)
1944-47	Employed as an advertising copy writer for Rumble, Crothers and Nicholas
1945	Publication of first detective novel, *The Immaterial Murder Case.*
1947-56	Reviewer for the *Manchester Evening News.*
1953	Co-Founder of the Crime Writers Association
1957	Crime Writers Association Silver Dagger Award for *The Color of Murder*
1958-59	Chairman, Crime Writers Association
1961	Mystery Writers Association Edgar Allan Poe Award for *The Progress of a Crime*
1974	Publication of The Object of an Affair and Other Poems
1974-77	Reviewer, the *Sunday Times,* London
1975	Fellow, the Royal Society of Literature
1975-76	Visiting Professor, Amherst College, Massachusetts
1976-Present	President, Detection Club
1977	Swedish Academy of Detection Grand Master Diploma
1982	Mystery Writers Association Grand Master Award

I: Social Critic and Man of Letters

Your three-months eyes outblue the cobalt sky
And stare at depthless images that lie
Cocooned in simple webs of sleep and hunger.

Their gaze reflects a fantasy of younger
And stranger days when friendly lions residing
Within the chintzy chair roared out of hiding

Before we knew the transverse alchemies
Corroding the bright Radicals to Tories
And turning poems to detective stories.[1]

Although this dedicatory poem affixed to Julian Symons' first crime novel, *Bland Beginnings*, divides his life into two disparate parts—poet and Radical in the 1930s, crime writer and Tory in the post-war years—an examination of his writings does not mirror that break. Merely to read the list of his publications is to see the limited usefulness of such a division.[2] Rather, there is a consistency to both his life and work. And, I suspect, this consistency has given his crime fiction its distinctive shape.

Symons has kept the Radical and the Tory, the poet and the crime writer together by subordinating each to two larger concerns. From the Thirties to the present Symons has been deeply involved in the world of letters and has cared greatly about the place of the individual in modern society. And it is as a man of letters and a social critic that, I suggest, he has held together his various literary, political and social commitments. Clearly, in the 1930s this man of letters was interested in the health and growth of poetry.[3] At that time Symons did what he could as a poet and as editor of the short-lived "little magazine" *Twentieth Century Verse* to extend and expand the range of modern poetry. At the same time, as a social critic, Symons was active in left-wing, anti-war activities. Since the war Symons has shifted his focus as both man of letters and social critic. As a man of letters he has expanded his repertoire to include **poetry, history, biography, autobiography, criticism and, of course,** crime fiction. So the man of letters has grown.

The social critic has also carried on. Since the war, however, Symons' most effective social criticism has been part and parcel of his writing, of his crime fiction. Nor is this by accident. Symons as man of letters has mapped and colonized new domains for crime fiction which, in their circumference, include the territory of the social critic.

II: From Detective Fiction to the Crime Novel

An assessment of Symons' place in the world of crime literature must include a discussion of his comments as critic and historian of the genre. His reviews, historical surveys and critical biographies are important in their own right; they also provide a perspective on crime writing which is useful to the critic of Symons' own work.

His most important contribution to the study of the genre was set forth in *The Detective Story in Britain* and amplified in his longer work, *Mortal Consequences*. At the heart of these works is his observation that crime writing has evolved from the detective story into what he calls the crime novel. Before World War II, he writes in *The Detective Story in Britain*:

> there was a belief that human affairs could be ruled by reason and that virtue, generally identified with the established order of society, must prevail in the end. The post-war writers did not identify themselves with such a point of view. They saw, instead, a world in which German force had been defeated only by the greater force employed by the Allies, and in which concentration camps and the atomic bomb mocked a liberal dream of reason. The new writers had no wish to create locked room puzzles. They have turned instead to stories which, while often retaining a puzzle element, are primarily concerned with crime in relation to character and motive (34-35).

While Symons has never pretended that the emergence of the crime novel has meant the total eclipse of the classical detective story, the social critic within him has spurred on the man of letters to do battle for the cause of the crime novel. And what is this crime novel? Symons defines it in contrast to the classical detective story. In *Mortal Consequences* he says that the detective story is built around a Great Detective and upon a plot of deception. It places great emphasis on crime clues and methods, is socially conservative and often takes it power from the puzzle which the crime poses. The crime novel, on the other hand, often has no detective, is based on the psychology of its characters, uses the lives of those characters (not methods, clues and puzzles) as the basis of the story, stresses the pressures of a particular way of life on a person who commits a crime, and often makes a radical critique of the social order (178-180).

The shift from the detective story to the crime novel frees crime literature, according to Symons, from the chains of formula and allows it to be taken seriously as both social criticism and as art. And Symons is firm in his belief that crime literature can become serious literature. To become so, however, it must be allowed to be realistic. As he puts it, "to exclude realism of description and language from the crime novel in a period when it has been accepted as normal in other fiction is almost to prevent its practitioners from attempting any serious work" (Critical Occasions, 152). To free crime literature from the restrictions of the detective story might have the effect of giving the crime novel "symbolic interest and value for our time" (Critical Occasions, 152). In short, Symons thinks that crime literature has reached a stage where it can and must be taken seriously as literature, although he concedes that "the crime novel must, even in its highest reaches, always be a work of art of a peculiar, flawed kind, since an appetite for violence and pleasure in employing a conjurer's sleight of hand seems somehow always to be blended with the power in delineating character and analyzing event that in the end make any novel worth reading" (Critical Occasions, 150).

A professional commitment to the practice of writing crime novels has not made Symons insensitive to the delights of the detective story, nor a poor historian of the genre. *Mortal Consequences* is a good history of crime literature, a term I use to include both the detective story and the crime novel. Perhaps the most reliable of them all. Its great appeal comes not only from its thoroughness and critical acuteness, but also from the sure sense page after page that a reader of crime literature, full of commitment to and prejudices within the genre, is the writer of the history.

The Tell-Tale Heart, Symons' critical biography of Edgar Allan Poe, is written in the same way. Perhaps it is even more effective since Symons and Poe share a spiritual kinship derived from Symons' own experience as a poet who has lived a good part of his life in financial debt to his journalist self, a poet known primarily to the public as a writer of crime fiction. Be that as it may, Symons' biography of Poe is a lively and readable study of the life and the work. It is meant for a non-academic audience and does not pretend to extend the boundaries of Poe scholarship. Rather, he contents himself with trying to make clear two contradictory sides of Poe's life and work: Logical Poe and Visionary Poe. On these two hooks the whole of the book is hung. Symons summarizes the results of his study neatly:

> The two are as nearly as possible identical. He had no subject except himself, and there are no characters in any of his serious stories except the fears, hopes and theories of Edgar Allan Poe. Several stories express his fear of madness, others are inhabited only by Logical Poe. All of the women are specters, idealized images drained of blood. The narrators sometimes embody the point of view of Logical Poe while the action is carried through by Visionary Poe, but there are few stories other than the merely trivial in which he is able to dispense with a narrator. As an artist he worked always in the first person, looking again at his personality in a glass that often gave back frightening reflections. Concerned wholly with the depths he discerned in the mirror image, Poe was altogether incapable of imagining what other people felt or believed ... (240).

I have quoted at length from *The Tell-Tale Heart* for two reasons. First, to give the reader yet one more experience of Symons' highly readable and perceptive prose and, second, because the mirror metaphor which winds through the paragraph is one we will find to be central to Symons' crime fiction, making the Poe of his biography appear as a character familiar to readers of Symons' novels. Here one is faced with a puzzle. Is Symons' biography flawed because he finds Poe to be very much like a Symons character, or does the parallel between Poe and Symons' own characters merely reveal a deep and lasting influence?

In both his fiction and non-fiction Symons has also shown a great interest in courtroom drama. Court transcripts seem to tease his imagination. On the one hand, they offer the allure of the intellectual puzzle. On the other hand, they offer detailed reflections of violent human behavior, a cracked mirror of the human self in conflict with the social order. In *A Reasonable Doubt: Some Criminal Cases Re-examined*, Symons applies the tools of the crime writing trade to an analysis of several actual cases. Through careful review and dissection of court transcripts, case commentaries and other available documents, he probes motive and character in an effort to set right the fact of the matter. But it is his deep and abiding concern for character which most informs his "verdicts."

Nowhere in the Symons' corpus is the distinction between fiction and non-fiction blurred more than in *Great Detectives*, a work handsomely illustrated by Tom Adams. There is really no ready made label for it. In the work Symons, as Symons, sets out to shed light on the lives of seven great fictional detectives. His knowledge of the genre and his playful wit gloss every page. He provides us with a very believable rendition of Holmes' last case, a case which may have been undertaken at the request of Miss Marple in her salad days. This is followed by the voice of the Reverend Leonard Clement, retired Vicar of St. Mary Mead, who ambles and rambles through his memories of life with Miss Marple. Archie Goodwin is then interviewed by Symons. In the interview Goodwin refuses to rule out the possibility that Nero Wolfe may still be alive. Next on the list is Ellery Queen. Writing in the voice of Julian Symons, literary critic, Symons explores the Queen corpus for internal evidence which will prove his thesis that there were, in fact, two Ellery Queens. The argument is quite convincing and leaves one wondering.

From there Symons turns his attention to Maigret, Poirot and, perhaps, the "original" from whom Marlowe was created. Each excursion into the life of a great detective is fresh, revealing and crackling with wit. Symons knows the territory of crime literature inside out, and *Great Detectives* proves it. Only a person whose life has become one with a genre can play in it with such zest, such versatility, such skill and such humor.

But what is there in Symons' non-fiction that is useful to the student of his fiction? First there is his working definition of the "crime novel." Second, there is the constant reminder that crime fiction is serious fiction, fiction capable of illuminating the human condition in the years following World War II. Third, there is a flag of caution against taking either crime fiction or the human condition too seriously—a reminder that the voice of the satirist, even when spoken through the teeth of a death mask, is a voice from the comic and not the ironic or tragic mode.[4]

A final note is in order before closing this discussion. Symons did not begin his career in crime literature by writing crime novels. Like the genre itself, Symons' crime novels emerge from the world of the detective story. Today Symons is embarrassed by his two early detective stories and is quite content to see them out of print. They merit passing attention here, however, because each was written according to the formula of the classical detective story and neither suggests the emergence of the crime novel.

The Immaterial Murder Case (1939) was stuffed into a drawer and not published until 1945. It was meant to be a spoof of trendy modern art and its followers. In fact, it is an unfortunate spoof of itself, an unintentional parody of the detective formula. Teake Wood, eccentric amateur detective and intentional parody of Sherlock Holmes, is the only interesting and accessible character in the novel. The rest either get lost in the tangled plot or fail to move successfully from Symons' circle of friends (who served as models for the characters) into his fiction.

Chief Inspector Bland who presides over the case is recalled to duty in *A Man Called Jones,* Symons' second detective novel. Bland is aptly named and hardly the Great Detective around whom a lasting series of novels is built. Dull and slow in the first novel, Bland is adequate in *A Man Called Jones*. The novel is also adequate. And therein lies the problem and, perhaps, that problem is the shape of the detective novel itself. One character in the book reflects on the purpose of the detective story saying that the essential thing about it is that "it isn't very much like life. It doesn't set out to be like life—that isn't its function. The detective story is decidedly a romantic affair ... it's fantasy. The future of the detective story is in the field of fantasy" (90).

The character speaks Symons' mind about detective fiction as he understood it at that time.[5] The formula is the fiction. Realism has no place in characterization or elsewhere. The result of this restriction is interesting here, for in this detective story Symons touches on a theme which is central to many of the better and later works which he calls crime novels. That theme is the theme of authentic existence symbolized through clever and intricate use of masked and multiple identities among his characters.

The basic puzzle in *A Man Called Jones* is the identity of a mysterious masked figure who calls himself "Jones." Had Symons broken from formula in this novel he might have created his first crime novel, pushing the quest for the identity of this character from clever puzzle to symbolic investigation of problems which prevent the formation of a stable and moral self in a world where the center will not hold. If *A Man Called Jones* had been written outside the bounds of the formula, then Bland's final comments about the identity of Jones would have had the ring of vintage Symons but, rather than being charged with psychological and social significance, Bland's comments are a mere summation of the thinking by which he solved the problem. Bland remembers that he had wondered whether "van Dieren when he saw me was playing some kind of part? And when I asked myself that question I asked myself another: was *not one impersonation involved* but two?" (185).

A departure from formula, a shift in form and intent is necessary for this detective story to become a crime novel. But the theme is there to be discovered, and Symons' shift from detective story to crime novel is, perhaps, not as radical as it first appears. The consequences of that shift are, however, far reaching for Symons the man of letters and Symons the social critic. For in the process of making this shift, Symons effectively adapts crime literature to the purpose of radical social critique while pushing the genre into the realm of serious literature.

III: *The Crime Novel and Social Criticism*

As Symons sprung his crime fiction loose from the classical detective formula, he was quick to put it to the service of social comment and criticism. In much of his best fiction this is done by replacing the classical setting of the detective story with the modern urban workplace. Gone is the world of people at leisure in great country houses, quaint villages or elegant townhouses. In their place Symons puts the working person—shopkeeper, clerk, professional or corporate executive. These characters are not only people who work but people who are seen at work. The shop or the office is the setting for the novel, and the violence in such novels is inherent in the work environment of the characters, not an anomaly as violence is in the peaceful, almost Edenic, landscape of classical detective fiction. In Symons' work violence is the condition under which people live and not a problem which they must solve. The violence portrayed in the works is spiritual, moral, psychological and continual. It is part of the hectic, untidy life that modern capitalism had produced. As noted earlier, Symons argues that peace and order departed with Hiroshima and the concentration camps. The problem posed in post-war crime fiction is not, then, who perpetrated an act of violence and how is the shattered order to be restored, but, rather, what happens to human beings who must live out their days under the conditions of violence.

Symons avoids both a simple and a simplistic answer to this question. His works show that there are many variables, some controllable but most not, which determine how an individual will respond to the violence, stress and pressure of life in modern society. He also knows that only the mix of variables separates one person's response from that of another, the response of the criminal and the insane from that of ordinary folks.

Seven of his crime novels are set squarely in the middle of the workplace and take their shape and meaning in large measure from their environment. These novels are *The 31st of February, The Narrowing Circle, The Killing of Francie Lake, The End of Solomon Grundy* and *The Players and the Game.* The world of work also figures importantly in *The Man Who Killed Himself, The Man Who Lost His Life, The Plot Against Roger Rider, The Blackheath Poisonings* and *Sweet Adelaide.* An examination of these works reveals Symons' wit and wisdom as a social critic while providing proof for his claims about the worth of crime literature as serious literature.

Symons' first real crime novel, and one of his finest, is *The 31st of February.*[6] It sets the pattern for his "world of work" novels. The first point in the pattern reveals the place of people in the world of work. Early in the novel, echoing T.S. Eliot's famous description of life in the "unreal city," Symons describes the world of work as a place peopled by automatons, human beings reduced to a series of interchangeable parts in a grand economic clockwork:

> At quarter to ten on Monday morning a small regiment of black Homburg hats marched own Bezl Street. Beneath the hats advertising men were to be found, respectably overcoated, equipped with briefcases, wearing highly polished shoes .... the hats shot into offices, right and left, and in five minutes Bezl Street was clear of them (4).

He turns the hat into a leitmotif and develops the image across the novel.[7] Machine-like people go through the daily grind indifferent to and destructive of the psyche of those around him. All of this is portrayed with a sense of realistic detail reserved only for the eye of the insider. The novel leaves little question as to why Symons quit the world of advertising as quickly as he could.

The destruction of the individual by the world of work is dramatized in the novel through the unfolding fate of its protagonist, Andy Anderson. Anderson is an advertising man whose smooth tick-tock existence is disrupted by the death of his wife. She dies as a result of a fall down the cellar stairs. A coroner rules it "death by accident" but Inspector Cresse, the policeman originally assigned to the case, believes that Anderson murdered his wife. Cresse pursues this belief to a cruel end. In close counterpoint, Anderson's colleagues at Vincent Advertising hound him out of the profession, insensitive to his burden of grief and guilt and protective of the great selling machine.

A second point in the pattern reveals the void that is life at work and at home in the modern world. The product of Vincent Advertising is worthless. Success in the field of advertising is defined cynically, in the following way, by one of Anderson's colleagues:

> You want to be a successful advertising man. All right. You've got to be able to draw and write a bit. But that's not much. You've got to be intelligent, so that you see it's parasitic, you see it's a bloody fleecing of the public. All right. But that's not all. In fact that's not much. Because *then* you've got to be able to believe it all while you're working on it (26).

A career spent knocking out phrases such as "Say Hey Presto. And forget shaving" (93) or developing jingles to say "AFTER LUNCH COMES CRUNCHY-MUNCH/CRUNCHY-MUNCH ROUNDS OFF YOUR LUNCH/LUNCH TIME'S ALWAYS CRUNCHY-MUNCH TIME/ALL THE BUNCH EAT CRUNCH-MUNCH" (22) hardly encourages a sense of great value and worth. While this relationship of person to work can hardly nourish the self, neither can relationships of the sort that Anderson had with his wife, Valerie. Symons first defines the relationship by describing the physical environment in which it exists:

> There is a part of London near the Buckingham Palace Road, behind Eccleston Bridge, where the large stucco seediness of once-fashionable squares, Eccleston and Warwick and St. George's, fades into a smaller shabbiness. There are streets here of small, identical red-brick houses, fronted by ugly iron railings; these streets branch off the main stem of Warwick Way, that backbone of Pimlico where large houses converted into a dozen one-room flats offer typists and secretaries the chance of developing an individuality untrammeled by the presence of parents or the inhibiting eyes of childhood neighbors. Such self-contained lives typify the decay that is spreading slowly over the fabric of our great cities; to be part of this decay, to visit the ballet frequently and to fornicate freely, to attain a complete irresponsibility of action—that is, in a sense, the ideal life of our civilization (45).

Then Symons turns to a description of their relationship as Anderson understands it. That relationship is experienced as a void he discovers in himself. He says,

> We lived together for several detestable years. For the whole of that time I had seen with irritation the grease on her face at

night, and her intolerable cheerfulness in the morning. I'd listened all that time to her inanities about clothes and film stars. Unconsciously, I must dozens of times have wished her dead. But now that she *is* dead, and the bathroom is free when I want to use it and I no longer find hairpins in the bed, I am oppressed by an extraordinary sense of loss. Not loss of Val exactly—that seems not to enter into it. Rather, part of myself seems to have disappeared (55).

To these two points in the pattern Symons adds a third which turns the novel from social satire to a chilling exploration of the structure of meaning in modern society. Using Inspector Cresse's vendetta against Anderson as a metaphor for the function of law in a modern society, Symons suggests that the forces of law and order are as irrational as the rest of society. Where one would expect reason, justice and benevolence to reside, there in a void is Inspector Creese, a gestapo sort described by a cohort as a person who likes to see people squirm, to "pull off their wings and see them crawl over the table under ... [an] omniscient eye ... a sadist" (206). To the charge that he is a sadist who likes to play God, Cresse coolly responds saying that "a policeman ... is God—or God's earthly substitute.... Justice should be intelligent. If we are obstructed by the forms of legality in reaching the ends of justice, the forms of legality should be ignored" (206).

The effects of these three points are telling when we discover the pattern is a blueprint for insanity. Meaninglessness, insensitivity and cruelty conspire to push Anderson from the fourth of February, the day his wife died, to the never-never time of the 31st of February. In a narrative aside Symons explains the modern predicament and Anderson's breakdown this way:

We all of us retain, for the greater part of our conscious lives, the impression that we are in control of events ... in the sense that the performance of certain actions have predictable results. The exact nature of the links that make up the chain of cause and effect is concealed from us, and to most people, indeed, the links are of no interest; but it is essential for our mental well-being that the chain itself shall not be broken .... It is upon this illusion of free will ... that our civilization has its slender basis; damage to this illusion in the case of an individual may render him incapable of dealing with the simplest problems, so that he is afraid to push the bell of a street door or to pull a lavatory chain because he has come to believe that life is in its essence illogical and irrational. Something like this loss of belief had been suffered by Anderson (164).

The Narrowing Circle repeats the pattern of *The 31st of February*, although the scene shifts from Vincent Advertising to the offices of Gross Enterprises, publishers of pulp fiction. Here as in the advertising world mass production and mass consumption overshadow individual expression, individual wants and individual lives. Interchangeable parts comprise the whole. Even the products produced at Gross Enterprises are interchangeable (formula) parts. Therefore, it is ironic that the presumed motive for murder in this novel is the cut-throat competition between Willie Strayte (the victim) and David Nelson (the protagonist) for editorship of a new Gross publication, "Crime Magazine." The spoils hardly seem worth the crime. To commit murder in order to control the publication of formula fiction for mass consumption seems cost beyond profit in any rational world. But, add to competition the fact that Nelson's wife, Rose, was having an affair with Strayte, and Inspector Crambo seems correct in his assumption of Nelson's guilt.

At first glance Crambo seems cut from the same cloth as Inspector Cresse. To Nelson he says,

> In my experience cases are almost always solved by the checking and rechecking that I talked about the other day. We often know the name of the murderer a long time before we arrest him. The rope is already hanging over his shoulder, you might say, but so lightly that he can't feel it. Every check we make on every minor point draws it just an inch tighter .... Every move and wriggle he makes now simply narrows the circle of the rope another inch... (125-26).

A wriggling insect, a gestapo cop and meaningless work toward a meaningless end—it all sounds familiar. And so the novel would be a repeat of *The 31st of February* were it not for Symons' ingenious power to puzzle and plot. Just when the reader has relaxed into the comfortable world of the known a double reversal occurs. First, Crambo turns out to be a decent policeman capable of releasing his grip on the innocent Nelson when confronted with the real murderer. This does not, however, provide a neat and happy ending. Instead through a second twist in the plot Symons shifts the title metaphor from Crambo's application to crime, quoted above, to a psychological and cultural application. By so doing he shows that Nelson escapes the gallows only to strangle in a more subtle noose pulled tight by the system. A friend of Nelson's offers a theory which explains this action of the system and the narrator repeats it at the end of the novel. This theory of the relation of the individual to the social order is based on the infinite capacity and adaptability of the infant mind. The circle of our actions that may seem "natural" to the infant ... is boundless because its concepts have not been compressed and distorted by the taboos of what we call civilized living. For the small child the possibilities of mind and imagination—of the personality, in fact—have no limits whatever .... the creation of the adult personality [is] a narrowing down of possibilities inherent in the infant mind. I am repressed, therefore I am. Every new taboo imposed by adults and by tradition narrows the circle of personality. Our actions move within a narrowing circle of possibilities, more and more things are forbidden us by the myths that we elevate into systems of ethics. We are like goldfish swimming in an ever-controlling bowl (96-97).

The Narrowing Circle descends a turn deeper into the works of modern society than does *The 31st of February*. Cruel, Hitlerian figures and an indifferent society are the primary agents acting against the interests of the individual in the first novel. In the second the organic relationship of the individual to society dictates a loss of self. It is one thing to make war on tyrants and to cry out against apathy, quite another to reconstitute the fundamental relationship of the individual to the social system.

Symons' award winning novel, *The Color of Murder*, is superficially akin to *The 31st of February* and *The Narrowing Circle*. The stress and pressure of life as an assistant manager of the complaints department of a big Oxford Street store prove to be too much for John Wilkins, the protagonist. However, the focus of the novel is not on the surface. Wilkins suffers from terrible migraines and periodic blackouts, symptoms of the stress and pressure of his life, emblems of the mental anguish which causes him to retreat from the real world into a fantasy life. And it is to the tension between reality and fantasy that Symons turns in this novel.

Form complements content in this well-crafted work. Symons chronicles Wilkins' journey into madness by using multiple narration, beginning with Wilkins' statement to a consulting psychiatrist, including extracts from letters written by other hands than Wilkins, and ending with a third person account of Wilkins' trial for the murder of Sheila Norton, a woman he imagines to be in love with him. The contrast between internal and external views of Wilkins' life heightens the tension between fantasy and reality in the work. So does a comparison between Wilkins and his defense counsel, Magnus Newton, Q.C.

Newton, who also appears in *The Progress of a Crime, The End* of *Solomon Grundy* and *The Man Whose Dreams Came True*, is described as

> a rising silk who welcomed a case that, whatever its outcome, was certain to bring him a lot of publicity. He was short, puffy and self-important, and in cross-examination sometimes produced the impression that he was a little slow to grasp obvious points. Yet witnesses who tried to take advantage of this apparent obtuseness almost invariably found themselves pulled up by a disconcertingly pointed and unpleasant question. His chief fault as a cross-examiner was that of occasionally ignoring an obvious line of questioning while pursuing some fanciful idea of his own (110).

Blending fantasy with reality, Newton's personality indicates how thin the line is that separates Wilkins' insane fantasies from the world of normality and also suggests that the stewards of order (barristers, the police, etc.) are scarcely to be distinguished from the denizens of asylums in the modern world.

The Color of Murder penetrates the surface of modern urban work-a-day life to expose a destructive presence more frightening than Cresse, the twisted tyrant of *The 31st of February* or the seductive social system operative in *The Narrowing Circle*—that is the presence of pure evil encapsulated in human flesh. Perhaps it takes a touch of madness to apprehend this presence; certainly it takes an imaginative mind capable of flights of fantasy. But the presence is there. A witness speaks of it on the stand to no avail. Later Magnus Newton apprehends it while vacationing on the Adriatic coast. Both times it is manifest in a laugh about which Newton says, "I tell you I know now what the old man [the witness] meant by saying it was a murderer's laugh. I know what he meant, I tell you, by saying that the laugh had in it the color of murder" (215).

While it is clear that Symons sees the clockwork of modern society as destructive of the individual, two of his world of work novels make it clear that the individual need not be destroyed by or succumb to the seductiveness of the system. Those novels are *The Progress of a Crime* and *The Killing of Francie Lake*. True to the pattern set forth above, these novels are set square in the world of work but in neither does Symons worry over suburban life or a bad marriage. Rather, the two share the newspaper world as a backdrop and offer up hope in place of the cynicism which dominates the earlier works.

The Progress of a Crime traces the growth of its major protagonist, Hugh Bennett, from helpless innocent cog in a machine to aware, assertive person willing to extricate himself from the machine which would use and destroy him. Although he does not free himself from the system before it has manipulated him, he nevertheless does get free.

While the plot of this novel is initiated by a bizarre Guy Fawkes Day murder, the heart of the novel is elsewhere. The gang of young men, including Leslie Gardner, who perpetrate the crime is caught and tried. But even as the action of the novel turns around their arrest, identification, interrogation and trial, the concern of the novel shifts to probe the cause of the crime and to examine the process by which justice is meted out. Several social institutions are savaged by the telling satire which marks the probe, particularly newspapers, the constabulary and the judicial system. Police brutality is exposed in the novel, a new departure for crime fiction. And the fourth estate figures as just another economic venture. Profit and not truth motivates the *Banner*, a large London paper which champions the cause of young Leslie Gardner. The *Banner* even goes so far as to retain legal counsel for Gardner. Enter Magnus Newton in his prime. Just as profit and not truth motivates the *Banner*, so public acclaim and not justice draws Newton to the case.

Truth and justice do have their champions in the back—backwater journalist Hugh Bennett and Gardner's schoolteacher sister, Jill. The pair persist in their belief that Leslie is innocent and eventually find "evidence" to prove it. But in the course of the novel cynicism is allowed its day. Because of this bit of "evidence" Leslie is acquitted, although he was, in fact, guilty. Then, after a quarrel with his father, Leslie hangs himself.

Against this cynical turn of events Symons sets the end of the novel. The ending suggests two things. First, the real crime in progress throughout the novel was not perpetrated by Leslie and his cohorts but by the system itself. Cops as interrogators, reporters as businessmen and lawyers as celebrities, these are the real criminals and their actions are emblematic of the real crime in progress.

Nevertheless there is an egress other than madness or suicide. It is tenuous and only pointed toward in the novel; both Jill and Hugh talk their way toward it as each rejects a place in the established order. The conversation runs as follows; Hugh speaks first:

> "I had a letter from the Banner. An invitation to lunch."
> "Are you going?"
> "No. But I'm not staying at the Gazette either."
> "What are you going to do?"

"I don't know. Do you think two temporarily unemployed people ought to get married?"

"Not when one of them is a meat and two veg girl."

"But you're not. If you were you would be staying here, staying in your job."

"I can't talk about it. Not in this house."

"Then let's go for a walk. You'd better put on your raincoat. It's pouring."

They went into the city (256).

The Killing of Francie Lake also shows that there is a way up as well as a way down. The novel is a chronicle of the fall of media tycoon Octavius Gaye and the rise to personhood of Boy Kirton. This double action plot dramatizes the theme of choice sounded in *The Progress of a Crime*.

As Boy Kirton investigates the murder of his colleague, and Gaye's former mistress, Francie Lake, Symons turns cynical social satire into a story of hope. This time the tale is one of redemption and not initiation. Boy Kirton, in spite of his name, is not innocent. Quite willingly he has subordinated his human and moral self as a flunky to the cause and career of Ocky Gaye. However, just enough of Gaye's early idealism survives in Kirton to prompt him to do a thorough muckraking investigation into Francie's death. In a marvelously written live television interview Kirton reveals what he has discovered. The act of courage and integrity seems sufficient to propel Boy Kirton and his Watson, Jennifer Masterson, beyond the destructive reach of the prevailing social order.

The End of Solomon Grundy is my favorite among the novels set in the world of work. Both title and plot are taken from a children's song which serves as the epilogue of the novel: "Solomon Grundy/Strangled her on Monday/Arrested on Tuesday/Tried on Wednesday/Acquitted on Thursday/Shot her on Friday/Arrested on Saturday/Ate his dinner on Sunday/Hanged on Monday/That was the end of Solomon Grundy"(241).

Considerable irony is generated by grafting his children's song to a crime novel. So grafted it becomes the perfect vehicle for a return to the pattern of *The Narrowing Circle*. Symons inverts the plot of *The Narrowing Circle* and appropriates the theory of self and society elaborated there.

Solomon Grundy lives in a suburban goldfish bowl called The Dell. There people are expected to speak and behave with the predictability Symons earlier assigned to advertising men in Homburg hats. Snippets of cocktail party conversation at The Dell nicely reflect the quality of life as it is lived there: "in any theory of gradual response"..."a wonderful hock, fruity and fragrant"..."a disgrace, of course, the whole garage question and the committee"... *"Beyond the Fringe,* yes, I loved the one who"... "Late again, I said to the porter, and he said..." (7).

Since Solomon Grundy is an advertising man we know that his working days provide no more meaning in Symon's world than his suburban nights. On The Dell and life in it Grundy says, "The whole place, community living, what anyone does is everybody's business, little committee living, what anyone does is everybody's business, little committee meetings to blather away about garages. Too much bloody order" (36). He also comprehends both the impossibility and necessity of breaking free from the narrowing circle, saying that one must try to do something else, "but what's happened is part of you, you're part of it. You can never cancel what's happened to you, you have to accept it.... You have to. You have to try" (36).

Grundy is in a position to try because he never really grew up. Not only is Grundy an advertising man, he is also a cartoonist. And as a cartoonist he keeps his childish self alive in the character of Tuffie McGuffie. This sign of "possibilities and imagination" points to a part of Grundy that is alive and twisted in The Dell, pushing toward violence against the established order. Grundy commits murder but fails to find in that awful existential act the freedom to will his own will. Instead he finds an empty and cruel freedom. In a letter from jail to his wife he describes it.:

> Prison is extremely interesting, a closed society, an image of what the world is going to be like in fifty years. Everything is ordered here for you by authority, it isn't like The Dells, where the residents were doing the ordering—that is the thing you like and I object to! Once you accept the fact that in all the trivial, inessential things you have to do what you are told, you have all of the time that's left to think about your life and errors. You are free! Do you understand what I mean?

A family of do-gooder neighbors rally around Grundy and hire Magnus Newton for his defense. The family discovers "evidence" sufficient to insure Grundy's acquittal. But like Leslie Gardner in *The Progress of a Crime,* Grundy was in fact guilty—so much for truth and justice. Unlike Gardner though, Grundy does not commit suicide when he's released. Rather, true to the plot of the children's song, he kills again.

Reversing the plot of *The Narrowing Circle, The End of Solomon Grundy* presents a protagonist who slips from the noose of social control only to hang at the end of a hemp rope. Rebellion seems to produce the same results as acquiescence—death.

The Players and the Game is Symons' most recent work set in the world of work. It tells two stories. One explores the fantasy versus reality theme of *The Color of Murder*, the other follows the pattern of *The 31st of February*. The first is presented in the form of a diary. Kept by a person who uses the pseudonym "Dracula," it records the gradual extension of fantasy into reality by Dracula who puts his Theory of Behavior as a Game into practice. The second story is a straight-forward narrative of the fall of Paul Vane, Director of Personnel for Timbals Plastics.

It is chance and fantasy which patch together the plots and personalities of Dracula and Paul Vane. But it is Dracula and not Vane who is aware of the power of fantasy in life. He puts it succinctly in his Theory of Behavior as a Game:

> The idea about the Theory of Behavior is that we all imitate somebody, but very few of us admit it .... We all think we're original, though we're really copies. Everybody pretends.... We're all playing games. The point is, you get more fun out of life if you admit it. You can let your fantasy run free, and that's exciting (2-3).

Distinguishing the two protagonists from each other is Dracula's ability to let his fantasy run free. This contrasts with Vane's vain effort to repress his fantasies and conform to the Timbals Plastics mould. Neither, however, is able to prevent the intrusion of fantasy upon reality and for both this proves, in the final analysis, disastrous.

In summary, Symons' crime novels portray a world at work which does not readily accommodate human life. As a result people are often destroyed by what ought to be their life-support machine. Sometimes they are crushed by the system (driven crazy or pushed to suicide): sometimes they are drowned succumbing to the Siren call of meaningless work in the void. Only one alternative is suggested and that is life lived according to the demands of love, cooperation and mutual respect.

IV. Dreams, Games and Masks

Dreams, fantasies, games and masks are all coping mechanisms commonly employed by Symons' characters. As the world at work is the essence of scene in his novels, so these devices are the soul of character. Dreams, fantasies, games and masks are all effective defenses against assault and battery from the social order, so long as characters do not confuse them with reality. For example, Magnus Newton's flights of fantasy only make him an interesting eccentric. Paul Vane's wife escapes from the emptiness of her marriage through endless games of bridge. Vane's boss, Bob Lawson, relieves his stress and tension by acting out his sex fantasies with a high priced "doctor."

More often Symons' characters blur the line between reality and fantasy as they employ these coping mechanisms. When they do the result is death in one of many forms. For example, David Nelson of *The Narrowing Circle*. Nelson is the first victim of these devices. He chooses the mask of financial and social success rather than the plain face of his desires. As a result, his wife, who would have supported him in his battle against the system, loses confidence in him as a person and believes he has sold out. Symons presents a haunting picture of their relationship as the novel ends:

> After he had gone down to the Rolls I went into the bedroom. Rose was putting on a cream facial mask and her face, one side white and the other side still flesh-colored, stared at me.
> "I didn't promise anything. I said I'd let him know. You heard that."
> She said nothing, but continued to spread the cream.
> "We'll talk it over, you and I. Don't think I was letting him sell me a line, Rose. It just might be worth putting off the trailer for six months, that's all, if there really is money in it...."
> Now Rose's whole face was white as a clown's. From the dead mask living eyes, in the glass, looked sorrowfully out at me (216-17).

The next victim is John Wilkins (*The Color of Murder*) who defies reality in his pursuit of Shelia Morton. Unwilling to read the obvious clues concerning her feelings toward him, he pushes himself into her world according to the dictates of his fantasy. Even as he misreads Shelia's clues, so the police and jury misread the evidence which links him to her murder. This irony drives home the point that, when it intrudes upon reality, fantasy behavior is dysfunctional.

In *The Pipe Dream* Symons pushes his protagonist out from behind a mask into the bright light of nightmarish reality. This character, Bill Hunter, is known to his TV audience as "Mr. X— Personal Investigator." Safe behind his mask, Hunter is a ruthless and popular muckraker; that is until a guest exposes him as a fraud. This guest, Nicholas Mekles, is a gangster whose sources have discovered that Mr. X is Mr. Hunter who is a Mr. O'Brien who did time in prison.

Hunter loses his job as a result of this revelation and retreats from the world under yet another alias, Mr. Smith. Wearing the mask of Smith, Hunter becomes involved in the fantasy world of Anthea Moorehouse. He agrees to help her turn fantasy into reality, and the two develop an elaborate game plan by which she will kidnap herself and demand ransom from her father.

The rest of the novel is a tangle of fantasy and reality—a nightmarish descent into the criminal self in which Hunter-Smith is no more able to escape the consequences of his life as Hunter than he had been able to free himself from his life as O'Brien. The novel snaps together with a loud crack when Hunter-Smith is brought face to face with the consequences of his life as both Hunter and O'Brien. At gunpoint he learns a truth central to Symons' vision of the self, that persons are wholes and not disparate parts, persons and not masks or roles. They cannot shed their skins like snakes. As Hunter learns this lesson he joins the protagonists from *The Progress of a Crime, The Killing of Francie Lake* and *The Man Who Lost His Wife* in that small circle of Symons' characters who get through the world alive and whole.

Two "everyman novels," *The Man Whose Dream Came True* and *The Man Who Lost His Wife* demonstrate the negative and positive functions of dream and fantasy in human life. *The Man Whose Dream Came True* recalls the pattern of *The Pipe Dream*. Anthony Jones, alias Anthony Bain-Truscott, alias Anthony Scott-Williams, is the protagonist. A fraud and a practitioner of fraud, Jones proves incapable of being or perceiving the real thing. The result is a plot of ironic twists, sometimes comic but finally deadly serious.

Unlike Bill Hunter in *The Pipe Dream*, Jones fails to integrate his many parts into a whole. Indeed he rejects as synonymous with anonymity his surname. The inability to accept the whole fabric of the self, as we have seen, is what causes Symons' characters to disintegrate. So Jones is doomed to exist as a series of aliases. And, being a shadow of a self he easily mistakes the shadows others cast for their substance. And it is in the shadows, dreamlike, that Jones makes his life. There others can easily persuade him that his dreams are reality. And during large parts of the novel Jones is allowed, even encouraged, to live out his dreams in order that very real and practical ends may be achieved by others.

Fantasy plays a very different role in *The Man Who Lost His Wife*. For the protagonist, Gilbert Welton, it becomes the means by which he begins to break free from an all to predictable life. At the outset of the novel Welton's wife, Virginia, leaves him because their relationship is stagnant. His dull, safe life is the reason for her boredom. She puts the matter succinctly: "I like marriage to be hills and valleys, a sort of switchback ride. You want to live on a plateau" (10).

Her departure for Yugoslavia puts "hills and valleys" into Welton's life. He convinces himself that she has gone there to have an affair with his partner, Max. Acting on this conviction, Welton follows her to Yugoslavia where his life becomes an adventure. Perhaps he even commits murder in his effort to win her back. When he returns to London, he has changed. He knows that. But he also knows that he is still the same man. He does not make the mistake of trying to kill off Welton the plateau dweller or banish Welton the adventurer. He knows his life is a continuum, the sum total of his experiences.

At the end of the novel he and Virginia are together again. He wears a new dashing Russian hat (gone is the Homburg). She perceives that he is somehow different, "more considerate, I suppose. Something like that" (203).

Fantasy, then, may be a restorative if it can be accepted as part of reality. It is only deadly when it is pursued as if it were reality, as if it were the self.

Fantasy, dreams, games and masks add up to considerably more than routes by which one may escape from reality. They may also be conscripted into a war against reality. Symons presents this function in *The End of Solomon Grundy, The Man Who Killed Himself, The Players and The Game, The Blackheath Poisonings* and *Sweet Adelaide*. In all these novels his protagonists are expressions of the Nietzschean *ubermensch*.

Solomon Grundy is in many ways a wise person. He knows that the fragmentation of self he experiences is not something from which he can simply move away. That Tuffie McGuffie and the advertising man are both Solomon Grundy he does not deny. But he does deny the real world setting in which the integration of the disparate parts of a personality must take place. And it is this denial which aborts his attempt to transvalue all values. Trivial matters, mundane chit-chat, the tick-tock of life are shelved by Grundy, as noted earlier, that he may get to the great questions. Those great questions are, however, inextricably a part of the quotidian. Grundy as *ubermensch* is a mask and not a person, a bold player strutting a stage, full of sound and fury signifying nothing.

The Man Who Killed Himself is a novel about masks, fantasies and freedom. It begins with a satiric portrait of life in the suburbs, focusing on silly Mr. Arthur Brownjohn, alias Major Easonby

Mellon. As Brownjohn, the character is presented as a terribly henpecked suburbanite leading a dull and marginal existence as a commercial traveler. As Easonby Mellon, he runs a matrimonial agency. Easonby Mellon is a flashy dresser with an eye for women. Brownjohn is constantly humiliated by his wife and regularly escapes from her by playing with electric racing cars in the attic.

An act of Nietzschean heroics unites Mellon-Brownjohn's divided self. In a moment of inspired fantasy Brownjohn takes it upon himself to transcend human values and posit his existence as he would have it to be. In the fashion of a Keystone-*ubermensch*, Brownjohn develops a scenario wherein Mellon kills Brownjohn's wife. The fantasy becomes reality and murder is committed. But in order to escape the consequences of his action as Mellon, Brownjohn must kill Mellon.

Self-murder, even when it involves destroying a mask of the self, always proves to be a heinous crime in Symons' works since oneself is viewed as a continuum of actions and indivisible. The long denouement of the novel explores Brownjohn's life after "suicide." Brilliantly written, it makes clear that the *ubermensch* is doomed to failure because the self cannot transcend the self.

Symons explicitly examines the appeal of Nietzsche's *ubermensch* in *The Players and the Game*. Dracula compares himself to Nietzsche's "lonely man who conceals his thoughts and lives in the cave of his imagination" (139). He goes on to quote Nietzsche's observation that "from time to time, we take revenge for our violent concealment. We come out of our cave with frightening looks, our words and deeds are then explosions, and it is possible that we collapse within ourselves" (139). Dracula, who at the end of the novel proclaims, "My name is Nietzsche Caesar .... I have effected in my own person the Transvaluation of All Values" (217), summarizes the plight of characters in Symons' social order. His fiction is populated by characters who conceal or mask their feelings and desires, making contact with parts of themselves only in the world of dream and fantasy, expressing those parts of themselves only as socially acceptable games and roles. The result of such repression is either violent explosion (most often murder) or implosion (madness in varying forms).

Sweet Adelaide gives new urgency to the problem of self and society by rendering the *ubermensch* as a woman. To this Symons couples the theme of fantasy versus reality heightened by a technique of blending fact (trial manuscripts, contemporary accounts, etc.) with fiction (invented biographical material, diary entries). The novel is a re-examination of the case of Adelaide

Bartlett. In real life Mrs. Bartlett was acquitted of the charge that she murdered her husband. Symons' probe of the evidence suggests that she was really guilty. Although he reverses the verdict he does not present her in the role of villain pure and simple. Rather he renders her as an *ubermensch*. As such she struggles to break bonds which hold her fast as a Victorian and a woman. She takes a lover, thinks thoughts, behaves assertively, cultivates her fantasies. Were she not so cruel and monomaniacal she would be endearing. But Symons' *ubermensch* is a failed heroic ideal precisely because he or she is an isolated individual with no concern for the rest of humanity.

The possible exception to this rule is Paul Vandervent. He is a young sensitive in *The Blackheath Poisonings* who dares to transvalue values, even to the point of committing murder. In his case Symons is sympathetic, casting neither guilt nor aspersions on his action. What sets the introspective Vandervent apart from other versions of the *ubermensch* is his personal integrity (in every sense of the word) and his willingness to take risks for the sake of others. His undeclared and unpunished act is committed out of love for another, even one he can never possess.

There are other instances of masks, dreams, fantasy and games playing significant roles in Symons' novels. False identities are crucial in *Bogue's Fortune* and *The Belting Inheritance*, but in these works masks primarily serve the purpose of plot and puzzle and rarely stand as metaphor or symbol for larger issues and problems. The same is true of the elaborate game contrived by and against Roger Rider in *The Plot Against Roger Rider*. As its title suggests, the book is a complex exercise in plot construction. It goes beyond that, but not very far when compared to the novels just discussed.

V: Concluding Observations

Symons' fiction has about it a sense of corpus—of being a solid and singular body of literature. It is marked by a realistic treatment of character and scene, a coherent and consistent view of self and society, and a penetrating analysis of the relation of masks, dream, game and fantasy to life in a systematized, sanitized, urbanized world. And through it all runs a vision of humanity informed by comedy, as distinct from the irony and absurdity which so often accompanies serious presentations of life in the post-war world.

Symons' fiction has not acquired this special flavor entirely by accident. He tried writing classical detective novels. Then he tried his hand at "the literary detective novel" in the manner of Michael Innes or Edmund Crispin. The result, *Bland Beginnings* is quite readable. Particularly successful is his characterization of two highly eccentric bibliographic experts. A third form which Symons explored early in his career was the espionage thriller: *The Broken Penny*, his only foray into the genre, looks back to the best of Buchan and forward to the fine works of Le Carré, suggesting that had he wanted to Symons could have worked the literary frontiers of that field too. In *A Three-Pipe Problem,* a more recent work, Symons makes clear his talent for comedy. This delightful novel projects a comic vision which underlies all his fiction. It tells the tale of an actor who has played Sherlock Holmes for so long that he has become Holmes. A Don Quixote in deerstalker, Sheridan Haynes confronts the post-war world. The subject matter is vintage Symons—masks, fantasy, games and social critique. But the mode and mood are explicitly comic. I, for one, hope there is a repeat performance in this vein some day.

Finally, it is with the crime novel that Symons has cast his lot. Along with Francis Iles and Patricia Highsmith, he has demonstrated in practice what he has so long preached—that crime fiction can be serious fiction.

Notes

[1] The editions of Symons' works used for this study are listed below, preceded by the original date of publication. All quotations are cited in the text:

1945	*The Immaterial Murder Case*, New York: Macmillan, 1957.	
1947	*A Man Called Jones*, London: Gollancz, 1947.	
1949	*Bland Beginnings*, New York: Harper Perennial Library, 1979.	
1950	*The 31st of February*, New York: Harper Perennial Library, 1978.	
1953	*The Broken Penny*, New York: Harper Perennial Library, 1980.	
1954	*The Narrowing Circle*, New York: Harper, 1954.	
1956	*Bogue's Fortune* (British title, *The Paper Chase*), New York: Harper, 1980.	
1957	*The Color of Murder*, New York: Harper Perennial Library, 1979.	
1958	*The Pipe Dream* (British title, *The Gigantic Shadow*), New York: Harper, 1959.	
1960	*The Progress of a Crime*, New York: Harper, 1960.	
1962	*The Killing of Francie Lake* (U.S. title, *The Plain Man*), London: Fontana Books, 1964.	
1962	*The Detective Story in Britain*, London: Longmans, 1969.	
1964	*The End of Solomon Grundy*, New York: Harper, 1964.	
1965	*The Belting Inheritance*, New York: Harper Perennial Library, 1979.	
1966	*Critical Occasions*, London: Hamish Hamilton, 1966.	
1967	*The Man Who Killed Himself*, New York: Penguin Books, 1977.	
1969	*The Man Whose Dreams Came True*, New York: Penguin Books, 1977.	
1970	*The Man Who Lost His Wife*, New York: Penguin, 1977.	
1972	*The Players and the Game*, New York: Harper, 1972.	
1972	*Mortal Consequences* (British title, *Bloody Murder*), New York: Shocken Books, 1977.	

1972 *Notes From Another Country*, London: London Magazines Editions, 1972.
1973 *The Plot Against Roger Rider*, New York: Harper, 1973.
1975 *A Three-Pipe Problem*, New York: Penguin Books, 1977.
1978 *The Tell-Tale Heart: The Life and Works of Edgar Allan Poe*, New York: Penguin Books, 1981.
1979 *The Blackheath Poisonings*, New York: Penguin Books, 1980.

[2]An excellent checklist of Symons' writings (novels, histories, radio and TV scripts, poems, stories, biographies) can be found in *Twentieth Century Crime and Mystery Writers*, ed. John M. Reilly, New York, 1980, pp. 1367-69. The list itself is partial proof that Symons should be called a "Man of Letters."

[3]The best account of Symons' life as a poet in the 1930s is his own autobiography, *In Another Country* London, 1972.

[4]See Northrup Frye, *Anatomy of Criticism*, Princeton, 1957, pp. 43-8.

[5]In his letter to me, of 31 March 1982, Symons says of this passage in *A Man Called Jones*, "I think I probably meant what I said about the detective story and fantasy at the time. Even now I'm by no means the strict adherent to realism that some people mistakenly think. The crime story **even at its most 'realistic' is a fictional confection, not *real*, and it is not made real by detailed accounts of blood and semen stains, analyses of hair or gun rifling, etc.** But of course the degree and kind of unreality are important. Christie is unreal in one way, Chandler in another and more interesting way. It's been important and useful to push toward realism in characterization, accounts of police procedure and other things, but deliberate fantasy has its place. I'd be inclined to say that most of my books are realistic in characterization, but much less so in the plots."

[6]In *Murder Ink*, ed. Dilys Winn, New York, 1977, p. 6, Ms. Winn ranks *The 31st of February* second behind *The Daughter of Time* on her list of "The Five Best" crime novels.

[7]Steven R. Carter's article "Julian Symons and Civilization's Discontents," *The Armchair Detective* (12 (January 1979), 57-64, called my attention to the hat device. His analysis of Symons is provocative and sound, making it required reading.

Dick Francis
Photo by Mary Francis
(courtesy of The Sterling Lord Agency)

Dick Francis

Marty S. Knepper

1920	Richard Stanley Francis born in Tenby, Wales, son of George Vincent and Catherine Mary Francis, on October 31.
	Learned to ride on a donkey, at age five, and grew up with a family that bought, bred, rode, showed, trained and sold horses.
	Educated at Maidenhead County Boy's School, Berkshire, until age fifteen.
1940-45	Served in the Royal Air Force in World War II, first as an airframe fitter and later as a pilot.
1946-48	Rode in steeplechase races as an Amateur National Hunt Jockey.
1947	Won first race May 3 on Wrenbury Tiger at Bangor-on-Dee.
1947	Married Mary Margaret Brenchley on June 21; later had two sons, Merrick and Felix.
1948-57	Rode in steeplechase races as Professional National Hunt Jockey.
1953-54	Became the National Hunt's Champion Jockey by riding 76 winners in 331 races.
1954	Rode Rose Park in the International Steeplechase at Belmont Park in New York.
1956	At the Grand National at Aintree, Francis' horse Devon Loch, owned by the Queen Mother and leading by six lengths or more, fell, for no apparent reason, just ten strides from the finish line, in front of 250,000 spectators, the bizarre fall becoming one of the most puzzling and highly publicized mysteries in British racing history.
1957	After 2305 races and 21 broken bones (not counting ribs), retired from racing with a record of 345 wins, 285 seconds, and 240 thirds.
1957	*The Sport of Queens* published, an autobiography and an insider's view of British steeplechasing.
1957-73	Worked as Racing Correspondent for the London *Sunday Express*.
1962	First mystery/suspense novel, *Dead Cert,* published.
1965	Received Crime Writers' Association Silver Dagger Award for *For Kicks*.
1966	Edited, with John Welcome, *Best Racing and Chasing Stories*.
1969	Edited, with John Welcome, *Best Racing and Chasing Stories 2* and *The Racing Man's Bedside Book*.
1969	Won Mystery Writers of America's Edgar Allan Poe Award for *Forfeit*.
1970	Francis' short story "Carrot for a Chestnut" appeared in *Sports Illustrated;* three other short stories appeared in magazines and anthologies in the 1970s, "The Big Story," "Nightmare" and "Twenty-One Good Men and True."
1973-74	Served as Chairman of the Crime Writers' Association.
1974	Film made of *Dead Cert,* directed by Tony Richardson, with screenplay by Francis.
1978	Sid Halley played by Mike Gwilym in Britain's Yorkshire Television production of "The Racing Game," appearing in the United States later as part of the PBS series *Mystery!*
1982	*Twice Shy,* Francis' twentieth novel, published.
1983	*Banker,* Francis' twenty-first novel published.

Dick Francis is not a man afraid of risks. In fact, the secret of Francis' success, both as a British steeplechase jockey from 1946 to 1957 and as a writer of mystery/suspense fiction for the past two decades, seems to be his willingness to take risks.

Each time Francis mounted a horse for a race, as an amateur and later a professional National Hunt jockey, he knew he was taking psychological, physical and financial risks. With each win came euphoria. But there was always the possibility of losing a race, for any number of reasons, and disappointing the owner, the trainer, the fans (especially those with heavy bets on his horse), and, of course, himself. In his autobiography, *The Sport of Queens,* Francis describes other risks steeplechase jockeys face.[1] A jockey runs about a one in fifteen risk of falling, Francis estimates, in any given race. Some falls do no damage, but many result in broken bones, and others cause even more serious injuries. Francis suffered twenty-one broken bones (not counting ribs) during his years as a jockey, and his friend and accountant, former jockey Lionel Vick, ended his racing career with a spinal cord injury that put him in a wheelchair for life. The risk of death, for steeplechase jockeys, is approximately one chance in five hundred. Because of the frequency of jockey injuries and the relatively high risk of permanent physical damage or death, insurance companies, Francis claims, generally refuse to cover jockeys or charge exorbitant rates. Jumping jockeys take an enormous financial risk just going into the profession because the pay is low, races are sometimes hard to find on a regular basis, and expenses are great. Naturally, given most jockeys' shaky financial status, they worry about financial survival in the case of a serious racing accident, despite the existence of the National Hunt Benevolent Fund that pays some money to injured jockeys. Two other very real financial fears are losing racing jobs, especially when successes on the race track are not forthcoming, and finding a means of financial support when the body can no longer take the hard knocks of the racing life (85-104).

Despite all these physical, financial and psychological risks, Dick Francis, for love of the sport, took up steeplechasing. Because of his nerve, stamina, riding skill and thorough knowledge of horses and courses, and because, too, of good luck and supportive friends and family, Francis became a top jockey. In 1953-54 he was

England's Champion Jockey. He rode some of the best horses in England, including Roimond, Finnure, Crudwell, Silver Fame and Devon Loch. In 1954 Francis represented England in the International Steeplechase held at Belmont in New York. For four years he rode horses for the Queen Mother (*The Sport of Queens*, 185-222). Francis ended his career, Robert Cantwell notes, with an impressive record of 345 wins, 285 seconds, and 240 thirds (in a total of 2305 races).[2] For Francis, in his riding, taking the risks paid off handsomely.

For Francis, taking risks has also led to success in his writing. Ironically, one of his worst moments as a jockey—the mysterious fall of the Queen Mother's Devon Loch just as the horse was winning the 1956 Grand National at Aintree—led to Francis' taking up a writing career. Because of the huge amount of publicity surrounding the Devon Loch debacle and because of his fame as a jockey, publishers were eager to market an autobiography of Dick Francis. At this point in his life, by refusing the services of a ghost writer and choosing to write the book himself (with the editorial assistance of his wife, Mary), Francis took a second major career risk, a risk that led him to become, eventually, one of the foremost contemporary writers of mystery/suspense fiction.

When Dick Francis made this decision to take up writing, few gamblers would have wagered on his success. He had no experience as a writer, and his education was weak. He freely admits in *The Sport of Queens* that he was an unenthusiastic student as a child, often playing hooky to ride horses. He left school at age fifteen (13-30). In spite of these handicaps, Francis completed his autobiography, which is a fascinating account of his life and draws a detailed picture of British steeplechasing, and he chose to become a professional writer. From 1957 to 1973, Francis was a racing correspondent for the London *Sunday Express*.

After four years as a journalist, Francis found he needed to supplement his income. Instead of choosing a safe job with financial security, he decided to take another risk, to write a mystery novel with a racing setting. This first novel, *Dead Cert*, appeared in 1962.

Since *Dead Cert*, Francis has gone on to write twenty more novels at an average rate of one a year. He has also written several short stories and edited anthologies of racing stories. Francis' novels are popular with critics and with the general public. *Forfeit* and *For Kicks* have won awards from the British Crime Writers' Association and the Mystery Writers of America, and reviewers have consistently praised his novels for their tight structure, imaginative use of racing plots and intriguing heroes. Currently, all twenty-one of Francis' novels are in print in the United States and selling briskly. His novels are also being widely translated. Even persons who are not enamored of the hard-boiled mystery genre are reading and enjoying Francis' novels. A startling case in point is Carolyn Heilbrun, mystery writer (under the pseudonym Amanda Cross), professor of literature at Columbia University and feminist. In *The Question of Max*, Cross' well-bred feminist academic, Kate Fansler, admits that, although she is becoming disenchanted with detective novels, she likes Dick Francis' books.[3]

Francis' popular and critical success as a writer may seem, at first, to be due to the fact that he does *not* take risks. It is true that he has chosen to write in the hard-boiled mystery/suspense genre, which has its established conventions and its devoted fans. And he has chosen also to write primarily about the two subjects he knows best, racing and flying. (Francis was a pilot in World War II.) The seeds for many of his plots, it is also true, can be found in *The Sport of Queens*. In his autobiography, for example, he notes that, in British steeplechasing, the National Hunt Committee are "the lawmakers,...the police, the judges, and the court of appeal for the wicked and the wronged" (96). In *Enquiry*, Francis presents this situation as a potential problem: jockey Kelly Hughes loses his license as a result of an unjust decision by a committee of National Hunt stewards, and he has no legal recourse because the National Hunt Committee is all-powerful. Violence sells books easily, and it is true that Francis' novels, especially his earlier novels, have scenes of excruciating, bone-cracking violence. What's more, Francis' heroes may, at first, seem to be carbon copies of each other, just one more example of the lonely knight walking down those mean streets—or, in this case, the lonely, compassionate jockey riding down those mean tracks.

A more careful analysis of Francis' twenty-one novels, however, suggests that he has, in fact, taken some rather amazing risks in his writing, and, in addition, one of the major themes in his books is risk-taking. For Francis the writer, like Francis the rider, success is the result of risk-taking.

The most obvious risk Francis has taken as a writer is to create a new hero for each novel. Most detective fiction authors create a series character—a Philip Marlowe, a Nero Wolfe, a Kate Fansler, a Mike Hammer—who is interesting enough and predictable enough that readers will buy book after book in a series just to see their hero in action one more time. The appeal of these heroes is precisely the fact that they do not change significantly from book to book. Marlowe will always wisecrack, and Kate Fansler will always quote from highbrow literary works; Nero Wolfe will always refuse to see clients during his orchid hours, and Mike Hammer will always lick his lips when a luscious lovely walks by. Because Francis has chosen not to recycle the same detective character in every book, with the exception of the character Sid Halley who appears in two novels, *Odds Against* and *Whip Hand,* he cannot count on reader loyalty to a particular detective hero to sell his books. Yet, by creating different heroes, Francis has given himself a great deal of freedom—specifically, the freedom to create heroes with a wide variety of personalities, occupations and backgrounds and the freedom to show these different characters developing and changing as a result of the events in each book. By taking the risk of not using a series hero, Francis has managed to write novels with a depth of characterization most detective novels lack.

Critics have looked for the characteristics Francis' heroes share in an effort, perhaps, to suggest that they are, in actuality, literary clones with different names but the same essential identity. In support of this point of view, there is the fact that many of the heroes are orphans, and nearly all have some connection with horse racing. What's more, all of them, more or less, fit the description of Edward Link, hero of *Smokescreen*: "patient, powerful, punctual, professional and puritanical" (59). While there is some validity and usefulness in this approach, it tends to blind the reader to the important differences among Francis' heroes and to underestimate his achievement as a writer.

One quality in people Francis admires is professionalism, the ability to do a job well and to do it responsibly. By creating heroes in a wide variety of professions, Francis can explore this idea more fully than he could if all his heroes were private eyes. (In fact, only three of Francis' heroes are investigators, Sid Halley, David Cleveland in *Slayride* and Gene Hawkins in *Blood Sport*.) The rest represent a cross-section of occupations, some involved with racing and some not: jockey, horse trainer, bloodstock agent, stable lad, artist, journalist, pilot, accountant, physics teacher, photographer, banker, actor, toy inventor, farmer. In presenting his heroes, Francis always examines their professions in some detail: What are the rewards, the challenges, the responsibilities of the job? What qualities does it take to become an expert in the field? Two examples will illustrate this point. In *Smokescreen*, Francis writes about film acting. He shows how everyone expects Edward Link, an actor featured in James Bond type adventure films, to be just like the characters he plays in the movies. Francis illustrates that actors have to deal, often, with egocentric directors, families who may resent long separations during on-location shooting, and publicity agents eager to exploit an actor's privacy to sell a film. He also demonstrates that actors need physical and mental endurance, keen observation and a willingness to reveal their innermost feelings to the camera. Because Edward Link is a private man, publicity events and exposing his emotions on film are difficult for him. In *Reflex*, Francis shows, in great detail, what skills are necessary for a person to be a professional photographer. Philip Nore spends much time in the novel in his darkroom, attempting to resolve the photographic mysteries created by George Millace by using different exposures, different chemicals and other tricks of the trade. Francis shows, too, that photographers face an interesting occupational hazard: the temptation to blackmail.

Francis also explores the issue of social class by having his heroes, and other characters, represent various social classes and various attitudes toward the class system in England. Sid Halley is "the posthumous illegitimate son of a twenty-year-old window cleaner who fell off his ladder just before his wedding" (*Whip Hand*, 237). Randall Drew, in *Trial Run*, is a gentleman farmer whose ancestors, for generations back, have served royalty; his lover, Lady Emma Louders-Allen-Croft, is a socialist in search of "social abasement" (5). Kelly Hughes, in *Enquiry*, is the son of a poor, working-class Welsh family who scorn him because he got a scholarship to the London School of Economics and then became, after graduation, a jockey. Roberta Cranfield, in the same novel, is the daughter of a "roaring snob" who inherited a fortune from his soap manufacturer father but has, so far, failed to buy a peerage (13). Henry Grey, in *Flying Finish*, is the product of a proud, but impoverished, aristocratic family who are desperate to marry him to a rich, socially acceptable wife. He reacts to this family pressure by becoming engaged himself to a working-class Italian woman.

Francis also uses his heroes to examine the nature of relationships between men and women. He shows Sid Halley suffering through an acrimonious divorce in *Odds Against* and *Whip Hand*. Rob Finn, in *Nerve*, is in love with his first cousin Joanna, who is willing to be a friend but not a wife. In *Bonecrack*, Neil Griffon has a comfortable, no-strings-attached relationship with his lover, Gillie, an overweight socialist. James Tyrone, in *Forfeit*, is fiercely devoted to a wife with polio who cannot, for physical and psychological reasons, have sex with him. In *Twice*

Shy, Jonathan Derry and his wife, Sarah, have a polite, loveless marriage, the result, in part, of their inability to have children. In presenting such a wide variety of relationships between women and men, Francis is a marked contrast to most hard-boiled detective fiction writers who rely, over and over, on the macho bachelor-*femme fatale* formula: Sam Spade-Brigid O'Shaughnessy, Mike Hammer-Charlotte Manning, et al.

Many writers fail to give their detective heroes much of a life history, though the detectives may have colorful personalities. We do not, for example, know much about Hercule Poirot's upbringing or Lew Archer's family. Francis gives each of his heroes a family background which helps to explain their different attitudes and personalities and which gives his readers some sharp insights into the psychological dimensions of family life. In *Risk*, Roland Britten's mother committed suicide after having been victimized by her accountant. This explains, in part, Ro's fierce commitment to the accounting profession and his affection for the competent, yet nurturing headmistress, Hilary Pimlock. Philip Nore's passivity, in *Reflex*, is a result of being abandoned, repeatedly, by a charming but irresponsible mother who left him to be raised by a succession of her friends and acquaintances and who eventually died of heroin addiction.

From the desperately suicidal spy, Gene Hawkins, in *Blood Sport*, to the happy, carefree jack-of-all-racing-trades William Derry, in *Twice Shy*, Francis has clearly made his heroes very different people. Because Francis has taken the risk of creating heroes as individual human beings rather than a single fantasy hero, he has been able to explore, in some depth, class, the demands of various professions, family relationships, interactions between women and men, and other issues. Ironically, his strategy seems to have worked in his favor; readers eagerly await each new novel to see what kind of hero he will have this time.

The other major advantage of using different heroes rather than one hero, over and over, is that the author can allow the character to develop. Not only is each of Francis' heroes a unique person, but each hero, to some degree, changes as a result of his adventures so that he is not the same person at the end of the novel that he was at the beginning. A case in point is Steven Scott in *High Stakes*, a toy inventor who achieved success in adolescence and who has grown in confidence and wealth ever since. The novel traces Steven's loss of innocence. At the beginning of the novel, he is suffering the first major disillusionment in his life: Jody Leeds, a friend and the trainer of his race horses, has been cheating him financially, playing him for a sucker. In the course of the novel, events lead Steven into carrying out an elaborate scheme that will regain him his horse Energise and destroy his enemies, Jody Leeds and his confederates, at the same time. By the end of the novel, Steven's scheme has succeeded, but at great personal cost. Although he has recovered Energise, found a wife, and made some new, true friends, he has spent huge amounts of money on his scheme; he has been lambasted by the press; his friend and employee, Owen Idris, has nearly lost his life; he has been beaten up, had gin shot into his veins, and been nearly killed himself; his toy factory has been demolished; and he has experienced intense hatred within himself and directed at himself. Since he is not the same man, he cannot lead the same comfortable, complacent life. He gives Energise to his friends and decides to take up riding race horses.

Unlike Francis, writers who have one repeating hero do not have the luxury of letting their characters grow and change. This is why we do not see Nero Wolfe going to a psychiatrist who can cure him of his phobias and his manias, and this is why Wolfe's sidekick, Archie Goodwin, never marries Lily Rowan. To be fair, it should be noted that the better writers of detective fiction, chafing at the restrictions created by one or more series characters, have shown their heroes changing and developing to some degree. Robert Parker's Spenser is not entirely the same man after he encounters lesbian-feminist Rachel Wallace in the novel *Looking for Rachel Wallace*. Marlowe is never the same after he is disillusioned by Terry Lennox in Chandler's *The Long Goodbye*. Dorothy L. Sayers has probably done the best job of showing a series character, her Peter Wimsey, developing and changing. Yet none of these characters—Spenser, Marlowe or Wimsey—changes to any significant degree in comparison to the changes some of Francis' heroes make.

Besides taking the risk of not using a series hero, Francis' novels are particularly interesting because of the ways in which he violates the formulas for mystery fiction, the ways he foils readers' expectations. Francis' novels fall within the general parameters of the hard-boiled mystery/suspense novel, as described by John Cawelti, George Grella and others.[4] Yet Francis breaks with writers such as Hammett, Chandler, Ross Macdonald and Spillane, especially in his portrayal of society, women and violence. Francis also surprises readers by his challenging of stereotypes, including the stereotype of the hard-boiled detective hero, and his treatment of unpleasant, painful or even taboo topics.

For a writer of popular fiction to violate the conventions of a particular popular genre, as Francis does, is a risk. People have expectations for their leisure reading that they want to see fulfilled; because popular literature is essentially escapist literature, people do not want reality to intrude too much, and they do not want plot or character surprises that shatter their fantasies. Readers of romance, for instance, would certainly rebel if a heroine chose not to marry but to pursue a career instead, while readers of westerns would protest if a rugged cowboy hero settled down to the domestic life. Yet, while violating rules may alienate readers, slavishly following a formula may bore them. Writers—Agatha Christie is a prime example—have often achieved notable successes by writing formula fiction that breaks one or two major rules. (Christie's *The Murder of Roger Ackroyd* outraged readers, but it is one of her most popular novels.) Certainly, too, as Dorothy L. Sayers discovered, the rules must be broken if a writer wants to go beyond escapist formula fiction into the realm of literature about the real world. In Sayers' *Strong Poison*, Peter Wimsey falls in love (a major transgression for a classic detective fiction writer, according to rules Sayers herself helped formulate), and, even worse, he leaves the bulk of the detecting to others, to his employees Miss Climpson and Miss Murchison. *Because* she breaks the rules, she manages to make *Strong Poison* not simply a whodunit/howdunit but a wonderful picture of life in the various segments of British society in the late 1920s, and she explores the attitudes of people in her day to marriage, women and sexuality. In similar fashion, Francis has used a popular formula but taken a risk in breaking the rules and going beyond the formula, and his risk-taking has paid off. He is more interesting and challenging because his work both follows and critiques the hard-boiled detective fiction formula.

Although Francis' heroes are usually amateur detectives, they are not eccentric, celibate intellectuals like Sherlock Holmes. Rather, they are like Philip Marlowe and Lew Archer: shrewd men of action, essentially lonely, fairly ordinary men, except for their extraordinary toughness, their unswerving loyalty to a personal code of conduct (often at odds with society's rules), and their willingness to jeopardize their own safety to protect the innocent.

Matt Shore, in *Rat Race,* illustrates these characteristics of the hard-boiled detective hero. He is a divorced man working as a pilot for Derrydowns, a seedy airplane transport service, and living alone in run-down quarters next to the Derrydowns airfield. Matt has been hurt in the past and has vowed "not to get involved. To be private, and apart, and cold. An ice pack after the tempest" (58). Besides suffering a painful divorce, Shore's career has been in a progressive decline. He left B.O.A.C. in disgrace when he was convicted, as captain of a plane, for negligently jeopardizing the lives of eighty-seven passengers, even though the lying first officer was responsible for the piloting error. Later, he was fired from a South American airplane company for cowardice when he refused to fly a plane he felt was unsafe. From there, he went on to run guns, medicine and refugees in and out of war-torn Africa and later to spray crops. At the beginning of the novel, Matt is depressed, alienated and poverty-stricken.

Events in the novel, however, prove Matt to be a man, like Humphrey Bogart's Rick in *Casablanca*, who cannot remain uninvolved, who is not, at heart, an emotional iceberg. When a bomb explodes in one of the Derrydown planes he has just landed, a plane full of racegoers, Matt starts an investigation that shows his toughness, his willingness to violate society's laws to do what he thinks is right, and his commitment to saving innocent lives, even at great personal cost. When a not particularly ethical jockey, Kenny Bayst, is besieged by two thugs, and no one else will help defend Kenny, Matt joins the fight and saves Kenny from a severe bashing. At another point in the novel, Matt breaks two Board of Trade rules and risks losing his pilot's license to save pilot Nancy Ross, a woman he is beginning to love, and her passengers, endangered because their radio communications system has been sabotaged. At the end of the novel, Matt, suffering from a knock on the head and a knife wound in his shoulder blade, manages, through sheer determination, to reach two innocents, the Duke of Wessex and his young nephew Matthew, in time to save them from being killed by a bomb planted in a candy box given to the boy by desperate con man Charles Carthy-Todd.

Although Francis writes about race tracks more than urban mean streets and although he is less cynical about modern civilization than some of the American hard-boiled mystery writers, he nevertheless portrays a world that is violent, in which greed leads to inhumane behavior, in which power, more often than virtue, is rewarded, in which the innocent suffer. Francis' world is not W.H. Auden's "Great Good Place"[5] nor exactly Cawelti's "glamorous high life of *Playboy* or ... *Esquire*.[6] Francis' novels are not just whodunits, how, why, where and when? His heroes must make moral choices, must resist temptation and refuse to be intimidated or bribed, must endure physical and psychological punishment. Often the identity of the criminal (or criminals) is revealed early, and the rest of the book is a battle of brain and brawn between hero and adversaries.

As Francis' *Odds Against* opens, it is clear that for Sid Halley, once Champion Jockey, it is not the best of all possible worlds he inhabits: his injured hand is grossly disfigured, he has had to give up racing and take up investigating, a job he does not relish, his wife is going to divorce him, and he has just been shot in the intestines by a two-bit crook. After he recuperates, while investigating the shady real estate machinations that led to the sale of Dunstable racecourse to private developers and what appears to be a similar plot to put Seabury racecourse of out of business, Sid confronts persons with corrupt values: the vicious, cruel gossip Mrs. Van Dysart; the suave sadist Howard Kraye and his beautiful, masochistic wife, Doria; the crooked accountant Ellis Bolt; the manager of Seabury, Leo Oxon, willing to allow his racecourse to be sabotaged to earn illegal money, the violent muscleman Fred, and the petty crook Smith, who will do whatever people are willing to pay for, with no questions asked. Although Oxon's involvement in the real estate plot is a surprise revelation at the end of the novel, Sid, and the readers, realize, early on, the guilt of Kraye, Fred and Bolt. The novel is, essentially, a physical and psychological battle of wits between Kraye and Halley. At first, Sid gets the upper hand by pretending to be an ineffectual idiot, encouraging Kraye to underestimate his opponent. Later Kraye and his confederates destroy Sid's flat, a psychological blow, and they physically torture Sid, by bashing his already damaged hand, to get him to reveal the whereabouts of some incriminating negatives. Sid, in the end, foils Kraye and his cohorts with a trick that delivers Bolt into the hands of Chico Barnes, Sid's assistant and a judo expert. Chico tortures Bolt, discovers where Sid is being held captive, and rescues him. The novel is suspenseful, especially when Kraye, Leo and Fred are chasing Sid through a Seabury racecourse building at night, with a boiler nearly ready to explode. Justice triumphs, but, as with other hard-boiled detective novels, the reader of *Odds Against* is not left feeling that all is right with the world. Rather, it is clear that, while there are good people in the world (Admiral Charles Roland, Sid's father-in-law; Chico Barnes; Bolt's secretary with the disfigured face, Zanna Martin), greed, lust and a mania for power will continue to cause innocent people to be victimized. It is clear, too, that Sid's triumph is not a triumph of ratiocination; rather, it is his nerve, his ability to withstand pain, his stubbornness, and his cunning that allows him to survive and see some justice done in a fallen world.

What is also fascinating and challenging about Francis' novels is the way in which he challenges readers to reassess the assumptions about men, women and society that underlie the hard-boiled detective fiction conventions. He joins such writers as Robert Parker and Joseph Hansen in developing this genre beyond its earlier parameters.

One particularly pernicious and widespread tradition has been to use women characters to symbolize perverted values in modern society. The message in one hard-boiled mystery after another is that women cannot be trusted: not intelligent, independent career women like Spillane's Charlotte Manning in *I, the Jury*; not beautiful, seductive women like Brigid O'Shaughnessy in Hammett's *The Maltese Falcon*; not "plain Janes" like Chandler's Orfamay Quest in *The Little Sister*, a doctor's secretary from Manhattan, Kansas; not even ostensibly devoted wives/mothers like Ross Macdonald's Marian Lennox in *Sleeping Beauty*. Women in hard-boiled mysteries are not allowed to be three-dimensional human beings. They are portrayed as flat and emotionless.

Francis' treatment of women characters is a notable contrast. No doubt influenced by the less misogynist traditions in British literature and by his wife, Mary, a woman undaunted by challenges (such as piloting an airplane), Francis developes his women as human beings as they exist in the real world, not nightmarish specters that haunt men's dreams or helpless, clutching, dependent creatures. For example, since women have relatively little power in the world of British steeplechasing, Francis does not, generally, make women his villains. This is not an indication he feels women are too pure or too unintelligent to be criminals. In *Blood Sport*, Yola Clive and her brother, Matt, are involved in horsenapping; in *Enquiry*, a mentally unbalanced Grace Roxford tries to kill Kelly Hughes. Francis shows bright women in all his novels, working the racing field and outside it: for example, Henrietta Craig, competent "head lad" in Griffons' Stables in *Bonecrack;* Sophie Randolph, an air traffic controller in *Knockdown*; Pen Warner, pharmacist in *Banker*; and Clare Bergen, the ambitious publishers' assistant in *Reflex*.

Another positive aspect of Francis' treatment of women is that he deals with problems women face as important human problems. In *Flying Finish*, Gabriella helps distribute birth control pills, which pilots and others smuggle into Catholic Italy. The pills are desperately needed by women exhausted physically and mentally by too many pregnancies. In *Twice Shy*, the problems of old and young women are examined. Mrs. Liam O'Rorke, a feisty 88-year-old widow, tells Jonathan Derry: "I look in my mirror. I see an old face. Wrinkles. Yellow skin. As society is now constituted, to present this appearance is to be thrust into a category. Old women, therefore silly, troublesome, can be pushed around ... unless of course ... one is an *achiever*. Achievement is the savior of the very old" (89). Ruth Quigley, a woman working on her doctorate in mathematics at age twenty-one, is frustrated because society holds her back from achievements because she is too young. She tells Jonathan's brother, William Derry: "I can't give much. I can't get jobs I can do. They look at the years I've been alive and make judgments. Quite deadly. Time has practically nothing to do with anything. They'll give me a job when I'm thirty that I could do better now. Poets and mathematicians are best before twenty-five" (264). Eunice Teller, in *Blood Sport*, at first appears to be a stereotypical aging, alcoholic nymphomaniac, living alone on a horse farm in Kentucky while her rich husband travels. But Francis treats her situation seriously. Eunice, like Gene Hawkins, the novel's hero, thinks she has nothing to live for. She is afraid to make a life for herself, afraid of failure, and afraid of loneliness. She has, Eunice admits to Gene, spent her life "playing games" to avoid the risks of real work and real commitment. She and Gene both learn from each other, become supportive of each other (as friends, not lovers), and, at the end of the novel, Eunice decides to stop playing games and to become a partner in a decorating business.

Francis not only explores the problems women face, but he also challenges the validity of some of the more unfair stereotypes of women, stereotypes that pervade literature, not just hard-boiled detective fiction. In *Nerve,* Rob Finn's mother, Dame Olivia Cottin, is a dedicated professional pianist, a chic, totally unmaternal woman who has ignored Rob most of his life. Rather than presenting Dame Olivia in a negative light for her coldness and her rejection of the maternal role, Francis suggests that having a professional pianist for a mother can have its advantages. Rob comments at one point:

> My mother might not have been a comforting refuge in my childhood nor take much loving interest in me now I was a man, but she had by her example shown me many qualities to admire and value. Professionalism, for instance; a tough-minded singleness of purpose; a refusal to be content with a low standard when a higher one could be achieved merely by working. I had become self-reliant young and thoroughly as a result of her rejection of motherhood, and because I saw the

grind behind the gloss of her public performances I grew up not expecting life's plums to be tossed into my lap without any effort from me. What mother could teach her son more? (87)

Another stereotype is of the skinny, sexless old maid, not very interesting, not very competent, not very useful. Francis shatters this stereotype in *Risk* with his characterization of Hilary Pimlock, the headmistress of a girls' school in Surrey. When Hilary first meets Roland Britten, a thirty-one-year-old accountant and amateur jockey, he has just swum ashore and collapsed on the beach next to her, exhausted, afraid and pursued by angry men on a boat. She is visiting Minorca on holiday; he has just escaped from the boat on which he has been held captive, in solitary confinement, for many long days and nights. Hilary saves Ro by hiding him in her hotel room. After feeding and clothing Roland, Hilary, between forty-two and forty-six years old, with glasses, wrinkles and flat feet, makes Ro a sexual proposition. Shocked, Ro asks, "Why?" and thinks both of his total exhaustion and his debt to Hilary for saving him from recapture. Hilary explains, and Ro questions her further:

"You will find it extraordinary, but I have never ... so to speak, slept with a man."
"In this permissive age?"
"There you are, you see. You find it hard to believe. But I've never been pretty, even as a child. And also I've always been ... well ... able to do things. Learn. Teach. Organize. Administrate. All the unfeminine things. All my life people have relied on me, because I was capable. I've always had health and energy, and I've enjoyed getting on, being given senior posts, and five years ago, being offered a headship. In most ways my life has been absorbing and gratifyingly successful."
"But?"
"But. I was never interested in boys when I was in my teens, and then I thought them callow, and at university I worked all hours to get a First, and after that I've always taught in girls' schools because frankly it is usually a man who's given the headship in a mixed school, and I've never fancied the role of male-ego-massager in second place. Nothing I've ever done has been geared to romance."
"So why *now*?"
"I hope you won't be angry ... but it is mostly curiosity, and the pursuit of knowledge .... For some time I've thought I ought to have had the experience. Of sexual intercourse, that is. It didn't come my way when I was young, but I didn't expect it, you see. I think now that I should have tried to find a man, but then,

when I was at college, I was half scared of it, and I didn't have any great urge, and I was engrossed in my work. Afterwards for years it didn't bother me, until I was thirty or so, and of course by that time all the men one meets are married, and in any case, teaching among women, one rarely meets any men, except officials and so on. I go to many official functions, of course, but people tend not to ask unmarried women to private social occasions" (62-63).

When Ro asks, fascinated, what changed her mind, Hilary explains she feels at a disadvantage teaching sex-education lessons to young girls who know more about the subject than she does and yet need good counseling. Also, she dislikes feeling patronized by married members of her staff. "Catholic priests may be respected for virginity," she remarks, "but schoolmistresses are not" (63). Ro, intrigued by this straight-forward, unusual woman, grateful to her, yet not sexually attracted to her, summons what little energy he has and gives her a lab course in sex education, that ends with Hilary achieving her first orgasm.

Hilary, no sex-starved spinster who craves repeat performances and no silly romantic who wants to marry Ro and give up her career, becomes Ro's "rock," the woman in his life who defies categorization (180). A deep bond of friendship, respect and love develops between them. Ro encourages Hilary to be daring, impulsively buying her a red cape at one point in the novel. On her own initiative, Hilary does some detective work and tracks down the man who held Ro captive. Ro explains accounting to her and consults with her on the detective work he is doing: he suspects he was kidnapped so that his partner and a client would not be exposed as embezzlers. Hilary also advises Ro on his developing relationship with the young, independent, emotionally skittish Jossie Finch.

At the end of the novel, Hilary saves Ro one more time from almost unendurable agony after five of his enemies have strapped him to a table and left him for hours, barely able to breathe. Ro ends up with his face against Hilary's chest, his "throat heaving with unstoppable half-stifled groans." Hilary says:

"It's all right, Ro .... It's all right, my dear, my dear."
Her thin arms [Ro narrates] held me close and tight, rocking me gently, taking into herself the impossible pain, suffering for me like a mother. Mother, sister, lover, child ... a woman who crossed the categories and left them blurred.
I had a mouthful of blouse button and was comforted to my soul (236-237).

Jossie Finch, watching this scene, is profoundly shocked, as perhaps are readers who cannot deal with a woman who does not fall into the stereotypes: a professional woman with nerves, brains, self-possession and common sense and yet with kindness; an older, single woman who can sleep with a man and yet not be a "dirty old woman" or a suffocating, jealous mother figure; a woman who is capable of love but who prefers the single, celibate life. Hilary Pimlock is Francis' most intriguing and most fully developed female character, and she illustrates the degree to which Francis has rejected the stereotypes of women found repeatedly in hard-boiled mysteries.

Francis also challenges the macho image of the hard-boiled detective hero. On the surface, it may seem that Francis' heroes are the epitome of stereotypical manliness because they are competent in their professions, they are in good physical shape, and they are too stubborn to give in to intimidation tactics. However, Francis' heroes are not Mike Hammers or James Bonds. They suffer a great deal of violence but administer very little. For example, in *Nerve*, the psychologically unbalanced Maurice Kemp-Lore hangs Rob Finn from a harness hook in a cold, deserted stable and leaves him there, after having doused him with cold water; when Rob gets a chance at revenge, however, he sets Maurice free, after making sure he will harm no one again. Francis' heroes, unlike most hard-boiled heroes, prefer women with lively minds with whom they can have long-term relationships rather than women with beautiful bodies with whom they can have one-night stands. Roland Britten's friend Johnny Frederick expresses his preference in women as follows: "Big boobs and not too bright .... When I get home, I want hot tea, a cuddle when I feel like it, and no backchat about women's lib." "Boring," is Ro's response (*Risk*, 192). Ro, like Jonah Dereham, William Derry, Philip Nore, Neil Griffon and most of Francis' other heroes, prefers independent women with brains and ambition. These men are not afraid of commitment either, in the form of marriage, ongoing friendship or the sharing of living quarters. Francis' men have deep, very human feelings. This is a contrast to the image of stoicism presented by heroes like Sam Spade. Charles Todd's cousin, Donald Stuart, in *In the Frame*, is devastated for weeks after his wife is murdered; his tears are not presented as a sign of unmanliness. Jonah Dereham, in *Knockdown*, suffers from loneliness and unrequited love. In *Whip Hand*, Sid Halley abandons a case he is working on because he is afraid.

Francis' undercutting of the hard-boiled hero fantasy is most obvious in *Smokescreen* and *Whip Hand*. In the former, Francis emphasizes the contrast between Edward Link's false image, the film screen macho man, irresistible seducer of women and invincible fighter of men, and the reality, Link's ordinariness. In the novel, we see that Link is essentially a domestic man, faithful to his wife and concerned about his children. When events force Link to take on the macho role for real—when he is trapped in a car for days in the African desert, with no food and water, his arms handcuffed to the steering wheel—Link makes no miraculous escape a la James Bond. Instead, for pages, Francis describes Link's incredible physical and psychological suffering. Link is a survivor and a bright, resourceful man, but he is no macho superhero, and this is, in large part, the "message" of this detective novel.

In *Whip Hand*, Francis portrays a hero, Sid Halley, who does, to a large extent, possess the "manly" attributes of pride, stoicism and physical stamina. However, Francis reveals with devastating irony both the falsity of the hard-boiled hero image and its physical and psychological dangers. Sid is perceived by crooks in the racing world (Trevor Deansgate, Lucas Wainwright) as a dangerous, invincible superhero. We see Sid, however, grappling, for six long days in Paris, with his cowardice, and we see him agonizing over the hurt he feels because of his divorce from his wife, Jenny. The image, clearly, is exaggerated; the man behind the image is human. Yet because Sid has assimilated "masculine" values, to a great degree, we also see the consequences of living according to the macho code of behavior. His enemies, because they are convinced and afraid of his supposed power and invulnerabilty, are driven to desperate tactics to stop him: Deansgate, for example, threatens to maim Sid's one good hand. Also, Sid learns, from Jenny, that it is his competitiveness and his inability to communicate feelings that, in large measure, destroyed their marriage. Jenny tells him:

> "No it was yours. [Your fault the marriage went wrong.] Your selfishness, your pigheadedness. Your bloody determination to win. You'll do anything to win. You always have to win. You're so hard. Hard on yourself. Ruthless to yourself. I couldn't live with it. Girls want men who'll come to them for comfort. Who say, I need you, help me, comfort me, kiss away my troubles. But you ... you can't do that. You always build a wall and deal with your own troubles in silence, like you're doing now. And don't tell me you aren't hurt, because I've seen it in you too often, and you can't disguise the way you hold

your head, and this time it's very bad, I can see it. But you'd never say, would you, Jenny, hold me, help me, I want to cry?" (285)

When Jenny says this, Sid desperately wants to say, "Hold me, help me, I want to cry" ... but he can't (286). Ironically, Sid's macho stoicism saves his life, when Trevor Deansgate threatens to kill him, but it loses him his wife. Francis, like Amanda Cross, is fully aware of the consequences of the hard-boiled hero's code—especially the precipitation of violence and the suppression of one's feelings—and, rather than glorifying macho heroes, Francis presents androgyny as a more sane and humane alternative than extreme "masculinity" or extreme "femininity."[7]

Readers are sometimes put off by Francis' many scenes of violence, torture and physical and psychological anguish. The significant difference between Francis and other hard-boiled writers is that Francis does not romanticize violence or make it exciting and titillating. In Francis' novels, pain hurts...intensely, and it does not go away in a page or two. Also, the heroes suffer the violence most often, forcing readers to feel the pain vicariously. What is more, violence in Francis' novels is not usually a matter of participation in gunplay and fistfights as much as it is a matter of enduring physical pain and psychological torment over a long period of time. For example, when Edward Link is locked in a car at the end of *Smokescreen,* Francis makes him suffer for twenty full pages before he is rescued. During the days in the car, we feel the heat, the headaches, the boredom, the aching body, the parched throat, the hunger, the cramps, the stench (the result of no convenient bathroom facilities), the desperation, the anger, the desire for death. By presenting torture scenes like this realistically, which he does in many of the novels, Francis runs the risk of alienating readers who are used to having the criminals, not the heroes, suffer the effects of violence and who are used to reading about violence mystery formula, his realistic, detailed presentation of violence is, in itself, a critique of the romanticized violence in many hard-boiled detective books. Francis is not naive; he knows violence is part of the real world, as a result of greed, selfishness, psychological aberrations, sociological factors; and yet he will not advocate violence or suggest that choosing violence is an option that is without devastating consequences for both victim and victimizer.

In his portrayal of society, Francis also rejects the simple answers provided by many other hard-boiled mystery writers, that society is corrupt and that, to exist as a moral individual, one must disassociate oneself from the institutions of society and live as a loner. Indeed, in hard-boiled novels, corruption is rampant and false values (such as money and lust) have replaced more humane values (such as justice and love).

Francis' world is not the "Great Good Place" of the classic detective novel. He shows, repeatedly, greedy, unscrupulous people victimizing other people. In *Knockdown*, Pauli Teska and his confederates manipulate bidding at horse auctions so that they can gain huge commissions from owners paying inflated prices, and they try to run out of business honest owners, like Antonia Huntercombe, and honest agents, like Jonah Dereham. But, and this is a crucial difference, Francis' heroes are, on the whole, not anti-establishment types. Randall Drew, after all, works at the bidding of royalty in *Trial Run;* David Cleveland, in *Slayride*, is chief investigator for Britain's Jockey Club; Steven Scott, in *High Stakes*, has reaped the financial benefits of the capitalist system. Society, in Francis' world, is not inherently corrupt, though individuals may be. Whereas, in many hard-boiled mysteries, the hero seems to be the only unsullied character in his world, in Francis' novels, the hero has allies, including representatives of the establishment, who are supportive, like Sid Halley's father-in-law, Admiral Charles Roland, in *Odds Against* and *Whip Hand*; the Earl of October in *For Kicks*; and banker Charlie Canterfield in *High Stakes*. For Francis, the answer to the problems of modern society is not separation from it, but working within it.

Francis deals with problems that exist in modern society seriously and in some depth. He treats modern social and psychological problems, including some topics generally considered unpleasant or even taboo, by making them a major part of his novels, by making the hero involved, in a personal way, with these problems. In fact, most Francis novels have double plots intertwining, one plot dealing with the racing-related mystery and one plot dealing with a psychological or sociological problem the hero must work through. Gene Hawkins, in *Blood Sport*, for example, battles against his own very strong suicidal urges. Jonah Dereham must deal with an alcoholic brother in *Knockdown*. Sid Halley, in *Odds Against*, must learn to accept a physical disability, his smashed hand. In *Twice Shy,* Jonathan Derry and his wife cannot have children, a situation that is destroying their marriage. In *Reflex*, Philip Nore must deal with his abandonment by his mother, with his mother's drug addiction, and with his sister's involvement with an exploitative religious cult. In exploring these issues, Francis writes with seriousness, sympathy and sensitivity, never minimizing the problems or suggesting easy solutions. Just as Francis makes his readers *feel* the effects of brutal, violent behavior, he makes readers empathize with persons experiencing these problems. To read *Blood Sport*, for example, is to learn what it feels like to be lonely, paranoid and suicidal.

Francis, then, has written novels that are in the hard-boiled detective fiction tradition, but he has taken the risk of violating the conventions of the genre, even challenging the assumptions on which it is based. He does this by presenting women as human beings, not just *femmes fatales* or pathetic, helpless victims; by dealing seriously with women's problems; and by exposing as narrow and false some of the common stereotypes of women. Likewise, Francis calls into question the macho man stereotype many hard-boiled mysteries perpetuate, and he shows the physical and psychic dangers of the macho mentality. Unlike many hard-boiled mystery writers, Francis refuses to romanticize violence, and he does not blame social institutions for the injustices and abuses of power individuals cause. Social and psychological problems Francis treats seriously, making them central, not just part of the background; he does not shy away from dealing with painful, unpleasant realities. Francis, like Robert Parker and Joseph Hansen, is moving the hard-boiled mystery away from escapist formula fantasy and into the realm of serious literature about life.

Besides using many detective heroes instead of one and moving away from the hard-boiled mystery/suspense formula, Francis has taken other risks as a writer, risks that have paid off. One is creating endings that violate readers' expectations. Strict moralists, for instance, will object to Philip Nore, in *Reflex*, finding his true profession as a blackmailer, even a blackmailer on the side of "good." Romantics will find the endings of *Knockdown* and *Trial Run* disappointing, for the two women, Sophie Randolph and Lady Emma, refuse to settle down with the men who love them, Jonah Dereham and Randall Drew. Many persons may question the ethics of Angelo Gilbert's lobotomy at the ending of *Twice Shy*. Conventional people will perhaps disapprove of the ending of *Forfeit* in which James Tyrone and his wife, Elizabeth, agree to Ty's having an extra-marital affair with a black woman, Gail Pominga, whom Ty cares for and respects.

Another risk Francis has taken is to move away from his areas of expertise (racing and flying, primarily) and to explore other subjects, other professions. He has, for instance, written about art (*In The Frame*), computers (*Twice Shy*), gold mining (*Smokescreen*), accounting (*Risk*) and the food industry (*Twice Shy*). When Francis decides to move into a new area, he does his homework well (always with Mary's help).

Francis has also taken risks with geographical settings. He has set his novels outside Britain in several cases: *Smokescreen* is set in South Africa; *Slayride*, Norway; *In The Frame*, Australia; *Blood Sport*, the United States; *Trial Run*, Russia. In each of these cases, Dick and Mary Francis have traveled to the locations for the books and researched social and political issues, history, geography, lifestyles, and other cultural information. The Russian setting in *Trial Run* was probably Francis' biggest risk. While the tone of the novel is depressing because of the details he gives about Russian life (the blank faces people must put on, the spying on each other, the cold, the bad food, the lack of freedom, the overwhelming government bureaucracy), Francis does not present the Russian people as villains or victims, but, rather, as human beings, who live under a different political system. One of his most interesting characters is Mr. Chulitsky, an architect who is "an unwilling mental traitor," a dedicated Communist who suffers guilt because of his love of luxury and his sense of humor (148). In *Trial Run*, Francis also cleverly contrasts the realities of life in Russia with Lady Emma's romantic ideas about socialism. In short, he uses the setting to paint a picture of another culture, but, while he decries terrorism, he does not explicitly condemn the Communist government of the U.S.S.R. Just as Harry Kemelman's insertion of Jewish materials enriches his mysteries, Francis' experimentation with subjects and settings adds an extra dimension to his novels.

Francis' recent books have been amazing because of their complexity of themes and structure. In the true spirit of adventure and risk-taking, he has not only examined new subject areas and geographical settings, but he has also experimented with multiple mysteries, with interrelated themes and with dual narrators. *Whip Hand*, for example, intertwines three separate plots: Lucas Wainwright and the horse-buying syndicates; Trevor Deansgate and the sabotaging of horses by inoculating them with a swine disease; and Nicholas Ashe and a phony charity solicitation racket. On top of this, Sid's relationships with two women (his ex-wife, Jenny, and a new friend/lover, Louise McInnes) and with two men (his partner, Chico Barnes, and his father-in-law, Admiral Roland) are explored. Besides all these characters, there are detailed portraits of minor characters: for example, young Mark Rammeleese and intrepid balloonist John Viking. All of this comes together, under Francis' expert manipulations, to become a well-integrated novel about love and courage.

Reflex deals with even more mysteries and subjects. Jockey and amateur photographer Philip Nore must solve the mystery of his past, the mystery of George Millace's personality and his death, the photographic mysteries he has inherited from Millace, and the mystery surrounding the universally disliked Ivor den Relgan's election to the position of racing steward. The novel deals also with heroin addiction, religious cults, homosexuality and homophobia, feminism, photography, and, of course, racing. What is more, Francis shows Philip's transformation from a passive, alienated, morally blasé boy to an active, caring, morally committed man. While this may seem like overkill—too many characters, plots and subjects—the novel works surprisingly well, except perhaps for too much emphasis on photography. The reason it works is that Francis is becoming more of a master, with each novel, at concise, detailed characterizations and at elaborate plotting.

Twice Shy is another complex, multi-faceted novel, and an even more successful experiment than *Reflex* because Francis uses the device of having two narrators, brothers Jonathan and William Derry, tell their stories, which take place fourteen years apart. Not only does this device allow Francis to bring in a number of subjects and issues, but it allows him to develop fascinating contrasts between the two heroes. Jonathan is a more conventional man: expert in his vocation (teaching physics) and his avocation (shooting), responsible, always in control, methodical, faithful to a wife he no longer loves. William is a free spirit: humorous, impulsive, loving, gregarious, stubborn, leery about either a steady job or a permanent relationship with a woman. The novel is rich in characterizations. For example, there is the memorable portrait of Bananas Frisby, William's friend, a corpulent, cynical chef. The book also explores the psychological aspects of gambling and, a favorite theme in Francis' novels, father-son relationships.

Francis' recent experiments in plotting have been risks—he certainly comes close to overburdening the reader with characters, issues, main plots, subplots, and technical information—but so far his risk-taking in this area has led him to push further and further the limits of the mystery form and to create books that are powerful and provocative.

Not surprising for a man who has chosen two risky professions, and who, most notably in his second profession has never been complacent, always experimenting and innovating, Francis' favorite subject in his novels is taking risks. Who, indeed, can speak with more authority on the subject? Francis presents positive images of risk-takers, he explores the reasons why people fear risk-taking and the consequences of not taking risks, and he examines, specifically, professional risk-taking and taking risks in human relationships.

A frequent plot pattern in Francis' novels is for a character who is in a nice, safe rut to find the courage to make a new, more satisfying life for himself or herself. Daniel Roke, in *For Kicks*, runs a successful stable in Australia and supports his orphaned siblings; yet his life is hard work and holds few psychic rewards. He has the satisfaction of working for others, but he has little else to make him happy. His home is a "prison" (17). When the Earl of October asks him to leave Australia and do undercover detective work in England, posing as a stable lad, Daniel agrees, although working as a stable lad holds little promise of being the good life. By risking his safety and his security, Daniel finds, ironically, through the utter brutality and degradation he must endure as a mistreated stable lad, that freedom lies within his own soul and that only by taking risks, and enduring hardships and danger for the cause of justice, can he be happy. At the end of the novel, Daniel accepts a permanent job as an undercover agent for the British government. Francis does not suggest that Daniel Roke will live happily ever after. In fact, the suicidal Gene Hawkins in *Blood Sport*, suffering from acute loneliness and paranoia, may be Daniel Roke a few years in the future. But Francis does suggest that for a person to be happy, to be sane, to be free, to be challenged, risk-taking is essential. Throughout his novels, Francis presents the risk-takers with great admiration and approval: Hilary Pimlock, Jonah Dereham, Liam O'Rorke, Steven Scott, Rob Finn, Henry Grey, Clare Bergen and others.

Those characters who are too afraid to take risks are presented by Francis as tragic figures; he examines, in his novels, the causes and consequences of their cowardice. Crispin Dereham, in *Knockdown*, cannot adapt when life proves disappointing, and he becomes an alcoholic. Eunice Teller, in *Blood Sport*, has been brought up to be dependent and decorative, not useful and independent. She takes refuge in meaningless, self-destructive game-playing. Philip Nore, in *Reflex*, had so little stability in his life as a child, passed from one set of his mother's friends to another, that passivity and going along with other people's expectations has become a way of survival. For Maurice Kemp-Lore, in *Nerve,* his family's unreasonably high expectations for him to succeed, as they had all succeeded, as riders or racers of horses, leads him to develop a fear of failure and an uncontrollable anger at persons, like Rob Finn, who have succeeded in steeplechasing. Francis sympathizes with these characters who do not have the nerve to take risks in life, even the psychopathic Kemp-Lore, and he does not minimize their suffering: depression, anger, feelings of meaninglessness, self-hatred, boredom, alienation. In most cases, Francis shows these tragic characters beginning to transcend their pasts and learning to live fully. Often, it is the example of a risk-taking character that motivates them to change and grow.

One of Francis' particular fascinations is professional risk-taking. Sometimes the characters take on new, challenging vocations, as Daniel Roke does in *For Kicks* or Neil Griffon does in *Bonecrack.* More often, they move from being amateurs, or what Henry Grey, in *Flying Finish,* calls "shamateurs," to professionals. Henry Grey, William Derry, and Philip Nore, for example, are all characters who, at first, prefer the safe, amateur, temporary, no-real-commitment status. But they find the courage to make a commitment professionally, to flying, to managing a horse empire, and to photography, respectively. Francis seems to feel that if a person is to be happy and fulfilled, he or she needs satisfying work, work that one does with intensity and one's full energies. Some jobs, like Sarah Derry's part-time job as a dentist's receptionist, in *Twice Shy,* are not enough to fill a life, not because they are part-time, but because they offer too little challenge and are entered into, understandably, without enthusiasm or commitment.

Risk-taking, for Francis, is important not only in people's work lives but also in their private lives as friends, lovers, spouses, relatives. Risks, Francis argues, are necessary to the building of honest communication, meaningful friendship, solid love. This means taking the risk of being real and open (rather than playing a safe role), having the guts to be assertive about needs and desires (as Hilary Pimlock is in *Risk*), and having the self-confidence to allow other people to be free (rather than clinging dependently or controlling through manipulation).

In *Forfeit,* Elizabeth Tyrone, a bed-ridden, ninety-percent paralyzed woman, is dependent totally on her husband, James Tyrone—financially, physically, emotionally. If Ty ceases to care for her and leaves, if he does not provide twenty-four-hour care for her and pay for the machines she needs to breathe, she cannot live. Understandably, Elizabeth feels she must play the role of saint; she does not feel she can risk being herself. Although she cannot, for physical and psychological reasons, have sex with Ty, she is not confident enough in herself or in him to discuss honestly the strain this puts on their marriage. And, while she acknowledges to herself that she is probably not being fair in expecting sexual fidelity from Ty, she is too insecure to allow him the freedom to build emotional or sexual relationships outside their marriage. By the end of the novel, however, Elizabeth learns that she does not have to be a saint for Ty to love her; that communication and assertiveness on her part will strengthen, not weaken, their marriage; and that, if she allows Ty more freedom, she will free herself from anxiety, guilt and jealousy. For all human beings, even for a person as physically limited as Elizabeth, Francis argues, risk-taking is as essential to life as breathing.

Francis' own life, as a steeplechase jockey and as a writer, is a testimonial to risk-taking. As a jockey, he faced psychological, physical and financial risks, but he pursued this challenging career, finding both disappointment (losing the 1956 Grand National) and success (becoming Britain's Champion Jockey). As a mystery novelist, Francis has taken risks from the very beginning: by using different heroes instead of a series hero; by altering and adapting, and ultimately transforming and transcending the hard-boiled mystery/suspense formula; by exploring a wide variety of subjects and settings; and by experimenting with increasingly complex plots. In his novels, Francis has examined the subject of risk-taking from the point of view of those who have nerve (the Hilary Pimlocks and the Rob Finns) and those who lack it (the Eunice Tellers and Crispin Derehams). Francis taps the sympathy we feel for those persons who are defeated by life and the admiration we have for those who beat the odds, those who have the determination and daring to live fully, whether they are jockeys or pilots, accountants or inventors, headmistresses or invalids. Given his achievements so far, it is a safe bet that Dick Francis will continue to take risks in his writing and to write about risks—unless, of course, he decides to take up the challenge of a new profession.[8]

Notes

[1]The editions of Dick Francis' works used for this study are listed below, preceded by the original publication date. References to Francis' works will be cited in the text.

1957	*The Sport of Queens* (New York: Harper & Row, 1969).	
1962	*Dead Cert* (New York: Pocket Books, 1975).	
1964	*Nerve* (New York: Pocket Books, 1975).	
1965	*Odds Against* (New York: Pocket Books, 1975).	
1965	*For Kicks* (New York: Pocket Books, 1975).	
1966	*Flying Finish* (New York: Pocket Books, 1975).	
1967	*Blood Sport* (New York: Pocket Books, 1975).	
1969	*Forfeit* (New York: Pocket Books, 1975).	
1969	*Enquiry* (New York: Pocket Books, 1975).	
1971	*Rat Race* (New York: Pocket Books, 1978).	
1971	*Bonecrack* (New York: Pocket Books, 1978).	
1972	*Smokescreen* (New York: Pocket Books, 1978).	
1973	*Slayride* (New York: Pocket Books, 1975).	
1974	*Knockdown* (New York: Pocket Books, 1976).	
1975	*High Stakes* (New York: Pocket Books, 1977).	
1976	*In The Frame* (New York: Pocket Books, 1978).	
1977	*Risk* (New York: Pocket Books, 1979).	
1978	*Trial Run* (New York: Pocket Books, 1980).	
1979	*Whip Hand* (New York: Pocket Books, 1981).	
1981	*Reflex* (New York: Putnam, 1981).	
1982	*Twice Shy* (New York: Putnam, 1982).	
1983	*Banker* (New York: Putnam, 1983).	

[2]Robert Cantwell, "Mystery Makes a Writer," *Sports Illustrated,* 25 March 1968, p. 78.

[3]In *The Question of Max* (New York: Knopf, 1976), Amanda Cross writes on p. 117:

In detective novels, which Kate had found herself reading less and less with the passing years, the detective would set out to discover. All sorts of other things would then happen, leading to one suspected criminal after another, not to mention other murders, attempted or achieved. (Kate thought particularly of Dick Francis, whose books she still did read, because she liked him and to discover how he would work the horse in this time.)

[4]John Cawelti, *Adventure, Mystery, and Romance: Formula Stories as Art and Popular Culture* (Chicago: Univ. of Chicago Press, 1976); George Grella, "Murder and the Mean Streets: The Hard-Boiled Detective Novel," *Contempora,* March 1970, rpt. in *Detective Fiction: Crime and Compromise,* ed. Dick Allen and David Chacko (New York: Harcourt Brace Jovanovich, 1974), pp. 411-428.

[5]W.H. Auden, "The Guilty Vicarage," in his *Dyer's Hand and Other Essays* (1948), rpt. in *Detective Fiction: Crime and Compromise,* p. 404.

[6]Cawelti, p. 154.

[7]Carolyn Heilbrun discusses masculinity, femininity and androgyny in *Toward a Recognition of Androgny* (New York: Harper, 1974).

[8]Since Dick Francis has demonstrated that he can write well about women, one obvious risk he could take would be to create a female hero. Also, although Francis is skilled at characterization, his criminals, on the whole, are a poorly characterized lot. If Francis took the risk of writing in the third person, he could explore the psychological dimensions of the criminal mind more fully than he has done so far.

Edmund Crispin
Photo credit, Nicholas Horne, Ltd.

Edmund Crispin

Mary Jean DeMarr

1921	(Robert) Bruce Montgomery born on 2 October in Chesham Bois, Buckinghamshire
1943	BA, Oxford University, in modern languages; also active there in musical organizations; had previously attended Merchant Taylors' School, London
1943-45	Schoolmaster, The Schools, Shrewsbury
1944	*The Case of the Gilded Fly,* first novel, written while at Oxford
1946	*The Moving Toyshop,* listed in "Haycraft-Queen Definitive Library of Detective-Crime-Mystery Fiction"
1948	*Love Lies Bleeding,* listed as alternate choice in "Haycraft-Queen Library"
1949	*Four Shakespeare Songs,* published under own name (as for all musical compositions and film credits)
1950	*Concertino, for String Orchestra*
1950	*An Oxford Requiem for Chorus and Orchestra*
1951	*The Long Divorce,* last of original group of detective novels
1952	*Concert Waltz, for Two Pianos*
1953	*Beware of the Trains,* short stories
1955-70	Edited seven anthologies, *Best Science Fiction*
1959	Film score, *Carry On Nurse;* very active in film in the following few years
1959-64	Edited two anthologies, *Best Detective Stories*
1962-65	Edited two anthologies, *Best Tales of Terror*
1967	Became detective fiction reviewer for *Sunday Times* (London)
1968	Edited science fiction anthology, *The Stars and Under*
1973	Edited anthology, *Best Murder Stories, 2*
1974	Edited science fiction anthology, *Outwards from Earth*
1977	*The Glimpses of the Moon,* last novel
1978	Died, September 15
1979	*Fen Country: Twenty-Six Stories,* most originally published in early 1950s

One of the last representatives of the Golden Age of detective fiction, Edmund Crispin created in Gervase Fen a detective worthy to stand beside such celebrated predecessors as Lord Peter Wimsey and John Appleby. Robert Bruce Montgomery (for that was Crispin's real name), was born too late: born in 1921 he was still a child during the great age of British detective fiction, and although his own career as a writer of fiction spanned the years between 1944 and his death in 1978, his characters, plots and situations always remained most akin to such forebears of an earlier generation as Dorothy L. Sayers and, especially, Michael Innes. The distinction of his style, the allusiveness of both narrative and characters, the unashamed concern for intellectual honesty, fused with a comic sensibility, marked Crispin's fiction as it marked that of Sayers and Innes. But Crispin's work is not excessively derivative; it bears a distinctive stamp.

Best known for his detective novels, Crispin also worked with distinction in several other fields. Under his real name he was the composer of serious music, a number of his compositions having been published, most of them between 1947 and 1952. This musical activity thus overlapped his first burst of writing in the detective genre: nine novels and one collection of short stories were published from 1944 to 1953. At about the time his publications in both serious music as well as, temporarily, in original detective fiction ceased, he became an active editor and anthologist in several fields, primarily science fiction and murder and detective fiction; several series of such collections appeared from 1955 to 1974, all these being published under the Crispin pseudonym. His third major creative activity was also musical, though of a different sort from his serious compositions—the creation of film scores. In this genre the best known films on which he worked were doubtless *Carry On Nurse* (1959) and a number of its successors in the *Carry On* ___ series. These musical activities, of course, gave him materials which he used with great effectiveness in his fiction, particularly in *Frequent Hearses*. Of greatest interest to his mystery readers is the fact of his long silence in that genre; after *The Long Divorce* (1951) and *Beware of the Trains* (a collection of short stories, 1953), his readers had to wait until 1977 for *The Glimpses of the Moon* and 1979 for *Fen Country*, the posthumous second collection of short stories, most of which, however, had previously been separately published in the early 1950s.

Crispin's indebtedness to his great forebears of the Golden Age is perhaps most obvious in his style—expecially if style is defined broadly to include tone as well as more limited matters of language. Crispin never took his materials seriously; his plots are ingenious, as carefully worked and as inventive as those of Agatha Christie, but his use of language, literary and allusive as well as witty, is more in the vein of Dorothy L. Sayers, Nicholas Blake and Michael Innes. His sense of discipleship is most dramatically revealed by the names he chose for himself and for one of the central characters in his first novel, *The Case of the Gilded Fly*. The character in Innes' *Hamlet, Revenge!* called Gervase Crispin gave him his pseudonymous surname and his detective's Christian name. In addition, one of the main characters, the one through whose eyes most of the action is seen, is called Nigel Blake, clearly a combination of the names of author Nicholas Blake and his detective Nigel Strangeways. And Inspector Humbleby, of the later novels and many stories, obviously pays homage through his name to Innes' Appleby.

One of the most obvious devices from the Golden Age which Crispin kept, though only for a time, was the use of maps and charts. His earliest three novels all contain them: thus *The Case of the Gilded Fly* has a plan of part of Fen's college at Oxford (75),[1] *Holy Disorders* contains a chart of part of a cathedral (90), while *The Moving Toyshop* rejoices in two diagrams—a simple map of part of Oxford and a chart of the murder scene (8 & 146). After these first three novels, however, Crispin dropped this device, perhaps a sign of his increasing confidence and independence of his masters.

Crispin's delight in language is everywhere apparent. Puns and wordplay abound, and the reader must be alert not only to follow clues but also to be sure not to miss much of the humor. Some jokes are extraneous to the plot proper and seem put there largely for the sake of the fun; for example, in *The Glimpses of the Moon*, Fen is engaged in writing a book on some contemporary British novelists and, jaded in that attempt, decides to write a novel of his own. Lonely in self-imposed solitude, he has been talking out some of his ideas to his only living companion, a cat; inspired perhaps by its lack of attention as well as by his own dislike of the novelists he has been studying, he decides his novel will be called *A Manx Ca* (287). The hasty reader, interested primarily in the extravagant plot of this novel with its many farcical twists and turns, or in the eccentric characters displayed in abundance, might skim past this passage, wondering only at the carelessness of the printers and proofreaders who had allowed such an obvious typographical error to slip past them. The more thoughtful and literary reader would pause to recall the oddity in conformation of the Manx breed of cats and then to become amused over the implied comment that something is missing from much of the most respected of contemporary fiction. But this subtle literary comment is unnecessary, not even clearly relevant to major concerns of Crispin's present novel, and it merely forms an added kind of in-joke for the observant reader to enjoy. Nevertheless, this sort of literary exuberance helps to create the very special kind of appeal that Crispin's novels have for their devoted readers.

Language is used with care by Crispin. His workmanlike narration moves his plots forward clearly and smoothly. His dialogue is also functional, generally being believable and helping to advance plots even as it is helpful in characterization, for his personages are generally given lines and manners of speech that are distinctive and appropriate. Crispin handles dialect particularly effectively. His pub scenes, for example, create local color through both narrative and dialogue even as they serve functions of exposition or narration. One rather extended quotation will illustrate. In *Buried for Pleasure*, Fen is campaigning for a seat in Parliament in a particularly benighted rural district. Early in his campaign he comes upon a pub, the Fish Inn, in a village full of ignorant but complacent souls. Both village and inn have pretensions to beauty, architectural and other, which they truly do not merit. A focal point of the decoration of the inn is a

> seascape, which showed, in the foreground, a narrow strip of shore, up which some men in oilskins were hauling what looked like a primitive lifeboat. To the left was a harbour with a mole, behind which an angry sky suggested the approach of a tornado. And the rest of the available space, which was considerable, was taken up with a stormy sea, flecked with white horses, upon which a number of sailing-ships were proceeding in various directions.
>
> This spirited depiction ... provided an inexhaustible topic of argument among the habitues of the Inn. From the seaman's point of view no such scene had ever existed, or could ever exist, on God's earth. But this possibility did not seem to have occurred to anyone at Sanford Angelorum. It was the faith of the inhabitants that if the artist had painted it thus, it must have *been* thus. And tortuous and implausible modes of navigation

had consequently to be postulated in order to explain what was going on. These, it is true, were generally couched in terms which by speakers and auditors alike were only imperfectly understood, but the average Englishman will no more admit ignorance of seafaring matters than he will admit to ignorance of women.

"No, no; I tell 'ee, that schooner, 'er's luffin' on the lee shore."
"What about the brig, then? What about the brig?"
"That's no brig, Fred, 'er's a ketch."
" 'Er wouldn't be fully-rigged, not if 'er was luffing."
"Look 'ere, take *that* direction as north, see, and that means the wind's nor'-nor'east."
"Then 'ow the 'ell d'you account for that wave breaking over the mole?"
"That's a current."
"Current, 'e says. Don't be bloody daft, Bert, 'ow can a wave be a current?"
"Current. That's a good one." (15-16)

Set pieces of this nature abound in all the novels, and they are often comic, as in this example, as well as functional in their revelation of character or their contribution to plot. In this case, a major function is that of setting up the background which is to play a particularly important role in the novel as a whole.

Quite noticeable in Crispin's work is a tendency toward the creation of long digressions which are enjoyable in themselves but which do not obviously move the plot forward and which therefore seem to some readers unnecessary interpolations. Usually, however, as in *The Case of the Gilded Fly* or *Holy Disorders*, they seem to have some connection, illusory though it may turn out to be, with the current case, and so they serve the function of misleading detective (and reader) and thus are justified—if justification be needed, for in each case the digressions are absorbing in themselves. And their inclusion is usually well motivated: least so, perhaps in *The Case of the Gilded Fly*, where Wilkes, the story-teller, simply insists on telling his tale rather in the manner of Coleridge's sailor to the wedding-guest—but for Wilkes this behavior is completely in character.

The allusiveness of the Crispin novels is everywhere apparent and explains a good deal of the delight taken in them by literary readers. In three of the novels, *The Case of the Gilded Fly, Holy Disorders* and *The Glimpses of the Moon*, each chapter is given an appropriate literary epigraph. Each of the novel titles, even those which first seem simply descriptive of some aspect of plot, turns out to be an allusion of some sort. *The Moving Toyshop* at first seems titled quite simply for its major plot device, and its epigraph has no connection with the title: *"Not all the gay pageants that breathe/Can with a dead body compare"* (from Charles Wesley, *On the Sight of a Corpse*). Thus title and epigraph together direct attention to plot device and to the fact of the novel's being a murder mystery. Eventually, however, on the novel's final page, we are given the origin of the title: lines from Pope's *Rape of the Lock* about women:

> *With varying vanities, from every part,*
> *They shift the moving toyshop of their heart*...(224)

And this alleged feminine flightiness is applied to the novel's first victim; but for her eccentricities, we are reminded, the crimes detailed in the book would not have occurred.

In plot, Crispin's novels are rather conventional stories of the Golden Age type. He delighted in apparent locked-room mysteries, and each one of his major cases, those detailed in novels rather than in short stories, at some time appears to be—and is usually referred to as—an impossible murder. Murder methods are sometimes ingenious, and on the way to the solutions we meet such strange and interesting phenomena as a "Kafka Cat" named Lavender which sees Martians in unexpected places (Divorce, 67); a church official with a bust of Pallas in a niche above his study door, a pet raven which, however, does not speak, and a wife named Lenore (Fen's bemused quotations only puzzle him, for he admits to no familiarity with Poe) (Disorders, 139-45); a surprisingly dull Black Mass (Disorders, 182-4); a nobleman improbably named Henry Fielding who has not heard of Tom Jones (Toyshop), and other assorted extravagances, some basic to plot and some mainly there for the sake of the fun, though they are generally tied into the climax in some ingenious way.

Indeed the exuberance of Crispin's imagination is nowhere more obvious than in his plotting, especially in the wild climaxes of his novels. Farcical in nature, they tend to become extended chases, as, especially, in *The Moving Toyshop*, and to draw together characters and motifs which have previously been disconnected and some of which may even have seemed merely unnecessary decorations to the main line of plotting. Crispin's last—and best as well as most complex—novel illustrates his work at its wildest and funniest. As the climax of *The Glimpses of the Moon* approaches, Fen and his friend, the Major, a stereotypical example of the type indicated by his military title, are up a large apple tree, where they wait to observe a fox hunt. From their vantage they observe not only the hunt—and, importantly, they can see almost all the locales which have previously been significant in the mystery—but a group of protesters against blood sports; both hunters and protesters are highly incompetent lots. While up the tree, Fen and the Major discuss the murders and characters involved, until interrupted by the appearance of various unexpected people and events. A conflict between hunters and saboteurs, as the protesters are referred to, is only one of the episodes to amuse them. This interchange, carried on in all the jargon of the time and striking blows in passing against both anti-war and feminist cant, is interrupted by the appearance of a herd of cattle, led by a cowman on a bicycle and followed by an eleven-year-old boy with a hazel switch. A disabled estate wagon deflects and scatters the herd. Then a motorcycle scramble arrives, and the melange now consists of milling, bellowing cattle, frantic cowmen, huntsmen and saboteurs still arguing, and motorcyclists, confused and angered at having their progress so ignominiously halted. Meanwhile, up their tree, Fen and the Major delightedly observe. Finally, the police arrive—a Cortina with the Detective Constable and his aid and a Panda with a "brace of uniformed constables" (217). A helicopter brings another familiar character, a bureaucrat who has been haplessly trying to understand why a locally famous electric pylon makes the strange noises which have caused it to become known as "The Pisser." The Rector discovers the bureaucrat apparently robbing his home and loudly raises an alarm—and only his "stentorian" voice can be heard over the general uproar. At this point, the Major comes to the rescue, dropping out of his tree, despite his arthritis, onto the back of a horse which happens to be standing conveniently beneath his branch, and taking off after the bureaucrat. Perhaps this is enough—to summarize these mad goings-on is impossible. The entire scene covers approximately fifty pages and is full of one extravagance after another; just when the convulsed reader thinks the limit has been reached, Crispin adds yet another fillip—and, most amazingly, everything fits together. Elements of all sorts from earlier episodes reappear here, and this madness leads directly to the solution of the crimes and their complete explanation. Surely the merging of fair-play solution with farcical, even slapstick, comedy is decidedly unusual, and few others (Tom Sharpe comes to mind) could have handled such disparate elements with such consummate skill.

Crispin created four significant series characters: Gervase Fen, his detective, is of course preeminent, but also significant in their different ways are Freeman and Humbleby, two professional detectives, and Wilkes, an aged Oxford don who is an almost purely comic character. Fen is central to all nine of the novels and to a majority of the short stories, in a number of which Humbleby, but not Freeman, also appears. He is always identified professionally as the "Professor of English Language and Literature in the University of Oxford" (as in his very first appearance, Fly, 9), and his behavior and attitudes as an academic place him squarely in the tradition of the eccentric detective as well as giving his creator great opportunities to satirize the academic world, matters at which we will look later. His physical appearance, consistently described in all the novels, sets him up as an eccentric: tall and lanky, with hair that tends to stand in spikes, he is blessed—or cursed—with excessive energy and wide, varied, though sometimes short-lived, interests. His fascination with insects in *Holy Disorders*, for example, is established rather tantalizingly in the novel's opening pages, is never suitably explained, but leads to a dramatic and comic, if implausible, climactic scene which seems its entire reason for being. Self-assured, self-centered, arrogant, he nevertheless has the gift of friendship, and his involvement in several cases occurs because he is called in by old friends or former students who place trust in him.

His domestic situation is established in the first of the novels, *The Case of the Gilded Fly*. Here we meet his wife, Dolly, learn of the existence of their small son, and even observe husband and wife at home with guests. His relationship with Dolly seems congenial; she is a "plain, spectacled, sensible little woman" (Fly, 63) who seems to spend most of her time knitting. While both clearly consider her prime function that of making his life comfortable, his patronizing affection for her despite their lack of common interests seems apparent: when she makes a particularly insightful remark, "Fen gazed at her with something of the triumphant and sentimental pride of a dog-owner whose pet has succeeded in balancing a biscuit on its nose" (Fly, 74). His condescending attitude toward her is another evidence of his arrogance; that she understands and herself is amused by him is made clear when, during a reconstruction of a suicide, she agrees to hold a gun to her head and then asks her husband, playfully, if she should pull the trigger. To the shocked observers she then remarks that she knows her husband's forgetfulness too well to follow his instructions blindly (Fly, 92-3). And she has no hesitation about telling him of her diagnoses of his behavior. Just after he has revealed to her the identity of a killer and has stated his own ethical dilemma, she tells him, "Nonsense, Gervase, you're exaggerating. Either way you'll have forgotten completely about it in three months. Anyway, a detective with a conscience is ludicrous. If you're going to make all this fuss about it afterwards, you shouldn't interfere in these things at all" (Fly, 181).[2] Dolly Fen is patient, sometimes amusedly forebearing with her husband, who is an obviously undependable and trying mate, but unfortunately after this first novel she hardly appears again, her existence being noted only in passing remarks. In fact, Fen's car, Lily Christine III, reminiscent of Lord Peter's automobile, which he drives with dangerous abandon, seems as close to his heart and has a larger role in the mysteries.

Fen always works in tandem with the police, though it is a matter of pride with him that he be the actual solver of the case. Frequently he drops hints early on, indicating that he has already worked out part of the solution. In quite conventional fashion, near the end of *Holy Disorders,* he challenges his friend and confidant: " 'Do you get it?' he asked." When Geoffrey confesses ignorance, Fen simply replies, "Nincompoop" (201). His arrogance, however, is justified, for his intuition and ability to sift through a mass of facts always leads him to arrive first at the solution (in the novels at least; exceptions exist in the stories). When he does, briefly, err or find himself baffled, his frustration is excessive and revealed by his hair becoming its spikiest and by his characteristic exclamations ("Oh, my dear paws!" or "Oh, my paws and whiskers!" or some other variation of the cries of Lewis Carroll's White Rabbit—see *Disorders*, 187, for example).

Although Fen is prominent in nine of the novels, his actual involvement varies somewhat. In a number of the books he shares the spotlight with a point-of-view character. In two novels, which come from near the middle of the series, there is no point-of-view character, and Fen himself thus becomes the single focal point. These novels are *Buried for Pleasure* and *Love Lies Bleeding*, both published in 1948. And in *The Long Divorce* (1951), the last of the original series, before the 26-year hiatus which was finally ended by the publication of *The Glimpses of the Moon,* Fen long seems absent, while a Mr. Datchery shares the spotlight with a woman doctor, Helen Downing. But the alert reader soon recognizes by his description that Mr. Datchery is indeed Gervase Fen, who has for some undiscernable reason disguised himself—and the reader who is not alert or knowledgeable is warned, first that Mr. Datchery has a "fictional namesake" (Divorce, 60) and then that the name comes from Dickens' *The Mystery of Edwin Drood* (102). The actual revelation comes approximately four-fifths of the way through the novel (188), but long before this it should be clear that "Datchery" is actually Gervase Fen and Helen Downing the point-of-view character.

One of Fen's more surprising characteristics is his awareness that he is fictional, and indeed the by-play between author and character sometimes becomes rather precious. The most obvious example of this sort of thing occurs in *The Moving Toyshop*. In this novel, which is itself distinguished by chapter titles all of which begin with "The Episode of ..." (for example, "The Episode of the Prowling Poet," "The Episode of the Malevolent Medium" and "The Episode of the Interrupted Seminar"), Fen spends much of his spare time, or claims he does, "making up titles for Crispin" (89). One of the titles is "A Don Dares Death (A Gervase Fen Story)" (89). A more interesting, because partly more functional, instance of this sort of interplay between author and character occurs in *The Glimpses of the Moon*, Fen's long-delayed final appearance: Fen

> paused by the mirror, from which, not unexpectedly, his own face looked out at him. In the fifteen years [sic] since his last appearance, he seemed to have changed very little. Peering at his image now, he saw the same tall lean body, the blue eyes, the same brown hair ineffectually plastered down with water, so that it stood up in a spike at the crown of his head .... At this rate, he felt, he might even live to see the day when novelists described their characters by some other device than that of manoeuvring them into examining themselves in mirrors. (47-8)

This passage both assures the reader of continuity in the treatment of the character and acknowledges the passage of time—and given Fen's own current occupation, the writing of a book on post-World-War-II writers, it seems appropriate for him to see himself in novelistic terms. But most obviously it is Crispin using Fen's long-established awareness of himself as a character in fiction to comment on the transparency of this particular device.

Occasionally a degree of testiness occurs in the relationship between author and character. In *Holy Disorders*, Fen describes a particular kind of knot, which he calls the "Hook, Line and Sinker .... Because ... the reader has to swallow it." A footnote, signed "E.C.," comments, "This is outrageous, tantamount to accusing me of invention. The knot does of course exist, is known as the sheet bend, and is much used in climbing" (89). And in *The Glimpses of the Moon* an even more pointed exchange occurs; Fen comments nastily that "Crispin writes those [Fen's cases] up ... in his own grotesque way" and "E.C.," again in a footnote, states, "I include this fragment of dialogue only at Fen's personal insistence" (263). Thus author and character come to seem almost equally real—and perhaps it is not irrelevant to remind ourselves here that "Edmund Crispin" is a pseudonym, the name created for the voice which narrates Fen's adventures.

Next to Fen, the most important continuing characters in the Crispin series are two policemen, Sir Richard Freeman and Inspector Humbleby. Freeman is Chief Constable of Oxford and appears in the three early novels set in that city, *The Case of the Gilded Fly, The Moving Toyshop* and *Swan Song*, though his role in *Swan Song* is minor. Although both Freeman and Humbleby are literate, even literary, Freeman is the more consciously, even ostentatiously, so. He and Fen are mirror images of each other: the one is a professional literary man and enthusiastic amateur detective, while the other is by profession a policeman but by avocation a literary critic. Their conversations sometimes seem comic exercises in cross-purposes, as each wants to discuss his hobby, the other's profession, while neither wants to talk shop. Each, in fact, has achieved a good deal of recognition in his sideline.

> Fen had solved several cases in which the police had come to a dead end, while Sir Richard had published three books of literary criticism (on Shakespeare, Blake and Chaucer)[3] which were regarded by the more enthusiastic weekly papers as entirely outmoding conventional academic criticism of the sort which Fen produced. It was, however, the status of each as an amateur which accounted for their remarkable success; if they had ever changed places, as a mischievous old don in Fen's college [probably Wilkes; see below] once suggested, Fen would have found the routine police work as intolerable as Sir Richard the niggling niceties of textual criticism; there was a gracious and rather vague sweep about their hobbies which ignored such tedious details. (Fly, 17)

Their relationship is partly a teasing rivalry, but the two men have a real respect and affection for each other and despite their sometimes acrimonious-sounding banter, they work together quite well. Crispin, of course, uses Freeman partly to poke fun at the pedantic earnestness of some literary critics, though Freeman's disinterested love of literature and the art of criticism remind us of their real worth.

Fen's relationship with Detective-Inspector Humbleby is not really very different from that with Freeman. Humbleby is a member of the Criminal Investigation Department, New Scotland Yard, and thus available to be called anywhere to work on a case, as Freeman, attached to Oxford, is not. He appears in *Buried for Pleasure* and *Frequent Hearses* as well as in many of the short stories, and if Freeman is an obvious derivative, by opposition, of Fen himself, Humbleby seems, as mentioned earlier, to owe his existence and some of his characteristics to the similarly named Appleby, the series detective of Michael Innes, Crispin's master. Appleby himself is referred to as a real person (again blurring the line between fact and fiction) in *Holy Disorders*, when Fen hopes fervently that the person to be sent from the Yard will not be the clearly to him repugnant Appleby (Disorders, 81). Crispin's pleasure in naming is obvious, and his making his detective a "humbler" version of Appleby is only one example. Humbleby is in no way an imitation of Appleby, in either appearance or behavior or social class. He is described, when we first meet him, as "a neat, elderly, mild-looking man with a round red face and a grey Homburg hat tilted forward over his eyes" (Buried, 85), who is easily at home in varied surroundings. His "habitual mildness of utterance" (Buried,85) and his intelligence make him a suitable foil for Fen. Despite some initial mistrust, they soon learn to respect and trust each other, and they work effectively as a team in their two novels and in a number of the short stories. In fact, in several stories, Humbleby works quite well alone, Fen either being completely absent or simply listening as Humbleby tells him of an interesting investigation. Humbleby remains, however, less colorful than either Sir Richard Freeman or John Appleby, and he is perhaps most interesting for Crispin's use of him to pay homage to Innes.

Another continuing character is very different. Wilkes, the aged don (for so he is always described) of St. Christopher's, Fen's college, appears importantly in the three Oxford novels (*The Case of the Gilded Fly, The Moving Toyshop* and *Swan Song*) and is mentioned in passing in others. He is usually a comic character, regularly butting in where he is not wanted—at least not by Fen who is at his rudest when he is around. In *The Case of the Gilded Fly*, Crispin uses him as the narrator of a ghost story which Fen does not want to hear but which it seems necessary that he and the reader know about. Despite Wilkes' age he is well informed and cogent in his narration, and through him we become familiar with an old tale which is, as he had promised, "interesting and even a little thrilling" (66). The comedy of his presentation lies less in anything he says or does than in his nonchalant ignoring of Fen's calculated rudeness to him.

In *The Moving Toyshop*, he again presents himself when Fen does not want him, this time to more comic purpose. He seems to have increased markedly in irascibility. When first we see him, he is engaged in discovering Fen, who has been attacked and left tied up. His first reaction is literary: " 'A rat!' he squeaked dramatically. 'A rat i' the arras!' " (91). Not surprisingly, Fen is irritated, but Wilkes refuses to become excited.

> "Some babyish prank, I suppose," Wilkes proceeded without perturbation. "Heh. Well, I suppose someone has to save you from the consequences of your follies." With shaky but determined fingers, he attacked the knot of the handkerchief which was tied round Fen's wrists. "All this detecting, that's what it is. People who play with fire must expect to be burned. Heh." (92)

From this point he attaches himself to Fen, following him through a series of comic chases which are made even more comic by the addition of this frail, but indomitable, elderly man in his academic gown who regularly comments on the action, sometimes cogently, sometimes irrelevantly, often irritably, but always with the disinterested interest of the scholar. And through it all, Fen keeps reiterating his annoyance at Wilkes' presence.

In *Swan Song* Wilkes' role is smaller, but it is nevertheless both comic and significant. His understanding is as keen and as malicious as ever, and his trenchant comments on some key characters, including his old antagonist Fen, are occasionally perceptive and helpful as in *The Moving Toyshop*. However, he is also responsible for misleading both Fen and the readers about a crucial alibi: when the clarification of the characters' actual actions occurs, Fen, "suddenly suspicious," inquires of the character who has misled him and is told,

> "I promised Wilkes .... He rang up on the morning after ... and particularly asked me to say I had left him shortly before the time of the murder. I admit ... that his motives were not clear to me, but he was so insistent that I thought it would be discourteous to refuse. He mentioned, I believe, that it would have the effect of confusing you, though I cannot understand why." (Swan, 191)

Here Crispin has skilfully used Wilkes to double purpose: as a comic personage and as a believable and consistent way to mystify Fen and the readers.

In the series generally, Fen is clearly the central character, Freeman, Humbleby and the others playing subordinate roles. But in some individual novels, Fen does share the reader's attention. The five novels with double foci are *The Case of the Gilded Fly, Holy Disorders, The Moving Toyshop, Swan Song, Frequent Hearses* and *The Long Divorce*. In each of these novels, although an omniscient narrative method is used, the primary consciousness through which events are observed is a character who is caught up in the mystery. In all cases they are likeable characters who either have or establish relationships of respect and affection with Fen. All are artistic or professional people and thus individuals whose sensitivity would be expected to be greater than average. Some are old friends or acquaintances of Fen's, from their Oxford days, while others are new acquaintances made during the course of a particular case.

Nigel Blake, of *The Case of the Gilded Fly*, is a journalist; a former student of Fen's, he travels to Oxford for a visit and then gets caught up in the activities of a repertory company that lead to murder. Geoffrey Vintner, of *Holy Disorders*, is an organist and composer of church music who has achieved some little reputation; an older man than Blake, he is a settled bachelor and an old classmate of Fen's. When the organist of Tolnbridge Cathedral is attacked and incapacitated during a visit by Fen to the locality, Fen calls him in as a replacement. Richard Cadogan, of *The Moving Toyshop*, is a poet who has, like Vintner, achieved reputation through his work but is unable to support himself by it. Talked out of committing suicide by his publisher, he travels to Oxford and stumbles upon a murder; he seeks help from Fen, his old acquaintance and first critic. In *Swan Song*, the point-of-view function is shared between a husband and wife team; Adam Langley is an operatic tenor involved in the first English production of a Wagner opera since the war, while his new wife, Elizabeth, a journalist, is interested in setting up a series of interviews with famous detectives (she is "hoping to do H.M., and Mrs. Bradley, and Albert Campion, and all sorts of famous people" [59]).

The use of two central consciousnesses in *Swan Song* enables Crispin to give us an insider's perspective from two different personalities with different special qualifications. Since the murders occur within an opera company, Adam's knowledge of opera and the world of music enables him to understand and interpret for us much that would be enigmatic to the outsider. Elizabeth, as an outsider, must learn much, and we learn with her, about operatic productions and personalities. But she too has special knowledge: she began her journalistic career with some popular works on criminology, and thus she is occasionally able to make perceptive comments on the action. Also, of course, the use of two narrative perspectives enables Crispin to present directly parts of the plot that otherwise might not be so easily accessible—and both Adam and Elizabeth at different times become potential victims. Also interesting is the experiment of using a woman's point of view, successfully represented by Elizabeth.

The final two novels using the device of the point of view character return to a single persona, in both cases a woman. In *Frequent Hearses*, she is Judy Flecker, secretary to the music department of a film studio—and clearly, as is the way with secretaries, the one person who keeps work and people organized. She is attractive and intelligent; and she is spunky. A long sequence, both comic and frightening, which climaxes the novel involves her in an unwanted dinner date; she feels sorry for the poor simp and agrees to have dinner with him at his family's country estate largely from pity. She borrows a car and sets off in a driving rain storm; arriving late—she has had a flat tire on the way—she is just in time to witness a murder. She instinctively pursues the murderer—into a maze. Crispin avoids the excesses of had-I-but-known-ism and, in fact, this entire episode may perhaps be read as a parody on that shopworn device.

The point-of-view character in *The Long Divorce* is Helen Downing, a young doctor striving to build a country practice despite the prejudices of the villagers. Her medical expertise is made use of and her self-possession, like Judy's, is remarkable, as she lives through a very trying time. Like Judy, she is a new acquaintance of Fen's, and like Judy she earns his respect and affection through her dignity and humanity.

Both of these female characters are potentially candidates to serve as love interest, but only Helen Downing actually fulfills this conventional function. Judy Flecker is an ingenue without a hero— for only Fen, the happily married and ineligible man, is truly a possibility; the other males are clearly not up to her standard or are otherwise disqualified. In *Swan Song*, Adam and Elizabeth do form a love-interest plot. However, only the opening chapter deals with their rather unconventional courtship, and the rest of the novel observes their adjustments to marriage. A central theme of this novel is that of healthy and unhealthy love, and they of course represent normal, if sometimes stormy, domestic love.

A rather ordinary love story is set up in *The Case of the Gilded Fly*. Nigel Blake has been attracted to Helen Haskell, an actress who is also a thoroughly nice young woman; his involvement in the case occurs, in fact, when he travels up to Oxford for the purpose of trying to meet her. He is eminently successful, and by the end of the novel they have become engaged. *The Moving Toyshop* at first seems to have a similar motif. Richard Cadogan, the poet, seems attracted to Sally Carstairs, a courageous and thoroughly nice young woman rather similar to Judy Flecker; the reader rather expects their relationship to become serious, but it never does. At the end of the novel, it is left hanging, and in *Love Lies Bleeding*, we learn that Sally has not married and that her friendship with Cadogan is just one element in her memory of a particularly exciting time (97).

Even more unconventional is *Holy Disorders*. Here as in *The Moving Toyshop*, the potential romantic male lead is in his middle age, but here he does in fact fall in love with a pretty, intelligent, eligible young woman. She is Frances Butler, daughter of the Precentor of Tolnbridge Cathedral. He torments himself with doubts about whether she could love a middle-aged man like himself and whether he wants to give up his comfortable, settled, selfish mode of existence. The reader is both amused and pitying and perhaps a bit impatient with his scruples and fears. However, it all works for the best—in a manner of speaking. Because Frances has been carefully set up as the ingenue and seems such a likeable and competent young woman (though some doubts are subtly hinted at), our irritation at Geoffrey and our concern that he might not be good enough for her are drastically and suddenly reversed when we learn that she is actually the ringleader of the gang of spies who have caused the various crimes with which the novel is concerned. The strength and ability which have made her seem admirable are now used against her and make credible the revelations of her evil activities and her leadership of the others involved. Geoffrey's doubts and hesitations now seem fortunate, and he is able to feel, rather more easily than might have been expected, that he has had a lucky escape.

Like some other detective novelists (the currently active American team writing as Emma Lathen comes immediately to mind), Crispin tends to take for a particular novel some special segment of society to examine. Thus *The Case of the Gilded Fly* describes the internal rivalries of a provincial repertory theater company, *Holy Disorders* the politics of an Anglican cathedral establishment, *Swan Song* an operatic production, *Buried for Pleasure* a parliamentary by-election, *Love Lies Bleeding* a school and *Frequent Hearses* the world of film. This list of his first seven novels reminds us of his special interests in the musical and theatrical worlds. The last two novels—*The Long Divorce* and *The Glimpses of the Moon*—cannot be so neatly categorized, though both are centered largely on Crispin's rather jaundiced view of life in the provincial English village, a theme also present in several of his earlier novels. It should also be noted that the apparent development revealed by the above listing is belied by the fact that *The Long Divorce* was published almost immediately after its predecessor, while a gap of twenty-six years separates it from *The Glimpses of the Moon*. And in addition to the themes mentioned above, through the characterization of Fen another constant theme is present—satiric treatment of the University and university life.

The University references are frequent, running through all nine novels, though seldom developed at great length. Three of the early novels are set in Oxford; in fact, the first, *The Case of the Gilded Fly*, was written while its author was still an undergraduate there. The city of Oxford is described as a "warren of relics, memorials, churches, colleges, libraries, hotels, pubs, tailors and bookshops" (9). But the actual life of the University or of Fen's college is little developed; we see into Fen's home and rooms at the college only briefly, and the theatrical settings are much more functional, even though one of the murders does take place in the college.

Crispin's disenchanted view of the University is revealed partly by his use of Wilkes, who steals Fen's whisky and his bicycle at various times in various books, following him around as he tries to detect, and telling long stories which add flavor to the novels and help to mislead the bemused reader. Alluding to the old question of how long it would take a group of monkeys, pecking at random, to type out the plays of Shakespeare, Fen tells of "a sort of enclosed pen, inside which [were] twelve typewriters on a table, and twelve monkeys, who sat about in attitudes of bored reverie or copulated in an uninteresting manner." When asked what this is, Fen replies,

> "Either the Junior Common Room,... or Wilkes' enclosure. The latter, I suspect... Wilkes, who has a practical mind, has hired it from the college for a very great number of years to come. But so far not a single Shakespeare sonnet, not a line of a sonnet, not a word of a line, or even two consecutive letters has been

produced. The monkeys have to be replaced as they die off, of course... In the meantime, they show little inclination to approach the typewriters, and content themselves with behaving in a normal though acutely embarrassing way" (Fly, 127).

The disinterested scholarship pursued at the University, then, is too often frivolous—or worse.

And Fen seems little more convinced of the value of his own work. He is versatile, moving throughout the periods of English literature, having published books on minor writers of the seventeenth century and on the Medieval poet William Langland, books described as "conventional academic criticism" (Fly, 17). But he maintains, doubtless shocking his more traditional colleagues, "maliciously, but with some truth that [detective stories] were the only form of literature which carried on the true tradition of the English novel" (Fly, 17). He always deprecates his serious work, and that this is not just modesty—indeed he is far from being a modest man regarding anything he really cares about, primarily his detecting—is indicated by his behavior in the last novel of the series, *The Glimpses of the Moon*. In this book, he is on sabbatical, trying to write a study of contemporary English novelists, and from time to time he struggles with phrases and evaluations of some of these writers, always rejecting each new inspiration.

> "Mortimer, Penelope," Fen said.
> "Different again," he told the cat, "different again in Penelope Mortimer, whose achievement is marred, is heightened, has been to, in part derives from ...."
> "In part derives from an acute apprehension of," Fen muttered...
> An acute apprehension of everyday reality," Fen said,...
> Whom had the sentence been going to be about? Never mind, it would do for almost anyone. (65-6)

Thus it seems clear that, to Fen in this study, what is important is the impressiveness of the language used, not the substance of its meaning—surely a severe indictment of this kind of scholarship. And Fen's dislike of modern literature and disgust with the prospect of writing about it are underscored at the end of the novel when he delightedly drops the entire project, explaining about "his publisher's voluntary liquidation. 'Now that there's not likely to be any money, nothing would induce me to go on with it .... I was only doing it to fill in time' " (287).

Fen seems to take his work as a teacher little more seriously than his scholarship. Only once do we see him actually at work as a don—and that one presentation is extremely brief. In *The Moving Toyshop*, as the plot is thickening and he finds himself in need of more confederates than he has already collected, he enters the lecture hall. But he uses his audience only as an opportunity to enlist several students to aid him and his friends in the chase which follows. He describes his lecture as a "troublesome duty" which he has no intention of carrying out. The women students diligently write in their notebooks the one phrase he utters which might accidentally have relevance to their academic pursuits, and the men students ogle the attractive young woman who is with him (158-9). At least the women do reveal some concern for their purported reason for being there, but even they seem rather unpleasantly earnest. In all, then, the novels seem to suggest that while Oxford is a very pleasant place to live, it is full of intelligent, dilatory people who have acquired their learning by some process resembling osmosis. Most of them certainly don't seem to work at it.

Like the treatment of Oxford, the depictions of the theatrical, operatic and film worlds come from intimate personal involvement. Crispin had special knowledge, derived from the experiences of Bruce Montgomery, serious composer and, doubtless for money, film composer. Thus his revelation of politics, in-fighting, backbiting and general mediocrity in these various spheres carries real conviction. In most cases, he contrasts those actors or musicians who are primarily concerned with the good of the production with those who are mainly involved with their own selfish egotism. Thus *The Case of the Gilded Fly* depicts a repertory company set at loggerheads by one beautiful but nasty young actress and *Swan Song* an operatic production nearly ruined by the demands and superciliousness of a leading male singer. *Frequent Hearses* adds to this gallery a prominent film family—an actress, a director, a cameraman and a worker in the script department, the latter the only decent one of the lot, who thoughtlessly destroy an aspiring young actress, unconcernedly driving her to suicide because she has gotten in their way. When they begin to be murdered, the reader cannot feel their loss very keenly.

Of these three novels, the most sharply satirical is *Frequent Hearses*, the one dealing with the film industry. Fen's initial involvement comes about because he is technical advisor for a projected film dealing with the life of Alexander Pope. The pretentiousness and shallowness of the film world are suggested in a brief exchange regarding the leading actress mentioned above; an employee of the studio defines her status as "one of the First Ladies of British films." "Well, I think it means that she's no longer obliged to make films in which she has to show her legs .... And that saves everyone a lot of trouble, because they always did have to be filmed very carefully if they were going to come out looking like anything at all" (27).

The chaos of commercial film production is vividly portrayed, and in passing we see glimpses of various stages of the process. There is, for instance, an extended description of the detailed and careful preparations for the shooting of what turns out to be only a snippet of action (*Hearses*, 44-5) and an explanation of the process whereby the music and action are finally melded together. The latter, depicting work with which the author was intimately familiar, is particularly interesting; the procedure is presented as mechanical, inhumane, unnatural and ultimately dishonest:

> Upon the screen ... two lovers, bereft of their sound-track, mouthed preposterously at each other; in the sound engineer's glass-fronted control-room, ... the composer sat complacently imbibing through a substantial loudspeaker the noises he had contrived. The ticker on the wall spelled out the seconds; Griswold, with headphones adjusted and a cigarette in his mouth, glanced rapidly and continuously from the players to the score to the ticker to the screen; and music appropriate to its erotic context—susurration of strings, plangency of French horns, the oily sweetness of tubular bells and the aqueous ripples of harps—filled and overflowed the room. Not a bad score, Judy conceded: in his concert works Napier was a somewhat acrid modernist, but like most such composers he unbuttoned, becoming romantic and sentimental when he was writing for the films. (Hearses, 150-1)

The late, and very complex, *Glimpses of the Moon*, though not set among theatrical people, subtly develops a related theme, by contrasting (implicitly at least) bad with good art, honest artists with sell-outs, and those who are naive with those who are knowing in their exploitation of bad art. There is, first, another film composer, Broderick Thouless, resentful over being relegated to the creation of music for monsters.

> For him, type-casting had set in with a highbrow horror film called *Bone Orchard*.... By nature and inclination a gentle romantic composer whose idiom would have been judged moderately progressive by Saint-Saens or Chaminade, Thouless had launched himself at the task of manufacturing the *Bone Orchard* score like a berserker rabbit trying to topple a tiger, and by over-compensating for his instinctive mellifluousness had

managed to wring such hideous noises from his orchestra that he was at once assumed to have a particular flair for dissonance, if not a positive love of it. Ever since then he had accordingly found himself occupied three or four times a year with stakes driven through hearts, foot-loose mummies, giant centipedes aswarm in the Palace of Westminster and other such grim eventualities, a programme which had earned him quite a lot of money. (38-9)

Fen's own abortive attempt at a study of modern novelists whom he dislikes has already been mentioned; he is another of the creative people in this novel who are doing, or trying to do, work that they know to be dishonest. More samples of meretricious art are supplied us by the wide variety of inane commercials innocently and joyously sung constantly by the stereotypical bluff Major. Mentioned in passing (another example of Crispin's exuberant and luxuriant fancy) is a Father Hattrick, a Catholic priest who, under the name of F.X. Christopher, writes books on Charles I and his era. These books are described as both scholarly and popular, but no value judgment is made on their worth (150).[4] At the other end of the spectrum are the Bale sisters, Titty and Tatty, elderly, dotty spinsters, who possess a picture that they fondly believe to be a Botticelli, though it is clear to everyone else that it is a late and very bad work. This portrait is annually trotted out for a summer festival at which the Bale sisters guard the tent in which it is placed, so that all who wish may, for a small fee, enter, view it, and meditate on religion. While the Botticelli is clearly as good an example of bad art as Crispin's works afford, the Bale sisters, though comic, are treated sympathetically, almost lovingly. They truly believe in the value of the painting and they wish to share it with others; there is nothing of dishonesty in them, unlike the film composer and even Fen. Crispin can be forgiving of those who are merely eccentric in their lack of esthetic sense—even while making them hilariously funny.

Crispin reserves some of his sharpest and funniest strokes for village life and villagers. And although the last two novels, *The Long Divorce* and *The Glimpses of the Moon*, are the most obviously centered around their depiction of village life, this theme also occurs in a number of other novels, especially in *Buried for Pleasure* (the political novel), *Holy Disorders* (based on a provincial cathedral) and *Love Lies Bleeding* (the school novel). In all cases we see the stupidity, cupidity and often brutality as well as the eccentricities and pleasures of small town life.

In *Buried for Pleasure* Fen is engaged in the totally

uncharacteristic activity of running for Parliament. He stumps a rural area filled with such characters as a naked escaped lunatic who frequently startles the unwary traveler, an innkeeper engaged in completely renovating his ancient inn (largely by destroying it), a surprisingly docile poltergeist and a "non-doing pig" which eats but does not gain and stubbornly finds its way home again each time it is sold, a kind of porcine Lassie-Come-Home. Fen engages a campaign manager, who must instruct him in the most elementary methods of winning the support of his potential constituents. Fen, however, learns quickly; as he observes, "The command of *cliché* comes of having had a literary training" (44). Although at first his cause seems hopeless, Fen gradually comes to fear that his evasion of all issues and the fulsomeness of his use of the cliché will prevail, and he may actually be elected. To make certain that this horrid eventuality does not come to pass, he tells an election rally exactly what he thinks of the voters. Instead of flattering them, as had been his wont, he now explains to them how stupid they are and how their silly acceptance of the political commonplaces he and the other candidates have been feeding them might lead them to fascism. It is a long and harsh indictment of the English public and its political system (157-61). But incredibly, the speech sways the election in his favor: because the insults are impersonal, the voters simply enjoy them, and, admiring the skill with which they are flung, reward the unhappy speaker with a one-vote plurality which Fen has some difficulty in upsetting.

The Long Divorce gives another perspective on village life. Here we become acquainted with a village plagued by anonymous letters which lead to murder and suicide. In an interesting revelation of the rules of village life, a young girl explains to an outsider why it is that the anonymous letters are so disruptive: "In a village, everyone knows all the scandal about everyone else—but of course people take terrific care it shan't get to the ears of anyone it'd hurt and upset" (19). Thus the writer of the poison-pen letters has broken the basic code, taking advantage of his inside-knowledge, and all sorts of suspicion and damage result. Additionally, the novel reveals the prejudices of the people. Two central characters are doctors, a woman and a man. The villagers, of course, distrust the woman's competence, while the man has a thriving practice; as it turns out, the woman is both a good doctor and a good person, while the male physician is an unscrupulous bounder.

The sorts of changes brought to such villages by "progress" are depicted and become crucial to the plot. As Fen ("Mr. Datchery") first sees Cotten Abbas, he observes its

> prosperous look—but its prosperity, Mr. Datchery thought, was less that of a working village than that of a village which has been settled by the well-to-do: in a population which could scarcely number more than a couple of hundred, it was obviously the invading middle class that ruled, badly weakened now by post-war conditions, but still hanging on. To them, no doubt, in their between-wars heyday, the preservation of the village's beauty must be ascribed. And their houses, eloquent of a time more prolific of servants than ours, were to be glimpsed through trees and past roof-tops, hemming the place in like an encircling force. (Divorce, 25-6)

The middle-class rulers are still, it develops, trying to enforce their standards of architectural purity, and as a result are at war with those who must actually work and live there. A saw-mill and a conventicle, eyesores to the snobs, are functional and in one case actually necessary to many in the village. But attempts to rid the village of these excrescences, as they seem to the middle-class citizens, cause enmities and ultimately wreak havoc with the peace of the village.

Much more horrid than the cluster of villages in *Buried for Pleasure* or the artificially preserved but troubled village in *The Long Divorce* is what we meet in *The Glimpses of the Moon*. When this novel opens, a particularly awful murder has already occurred; after death the body has been decapitated and otherwise mutilated. We learn that the victim had merited his fate—his great hobby was torturing animals, killing them in particularly refined ways. The man accused of the murder is a stupid but pathologically hard-working man who loves animals and has been outraged by the evidences of abuse he has discovered. Another murder follows, and in this case also the head and other parts of the body are removed. It turns out that two separate murderers are at work—but those sadists and killers are not the only particularly distasteful inhabitants of the community. Two women of voracious and depraved sexual tastes are involved, as are a number of other eccentric and often unpleasant characters. By contrast the Misses Titty and Tatty Bale and the Major of the constantly sung commercials seem almost ordinary and endearing.

Other elements of satire are brought into the climax of the novel, partially described above as a typically wild Crispin melange of characters, chases and general craziness. The fox hunt by a particularly inept cadre and the group of protesters against the hunt allow Crispin to underscore both the theme of cruelty to animals and his distaste for several social phenomena of the 1970s. Two especially amusing characters are Mr. Dodd, the pharmacist, who is putative leader of the protesters but who is ineffectual and finally flees when his reformist attitude angers his co-protesters, and a young woman usually referred to as the "hunt saboteuse." When Mr. Dodd's treachery becomes apparent, she hisses, "Male chauvinst mouse," at him, inspiring Fen to the realization that

> Although she could only be about sixteen or seventeen, her package of progressive *idées reçues* was already a bit out of date, not to say rather blurrily cross-referenced. What would it be next, he wondered? Namibia? The perennial C.I.A.? Chile again? The Black Papers on Education? (Glimpses, 216)

Crispin's scornful attitude toward faddishness in political action is apparent.

Life in rural England, then, as depicted by Crispin, is far from idyllic, as also, however, life in Oxford. Throughout these studies of the inanities and insanities of mid-twentieth century life, Crispin frequently attacks pretentiousness and dishonesty: in art of various sorts, in relationships between people, and in individuals' senses of their own identities. But almost always these attacks are made in good humor. Crispin reserves his harshest treatment for those who are knowingly cruel, whether physically or emotionally, to other living beings. Unfortunately, he finds much cruelty to be observed. In fact, he generally reserves the position of first victim for such a cruel person. But the tone of the novels, as I hope my quotations have suggested, is not bitter or harsh; the good-natured satire of the foibles of the worlds their author knew is what most readers most clearly remember.

In 1974 and thus before the long-awaited publication of Crispin's masterwork—though he was aware of rumors about it and even of the existence of chapters—another master in the field of detective fiction summed up Crispin's contribution, calling him "the last and most charming of the Farceurs":

> Crispin's work is marked by a highly individualistic sense of light comedy, and by a great flair for verbal deception rather in the Christie manner. If he never gives the impression of solid learning that can be sensed behind Innes' frivolity, he is also never tiresomely literary. At his weakest he is flippant, at his

best he is witty, but all his work shows a high-spiritedness rare and welcome in the crime story.⁵

This even-handed assessment accurately indicates both strengths and weaknesses of Crispin's detective fiction. One does not, perhaps, go to a Crispin novel for profound comment on the world, though comment there is. One goes to Crispin for the delight to be found in skilled, witty, allusive use of the English language, for the fun of observing people and events a good deal exaggerated from ordinary life, and for good-natured amusement at our human foibles. But most of all, one goes to Crispin for laughter. One may regret that he wrote no more, but what he did write is sufficient to give many readers much pleasure and to make secure his place in the canon of detective fiction.

Notes

¹Crispin's detective fiction is listed below, each title preceded by year of original publication and followed by bibliographical data for the editions used in this study. Additionally, since several novels originally had other titles in the United States, those alternate titles are listed. All quotations will be cited in the text, using, when clarity requires, the abbreviations given after the entries below:

1944	*The Case of the Gilded Fly* (Elmsford, N.Y.: London House & Maxwell, 1970). US: *Obsequies at Oxford* (Fly)
1945	*Holy Disorders* (New York: Walker & Co., 1979) (Disorders)
1946	*The Moving Toyshop* (Elmsford, N.Y.: London House & Maxwell, 1970). (Toyshop)
1947	*Swan Song* (New York: Walker & Co., 1980). US: *Dead and Dumb* (Swan)
1948	*Buried for Pleasure* (Philadelphia and New York: Lippincott, 1949). (Buried)
1948	*Love Lies Bleeding* (New York: Walker & Co., 1981).
1950	*Frequent Hearses* (New York: London House & Maxwell, 1971). US: *Sudden Vengeance*. (Hearses)
1951	*The Long Divorce* (London: Victor Gollancz Ltd., 1951). US: *A Noose for Her* (Divorce)
1953	*Beware of the Trains* (New York: Walker & Co., 1962).
1977	*The Glimpses of the Moon* (New York: Walker & Co., 1977). (Glimpses)
1979	*Fen Country: Twenty-six Stories* (New York: Walker & Co., 1979).

²The contrast with Lord Peter Wimsey's pains and scruples at the end of *Busman's Honeymoon* and Harriet's sympathetically delicate treatment of him is doubtless an implied comment on the excessively complex and sensitive sensibilities of Sayers' characters.

³Fen, the professional, seems to stick to safer, because less known or minor, writers, but Freeman, the amateur, attacks three of the most complex and thoroughly studied figures of English literary history. And we are led to believe that the amateur's contributions are at least as valuable as those of the professional—in clear denigration of the pretensions of academic critics.

⁴References to Charles I are frequent in this novel, which contains two corpses beheaded after death, but these allusions to the only English king executed by beheading seem merely playful and are not linked except thematically to the mutilations of the present bodies. Crispin's humor, in this novel especially, becomes rather macabre.

⁵Julian Symons, *Bloody Murder: From the Detective Story to the Crime Novel: A History* (London: Faber & Faber, 1972), p. 152. Symons' respect for Crispin is additionally shown by the fact that Symons' self-deprecatory comment on himself has appended to it a complimentary but fair and objective evaluative footnote signed Edmund Crispin (188-9).

H.R.F. Keating
Photo copyrighted by Fay Godwin. Reprinted with permission.

H.R.F. Keating

Meera T. Clark

1926	Henry Reymond Fitzwalter Keating born on 31 October in St. Leonards-on-the-Sea, Sussex.
1940-44	Attended Merchant Taylor's School, London.
1945-48	Served in the British Army
1948-52	Attended Trinity College, Dublin; received Vice-Chancellor's Prose Prize
1953	Married Sheila Mary Mitchell; three sons and one daughter.
1953-56	Sub-Editor, *Wiltshire Herald,* Swindon
1956-58	Employed by *Daily Telegraph,* London
1958-60	Employed by *Times,* London
1959	Published *Death and the Visiting Firemen,* first mystery
1964	Published *The Perfect Murder,* first Inspector Ghote mystery; recipient of Crime Writers Association Golden Dagger
1965	Recipient of Edgar Allan Poe Award of Mystery Writers of America
1967	Crime books reviewer, *Times,* London
1969	Published with Maurice Keating *Understanding Pierre Teilhard de Chardin*
1970	Recipient of short story prize of *Ellery Queen's Mystery Magazine.*
1970-71	Chairman of Crime Writers Association
1981	Published *Go West Ghote*

(For a listing of Keating's non-mystery fiction, his radio plays and his mystery criticism, see footnote 3 to this essay.)

H.R.F. Keating—the name may not be as well known as those great money spinners like Agatha Christie and Ngaio Marsh, but among the cognoscenti of detective fiction it is well known and loved. Indeed, Keating's novels featuring Inspector Ghote (pronounced Gotay) of the Bombay C.I.D.—on which his claim to distinction rests—can be read as perfectly orthodox whodunits in the British genteel tradition as well as satirical protraits of the variegated aspects of that dauntingly complex country—India.[1] Keating's Ghote novels, however, go beyond the narrow constraints of satire, for each novel, while it is very specific in its local settings, also deals with a universally applicable philosophical theme.

Fortunately, this underlying philosophical concern never becomes too weighty for the traditional whodunit form, because Keating has a delightful and unfailing comic sense reminiscent of the great eighteenth century novelists. The chief instrument in Keating's comic vision is his mastery of that curious linguistic mutation—Indian English. Keating's ear for the nuances of Indian English and the epistemological assumptions implicit in its contortions make him a genuinely original stylist.

Of the twenty detective novels Keating has written, thirteen feature Inspector Ghote of the Bombay C.I.D. Besides the novels, Keating has published innumerable short stories, most notably in *Ellery Queen's Mystery Magazine*.[2] Most of them feature Inspector Ghote, and some Mrs. Craggs, the cockney charwoman, whose powers of observation and reasoning surpass those of her social betters. Besides detective fiction and several essays on his craft, Keating has written three novels, three radio plays, and in collaboration with Maurice Keating, a guide to Pierre Teilhard de Chardin's *The Phenomenon of Man*.[3] However, in spite of his varied and sizable output, Keating's fame rests mainly on his creation of Inspector Ghote.

Keating's philosophical approach is consistent with his interest in the philosophy of Teilhard de Chardin, a French philosopher who is notable for his effort to trace the evolution of man both, as he puts it, from "within and without." A Jesuit by training, and a competent paleontologist by choice, Teilhard's philosophy is notable for his synthesis of evolutionary biology, derived from Darwin, with his formulation of how man's consciousness evolved from his origins in the humble amoeba. While tracing the biological history of man in accordance with scientific facts, Teilhard emphasizes the importance of the origin, the growth and the complexity of man's interior life. According to Teilhard:

> With the advent of the power of reflection everything is changed. The phenomenon of man takes definite shape. The cell becomes someone. After the grain of matter, the grain of life, and then at last we see the grain of thought.
> ... What is spontaneously mental (or spiritual) is no longer an aura round the physical; it becomes a principal part of the phenomenon (46-47).

In other words, Teilhard sees man's power of reflection, and his awareness of that power, as of primary importance in his evolutionary history.

It is no wonder then that Keating's Ghote novels are notable not for their fast-paced action or intricacy of plot but for the complexity of his characters' interior lives. This is particularly true of Keating's portrayal of Inspector Ghote. The central paradox about Ghote is that while his physical presence remains shadowy—we never learn what he looks like—we come to know every shade, every nuance of his feelings, be it his acute discomfort at the overwhelming stridency of the American voice or his embarrassment at being caught by his superior officer giving money to an itinerant beggar. Keating is not above devoting a whole page to every permutation of Ghote's inner life, so that although Ghote's physical presence is elusive, his thoughts and feelings are brought vividly to life.

Although Ghote is enshrined in the pantheon of great detectives of literature—Otto Penzler has included an essay by Keating on Ghote in his book *The Great Detectives*—Ghote's very presence among the heroes of detection like Sherlock Holmes, Lord Peter Wimsey and Roderick Alleyn redefines the concept of greatness.[4] For great in the old traditional sense, Ghote is most definitely not. He does not command an imposing physical presence like Holmes, nor is he aristocratic like Wimsey, nor outre in appearance like Hercule Poirot. Not only is Ghote's physical presence innocuous, even his intellect does not inspire awe in the reader, his colleagues or his wife. In fact, everyone Ghote meets tends to have the upper hand over him; he is a much put-upon man.

How then has Ghote managed to take his place among the colorful, showy great detectives of tradition? Ghote is great simply because he is so intensely, ordinarily human. And that, in an increasingly dehumanized world, is no mean feat. Indeed, he redefines the meaning of greatness by his very lack of anything outstanding, anything heroic—for greatness according to Keating resides in being intensely human with all the heart-searching it implies. Indeed, if we agree with Teilhard de Chardin that consciousness is the measure of man, then Ghote, whose consciousness is exceptionally complex and constantly growing, exemplifies what it means to be human.

In his essay on Ghote, Keating assumes the point of view of a supposedly real inspector of Bombay Police who speculates, in his inimitable Indian English, on the authenticity of Ghote, "I am always wondering: is the fellow a real top-notch C.I.D. Inspector at all? Sometimes I am thinking he must be no more than an idea in the writer fellow's head" (112). With fiendish cleverness—a characteristic of most of his work—Keating goes on to reveal the genesis and development of Ghote's character through the irate speculations of the supposed inspector of police who is angry because Ghote gets all the best cases and gets sent abroad, regardless of his junior position.

What emerges from these speculations is that Ghote is as vague physically to his creator as he is to the reader. "Mr. Keating in the beginning saw a pair of shoulders only, thin and bony shoulders with a burden always upon them .... I do not believe the fellow altogether knows what like are Ghote's feet." Ghote's age, like his feet, is nebulous, and he has a son, Ved, who "has grown from five years to twelve only during the whole eleven-twelve years of Ghote's cases" (113). Then there is the question of Ghote's wife, Protima, consistently described as beautiful and elegant, although how Ghote, a Mahrashtrian, came to have a Bengali wife is not explained. Also, Keating who has an uncanny ear for the comedy of Indian English, apparently came very close to committing an outrageous blunder when he almost called Ghote, Ghosh—a Bengali name which "would be like saying that that so famous Commissaire Maigret of the Paris police force was called all the time Boris Ivanovitch" (114). Finally, it appears that Keating had no intentions of writing a series featuring Ghote when he wrote the first Ghote book, *The Perfect Murder*; however, when the book won the Crime Writer's Association award, it set him off on a Ghote odyssey.

This odyssey—both physical and mental—fleshes out Ghote's shadowy physical presence. What his physical description lacks in concrete detail is more than made up for by Keating's acute eye for the Indian landscape, both physical and cultural, and his finely tuned ear for Indian speech patterns. In every Ghote novel, the climactic scene describes with vivid detail a uniquely Indian scene or event; for example, the first thunderstorm heralding the monsoon at the end of a long hot summer in *The Perfect Murder* and the colorful festival, Holi, in *Inspector Ghote's Good Crusade*. What is more remarkable, the scene functions as a dramatic turning point in Ghote's own psychological resolution.

Keating's ear for Indian English which encompasses all the comic and epistemological possibilities inherent in it enables him to register every vibration in Ghote's very intricate psyche. And it is this minutely detailed portrait of Ghote's inner life which makes Ghote so real and human. For example, how can we not identify with Ghote, not only in his specific Indianness but in his universal humanness when he agonizes over his cheap suitcase at Heathrow airport: "With a growing feeling of hot shame, he saw that every single piece of luggage that had so far appeared was infinitely more respectable in appearance than the big, light brown, rather cardboardy—no very cardboardy suitcase" (Peacock, 8)? After an extended, very funny scene in which Ghote tries pathetically to avoid owning up to the cheap suitcase, but is finally forced to when the porter holds it up for all to see asking if the owner would come forward and identify it, Ghote has to face another humiliating contretemps. This time he finds that "his feet were being weepingly embraced" by the plump, noisily emotional form of Vidur Datta who claims to be his "wife's cousin's husband" and who wants him to investigate the disappearance of his wife's beautiful and westernized niece known as the Peacock. Just when the scene is at its noisiest, a British bobby sent to receive the Indian representative to the Emergency Conference, The Smuggling Of Dangerous Drugs, accosts him. Ghote's humiliation is complete:

> But why, oh why, had Cousin Vidur chosen just the very moment when he was being sought out to make that ridiculous, undignified, over-emotional un-British scene? The constable could not but have heard and seen. At the very outset of the visit he had become a figure of fun. (Peacock, 17)

What is involved here forms the underlying theme of the novel—Ghote's pathetic lack of self-assurance attributable both to the colonial heritage which has taught him that everything British (including their famed glacial persona) is necessarily superior to his middle class status which enables him to *recognize* but not *buy* quality things like a genuine leather suitcase. However, by the end of his stay in England during which he successfully investigates the disappearance of the Peacock, a case which even Scotland Yard had failed to solve, Ghote is disabused of his illusions about England. He finds that the real England, as opposed to his dreams of England based on readings in English literature, is as flawed as any other place in the world. Ghote's voyage to England becomes one more voyage of discovery—of truth in its various, elusive forms.

One of the truths—the vindication of Ghote's essential integrity and humanness—is put to the test in every novel. Ghote's humanness receives a constant battering, because, although he is persistently and courageously human, he is constantly afraid of exposing his humanness in a society so bound by orthodoxy and bureaucracy that being human is perceived as a sign of weakness. The police force, of which Ghote is a diligent member, has to maintain the image of being tough, and Ghote is always afraid of being found too soft-hearted. Thus, in the opening chapter of *Inspector Ghote Trusts the Heart*, Ghote has just succumbed to the whiny machinations of a little beggar boy with a withered leg:

> He pulled out the two-paise piece and pressed it hastily, stealthily, into the boy's thin-fleshed hard, little expectant hand. There. It was done.
> Freed of a burden, he swung sharply away and prepared to mount the steps at a trot.
> "Ah. It is Ghote. Inspector Ghote."
> A cold lurch of dismay froze him into stillness. Spotted. Found out. A hardhearted inspector of the Bombay C.I.D. seen falling for the totally transparent wiles of a mere boy of a beggar (Heart, 2).

However, as it turns out, the Commissioner of Police, who catches him in the act of giving money to a beggar, wants him for a special job for which Ghote's compassionate nature is precisely suited:

> "Inspector, this is a job that may well require the utmost tact. It needs a man of feeling. I saw you giving to that beggar boy as I drove up: I'm glad to find at least one of my officers hasn't let his duties rub away all the heart in him" (Heart, 3).

The Commissioner wants Ghote to investigate a kidnapping in the household of his friend, a wealthy industrialist. The kidnappers, who had obviously intended to kidnap the industrialist's son for ransom had, instead, taken a poor tailor's son by mistake, because the rich man's pampered son and the poor tailor's ragged little boy who had been playing together had exchanged clothes.

The crux of the novel hinges on whether the poor tailor's son is dispensable and therefore should be used as a pawn in stern police measures to punish the kidnappers who would not hesitate to kill the boy if the industrialist did not pay ransom and called the police instead. Ghote has a doubly onerous task: he must induce the industrialist to dredge up the remnants of compassion unextinguished by his long ruthless financial climb and pay at least half the ransom asked for, and he must convince the Commissioner not to take drastic police action which would scare the kidnappers into killing the boy. His task is further complicated by the uxorious industrialist's beautiful and greedy young wife who is loath to see one *paise* of her husband's money go to succor of the poor, and who uses all her sexual wiles to harden her husband's heart.

The industrialist vacillates between compassion and rationalization, but, finally, the Commissioner's and his wife's counsel to leave it all to the police and deny ransom prevails. Ghote is dismissed from the case. However, in the middle of his professional and personal defeat, he has a blinding insight about the location of the kidnappers (no mean task in the teeming city of Bombay) and decides to follow up the clue on his own. He finds the kidnapped boy—a starved, filthy, apathetic, barely breathing huddle of bones. At this exact moment the Commissioner appears, successful in his own ruthless, efficient methods, and rewards Ghote for his intelligence and disinterested humanitarianism by sending him up against the Disciplinary Board for insubordination: "Nobody, Inspector, nobody slides out of obeying orders I give him and then goes off on his own sticking his dirty little fingers into my case" (Heart, 200).

The Commissioner's attitude—punishing Ghote for insubordination rather than rewarding him for "trusting his heart" and showing his initiative—devastates Ghote. But again, what provides a catharsis for the novel and personal redemption for Ghote are brief flashes of human contact. In the middle of arresting the kidnappers, Ghote manages to buy a bobbing red balloon and put it in the hand of the little boy in an attempt to rouse him from his apathy. The Commissioner's rigidity is contrasted to little Pidku's flicker of life nurtured by Ghote's wonderful understanding of the child's needs:

> He took Ghote's mute burden from him with stiff precision, turned and walked smartly out into the street, the red balloon still clutched in Pidku's hand bobbing and bouncing absurdly about him. Outside the proprietor of Trust X stood with the old tailor, the richly suited tall figure and the lean-shanked, single-darned one side by side. As the ambulance driver waited for his companion to open the back door of their vehicle, Ghote saw the tailor put out a tentative hand to his son and gently touch him. And then at last Pidku smiled.
>
> * * *
>
> Ghote felt his lethargic gloom sliding away like great, stiff cakes of dust under the first rain of the monsoon (Heart, 200-201).

Over and over again, Keating makes the point that humanness consists not in following abstractions, bureaucratic or philosophical, but in one individual confronting another and doing his duty by the other. As the wealthy proprietor of Trust X explains his decision to pay the ransom for the tailor's boy: "It is that I have spoken to the father. He and I have spoken face to face. I must pay. I will pay" (Heart, 69). In Inspector Ghote's Good Crusade this theme is set in the context of a larger, very current subject—American philanthropy. An American millionnaire, Frank Masters, who has set up a Foundation for the care of juvenile vagrants in the city of Bombay and who is described by everyone as a good man, is murdered. No one can understand the motive for this murder—a quantity of arsenic has supposedly been slipped into the meal he has eaten.

The novel shows Ghote's deductive powers turning into sentimental mush by his admiration for Master's philanthropy. Wonderful comedy follows as Ghote, neglecting his real duty—that of investigating the murder—attempts to emulate Master's philanthropy by giving five hundred rupees, saved over many months in order to buy his wife a much needed refrigerator, to a fisherman's paramour who spins him a tale of woe. When Ghote looks back at the woman, "It came as no real surprise to see that the enormous paramour was sitting visibly quivering, even at this distance, with great tides of irrepressible laughter" (Crusade, 186). Not only is the paramour overcome with hilarity at Ghote's gullibility, she spends all the money not on paying off her debts, but on a riotous festival—Holi. This great, rambunctious, Bacchanalian festival, as anthropologists have shown, is designed to reverse conventional social hierarchy. In the colorful free-for-all of this festival, license is granted to generally humiliate those in power.

Ghote, appropriately enough as the prime representative of the law, is gleefully pounced on by the revellers:

> Tossing powder by the handful, squirting ink by the bicycle pumpful, they came at him from every side. In seconds he was through, red wet, blue wet, yellow wet. And on to the wetness the coloured powders, pink, turquoise and orange, clung and smeared .... I have deserved this he thought. This is a fit punishment for coming here with my money and telling people how to live their lives. Exactly fit (Crusade, 226).

This insight into the arrogance inherent in philanthropy helps him to knock Masters off his saintly pedestal and to see clearly that he was a fallible human being; this gives him a further insight into the motive for his murder. From finding the motive to finding the murderer proves a short, logical step.

That perfection is incompatible with being fully human is a theme most fully and comically explored in Keating's very first Ghote novel, *The Perfect Murder*. As Keating explains: "whether you should strive to be perfect, or whether you should settle for the halfway, which applies in even the smallest things in life. You're typing a sheet of paper and make one mistake; do you rip it out of the typewriter, or do you erase the error?" (*The Great Detectives, 110*). Keating's choice of locale is perfect for the exploration of this theme, for where else but in India, so monumentally imperfect and so indubitably human could you sound all the variations on this theme? If Keating had set this theme in super-efficient Germany, for example, he would have run into trouble. What is remarkable about this novel is that Keating pulls off every blatantly farcical device to reinforce his theme. For example, when Ghote is sent to investigate a murder which has splattered headlines over every newspaper as *The Perfect Murder*, he finds that the murder is far from perfect—it is a botched up affair and the victim named Perfect, secretary to a gross, wealthy businessman Lala Varde, is alive though concussed and unconscious.

If Ghote, a diligent student of Hans Gross' *Criminal Investigation* expects to apply the rigorous investigative methods of Scotland Yard of which he is a colonial heir, he is quickly disillusioned. No one cooperates with Ghote. Lala Varde considers that his enormous wealth places him above the obligations of ordinary citizens; his spoiled sons, Dilip and Prem, and his fearfully imposing wife, Laxmi, obstruct Ghote at every step for their own devious reasons. As if all this obstreperousness were not enough,

Ghote is entrusted with another case—a laughable one concerning the disappearance of one rupee (about 11¢) from an austere minister's desk.

The final straw that threatens to break poor Ghote's bony back is the fact that a great big Swede, Axel Svenson, from UNESCO attaches himself to Ghote in order to study Indian police methods. Svenson blunders after Ghote like a bumbling St. Bernard, adding to Ghote's problems, but a genuine friendship develops between them when Ghote risks being a little late for an appointment with the fanatically punctual Minister for Police Affairs in order to help Svenson—thus once again putting humanness above an abstract idea. Nature plays its own inexorable role adding to the general muddle in India—a heatwave is on, a prelude to the spectacular tropical thunderstorm which, when it breaks, clears the muddle in Ghote's own mind, and helps him, in a burst of brilliant insight, to solve the case. The solution, like the crime, is absurd in its imperfection, but the very imperfection is responsible for saving a life.

In *Inspector Ghote Goes by Train*, the other facet of perfection is portrayed—arrogance, playful self-assertion turning to anarchist villainy and disruption of the social order. Ghote is sent to Calcutta to nab the master criminal A.K. Bhattacharya, who has amassed a fortune by selling fake antiques. By choosing to travel by the slow, humble train when he was empowered to fly, Ghote is the opposite of the mythical Icarus who flies too close to the sun and is burnt for his pains. As he explains to the scornful, disguised Bhattacharya who sits opposite him and baits him unmercifully: "That is what is wrong. I tell you it is wrong. Wrong to go so high, wrong to like to see so much wrong, wrong" (Train, 20). Bhattacharya's reply brings the classical motif underlying the novel to the forefront: "You cannot be meaning to tell me that you equate the simple act of travelling by air with the presumption of Icarus?" (Train, 20).

In *Goes by Train* Keating again manages to integrate a characteristic feature of the Indian scene—travel by train—with philosophical concerns and the form of a suspense novel. *Goes by Train*, however, departs from an orthodox whodunit in the fact that the identity of the criminal is known, and although Ghote initially has trouble identifying him positively as the man he wants, halfway through the novel the criminal reveals his true identity in a characteristic moment of hubris. The rest of the novel becomes a duel of wits. All the people in Ghote's compartment are stuck with one another for the duration of the train journey, and this allows

Keating to draw a comic picture of two American hippies, Red and Mary Jane, their Guru and Mr. Ramaswamy from Madras whose inimitable accent—he prefaces every word with an e (for example, "e-Sir")—Keating catches with great accuracy. The charactization is neither subtle nor deep. All the travelers with the exception of Ghote and Bhattacharya are stereotypes, but they are great fun, and Keating satirizes stock types with gusto. Besides evoking the claustrophobic intimacy and the illusion of timelessness which train travel induces, Keating has a marvellous chase scene, reminiscent of Hitchcock, in which Ghote chases Bhattacharya over the roof of the train—a scene which provides a thrilling climax to the novel.

Ghote, as usual, is subjected to every humiliation and near defeat: he nearly dies of opium poisoning; Bhattacharya continually and cruelly baits him; and in a macabre scene, a one-eyed barber at a wayside station (bribed by A.K.B.) holds Ghote helpless by his nose while he brandishes a knife, nearly causing Ghote to miss the train and lose A.K.B. Of course, Ghote emerges modestly triumphant at the end, his integrity and humanity intact. For unlike his fellow officers, Ghote never uses third degree methods nor does he ever use torture to extract confessions from even the most brutal suspects. Ghote's unfailing weapons are his patience and persistence. Even the most hardened criminal who has withstood the sadistic Inspector Phadke's torture gives in to Ghote's quiet determination. Even A.K.B.'s will, so strong, so arrogant, breaks before Ghote's power, and he makes a long and detailed confession of his fraudulent dealings.

From where do Ghote's infinite patience and persistence come? They come from the fact that in spite of the constant humiliation he suffers, in spite of his comic bumbling, in spite of the fact that his superior officers, and even his charming wife constantly bully him, Ghote manages to do his duty by his job, by his family, and those around him. Confronted by an investigative problem or a human contretemps, Ghote, with a quiet, deceptive stubbornness, never gives up. Like a dog worrying a bone, Ghote keeps at it till the problem yields a solution.

A very clearly defined sense of duty leads Ghote in *Inspector Ghote Breaks an Egg* to redefine himself in a way which lifts him above a specific Indian context to a larger, universal one. In India, the predominant religion of the country, Hinduism, defines every individual according to an intricate hierarchy of caste and family distinctions. Self-definition according to one's work is a recent acquisition. In the traditional Indian context loyalty to one's family and caste is placed above loyalty to the state. Ghote's investigation of a possible murder committed fifteen years earlier takes him to a remote Indian village where inherited values fight a vigorous battle before yielding to new, Western ones.

As the title indicates, the *deus ex machina* is a brightly colored box of eggs. Because the suspected murderer is the powerful Municipal Chairman who keeps the village in order with his personal band of hoods, Ghote has been ordered to disguise himself as a chicken feed salesman advertising a new company: "Grofat Chicken Feeds Ltd." As the eminent political figure who orders the investigation tells him, "The average size of the Indian egg, did you know, is disgraceful as compared with the American and British egg. It is nothing less, indeed, than a national disaster" (Egg, 2). The eminent figure, as it turns out, is concerned not so much with the national disaster as with promoting his nephew's interests—the nephew owns the factory manufacturing the chicken feed. From the beginning, Keating sets the comic tone of the novel—India's perennial conflict between the personal and the public, between the old and the new fought out in terms of the absurd, a box of eggs. Absurd and trivial as it may be, the box of eggs plays a crucial role in the violence charged climax of the novel.

After a great deal of agonized self-questioning, Ghote has to decide what his values are and where his loyalties should lie. The test comes when Ghote is ordered to drop the investigation when he is very close to the truth. The eminent figure is not interested in truth; he is interested only in discrediting the wealthy, powerful Municipal Chairman so that his clout in party politics is undercut. As he tells Ghote, it is not necessary to find out if the Chairman poisoned his first wife because the discovery that the Chairman is really the son of a Harijan beggar woman, and not a Brahmin as he has passed himself off, is enough to destroy him. For in caste-ridden India the mere fact of being an untouchable has terrible consequences, and that is enough to destroy the Chairman. However, Ghote "knew that he would not have been able to live with the thought of abandoning a case of murder at the whim of a politician when the whole case was within hours of being satisfactorily completed. His whole reason for existence would have crumbled up to fragments inside him" (Egg, 164). Ghote's awareness that his reason for existence lies in his pursuit of truth as his job dictates marks him out as a human being able to choose and accept the risks and responsibilities of that choice.

Ghote's heroism stems not so much from spectacular encounters with danger and death, from shooting from the hip, or jumping off cliffs a la James Bond, but in quietly and stubbornly attending to and completing the task immediately at hand. In *Breaks an Egg* for example, Ghote takes a few very precious minutes off to talk a troubled adolescent out of drowning himself. Ghote is surrounded by the Chairman's hired thugs and a few minutes spent talking to the boy might cost him his life: "But in front of him was a tormented young man, and it was more than probable that his torment was one of the self-inflicted ones of youth. Ghote addressed himself to the immediate task again" (82).

Doing what has to be done, Ghote braves the incandescent wrath of a holyman who has begun a fast unto death to oppose the government investigation of the Chairman. In a country as remorselessly religious as India, the holyman's death, construed as martydom, might cause a riot. Ghote commits an egregious *faux pas* by bringing into the sacred precincts of the temple a box of eggs. The Swami explodes at Ghote: "It is carried to disgust me .... Well you are knowing that the egg is equally forbidden to pass the lips as any meat. And into this temple you bring them. Go. Go now. Go this instant. Or I will curse you" (Egg, 60). However, when the holyman is on the point of death, Ghote does not hesitate to force the whites from the despised egg down his throat and revive him with the help of the fortunately "irreligious Sikh" doctor. In the extended and wholly believable descriptions of the confrontation between Ghote and the Swami, Keating accomplishes three things with masterly economy: he etches in one more fine point about Ghote's heroic persistence and pragmatism, he illustrates the everpresent conflict between the spiritual and the secular in India, and finally the box of eggs comically vindicates its existence as a *deus ex machina.*

Another novel in which the form and theme are beautifully woven together is *Bats Fly Up for Inspector Ghote.* BATS happens to be the acronym for the Black Money and Allied Transaction Squad—a band of elite police officers assigned to fight the extensive circulation of black money made from smuggled and illegally sold gold. Real bats, black, with outstretched wings, swoop down on the city of Bombay heralding the darkness which shelters the pick pockets. Bats also rest in the banana tree in Ghote's backyard and destroy the precious green bananas Ghote hopes will ripen soon. Bats of suspicion and jealousy flit around and cloud Ghote's mind as his wife, Protima, constantly praises Inspector Rhadwan, the dashing Moslem member of the BATS. Rhadwan who has moved in as Ghote's neighbor is gallant to Protima and is rich enough to send his ailing wife to an expensive resort town. He is also, as Protima never fails to point out, home much more than Ghote is. In addition to his sense of all these shortcomings, Ghote's mind is tainted by the constant suspicion he has to direct against his colleagues—he has the job of nosing out the traitor among his colleagues who is serving as an informer, for the blackmarketeers always manage to elude the net cast for their capture. Surely one of the BATS is a traitor.

The climax is reached in a nice blending of the professional and domestic. Their quarry has once again escaped the elaborate and super efficient schemes laid by the BATS, and Ghote is no wiser about the identity of the traitor. All five members of the Squad seem equally innocent or guilty. His preoccupation with the case has made Ghote neglect his wife, Protima, and son, Ved. They are resentful of him and he is suspicious of them—a carry-over from his profession. The domestic kettle boils over when Ghote quite unjustifiably suspects little Ved of stealing money. Ved bursts into tears. Protima is furious. Ghote feels a failure, as a detective, as a father and as a husband. Realizing that his mind is so tainted with suspicion that it is in danger of becoming quite unhinged, he decides to resign from his job. Coming home tired and dispirited, Protima's taunts about how the dashing Rhadwan dealt efficiently with the bats ignite the last embers of his courage. Risking his life, he climbs the tree, dislodges the bats and sustains a fall. The fall, however, turns out to be fortunate—a forgotten wallet which he confiscated a long time ago from a pickpocket drops out of his pocket. Protima's tenderness and solicitude over his fall, and her faith that he will, with his superior intelligence, be able to find the owner of the wallet among the teeming millions of Bombay, dissipates the fog of jealousy and suspicion which had clouded his mind and prevented him from seeing the truth. He solves the case in a burst of brilliant intuition, and, in a final scene in the Natural History Section of the Prince of Wales Museum, lays bare the culprit. On his way out, he halts before a painting of a forest scene:

> the jungle round a forest pool in Assam, two tigers were crouched drinking. But it was not on these powerful and sleek forms that Inspector Ghote's gaze came to rest. It fixed, instead, on one tiny characteristic detail that the artist had incorporated in their scene. Up in the shadowed branches of one of the trees overhanging the pool there had cunningly been placed the

stuffed bodies of a cluster of bats. And they were deep and safely in their noonday sleep (180).

Keating has claimed that he wrote the first ten Ghote books before he ever went to India. He visited India briefly in 1974 and 1975, the second time invited by the BBC which had made a movie on Ghote. Perhaps inspired by these visits, his post-India novel published in 1976, *Filmi, Filmi Inspector Ghote* deals with the murder of an Indian actor in a Bombay film studio. The book is the least subtle of the Ghote books. It is tempting to speculate that Keating's contact with India in its most tinsellish aspect—the Bombay film world which Keating, with heavy handed satire, terms Bollywood—has prevented him from exercising the detachment so necessary for the exercise of the creative imagination. The truth of Keating's satire of the Bombay film world cannot be disputed, but it is too easy and self evident a truth. Bollywood is, even to the most star-struck dimwit, a sleezier, stupider Hollywood, if that can be imagined, and, as Horatio would say, it needs "no ghost ... come from the grave to tell us this." Keating's knowledge of the Indian social hierarchy: for example, the fact that hangers-on of public figures are called *chamchas*, spoons, is again on display here, but all the characters are cardboard or rather, celluloid, figures. Even the Bombay film version of *Macbeth* as *Maqbet* is funny, but at the level of slapstick, not at the level of the subtle comedy of earlier books.

When Keating relies on his fertile imagination to flesh out India's colonial past as he does in *Murder of a Maharajah*, he excels. *Maharajah* is not strictly a Ghote novel, though there is a diabolically clever link established with Ghote at the end, but I shall consider it a Ghote novel. It is set in the 1930s during the heyday of British rule when despotic maharajahs spent much of their time organizing spectacular tiger shoots and entertaining their British overlords in a style to which they were not accustomed.

The central figure, the Maharajah, as in most orthodox whodunits, is both the prime mover of the plot and victim. He is also a believable character, both as a stereotypical tyrant and as a complex human, being minimally attractive because of his appetite for life and wholly repulsive because of his all-consuming ego. His ego will brook no opposition when it is suggested by an American engineer that the dam he built for millions of dollars should be used to irrigate vast areas of land lying arid and useless to his starving subjects. The Marahajah refuses to put the dam into use for fear that the water level in the lake used by sandgrouse will go down too low to attract the birds and ruin his favorite sport—sandgrouse shooting.

The novel begins with a piece of arcane folklore of sufficient interest to involve the reader's attention immediately. A humble villager is on his way to the Maharajah's palace to present him with a rare tribute—a piece of Sapura bark which grows on a tree once in a hundred years, and which has the even rarer attribute of stiffening into the hardness of iron when it comes into contact with water and coloring everything it touched with an indelible orange dye. Both these properties are crucial to the development and resolution of the plot.

As a counterpoint to this piece of ancient folklore, there is a thoroughly modern, thoroughly enjoyable contrivance—the Maharajah's favorite toy, a huge silver electric train which runs around the dining table carrying delectable desserts and liqueurs, all listed with an almost medieval relish in enumerating gastronomic delights. Not content with playing a perfectly infantile joke on little Michael, the Resident's son, on April Fool's Day, the Maharajah uses the train to play a joke on one of his twelve (Last Supper?) dinner guests. As Henry Morton III reaches over to one of the silver carriages to help himself to a bottle of creme de cacao, a hidden spring sends the bottle shooting up spraying a "thick stream of dark, chocolaty, sticky liquid all over him." Henry Morton, the "soft metals king of the American midwest" who had been summoned to reopen negotiations on the zinc-mining in Bhopore becomes the last victim of the Maharajah's April Fool's Day jokes.

The Maharajah's first victim, little Michael, is about to get into his chauffeur driven Rolls after a protracted and difficult audience with the Maharajah when there is an explosion—the exhaust pipe is found to be blocked by a piece of Sapura bark. These two practical jokes turn against the Maharajah in a distinctly unfunny way and cost him his life. Someone, taking a lesson from the Maharajah's macabre ingenuity, stuffs the Maharajah's gun with a piece of bark, so that the next morning during the sandgrouse shoot it explodes in his face and kills him.

The excitement, the primitive thrill of the sandgrouse shoot in the beautiful light of an Indian dawn is vividly described:

> Then, quite suddenly, the sky on its first tinge of pink-red. And the whole huge dome of the heavens above, which when they had set out had still been pricked with pale stars, moved imperceptibly from blue-black to an overarching pallor. The shape of the land round the unmoving water of the lakes began to be just discernible.

And then, after a single long hush, the first heralds of the sandgrouse could be heard as a tiny insistent drumming of wings (76).

Even if one were not a fan of detective fiction, *Maharajah* would be worth reading as a satirical evocation of India's colonial past. Keating juxtaposes, with tongue-in-cheek irony, the beauty of the well orchestrated hunt and the appalling cruelty to the poor on which it rests. As mentioned earlier, the water level in the *jheel* which attracts the birds is maintained by denying the peasants the use of the dam which they have built at enormous cost and hard labor. The peasants are denied water so that the sandgrouse may drink and be shot.

The man summoned by the Resident to investigate the murder of the Maharajah is District Superintendent of Police Howard who despite his "remarkable record of successes" is regretably "country-born":

To be "countryborn," not to have been subjected, if by chance your actual birth had occurred in India, to the bracing climate of the mother country, that climate that was always thought of as being not simply physically bracing with its cold winds, its hard driving rain, its pure snows, but also as being morally bracing. A man who had not had that was somehow suspect (93).

Keating's understanding of the intricacies of colonial snobbery adds one more dimension to the book, and makes D.S.P. Howard an interesting figure who, as a social outcast, belongs nowhere and yet is at home everywhere. He plays tennis with his ultra-British Resident, whose often reiterated advice to his son to "keep your mouth shut and your bowels open" surely epitomizes the moral simple-mindedness on which imperialism rests, and he is at home with the Maharajah's circle and can befriend on equal terms the austere, acute schoolmaster who serves as his sidekick in the investigation.

The investigation itself turns out to be unexpectedly tricky. All twelve of the Maharajah's guests have equally strong motives for murdering the host: the son and heir, the new Maharajah, whose love for Dolly Brattle, an aging chorus girl, had been contemptuously dismissed by his father who had urged him to marry a princess and keep Dolly where she belongs—in a harem; Joe Lloyd, the fiery engineer, whose dam lay useless because of the old Maharajah's whim; Dolly, whose brassy blonde person was not proof against the Maharajah's insults; and Henry Morton, who had been summoned all the way from the Midwest only to be made a fool of. In this novel, as D.S.P. Howard and the schoolmaster explore the palace and the motives of its guests for clues to the murder, Keating manages to avoid the tediousness often present in his and in other redoubtable whodunits of the investigative process—the patient questioning, the elaborate mathematical juggling of clues, timetables and alibis. The uncovering of the clues also becomes an expose of a way of life so exotic, so grotesquely splendid, that the novel holds the reader's interest from first to last. It is also, unlike conventional "period" novels which tend to take themselves too seriously, utterly playful, and, therefore, unpretentious and delightful. And playfulness is and should be a feature of the whodunit as it is, above all, a puzzle which *Homo Ludens* likes to solve when he is not trying, with his usual lack of success, to solve the mystery of existence.

In a letter to me Keating professes to be surprised at the success of *Maharajah* which he terms, rather dismissively, a "conventional mystery": "I did it at what I thought was a good deal more superficial a level and to my embarrassment my editor here liked it more than anything I had done."[5] Ironically, Keating's most superficial novels are *Filmi, Filmi Inspector Ghote* and *Go West Inspector Ghote*, both written after brief contacts with the reality they try to depict, and both lacking the panache which distinguishes *Maharajah*, written from a considerable distance in time and place. Indeed, Keating's brush with reality, whether it be dusty and dirty Bombay or the plastic and shiny Los Angeles, seems to hamper his inventive powers, for like *Filmi, Filmi, Go West* is rather superficial and contrived. As in all Ghote novels, Keating explores an interesting theme—the export of instant Indian spirituality to the West. Ghote is sent to Los Angeles to bring back the only daughter of a Bombay businessman who has dropped out of college in California to join the Ashram of an Indian Swami. Keating's portrayal of the Swami, who recalls Jim Jones who led hundreds of people to suicide in Guyana in the absolute charismatic power he wields over his mindless followers, is unerringly accurate. He is also very good at portraying Ghote's bemused response to the stridency of the American scene, but the kind of depth of understanding he reveals in his understanding of Indian village politics in *Breaks an Egg* is missing here, and the solution to the murder is contrived and implausible.

While Keating does not try to delve into the question of why the devotees of these so-called spiritual leaders behave like half-witted sheep, the Swami himself comes alive in all his complexity. Incipient sadist, blatant lecher and complete fraud that the Swami is, Keating, however, entertains the possibility that there are more things in heaven and earth than are dreamt of in our super-rational age. As Ghote puts it, "events do occur which can be called magic events which cannot be accounted for by logical, scientific means" (West, 75). Demonstrating his power, the Swami singles Ghote out in a vast crowd as "someone who has come and is not happy. His head is paining. He needs help. You there, at the back of the doors, come here to me" (32). Indeed, Ghote ever since he has landed in California has been suffering from a throbbing head. Reluctantly he goes up to the Swami who puts his right hand on his shoulder:

> Ghote at once felt a sensation of peculiar warmth there .... It was as if, he felt, there was an actual source of heat within that dense, soft flesh. And immediately as the weariness and grittiness accumulated over hours of being swept through the skies at hundreds of miles an hour began seeping out of him through it seemed, some sump-hole in the back of his neck.... Damn him. Why should he be endowed with a power like this? (33-34).

While one must admire Keating's open-minded attitude to the mystery of spiritual powers, his explanation of the Swami's final degradation as voiced by Johananda, a believable observer, is far too facile:

> When he came out here to California first he was a truly God-realized person. A true yogi. But, you know, one of the great masters once said that everything on this earth is like a mingling of sand and sugar. But, poor Swami, after a while he began to think that California sand was sweeter than sugar (175).

Keating takes the easy way out; instead of tackling the difficult subject of the authenticity or inauthenticity of Indian mysticism, or ignoring the subject because it may be too large for the scope of a detective novel, he "solves" the problem, as it were, by blaming the potential for corruption inherent in it on the influence of the West. It boils down to that old chestnut—the West is materialistic, the East is spiritual. Why the West is so anxious to exchange its relatively solid dollar for the essentially light weight brand of spirituality exported from the East may not be as easily solved as the Swami's murder.

It should be obvious from this survey of Keating's Ghote novels that his philosophical and satirical themes have immense variety. What gives authenticity to his approach, and prevents the unpretentious whodunit form from sinking under the philosophical freight it carries, is his unfailing comic vision conveyed chiefly through his mastery of Indian English. The comedy springs from the fact that Indian English is the result of an uneasy marriage between a world view handed down from India's Vedic past and an essentially alien, even inimical, structure of thought embodied in the English language. For in this post-Wittgenstein and post-structuralist era we know that language, far from representing reality, shapes and reconstructs reality according to the demands of its inherent order and the values and assumptions of the people who use it. Much of the comedy of Indian English springs from the fact that the English language, homegrown over centuries in the sceptered isle, was roughly grafted to an entirely different culture in an entirely different climate.

This rough grafting has produced innumerable saplings. For apart from its political unity (imposed by the British) India is not really one country; rather, it is a loose federation of states each of which has a distinct linguistic, ethnic and cultural character, all reflected in the syntax and rhythms of its English. For example, a Northerner and a Southerner (and their sub-varieties) can immediately identify the region the other comes from by the accent and structure of the English he speaks. And ironically they can communicate only in English, for although Hindi has been declared the national language of India, Southerners refuse to learn it because they see Hindi, the language of the North, as an instrument of domination of the South. For all intents and purposes, even after nearly forty years of independence from British rule, English remains the national language of India.

In addition to the varieties of English spoken by different ethnic groups, there are variations created by differences in economic class and education. Roughly, there are three kinds of English spoken in India which reflect a person's economic and educational background. They are the monosyllabic sentence fragments consisting mostly of verbs and nouns spoken by taxi drivers, waiters and others who deal with those economically better off than themselves; the fluent English spoken by those who have attended vocational and professional colleges which, however, bears the imprint of their regional language in its grammar, syntax and accent; the idomatic, almost British English lightly spiced with a distinctively Indian lilt spoken by westernized Indians who have degrees in the humanities. There are many other variations, of course, but these three categories provide a convenient way of dealing with the social framework of Keating's novels.

Ghote is a police officer trained in the British judicial system, and his English is representative of the second category. Whenever his professional ethics show signs of weakening, he fortifies himself with a glance at his Bible—Han Gross' *Criminal Investigation*. The chief characteristic of Ghote's English is the use of a present participle without its object. For example, in *Breaks an Egg*, when an old woman drops a *Time* magazine, Ghote picks it up and delays handing it back because a picture of himself has caught his eye. The woman screams "Mine, mine," and Ghote reassures her with, "Yes, yes, I am giving" (4). Keating does not make it clear whether this exchange is in one of the Indian languages, or in English. It does not matter. Ghote's reply catches the authentic flavor of the syntax of an Indian language and the way it is transferred to English. The encounter between the local Superintendent of Police and Inspector Ghote further illustrates Keating's grasp of all the nuances of Indian English. When Ghote demands a room to work in, the Superintendent replies: "Very well, my dear fellow, if you are insisting, I will see that it is done. But we are faced with a problem here, I do not mind telling" (16). Once again, we notice the use of the participle "insisting" instead of the verb "insist." Also, the Superintendent transforms the phrase "I must confess" into its Indianized version "I do not mind telling." Ghote also drops his articles when he asks about the state of the prison cells: "Are they in dirty condition?" (16). Ghote often sounds stiffly formal because, lacking idomatic ease in English, he uses the jargon of bureaucracy; "Then shall we go and select one as office for me? . . . And perhaps you could see that a stronger-than-regulation bulb is found for it. I expect I shall be working all night" (16).

This Indianization of the structure of English indicates something very important: the Indianization of Western epistemology. A good example is the use of a present participle for a transitive verb. The average Indian's inability to use a past perfect or future perfect verb, his reliance on the present participle, reflects his attitude to time—he finds it hard to grasp a linear, historical time segmented into a past, present and future. (I shudder at my generalizations. Is there such person as an average Indian or an average Englishman? But, for the purpose of this analysis, I have to make these generalizations and risk becoming formulaic and reductive.) He lives in an eternal present, the *now* of mythical time which in T.S. Eliot's words "contains a time past and a time future." The Indian concept of reincarnation perceives life as an endlessly recurring cycle of existence on earth, a cycle you can bring to a halt only if you dissolve your individual soul, your *Atman*, into the universal soul—the *Brahman*. Death does not, as in the West, cut you off forever from life on earth. All the *carpe diem* in the lyrics of the seventeenth century English poets dwells on this brevity of human life on earth unconsoled by the promise of continued life in heaven or hell or purgatory. There is no sense of urgency in an Indian's attitude to life because he has the assurance that he will taste its pleasures over and over again.

If Ghote's English reveals the remnants of Hindu epistemology clinging to the rough and ready translation of his thoughts from a native idiom to an alien one, there is the even funnier English spoken by the street urchins of Bombay. Born and bred on the teeming streets of that cosmopolitan city, these delinquents manage to cope with the appalling cruelty of their existence by taking refuge in the fantasy world of Hollywood movies. The leader of a gang who has "the head of a twelve-year-old boy: the face of a man of sixty" because of "the spread of some sort of infection which had crinkled the skin of the boy's face into a thousand etched tortuous lines" (Crusade, 11) calls himself Edward G. Robinson. The boy is so street wise, so distrustful of authority that Ghote is continually foiled in his attempts to extract information from him. It is only when Ghote with characteristic insight realizes that if he resorts to the boy's old Hollywood idiom he might be able to break down the boy's resistance, that things begin to move. What follows is an extremely funny, yet pathetic dialogue:

> "Nah," he [the boy] said, "When I keep watch on a fella he don't know there's nothing there."
> "Smart guy," Ghote said. "You gonna say what this fella did?"
> "Maybe."
> "Fill you full o' lead if you don't. (Crusade, 63).

The farcical humor of the dialogue springs, of course, from the encroachment of Hollywood tinsel glitter into the slums of Bombay, and the pathos lies in the fact that it is precisely these incongruous fantasies that enable these poor naked forked animals to survive in a world where they are indeed as flies to the wanton gods.

At the other end of the social scale are the Westernized, upper-class Indians who are not Hindu, and who, therefore, speak an ultra British, though comically dated, English. Here is an "irreligious Sikh": "Give me a hand, old boy, and we will have something in him in a jiffy. We'd better mix it with a bit of water, digests easier that way..." (Egg, 170). The Sikh punctuates his sentences with "old boy," "jiffy," "old chap" in the best Colonel Blimp manner. Then there is an amazingly believable portrait of a judge, a Moslem, who though retired and almost a recluse, does not bend an inch from his former eminence, and whose antediluvian attitudes are revealed in the precise cadences of his speech: "I had allowed myself to hope that the plain expression of plain facts, however few the ears that heard them, would do some good in these dark times, that with lies and corruption all around us a few grains of truth would show up like specks of white on the universal blackness" (Line, 29). The antithesis of an aristocratic Moslem judge is a South Indian Brahmin, Mr. Ramaswamy, a mere cog in the vast bureaucratic machinery handed by the British. Mr. Ramaswamy's speech with, as Ghote is quick to note, its "intrusive 'e' in front of words beginning with an 's' " (Train, 78), marks him out as a Southerner, and the futility of his profession is conveyed perfectly in the windy formality of his speech:

> That is precisely the nature of my occupation. I travel all around the area of the Central Railway and sometimes make forays into other areas, and e-Sir, I inspect the forms kept at my station I choose to descend upon. And, of course, the stationary. It is, you will agree, a curious form of existence (81).

In *Go West Ghote*, Keating catches the exact cadences of the dangerously manipulative rhetoric that flows from the bogus Guru and engulfs the audience like warm treacle:

> My friends, today I have something to give to you. A present from Swami. Is it a little, little present? Oh no. Swami is feeling very kind. He is going to give each of you a present that is very, very valuable. It is a present that he knew he was going to give long, long ago when he was meditating in the Himalayas and an inner command came to him that said: Go West, young man, go West. Yes, Swami is going to give you now—a future. It will be a future guarded more wisely than your future ever could be by an insurance company however, careful. Yes, I am giving it ... (35).

Keating not only strains the traditional puzzle form of the whodunit, but spoofs it. For the basic puzzle in Keating's novels is not the puzzle of the murder, but the much more disconcerting puzzle of man's ontological position. Indeed, he carries the British Golden Age tradition of keeping the murder to a minimum to its logical absurdity—in at least five of his Ghote novels there are no murders. Indeed, Keating could very successfully enter a competition suggested to him by Julian Symons to see "who could get least murder in a murder novel."[6]

This self-parodic strain may be explained by the fact that Keating chose to write detective fiction in apparent rebellion against his father who in the expectation of his son becoming a great writer gave him a battery of forenames—Henry Reymond Fitzwalter—because they would look good on the spine of his books. Writing detective fiction satisfied his need to rebel because he saw the form as "deeply flawed" and as "a way of writing without saying anything."[7] But of course by choosing to put in as little crime as he could possibly get away with, he gives himself room to say a great deal. As Northrop Frye points out, "If the general shape of structure of the story is prescribed in advance, then—all the literary merits of the story, the wit in the dialogue, the liveliness of the characterization, and the like are a technical tour de force."[8] And this is exactly what Keating has achieved. If the puzzle form of the whodunit harks back to the tradition of playing so dear to the heart of *Homo Ludens,* Keating plays the ultimate game by inverting all the rules to present the human comedy in all its unpredictability.

Notes

[1] The editions of Keating's novels used in this study are listed below, preceded by the original date of publication. All quotations will be cited in the text using, where necessary, the abbreviations given after each entry:

1964	*The Perfect Murder,* New York: Dutton, 1965 (Perfect).
1966	*Inspector Ghote's Good Crusade,* New York: Dutton, 1966 (Crusade).
1967	*Inspector Ghote Caught in Meshes,* New York: Dutton, 1968 (Meshes).
1968	*Inspector Ghote Hunts the Peacock,* New York: Dutton, 1968 (Peacock).
1969	*Inspector Ghote Plays a Joker,* New York: Dutton, 1969 (Joker).
1970	*Inspector Ghote Breaks an Egg,* New York: Doubleday, 1971 (Egg).
1971	*Inspector Ghote Goes by Train,* New York: Doubleday, 1972 (Train).
1972	*Inspector Ghote Trusts the Heart,* New York: Doubleday, 1973 (Heart).
1974	*Bats Fly Up For Inspector Ghote,* New York: Doubleday, 1974 (Bats).
1976	*Filmi, Filmi Inspector Ghote,* New York: Doubleday, 1977 (Filmi).
1979	*Inspector Ghote Draws a Line,* New York: Doubleday, 1979 (Line).
1980	*The Murder of a Maharajah,* New York: Doubleday, 1980 (Maharajah).
1981	*Go West Inspector Ghote,* New York: Doubleday, 1981 (West).

[2]Uncollected Short Stories:
"The Justice Boy," in *Ellery Queen's Mystery Parade,* New York, New American Library, 1968.
"Inspector Ghote and the Test Match," in *Ellery Queen's Mystery Magazine* (New York), Oct. 1969.
"An Upright Woman," in *Winter's Crimes 2,* edited by George Hardinge, London, Macmillan, 1970.
"The Old Shell Collector," in *Ellery Queen's Headliners,* Cleveland, World, 1971; London, Gollancz, 1972.
"The Old Haddock," in *Ellery Queen's Mystery Magazine* (New York), June 1971.
"Insector Ghote and the Miracle," in *Ellery Queen's Mystery Magazine* (New York), Jan. 1972.
"A Little Rain in a Few Places," in *Ellery Queen's Mystery Magazine* (New York), Sept. 1972.
"Memorial to Speke," in *Ellery Queen's Mystery Magazine* (New York), Nov. 1972.
"Inspector Ghote and the Hooked Fisherman," in *Ellery Queen's Magazine* (New York), Jan. 1973.
"The Butler Did It," in *Ellery Queen's Mystery Magazine* (New York), May 1973.
"Torture Chamber," in *Ellery Queen's Mystery Magazine* (New York), Sept. 1974.
"The Five Senses of Mrs. Craggs," in *Ellery Queen's Murdercade.* New York, Random House, 1975.
"Inspector Ghote and the Noted British Author," in *Winter's Crimes 7,* edited by George Hardinge. London, Macmillan, 1975.
"Liar, Liar, Pants on Fire," in *Ellery Queen's Mystery Magazine* (New York), April 1976.
"Mrs. Craggs and the Lords Spiritual and Temporal," in *John Creasey's Crime Collection,* edited by Herbert Harris. London, Gollancz, 1978).
"Mrs. Cragg's Sixth Sense," in *Ellery Queen's Mystery Magazine* (New York), Sept. 1978.
"The Adventure of the Suffering Ruler," in *Blackwoods* (Edinburgh), May 1978.
"Gup," in *Verdict of Thirteen,* edited by Julian Symons. London, Faber, and New York, Harper, 1979.

[3]Other works by Keating include:
Novels:
The Strong Man, London, Heineman, 1971.
The Underside, London, Macmillan, 1974.
A Long Walk in Wimbledon, London, Macmillan, 1978.

Plays:
Radio Plays: *The Dog It Was That Died,* from his own novel, 1971; *The Affair at No. 35,* 1973; *Inspector Ghote and the All-Bad Man,* 1972; *Inspector Ghote Makes a Journey,* 1973; *Inspector Ghote and the River Man,* 1974.

Other:
Understanding Pierre Teilhard de Chardin: A Guide to "The Phenomenon of Man," with Maurice Keating. London, Lutterworth Press, 1969.
Murder Must Appetize (on detective stories of the 1930s). London, Lemon Tree Press, 1975.
"I.N.I.T.I.A.L.S.," in *Murder Ink: The Mystery Reader's Companion,* edited by Dilys Winn. New York, Workman, 1977.
"New Patents Pending," in *Crime Writers,* edited by H.R.F. Keating. London, BBC Publications, 1978.
Sherlock Holmes: The Man and His World, London, Thames and Hudson, and New York, Scribner, 1979.
Editor, *Blood on My Mind,* London, Macmillan, 1972.
Editor, *Agatha Christie: First Lady of Crime,* London, Weidenfeld and Nicolson, and New York, Holt Rinehart, 1977.
Editor, *Crime Writers: Reflections on Crime Fiction,* London, BBC Publications, 1978.
Editor, *Whodunit? A Guide to Crime, Suspense & Spy Fiction,* New York: Van Nostrand Reinhold, 1982.

[4]"Inspector Ghote," in *The Great Detectives,* ed. Otto Penzler (Boston: Little Brown, 1978). Further references will be cited in the text.

[5]In a letter to me dated 28 December 1978, the full reference to *Murder of a Maharajah* reads: "Meanwhile (have I told you?) I have a different sort of crime book coming out next, a rather conventional mystery set in a Princely State in 1930, written originally because it's the 50th anniversary over here of Collins Crime Club, our equivalent of Doubleday. I did it at what I thought was a good deal more superficial level and to my embarrassment my editor here liked it more than anything I had done ...."

[6]"Pooter," *The Times,* 7 Jan. 1971, p. 7.

[7]"Pooter," p. 7.

[8]*Natural Perspectives* (New York: Columbia University Press, 1965), p. 4.

Simon Brett

Simon Brett

Earl F. Bargainnier

1945	Simon Anthony Lee Brett born on 28 October in Worcester Park, Surrey, son of John and Margaret Brett, a surveyor and a schoolteacher.
1956-64	Attended Dulwich College, London.
1964-67	Attended Wadham College, Oxford University; while there, President of the Oxford University Dramatic Society; graduated with B.A. in English with First Class Honours.
1967-77	Producer of radio programs for British Broadcasting Corporation.
1970	*Mrs. Gladys Moxon,* first play, produced in London.
1971	Married Lucy Victoria McLauren; one daughter and one son; *Did You Sleep Well* and *A Good Day at the Office* produced in London.
1972	*Third Person* produced in London.
1973	Recipient of Writers Guild of Great Britain Award for Best Radio Feature Script.
1975	Published *Cast, In Order of Disappearance,* first Charles Paris mystery.
1977	Librettist for *Drake's Dream*, musical produced in London.
1977-79	Producer for London Weekend Television.
1982	Published *Murder Unprompted,* eighth Charles Paris mystery.

Since 1975 Simon Brett has written yearly a novel featuring actor-detective Charles Paris, and those novels have made Brett one of the principal younger writers of detective fiction in Great Britain.[1] On more than one occasion he has made some variation on the statement his novels are intended as entertainment. They are indeed that, for they are a continuation of that long tradition of the seemingly easy—but treacherously difficult—sophisticated, comic British detective novel. Using his own experience and knowledge of the theater, radio and television, Brett has also added, with much more expertise than most, to that large and popular sub-genre: the theatrical murder mystery. Whereas earlier writers in that sub-genre, most notably Dame Ngaio Marsh, presented the theatrical murder as comedy of manners, Brett surrounds it with social satire. In fact, it is as a social satirist that Brett shows his greatest distinctiveness as a mystery writer. He is not just a satirist of the theater and the media; rather, the satire provided by Charles Paris' acting jobs and the resultant murder cases is of contemporary British life with British show business serving as a microcosm of the problems, frustrations, stupidities, dislocations and antagonisms present in that larger world outside the theater or studio. In both his adherence to the conventions of British detective fiction—even when breaking those conventions—and his contemporaneity of attitude, Simon Brett is most significantly the detective novelist as satirist of his society.

At the center of Brett's satire is Charles Paris, for as S. S. Van Dine propounded years ago, "the detective novel must have a detective in it, and a detective is not a detective unless he detects." Fortunately for Charles Paris, Van Dine says nothing about the nature of the detection, for Charles (to use his last name would be unnaturally formal for someone so informal as Charles Paris) is an amateur in the most literal sense: his hobby is detection, but much of the time he is not sure what he is doing or whether whatever it is is right. But in spite of his bumbling, he never fails to discover the murderer before anyone else does—sometimes when no one else has even considered that a murder has been committed. In his profession and lifestyle, his methods of detection, his views of himself and others, and his humanity, Charles is an original and—

though he would be irritated, if not disgusted, by the description—a lovable old dear.

The *old* does not refer to age, though that would be a major reason for the irritation. Born on Guy Fawkes Day, 5 November, Charles ages in the novels from forty-seven to fifty-two, and the onset of elderly infirmities is one of his many worries. However, it is just one, for Charles finds "the basic challenge of getting from day to day" occupies most of his time (Trap, 11). The reasons are many, ranging from his excessive drinking and unsatisfactory casual affairs through unpaid taxes, an incompetent agent, and a minimal career as an actor to his off-and-on relationships with the wife and daughter he deserted in the early 1960s. In other words, Charles Paris' personal life is a mess.

On his first appearance, he is dozing over a boring script at a radio rehearsal as a result of too much wine at lunch and almost immediately has to relieve his inflated bladder—another recurrent problem. In the course of the novels, readers learn how he has arrived at this less than dignified point in his life. He graduated from Oxford in 1949, wrote one successful London play, *The Ratepayer,* and over the years has acted and directed throughout the British Isles; such a background would seem to provide the basis for much more success than Charles has or expects. His lack of success has the same cause as the failure of his marriage: his determination to have if not utter freedom of action, at least as much as is humanly possible. Even his appearance reflects this determination. Though still handsome with thick hair only slightly silvered at the temples, he makes no effort to capitalize on his looks. In 1979 he has one sixties suit, which he wears only when absolutely necessary. A friend describes his "usual guise" as that of "an out-of-work gamekeeper who's just spent a long night with Lady Chatterley" (Corpse, 70), and a fellow actor calls his sports jacket, "a sack with an identity problem" (Tragedy, 19). Charles is hardly a walking advertisement for Bell's scotch whiskey, his favorite tipple, though he never refuses anything available. His living quarters similarly reflect his desire for freedom. Since leaving his wife, he has lived in a one-room bed-sitter in Hereford Road, Bayswater, surrounded by lumpish Swedish girls, who are usually in the bath when he wants it and who leave him nearly incomprehensible messages from the telephone in the hall. His room contains the barest essentials for existence, but since he is usually there only to sleep off the effects of his drinking, he accepts the discomfort, for he is not tied down by possessions or obligations.

The obligations of marriage, especially fidelity, were too restrictive for Charles, and so he left his wife, Frances, and their daughter, Juliet, for freedom: "A cliché of freedom, perhaps. Certainly an accepted stereotype of freedom" (Mike, 46), but guilt goes with that freedom in spite of his sense of a "perverse integrity." What is unusual is that his relationship with Frances did not end when he walked out. They have never taken the final step of divorce because of "the fraying but resilient umbilical cord that joined him to her" (Blood, 85). Instead, "there had been so many attempts to mend it that the marriage, like an old tea-service, was bumpy with rivets" (Comedian, 7). They take vacations together in *So Much Blood* and *A Comedian Dies* and come to New York for her mother's funeral in *The Dead Side of the Mike*. Frances is a teacher and lives at Muswell Hill, where Charles retreats whenever he feels the need of, as he puts it, "the great calm that emanated from her" (Cast, 13). He generally feels sentimental when they meet, but in a few days the old claustrophobia sets in, and he is off. His ambivalence toward her is perhaps best expressed as follows: "Two things about Frances—she was always busy and she was never surprised. These, in moments of compatibility, were her great qualities; in moments of annoyance, her most irritating traits" (Cast, 12). He can wish for her presence and wish her away at almost the same time. He can admire her efficiency and resent it. He can be worried by rumors that she has a boyfriend and be astounded when he learns the boyfriend is a scout-master. Frances rather wistfully accepts Charles' attitude, sends him shirts for Christmas, asks him to test drive her new car, and discourages him from investigating crime. The failure of the marriage is Charles' fault, as he is occasionally willing to recognize, for he is an impractical idealist as far as marriage is concerned:

> If marriage were all making love and comforting wives when they cried, he would have been very good at it. But that was only a small part; there was all the waking up in the morning and going shopping and washing up and paying the mortgage and replacing fuses in plugs and spending evenings when there was nothing on the television watching it. Those were the bits that killed.

* * *

> [he felt confused] by the whole system of marriage. Once again, he concluded that it was a generalized system, designed to suit everyone in general terms all of the time, and suiting no one in detail any of the time (Mike, 78 & 89).

Charles' relationship with Juliet is one element of the novels' social satire. He can be "surprised by the power of feeling for his daughter" when he fears for her safety (Mike, 34), but basically he finds her "irredeemably boring" and his feelings for her just "a cumbersome bulk of undefined emotion" (Mike, 74), the result of "a life-time of non-communication" (Trap, 124). Juliet's attitude toward Charles is summed up by her "Daddy, I do wish you'd get yourself sorted out" (Cast, 64), while his toward her in the phrase: "a middle-aged daughter of twenty-one" (Cast, 65). Juliet is married to Miles Taylerson, an ultra-stuffy young man who sells insurance—but not to Charles—and calls his father-in-law "Pop." They live in the suburb of Pangbourne, have an "odious yellow Cortina," belong to the "Scampi and Mateus Rose crowd," and have all the amenities of a rising young couple, without a thought for anything but material and social success: "They bought every possession (including the right opinions) that the young executive should have and their lives were organised with a degree of foresight that made the average Soviet Five-Year-Plan look impetuous" (Trap, 124). Naturally, Charles is fascinated by thoughts of their sex-life: "Perhaps a regular weekly deposit with a family protective policy and a bonus of an extra screw at age twenty-five" (Cast, 66). He even asks Miles about possible children and is told they intend to wait for Miles' next promotion, but a "mistake" intervenes. Juliet is pregnant in *Star Trap*, twins Damian and Julian result and are christened in *An Amateur Corpse*, and Julian delights his grandfather in *The Dead Side of the Mike* by "peeing against his father's Marks and Spencer's checkered trousers" (75). Obviously Charles is not suited to conventional domesticity. Brett makes him unfair to Frances, but makes Juliet and Miles such utterly bourgeois twits that the reader agrees with Charles' view of their insipid, stultifying lives.

His inability to be monogamous is evidenced by the number of bed-partners, including Frances, that Charles has, but they do not solve his sexual quandary: "Casual sex didn't give him enough and anything deeper soon got claustrophobic" (Trap, 79). Nevertheless, he is always looking for a new "crumpet" and is generally successful—for a short time. Whether it is a one-night stand with a married woman in *A Comedian Dies*, his seduction by a blackmailer in *Cast, In Order of Disappearance* or the strange hate-love relationship with a former lover in *Star Trap*, Charles' sexual adventures never last.

His only intense affair is with the young actress Anna Duncan in *So Much Blood*, but he finds that her apparent passion is solely for the advancement of her career. The same is true of the Production Assistant in *Situation Tragedy*, who begins as Jane Lewis and successively changes her name to Janey, Janie, Jay and Jan to look better on program credits. Like these two, most of his bedmates are young, such as Jacqui—with whom he is impotent because of "the dreaded Distiller's Droop"—and Felicity Newman of *Cast, In Order of Disappearance*, and so is Steve Kennett of *The Dead Side of the Mike*, who because of her problems and his circumspection never goes beyond a kiss. He realizes that their youth is a great part of their attraction, though ultimately self-defeating for himself: "Women could alleviate the awareness of the approach of death, but they could not delay it" (Trap, 106); even more, he realizes that he is "bad at the sort of insouciance that should have accompanied his style of sex life. Feelings kept snagging, he kept feeling sorry for people, kept feeling he was using them. And, as always, lacking the self-righteousness necessary for anger, he ended up feeling self-disgust" (Trap, 95).

Such self-awareness is a significant aspect of Charles Paris, in spite of his continuing habits that will hardly improve his situation. Though he has a veneer of cynicism, it is not very thick: "His cynicism could still be unexpectedly erased by the sight of a child or the shock of a sudden kindness or a moment of desire" (Trap, 61). He can show great compassion for those who are helpless, as Jacqui in *Cast, In Order of Disappearance* or Hugo Mecken in *An Amateur Corpse*. He is totally without envy—something most unusual in an actor. His best friend is a rich lawyer whom he first met when they were students at Oxford, Gerald Venables. Gerald is a successful Miles, with all of the material goods and social status that Charles lacks, and looks "like the ideal executive in an American Express advertisement" (Tragedy, 19). Yet Charles is not envious, but amused by Gerald's unashamed love of money and his boyish delight in aiding Charles in his investigations. The verdict has to be that, with all his moral lapses, Charles Paris is a decent man. He has chosen personal freedom over security, wealth and fame, and though he is occasionally depressed by his life, he is a character whose frailties are human. In *Star Trap*, the novel in which he is most unhappily introspective, he gives a summation of his life:

> He saw himself with the deadly X-ray eye of a third person. A middle-aged actor play-acting on the front at Brighton. Someone who'd never managed to create a real relationship with anyone,

a man whose wife was forced to take solace with a scout-master, a man whose daughter spoke the language of another planet, a man who would sink into death without even disturbing the surface of life, unnoticed, unmourned (162).

Fortunately, such thoughts are only intermittent, and he shakes them off to continue that "basic challenge of getting from day to day."

For in spite of his personal problems and the lack of help from Maurice Skellern, his useless agent who spends his time gathering gossip rather than jobs for his clients, Charles does somehow find work as an actor. Interspersed throughout the novels are capsule reviews, good and bad, of Charles' theatrical work: in *Richard III* ("nicely understated"—*Yorkshire Post*), in *Look Back in Anger* ("a splendid Blimp"—*Worcester Gazette*), in *Arturo Roi* ("grossly overplayed"—*Glasgow Herald*) (Cast, 44). At the beginning of *Cast, in Order of Disappearance*, he has just completed "a ghastly television series in which he'd minced around some unlikely Tudor monarch in doublet and hose for a couple of months" (3). Though he finds them necessary for money, Charles despises film and television. In the novels themselves, he is Tick the deformed coachman in a horror film, *The Zombie Walks*; presents his one-man show at the Edinburgh Festival; does voice-over commercials and serves as consultant critic for an amateur group; plays Sir Charles Marlowe in *Lumpkin!*, a musical distortion of Goldsmith's *She Stoops to Conquer*, which he has previously directed; has a chance at a television series; does a program on Swinburne for the BBC and acts as the Mystery Voice on a quiz program; and has a small role in a situation comedy. His career, which he has ceased to call it, may be minimal, but it does plod along and certainly fulfills his aim of "variety rather than stardom" (Trap, 122). His one-man show on the poetry and prose of Thomas Hood in *So Much Blood* indicates his seriousness as an actor, when he has a vehicle worthy of his ability. Though luncheon performances sponsored by a university group cannot be considered a money-making venture, Charles prepares for it as carefully as for a London opening and deservedly receives a rave review and continuously increasing audiences. He can justly claim that, star status or not, he is a professional.

Fantasies of stardom can still make him "deliciously nervy and excited," he can still count the number of lines given him, an enthusiastic audience can "cut through all his layers of cynicism and [leave] him exposed like a stage-struck teenager" (Comedian,

61), and his realistic view of his position in the theater no longer lets him aspire to stardom, but cannot "stop him from finding small parts boring" (Tragedy, 34). In other words, the theater, whatever its manifestation and whatever his role, is deeply a part of him; he is in the theater and the theater is in him. Most important, his years of experience in the world of the theater—and that hard-won personal freedom—have given him a clear-eyed view of his colleagues: writers, producers, directors, actors, etc., which enables him to see them as a detective must.

At the end of *So Much Blood*, Frances asks Charles why he has chosen "this very dangerous hobby," detection. His answer is "It's not deliberate. It's just if I get into a situation I have to find out what happened, find out the truth, I suppose" (191), and in *An Amateur Corpse* he says, "I just want the truth to come out" (188). This desire to know the truth is a personal drive; it is for his own peace of mind, rather than from any sense of abstract justice or protection of society. At one point the comment is made that "violent death had begun to exercise an almost unhealthy fascination on him" (Comedian, 21). Unhealthy or not, that fascination causes him to undertake investigations on his own, sometimes, as in *A Comedian Dies* or *The Dead Side of the Mike*, when no one but Charles sees the necessity. (The police play almost no part in the novels. In *So Much Blood* Charles has "an outdated image of the police as thick village constables whose only function was to have rings run around them by the brilliant amateur sleuth" [147]. Actually, he realizes that he has no standing as a detective and only proof will give him any believability with the police.) His working alone makes Frances' statements about danger quite true. He is shot, suffers several nasty falls from traps or being pushed, is shocked by a rigged electrical switch, and has his leg torn by the hooks of a salmon ripper thrown by a murderer's faithful retainer. But in spite of such dangers, Charles remains tenacious in his search for the truth. His determination to know all the facts keeps him going no matter the obstacles.

In fact, that tenacity is his single most important characteristic as a detective, for he is not a Sherlock Holmes or Hercule Poirot, and he recognizes the fact and is often despondent over his lack of ability as a detective. He becomes depressed about his mistaken suspicions that seem to drag on "like a Whitehall farce, with him as the over acting protagonist, always opening the wrong door after the crooks had fled, after the pretty girl had put her clothes back on again, or after the vicar's trousers had been irrevocably lost" (Blood, 143-44). He asks himself "the point of playing at detectives when his performance was so abysmal on the occasions that required real detective abilities?" (Trap, 79). He explains to Gerald Venables, "I'm an actor, not a detective. If I were a detective, I'd have been sacked years ago for incompetence.... I now know that I have as much aptitude for detective work as a eunuch has for rape" (Blood, 135), and when on another occasion, Gerald says, "True detective work is the product of endless painstaking research, of enquiry and counter-enquiry," Charles' sour reply is "So I've heard. Maybe that's why I'm not a true detective" (Comedian, 126). After having saved Hugo Mecken from a murder conviction in *An Amateur Corpse*, only to hear later that he is drinking himself to death, Charles wonders, "What was the point in his dabbling in detection when his efforts brought so little happiness to the people involved?" (Comedian, 30).

The reasons for so many such statements are that Charles is hopelessly subjective in his judgments; he has a fickle logic and a vivid imagination; depends upon "educated guesswork," that is, theories without facts; and is lavish in accusing people of murder. That vivid imagination creates all sorts of possible scenarios; then new ideas require him to recast the script. He will choose a suspect, work out how that person must be guilty, confront the person or find new evidence proving his theory wrong, and then proceed to someone else and follow the same pattern until he finally stumbles on the real murderer. As stated in *A Comedian Dies*, "Charles [finds] it difficult to concentrate on more than one suspect at a time" (54). As a result, he simply chooses the most likely suspect—on the basis of insufficient evidence—and goes after that person, usually ending in a direct confrontation. In *A Comedian Dies* the process involves six people, and in *The Dead Side of the Mike* and *Situation Tragedy* four—sometimes with the same person twice. Charles' ease at making such wrong, or at least inadequate, assumptions provides the basic investigative structure of the novels. However, he perseveres. (It must be noted that his mistakes can be helpful. First, they provide additional information; second, his mistakes can cause the murderer to assume Charles knows more than he does and result in that murderer's discovery, as in *Cast, In Order of Disappearance* and *So Much Blood*.) Charles can be fooled by surface appearance: if he likes someone, that person is removed from suspicion unless evidence is overwhelming, then he is unhappy. He can be sure he is right when he is totally wrong, for he often sees what he wants to see. A "watertight alibi" can immediately send him to another suspect, as in *An Amateur Corpse*:

> He saw all his ideas suddenly discredited, he saw that he must flush every thought he'd ever had about the case out of his mind and start again with nothing.

* * *

> The void which had been left in his mind by the confirmation of Vee's alibi had only been there for a few seconds before new thoughts started to flood in (145).

But though a murderer may tell him that "as a detective ... you're rubbish" (Comedian, 157), to repeat, Charles perseveres.

Second only to his tenacity as a detective is Charles' acting ability. In every novel he uses disguise, vocal impersonation, or both to gain evidence. His favorite role is Detective-Sergeant McWhirter of Scotland Yard, for which he uses a Glaswegian accent, but he uses others as well: insurance salesman, reporter, Yorkshire manufacturer, etc. These disguises enable him to question people incognito, which is a major method of detection, for though he collects physical clues when available, most of his time is spent asking questions or engaging in supposedly innocent conversation with people who can tell him something about the victim or his present suspect. Haphazard the method may be, but it ultimately succeeds, and in spite of Charles' considering detective work "a slow and unrewarding business, like reading Dickens for the dirty bits" (Blood, 144), he remains a tenacious, if frequently fallible, seeker of truth.

Charles finds murder in the world of the theater and the media. In the principal elements of a murder case—murderer and motive, victim, type of murder, clues and misdirections—Brett's novels follow traditional patterns. However, in the presentation of those patterns—point of view, structural devices and particularly the use of setting and humor—Brett adds qualities which justify their being described as social satire.

Brett uses the closed circle of suspects, and his murderers are always within that circle. With one exception (insanity), the motives of his murderers are either some form of fear or some form of revenge. The fear may be of loss of money, marriage or position, and the revenge may be for a slighting remark about a loved one or a belief in a person's inherent evil. Some of the murderers are quite clever in hoodwinking Charles: one becomes his "Watson," another he considers a good friend, and he has great professional admiration for a third. (A fourth develops a very tricky double-alibi, but Charles finally cracks it.) In each of the three cases, the murderer uses Charles' attitude toward him or her to mislead him and to place the suspicion of guilt upon someone else. In only one case is the murderer partially successful, in that Charles does not reveal his identity, but tells Gerald Venables that the murderer is the second victim, dead of heroin poisoning. Nor does Charles reveal the "saboteur" of the show in *Star Trap;* although that person never murders anyone, his actions contribute to events leading to a suicide. Three of the other murderers are presumably arrested, and those in *Cast, In Order of Disappearance* and *Situation Tragedy* die. The conclusion that can be made about Brett's murderers is that, excluding the one in the first novel, they are generally likeable people, for Charles likes, or at least does not dislike, them.

Unlike the murderers, Brett's victims are not particularly likeable, but they and the methods of their deaths are conventional. Of the twelve victims in the seven novels, four are never met by the reader, five fall into the category of unpleasant or worse, and one is a total cipher as repeatedly stated. Only the remaining two, Charlotte Mecken of *An Amateur Corpse* and Andrea Gower of *The Dead Side of the Mike,* are in any way sympathetic, but both are killed early. There is little grief for any of them; Brett follows the classical school of detective fiction in not requiring the reader to care about victims. Of the first victim in *Situation Comedy,* this statement is made: "It was more as if the communal will had been so unanimously hostile that an indulgent God had given her a little nudge on the fire escape as a gesture of magnanimous serendipity" (32)—hardly a statement of mourning. These victims meet their ends, with two exceptions, not in unusual ways: they are shot, strangled, asphyxiated, crushed, pushed from heights, run over by cars or have their cars wrecked, have their wrists cut while drugged, and are given "bad" heroin. The two which are less typical are the public murders in *So Much Blood* and *A Comedian Dies,* and even their basic premise was used by Dame Ngaio Marsh: the detective in the audience when murder takes place at a performance. In the first a real knife is placed among stage ones so that at a rehearsal of a play, in which one of the characters is to be stabbed by a number of others, one wound will not be fake and an unsuspecting actor will become an instrument of murder. In *A Comedian Dies* Charles and Frances are watching a variety show; when a rock comedian grasps the microphone and strikes a chord on his guitar, he is electrocuted as a result of switched electrical leads. That victim's valedictory is the following exchange between Maurice Skellern and Charles: "He was a real live wire, I believe." "You can say that again" (25).

The principal method of misdirection in the novels has already been indicated: Charles' wrong assumptions. Whether they are the result of the murderer's trickery or Charles' willingness to jump to conclusions with insufficient evidence, they not only complicate matters for him, but they also lead the reader astray. Since the novels are presented from Charles' perspective, the reader accepts his assumptions—after all, he is the detective—and thus follows him down blind alleys. He can assume that a psychotherapist is a hired killer with himself as target, that faked evidence is the real thing, that a heart attack is murder and any number of other possibilities that prove to be wrong. Perhaps the most effective use of such an impression is in *Star Trap*, where a murderer is apparently present and ready to strike, but there is no murderer and no murder, only the threat, an unusual twist for a contemporary detective novel. The false assumptions provide a method for hiding clues that are present. Brett is scrupulous in adhering to the "fair play" convention. All clues are given to solve each case. In *So Much Blood*, the major clues are given in the first chapter—before the murder is even committed. However, most of the significant clues are the double-edged type of character and behavior, and since they can be interpreted in more than one way, they often lead to those false assumptions by Charles and the reader.

All in all, most of the elements in the past few pages are essentially traditional for British detective fiction. Brett is more innovative in his treatment of point of view and structural motifs. The novels are told in the third person, but the sense is of seeing the action through the mind of Charles Paris. It is as if the narrative voice is his shadow, for Charles is never left for even a paragraph, and much of each novel is given to his thoughts, conjectures, emotions and observations. Whereas in earlier British detective fiction a reader rarely entered the detective's mind until he was ready to reveal all, Brett's readers are able to follow every step and mis-step in Charles' search for answers. Brett's strong grasp of narrative structure is undoubtedly a result of his years of working with the rigid requirements of radio scripts. Only *An Amateur Corpse* and *The Dead Side of the Mike* do not have some controlling motif (some might condescendingly say, "gimmick"), and the messages by song titles in the latter almost qualify. Since Charles and Jacqui have appeared together in a pantomime of Cinderella, the chapter titles of *Cast, In Order of Disappearance* are from the characters, action or form of pantomime: "Prince Charming," "Transformation Scene," "Inside the Giant's Castle," "The Ugly Sisters," etc. More significantly, Charles' role was Baron Hardup, Cinderella's father, and in the novel he is essentially father-protector to the waif-like Jacqui, even saving her from a forcible abortion. In *So Much Blood* he is presenting his one-man show on Thomas Hood at The Edinburgh Festival, and each chapter is prefaced by an appropriate quotation from one of Hood's pun-filled poems, there is discussion of Hood as man and writer, and his *The Dream of Eugene Aram* is a neat parallel to the murder situation in the novel. More conventional is *Star Trap*, whose structure is based upon the rehearsal and tryouts of a new musical. From early rehearsals in London to the tryout tour of Leeds, Bristol and Brighton, the reader follows the development for better or worse of *Lumpkin!*, while Charles tries to find the person attempting to sabotage it. Obviously, *A Comedian Dies* has comedy as its motif, from the pun in the title and the stale jokes that preface chapters to Charles being the "feed," or straight man, for an old-time comedian. The intense nature of a comedian's work is explored, and there are more comic set-pieces than in any of the other novels. *Situation Tragedy* offers two motifs. Interspersed through the novel are letters to Charles from the producer of the situation comedy in which he is appearing; though their principal purpose is satire, they also serve to provide information and summarize previous action. The second motif is the detective fiction of R.Q. Wilberforce, a Brett-invented minor writer of the thirties. As Charles learns, the multiple murders of people involved in the production of the television program parallel the murders of Wilberforce's novels. Chapter Fourteen consists of excerpts with connecting summary of Wilberforce's *Death Takes a Short Cut*, a parody-pastiche of a thirties thriller, with an aristocratic hero named Maltravers Ratcliffe, his beautiful wife Eithne, servants Podd and Smithers, a master German villain named von Strutter, a foreign gentleman named Mr. Akbar, and such prose as "With a merry laugh, Maltreavers cried, 'I've had my fill of crime for a while! Let's away to Derbyshire to play cricket'" (143). The relationship between this hilarious parody, the other Wilberforce works, and the murders is clear evidence of Brett's narrative skills, his comic gift and his ability to combine them.

The comedy in Brett's novels ranges from wit to farce, with all sorts in between. Though Brett's wit is occasionally the result of sheer incongruity, as in "two eighteenth-century go-go dancers" (Trap, 145), or of the ludicrously stated observation, as in "long hair of a redness unavailable on the colour chart offered by God" (Mike, 9), most of the best examples are epigrams or comic similes:

> Marriage is the last refuge of the impotent. (Cast, 9)
> ...the art of meetings is not what you do or say at the time but what you manage to get minuted. (Mike, 87)
> She spoke of money as if it were an unfortunate skin condition. (Corpse, 169)
> It was horrible, like being groped by liver. (Cast, 142)
> She turned on her husband the sort of smile snakes reserve for rabbits. (Comedian, 27)
> Steve Clinton could be guaranteed to be the life and soul of any party, a characteristic which Charles found about as appealing as a slug in a salad. (Comedian, 86)

Whereas such wit is a form of verbal humor, farce is humor of action. The farcical incidents of the novels are both comic in themselves and, at their best, effectively juxtaposed to the criminous activity. The rehearsal and filming of Charles' big scene in the horror film of *Cast, In Order of Disappearance* is utter farce, but ends with Charles' being shot. Similarly in *Situation Tragedy*, when a television crew goes on location in a slum area and their caterer's van is attacked by a mob of insulted residents, the presentation is farcical, but murder results:

> Terrines of pate cracked against skulls, rare beef slices slapped in faces, glazed chicken wings rediscovered flight, strawberries splattered, mayonnaise flowed down denim shoulders, coleslaw matted into layered hair.
> How the fight would have developed was impossible to say. An awful thud and a scream froze the action and drew everyone's attention back to the lit area.
> In the middle of it lay the still body of Robin Laughton, pinned beneath the metal mass of a toppled light (108).

But whether the farcical incidents are joined as these are to the novels' crimes or are just set-pieces, as when Charles serves as babysitter in *Star Trap* and pacifies an infant by continually offering it his finger dipped in scotch, they always provide laughter.

The various forms of comedy are obviously significant in creating the tone of the novels, but just as important is that they are usually related in some way to Brett's satiric purposes. The satire is centered upon the forms of show business which provide Charles with his livelihood. The variety of Charles' work allows Brett to satirize actors, writers, directors, producers, technicians, agents and hangers-on in professional and amateur theater, radio, film and television. Since fame has passed Charles by, he becomes the observer of those who have it and those who want it. He realizes its fleeting nature: "show business biographies must be the most quickly dated and evanescent forms of literature" (Tragedy, 95). Charles' encounters with such stars as Christopher Milton in *Star Trap* and Bernard Walton and Dame Aurelia Howarth in *Situation Tragedy* provide Brett the opportunity to comment satirically, and in *Star Trap* straightforwardly, on the meaning of theatrical fame. The presentation of Christopher Milton is an acute analysis of the megalomaniac star who lives only for his audiences and requires a daily session with a psychotherapist to face that audience. Bernard Walton opens supermarkets, appears at benefits and on quiz shows, visits hospitals and has stories about himself planted in newspapers—anything to keep his name before the public. The maliciously funny dissection of Alexander Harvey, a talk-show host in *A Comedian Dies* is another instance. Harvey is a man who keeps a high profile "to the point of irritation," and who is a snob of doubtful sexuality. His humiliation by an elderly comedian whom he is trying to ridicule is a prime illustration of taking one's fame too seriously.

The pretensions and phoniness of those in show business is a major object of satire. From something as minor as Charles' observation that "the new generation of actors never used the word 'audition'," but instead "interview" (Tragedy, 52) to the extended description of a television awards ceremony, Brett punctures the pretense and lambasts the phoney. That awards ceremony receives over three pages of deadly attack: "simulated consternation," "sycophantic laughter," "the mindless pattern that was fixed for such occasions," "well-feigned amazement," and, most telling, "a very cheap way of making a television programme" (Comedian, 103, 105-06). Brett plays with a character like George Birkett, who finally stars in a television series and hypocritically claims to detest stardom; he refers to "media mushrooms," those "stars" who spring up over night as a result of a television hit; he can have Charles think that Noel Coward "has a lot to answer for. Generations of actors who, without a modicum of the talent, have pounced on the mannerisms" (Cast, 26); or he can present a producer who strikes a false anti-Establishment pose: "The donkey jacket wasn't a real donkey jacket, but a well-cut coat in donkey-jacket style from a Hampstead boutique. And the jeans weren't worker's jeans, but expensively aged denim trousers, finished with curlicues of yellow stitching" (Mike, 26). In every case, it is hypocritical pretension that masks insecurity or lack of ability at which Brett aims his satire. Other targets are lack of professionalism, purposeless extravagance, and the sometimes total inanity or tastelessness of what is presented to the public, such as a rock musical about the Boston strangler.

Such inanities are most evident in Brett's treatment of the media. The mentality controlling the media is summed up by Brett, after twelve years of working in radio and television, in the epigraph he chose for *Situation Tragedy*, Ernie Kovac's definition: "Television: A medium, so called because it is neither rare nor well done." In the same novel, Peter Lipscombe, the producer of Charles' sitcom is an ineffectual, optimistic ass, as evidenced by his cheery letters, no matter the disaster, his everpresent greeting of "Everything okay?" and Charles' conclusion that his only function is to buy and serve drinks. In fact, Charles' opinion of producers is that though many "can read scripts, it's a very rare one who can manage a whole book" (93). If they are not as fatuous as Lipscombe, they are like the ambitious John Christie of *The Dead Side of the Mike:*

> So he continued his urbane climb up the Management ladder, forgetting none of the people with whom he had made contact.... Oh no, they would all come in useful, their opinions would be quoted at Management meetings, their Christian names would be invoked to demonstrate his common touch, their ideas would be presented as his own. Nothing would be wasted in what he saw as his inexorable climb to Director-General (172).

In the same novel Charles attends a number of BBC committee meetings in which network infighting and jargon are rampant. The acronyms used make Charles think of "a game of Etruscan Scrabble" (18). There is a "licensed BBC intellectual" who is Germanically unintelligible; a provincial executive who natters, "I think it may be that I have a, as it were, solution to what can only be defined as the problem which we are, in a sense, talking about" (91); and a woman producer who seems obligated to use every trendy expression possible: "that's the scene he's into, but I think, whatever your bag, features could still be where it's at, creative-wise, because it's a matter of vibes ..." (21). Without question Brett places much of the blame for the media's inadequacies on those making the decisions at the top.

In *Situation Tragedy* he turns to the writers and their products. Prime illustrations are Willy and Samantha Tennison, "the archpriest and priestess of the arch" (113). They pour out interchangeable shows dramatizing "the small happenings of their own lives" (89), with a trite and silly cuteness that ensures commercial success. Another writer is Rod Tisdale, who counts the number of laughs in each of his scripts. The titles of the shows these writers turn out indicate their nature: "that smashing show set in a municipal rubbish dump, *Hold Your Nose and Think of England!*," "that charming show set in a cookery college, *Oh, Crumbs!* and *Oh, What a Pair of Au Pairs!* (64 & 88). As can be seen, exclamation marks are popular. Charles mentally develops series to cover the remainder of the Tennisons' lives: "There'd be *Mum's the Word!* for when their tongues were cut, *There's a Funny Thong!* for when they were garrotted, and, to cover their funerals, *We're Only Here for the Bier!*" (90). However, Charles' inventiveness is wasted, for at the end of the novel Lipscombe writes Charles that the Tennisons have split up and that he has received "a very exciting new script from Willy, provisionally titled *Marriage on the Rocks*" (170). The capsule summaries of the sitcoms *The Strutters* and *Dad's the Word* and the film *The Zombie Walks* are further examples of Brett's knowledge of entertainment cliches and his satiric exposure of them. The media in his novels are worlds of banality and bathos.

Two of the novels, *So Much Blood* and *An Amateur Corpse*, satirize amateur performers, and again unjustified pretension is the target. Charles' experience with the Derby University Drama Society—D.U.D.S. for short—at the Edinburgh Festival provides Brett the chance to skewer the arty "experimental" theater. (Brett directed the Oxford Theatre Group's late night show at the Festival in 1967.) He is particularly good with overstated publicity of such ventures:

> There were dress rehearsals for at least a dozen "funniest revues on the Fringe," some twenty "revolutionary new plays," and three or four "new artistic concepts which would flatten the accepted barriers of culture." If all these ambitions were realised, British theatre would never be the same again (72).

When Charles reads the blurb on Michael Vanderzee, a young director whose forte is the "perception through inanimate transference of pure emotion"—that is, pretending to be a banana—his reaction is "Huh" (39 & 15). Also present is Sam Wasserman, American author of *Mary, Queen of Sots*. Charles has to listen to Wasserman explain his play:

> "Now Mary's two husbands, Lord Darnley and the Earl of Bothwell, I take to represent England and the good old U.S. of A., the two countries who want to control her health. Queen Elizabeth, who ordains her execution, is the Arab states, who hold the real power in oil politics. Neat, huh?"
> Charles, suffering from mental indigestion at the thought of this laboured allegory being expounded in Creative Writing, nodded feebly (100-01).

Mental indigestion, indeed, but at least these young people are sincere, as Charles realizes. He encounters a more hypocritical group in *An Amateur Corpse*. The Breckton Backstagers' production of Chekhov's *The Seagull* is assumed by the company members, with much false modesty, to be a major achievement. The opinion of Charles, who is acting as consultant critic for the production is quite different:

> Such a pity that amateurs are always tempted by classic plays. Just because they're classics, it doesn't mean they're easy to do .... Amateurs should stick to what's within their range—Agatha Christie, frothy West End comedies, nothing that involves too much subtlety of characterization (7).

As with the professionals, Brett expects the amateurs to know their limitations and not make grandiose claims about their "art."

Many other satirical comments are present. A director named David Meldrum is so weak that he is known as David Humdrum. Gin is described as the "middle-aged actress' little helper" (Trap, 90). Much of television is just "viewzak" and "jokezak." Charles' comedy *How's Your Father?* is rejected by the Backstagers in favor of *Amniotic Amnesia*, which "concerns the thoughts of a group of foetuses awaiting a fertility drug-induced multiple birth [and supposedly] raises many interesting questions about philosophy and ecology" (193). Charles can be puzzled by voice-over commercials, even when making money from them: "Giving a couple of dozen readings of a banal endorsement for some product which no self-respecting housewife would be without didn't fit into his definition of acting" (Corpse, 27). Some of the satire is gentle when the targets are relatively unimportant, such as the elderly drama coach Ellen da Costa of *Star Trap*, but whatever his targets and however sharp his shafts, Brett's exposure of the sins and follies of show business is a reflection of his view of contemporary British society.

When Charles reads the Sunday papers, he is not cheered: "Bombs in London restaurants and the continuing apparent helplessness of the Herrema siege led to fears of the imminent collapse of society, that terrible plunging feeling that tomorrow everything will stop and animal chaos will reign" (Trap, 95). A similar reaction results from Christmas shopping during an energy crisis: "The cold shops with their sad gas-lamps were full of Christmas shoppers feeling sorry for themselves, and shoplifters having a field day. The ever-present possibility of bombs made buying presents even jollier" (Cast, 123). Such is the England of the novels, an England of "the aerosol artist," *kung fu* films, tape copying, Reggae, large Pakistani families, petrol crises, mansions "converted into hotels with very British names for German tourists, private nursing homes for Arabs or ... honeycombs of small flats" (Mike, 38), sex scandals, frozen dinners, panic buying of toilet tissue, building slumps, terrorist bombs, Jean Plaidy paperbacks, an area of London with "not too many friendly white faces" (Comedian, 133), television off at ten thirty to save power, "interfaces" with wine bottles, *I, Claudius* as "bourgeois commuters' wish fulfillment. Lots of rapes and murders" (Corpse, 39), and a commercial featuring Mr. Bland in top hat and tails offering his bedtime drink to "a tribe of little fuzzy red creatures called the Wideawakes," who turn pale blue and fall asleep (Corpse, 28). As a social satirist, and commentator, Brett presents this England as the background for his mysteries, but even more he parallels and connects its problems and antagonisms with those he specifically treats in the theater and the media. It is not possible to examine all aspects of this satire, but three areas deserve some consideration: the satire of unionism in *Situation Tragedy*, of middle-class tackiness and trendiness in *An Amateur Corpse*, and of places in *A Comedian Dies* and *The Dead Side of the Mike*.

There is a threatened strike in *Situation Tragedy*, and Charles comments: "The BBC went on strike to achieve parity with ITV, so it's only a matter of time before ITV goes on strike to achieve greater disparity from the BBC" (12). This anti-union attitude runs throughout the novel. Though Brett has claimed that he is not political, his experience in radio and television has given him a jaundiced view of unionism. The amount of control unions have as to time of work and their number on any job and their demands for every possible perquisite form a major theme. Union members are characterized again and again by their shirts and their laziness: "The men whose only function seemed to be to wear lumberjack checked shirts wore their lumberjack checked shirts and discussed overtime rates ominously" (54). Overtime, the requirement of a plumber when sprinklers are used on the set, cheating on their travel allowances: these are what they talk about instead of working. The result is "the slow pace of everything, which is *de rigueur* in television" (54), except when the filming is over, for since there is fixed payment for "tidying-up time," the union men then work "with a speed and efficiency" not otherwise evident (61). The bluntest satire occurs when Charles is pushed from a bank of studio seats and falls on two union men. They are not sympathetic to his possible injuries:

> "Fall down on top of union members—that's the sort of thing that could cause a strike."

* * *

> The speaking shirt turned accusingly to Charles. "Ere, you really hurt him. I reckon falling actors comes under industrial accident. We'll take the company for a lot of insurance on this."
> That thought seemed to make his own injuries worse, and he too groaned (157).

Unfortunately for the two, their being already on strike relieves the company of any liability, and they can only stop groaning and say, "Bloody hell." Unionism is the major illustration of the greed and waste which Brett satirizes in *Situation Tragedy*, but it is only one. There are, for example, the caterers on location, who throw away good food and who, when Charles offers to pay for a bottle of wine "to see him through the afternoon," look at him "as if he were the first of some newly hatched species hitherto unseen on the planet" (60).

Charles comes in contact with all sorts of people in the novels. Some are presented in a sort of comic-pathetic way, particularly old people, such as the studio audiences and the unbalanced radio fan, Mrs. Moxon, of *The Dead Side of the Mike*. But the major type of person satirized is the member of the middle class who is either too trendy or too conventional; both are present in *An Amateur Corpse*.

Ian Compton, a young advertising copywriter, is trendiness personified:

> He was wearing a double-breasted gangster-striped suit over a pale blue T-shirt. Around his neck hung a selection of leather thongs, one for a biro, one for a packet of Gauloise, one for a Cricket lighter and others whose function was not immediately apparent. His lapels bristled with badges, gollies, teddy bears, a spilling tomato ketchup bottle and similar trendy kitsch (33).

Another instance is the marriage of a man of Charles' generation to a young actress; they dress in identical oyster-grey velvet suits. Such trendiness is a sign of insecurity: Compton is a homosexual and the groom is attempting to fight his aging. Utter conventionality is another form of insecurity. The example of Miles and Juliet has already been noted. In *An Amateur Corpse* suburbia is the principal target. Charles thinks that the class levels of a suburb are such "that a full understanding of the society would be a lifetime's study" (150). Charles finds the rich Mr. and Mrs. Hobbs "infinitely pathetic" in "trying to buy friendship with a constant supply of free drinks" (171), but their mock-Tudor house with jungle wallpaper, Raspberry Ripple carpet and three-foot high china pony is hilarious tackiness. Charles also visits Gerald Venables' home. It is definitely not tacky: "It was exactly the sort of house that anyone in Georgian England who happened to own two cars, a central heating oil tank, a television and a burglar alarm would have had" (138). Gerald greets Charles "dressed in a pale blue towelling shirt and evenly faded jeans ... [and] navy blue sailing shoes and a Snoopy medallion hung around his neck. This last was worn a bit self-consciously" (138). When he offers Charles a beer, it is predictably Lowenbrau. All very proper for a wealthy executive, but to Charles the atmosphere of Gerald's Dulwich is the same as that of the Hobbses' Breckton, "quiet desperation":

> Paranoid car-cleaning, wives pulled in every direction by children, buggies and shopping, determinedly jovial husbands taking the kids for a walk, track-suited executives sweating off some of the week's lunches in unconvinced jogging, others bearing their loads of wood and ceiling tiles from the brochured neatness of the Do-It-Yourself shop to the bad-tempered messes of a constructive weekend (138).

The above example indicates that places are important for Brett's presentation of satire.[2] Tastelessness is not limited to homes;

the Balmoral bar contains "a prickly tartan bench beneath a plastic spray of dirks and claymores behind a buckler" and "a Formica 'Monarch of the Glen' table-top" (Mike, 136). The Great Expectations restaurant carries its Dickensian theme to excess and becomes ridiculous, with waiters and waitresses who look "as though they had escaped from the chorus of *Oliver!*" (Comedian, 32). The menu consists of such dishes as Tale of Two Cities, poached eggs on spinach; Fanny Squeers' Pate; Quilp Fritters; Martin Chuzzlewit, toad in the hole; Sidney Carton, tomato soup—straight from the guillotine?—and so on. Such obvious fakery and pretense are attempts to cover the often drab and ugly in modern life, but their inadequacy in doing so makes them ludicrous. On the other hand are those places where Brett emphasizes the drabness, such as the shabby resort of Hunstanton in *A Comedian Dies*, with its sad elderly retirees and tourists, or The Leaky Bucket, "one of those little clubs which closes and reopens every six months or so under a different name .... In its recent incarnations it had been The Horseshoe, a drinking club, Kickers, a discotheque, The Closet, a gay club (much to the fury of the local residents), The Safety-Pin, a punk-rock club, and The 39 Steppes, a club with an emphasis on vodka and Russian cuisine" (85). In *The Dead Side of the Mike* Charles has to make one of his infrequent trips to a launderette, which he considers "the most depressing place in the world," suggesting "the set of some Beckett paean to despair" (52). Brett's treatment of places—like that of people, unions, the theater and the media—can be comic or bleak, but it is nearly always satiric. The world in which he places Charles Paris is the world of today: insecure but pretentious, materialistic but often tasteless and ultimately frightening in its seeming lack of purpose.

How far Brett will take Charles Paris, theatrical murder and satire of contemporary Britain is unknown. (If he continues his yearly pace, by the time this essay is published, there will be at least one more novel.) Already he has shown that he ranks among the most innovative of recent mystery writers. His insider's knowledge of the British entertainment world and his sharply focused observations of people, institutions and manners have been employed within the framework of the detective novel to satirize, with the full range of comedy, both implicitly and explicitly life in contemporary Britain. As a social satirist in the detective genre, he has fulfilled his expressed purpose of entertaining and, in doing so, has produced a distinctive body of work which is a reflection of and comment on his time. Finally, there is Charles Paris. He may not be a star as an actor, some might even say he is not a star as a great detective, but he is a star as a fictional character for whose appearances readers eagerly await, and with just eight novels his creator rightly deserves a place with his predecessors among these dozen Englishmen of mystery.[3]

Notes

[1] The editions of Brett's novels used for this study are listed below, preceded by the original date of publication. All quotations will be cited in the text using, where necessary for clarity the abbreviations given after each entry.

1975 *Cast, In Order of Disappearance* (New York: Berkley, 1979). (Cast)
1976 *So Much Blood* (New York: Scribner's, 1976). (Blood)
1977 *Star Trap* (New York: Scribner's, 1977). (Trap)
1978 *An Amateur Corpse* (New York: Berkley, 1980). (Corpse)
1979 *A Comedian Dies* (New York: Scribner's, 1979). (Comedian)
1980 *The Dead Side of the Mike* (New York: Scribner's, 1980). (Mike)
1981 *Situation Tragedy* (New York: Scribner's, 1981). (Tragedy)

[2] Brett is surprisingly mild in his comments on the United States. The visit of Charles and Frances to New York in *The Dead Side of the Mike* could have offered much more than Charles' embarrassment on wandering into a gay bar, his encounter with a Puerto Rican security guard, and his "channel-hopping with glee from the confessional mania of breakfast-time evangelists to patronising children's programmes and endless cartoons" (76), but Brett obviously feels that his knowledge of America is inadequate for satire: "Charles realised that a lifetime of hearing about the States and not being there had filled him with a lot of silly prejudices" (77).

[3] Brett's latest novel, *Murder Unprompted*, was published in October 1982, three months after the completion of this essay. Unfortunately, its detection is the weakest of the novels, though the characters and action continue the Brett satirical hilarity. He uses his usual elements, but *Murder Unprompted* seems a somewhat perfunctory work. Charles Paris is now fifty-four and starring in a provincial production of a new play, *The Hooded Owl*. When the play is moved to London, he is pushed aside for a "name" star, but that star is murdered on-stage at the opening performance—a repeat of the situation in *A Comedian Dies*. Charles then retakes the role and has one of his greatest successes, but for non-artistic reasons the show soon closes. The murder occurs late—on page 94 of 160—and detection is slight, and the revelation of the murderer's motive and method difficult to accept. Following the Brett formula, Charles is shot at, has unsatisfactory sex: "It had reduced him to ... just another anonymous treatment that her body had required" (129), and beds more successfully with Frances, who plays a larger role than in most of the novels. In spite of the novel's less than satisfactory detection, Brett's skewering of the egos and double-dealings of producers, agents, writers, directors and actors is as brilliant as ever, and again justifies the epithet: the detective novelist as social satirist.